PIERRE GILLES'
CONSTANTINOPLE

PIERRE GILLES'
CONSTANTINOPLE

A Modern English Translation
by Kimberly Byrd

৵

ITALICA PRESS
NEW YORK
2008

ITALICA PRESS, INC.
595 MAIN STREET
NEW YORK, NY 10044
HTTP://WWW.ITALICAPRESS.COM

Library of Congress Cataloging-in-Publication Data
Gilles, Pierre, 1490–1555.
  [De topographia Constantinopoleos. English]
  Pierre Gilles' Constantinople : a modern English translation / by Kimberly Byrd.
     p. cm. — (Italica Historical Travel Guides)
  Summary: "This new edition of Pierre Gilles' 'De topographia Constantinopoleos' includes a new English translation of the entire work with references to Gilles' sources and to the most important recent scholarship on the city and its monuments, with illustrations, notes, bibliography and index"—Provided by publisher.
  Includes bibliographical references and index.
  ISBN-13: 978-0-934977-69-2 (pbk. : alk. paper)
  1. Istanbul (Turkey)—Description and travel. 2. Istanbul (Turkey)—Antiquities. 3. Turkey—Antiquities. I. Byrd, Kimberly May. II. Title.
  DR720.G513 2007
  949.61'8—dc22

                                                                    2007022698

Paperback
ISBN: 978-0-934977-69-2

Cover: View of Constantinople. From Hartmann Schedel, *Nuremberg Chronicle*. Nuremberg: Anton Koberger, 1493.

CONTENTS

❧

ILLUSTRATIONS

Unless otherwise noted, all photos were taken by the author.
Note: DAI refers to the photographic archive of the German Archaeological Institute of Istanbul; MW Archive to the plans in Müller-Wiener, *Bildlexicon*.

Cover: View of Constantinople. From Hartmann Schedel, *Nuremberg Chronicle*. Nuremberg: Anton Koberger, 1493.

❧

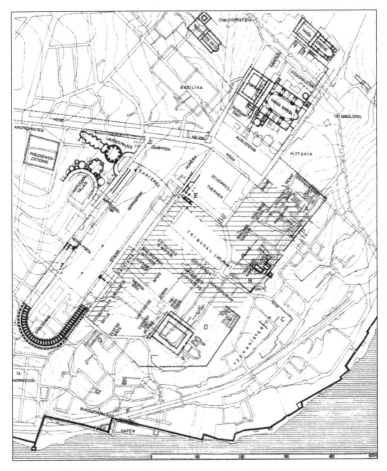

2. Plan of Hagia Sophia and Great Palace area. Plan, MW 1.

INTRODUCTION

In the 1540s, in the glory days of the Ottoman Empire, a French antiquarian named Pierre Gilles arrived in Constantinople (modern Istanbul). Although dispatched to the Ottoman capital by his sovereign, François I, his mission was not diplomatic in nature. Instead, he was charged with purchasing ancient Greek and Latin codices to add to the French king's new library. Unfortunately for our traveler, François died shortly after Gilles reached his destination, and funds earmarked for the purchase of ancient manuscripts were never dispatched. Somewhat at loose ends, Gilles' excursion took on an entirely new dimension. Deciding that this opportune period in one of the world's greatest cities should not go to waste, he resolved to write a book that would become the first scholarly study ever produced about this magnificent metropolis.[1]

Istanbul was then and remains today one of the world's great cities. In Gilles' day it went by another name: Constantinople. At the time of his arrival in 1544 it was the largest and wealthiest city in Europe — as it had been in the period of the Byzantine Empire. With a population of nearly 700,000, Constantinople's inhabitants outnumbered the combined populations of western cities such as Venice, Palermo, Messina, Catania and Naples. Furthermore, Constantinople was home to a truly international population of Turks, Greeks, Jews, Armenians, Gypsies, Arabs, Africans, Slavs, French and others who lived side by side, for the most part in peace. They worshipped in over 400 mosques and dozens of Christian churches, engaged in commerce in tens of thousands of small ateliers and shops, and sailed the waters of the Bosporus, Golden Horn and Marmara Sea in thousands of small boats, ferries and ships. Each year the populace consumed over 100,000 tons of wheat and other grains and hundreds of thousands of head of cattle and sheep.[2]

The city Gilles explored and wrote about was not, however, the contemporary Ottoman one. The city he searched for was largely below the surface or crumbling into ruins around him even as the splendid monuments of the great Ottoman architect Sinan were progressing skyward. Pierre Gilles was a humanist scholar and antiquarian interested above all in Constantinople's brilliant past under the great Emperors Constantine I (fourth century CE) and Justinian I (sixth century CE). He sought to discover and reconstruct the topography of the long-lost imperial capital, its temples, churches, public buildings, theaters and circuses, palaces, harbors and markets.

The task he set himself was prodigious, for the project involved much more than exploring the Ottoman capital and recording the location and condition of known ancient monuments and ruins. Gilles sought out both the seen and the unseen; he wanted to pin down precise attributions and dates, and he endeavored to reconstruct a portrait of ancient Constantinople that was as accurate as possible. To do this Pierre Gilles drew upon all his experience and resources as a scholar trained in the Renaissance humanist tradition, for he had a long career studying the ancient pagan and Christian texts his fellow humanists prized. Indeed, it appears that Gilles approached his investigation of Constantinople's ancient topography rather as he would have analyzed a text: by verifying one source against another and carefully testing in the field what the ancient authors said about the urban geography of the city's monuments and streets. His final reconstruction of Constantinople in the late Roman and early Byzantine period is surprisingly accurate given that he was the first scholar to have ever undertaken such an important and, indeed, such a colossal project.

BYZANTIUM, CONSTANTINOPLE, ISTANBUL

Constantinople was born of humble origins. It began life as a Greek colony called Byzantium, which was established by settlers from Megara in about 667 BCE. By the fifth century BCE, however, the small colony became a major player in the Mediterranean world when it allied with Athens against Sparta in 431 BCE at the start of the Peloponnesian War. Its geographical situation was and is superb, for Byzantium was set up on a promontory of land where the Bosporus joins the Sea of Marmara. The site had good natural harbors and its situation allowed its inhabitants to take advantage of trade routes running from the Dardanelles to the Black Sea. The Romans certainly appreciated the city's advantages as early as the first century CE. Even Emperor Septimius Severus, after taking the city in 196 CE in a bitter siege that resulted in great destruction, was quick to rebuild the ancient polis so as to benefit from the commercial and strategic importance of the colony's location.

The town on the Bosporus truly came into its own and embarked upon an entirely new course early in the fourth century CE when the first Christian emperor, Constantine the Great, became sole ruler of the Roman Empire. As his immediate predecessors before him, Constantine acknowledged that the East's high population, rich cultural heritage and fabulous wealth constituted the major strengths of a vast empire that stretched from Spain in the West to the borders of the Persia in the East. Rome, the original capital of the empire, was simply too far away to deal effectively with the governance of the vast areas in the East. What was needed was a second or "assistant" capital. Diocletian had recognized this necessity in the late third century when he established permanent headquarters in the East not only at Split in Croatia but also at Nicomedia in Anatolia (modern Izmit, Turkey). Constantine followed suit in setting up a permanent Eastern base of his own. After considering several locales on the southern coast of Turkey (including Troy), he finally settled upon the colony of Byzantium as his new capital.

In 330 work began on New Rome, or Constantinopolis, "the City of Constantine," as it came to be known. It was never Constantine's intent to wholly replace the *first* Rome, yet even so the emperor spared no expense or effort in stripping old Rome and many of the richest urban centers in the East of art and costly ornaments deemed worthy to embellish his new imperial capital and namesake. The city grew rapidly not only in population but in importance, especially after the division of the empire into East and West by Theodosius in 395. By the end of the sixth century Constantinople was the center of a predominantly Christian empire, steeped in Greek cultural and artistic influences, yet founded on and maintained by a Roman legal and administrative system. Despite the amalgam of Roman and Greek influences, however, its language was definitively Greek. Constantinople truly was the capital of the Roman Empire in the *East*, and from its founding under Constantine to its fall in

1453 the inhabitants always called themselves "Romans" (*Romaioi* in Greek). Over its long history the empire and its capital experienced many vicissitudes that included several periods of growth and decline and more than one "golden" age. The first and most famous zenith was reached under Emperor Justinian I (527–68). During this period plague and riots decimated the capital on the one hand, while fantastic building projects were carried out on the other. Foremost among these was the erection of the church of the Holy Wisdom, Hagia Sophia, still one of the world's most breathtaking architectural marvels. Centuries later the city suffered the worst disaster in its history as the result of the Fourth Crusade. The Venetians played a prominent role in the attempt by western Latin Crusaders to win back the Holy Land from the Muslims. On this occasion, however, the Crusaders, unhappy with the alliance they had made with their fellow Christians, the Byzantines, became involved in Byzantine politics, which led to their supporting a usurper and helping him to gain the throne. So the Crusaders, diverted from the Holy Land, conquered and sacked Constantinople in 1204. Such a disaster had never been visited upon Constantine's city; it was worse even than the final Turkish conquest of 1453 was to be. The richest city in Christendom was looted by the Crusaders of its fabulous wealth and artistic treasures, with much of the booty being shipped to Venice. One prize, for example, was the quadriga of ancient Greek bronze horses from Constantinople's Hippodrome. These ended up atop the façade of San Marco. Likewise disastrous to the Byzantines was the temporary loss of their capital, which became the center of a Latin empire in the East.

In 1261 the Byzantines under the Palaeologan Emperor Michael VIII regained Constantinople from the Latins, but by the fourteenth century the restored Byzantine Empire had shrunk to a mere shadow of its former self. Byzantine realms were slowly being eaten away by the empire's last and greatest foe, the Ottoman Turks, who crossed the Bosporus and occupied Thrace in the early 1300s. By 1450 the situation was worse: the only territory the empire controlled was nothing more than Constantinople and its suburbs. In April of 1453 the final Ottoman assault began under the leadership of the young Ottoman Sultan Mehmet II. The Byzantines, with a much reduced defensive force and desperate but unfulfilled hopes of aid from the

Latin West, held out for fifty days against the Ottoman onslaught of not only soldiers but of a new weapon: artillery. Constantinople's double-walled defensive system, the greatest in Europe since the time of Theodosius in the late fourth century, was no match for the sultan's cannon. The last Byzantine emperor, Constantine XI refused to surrender. He was last seen fighting hand-to-hand in the final, desperate battle at the Romanus Gate; his body was never found. Early the next morning Mehmet II, now hailed as Fatih, "the Conqueror," entered the city in triumph and immediately reconfirmed Constantinople in its role as imperial capital — this time a Muslim Ottoman one.

The Ottoman sultans, as new emperors of Constantinople, continued their westward expansion and directed it into the heart of Europe. By the death of Sultan Selim I in 1520, the Ottoman realm stretched from Alexandria in Egypt to Mosul in Syria and from Bodrum in southwestern Turkey to the Danube. When Ottoman armies advanced upon the very gates of Vienna, terror of the Turks reached new heights in western Europe.

How to halt the advance of the heathen and bloodthirsty Turk became the obsession of European rulers during the mid-sixteenth century, an age of great fear and struggle throughout Europe and the Mediterranean. In this period the Ottomans captured Belgrade (1521) and Malta (1565) and nearly took Vienna by siege (1529). Famous battles between Western armies and the sultan's warriors and Janissaries included the battles of Mohacs (1526) and Lepanto (1571). Europe's most renowned and powerful leaders, from the Hapsburg emperor Charles V to Philip II of Spain, and from Pope Leo X to François I of France, wrung their hands in despair. Indeed, the specter of "the Turk" and what to do about this new and threatening "evil empire" obsessed the entire population of the Christian West.[3] The Turk was reputed to be cruel and tyrannical, and, furthermore, uncivilized to the point of murdering not only Christians but his own people. Western Europeans shuddered in horror at accounts of the treacherous and sadistic infidel who kept slave harems and captured Christian boys, forcing them to convert to Islam and molding them into murderous Janissaries. The general consensus in the West was that the Turk was a creature fixated on conquest, in love with blood and torture, and was, in fact, a demon capable of any imaginable atrocity.

The reality could not have been more different. The Ottoman Empire was populated by a people and led by a sultan far away from the stereotypes western Europeans took to heart. In the sixteenth century Constantinople was the center of an empire whose citizens created bold and lasting architecture, alluring ceramics and textiles, and richly illuminated manuscripts. Ottoman authors penned vivid literature and histories, and the empire's thinkers produced inspired and influential religious and philosophical views. What is more, Sultan Suleyman, one of the greatest rulers in Ottoman history, was beloved by his own people. They fondly referred to him as the "Lawgiver," a just ruler who constructed and funded hospitals, schools, orphanages and havens for the poor, and who unsparingly protected and beautified the empire's holy places: Jerusalem, Mecca and Medina. Not since the era of the Byzantine emperor Justinian in the sixth century had Constantinople been the site of such wealth and activity, or such building and innovation. Nor had it been home to so many schools and artists creating anew and crystallizing the beauty and genius of a cultural tradition. This brilliant age of arts and material culture was the expression of the power, wealth and intellect of a Muslim empire centered on Constantinople. Suleyman's age was indeed another golden age.[4]

PIERRE GILLES AND THE TOPOGRAPHY AND ANTIQUITIES OF CONSTANTINOPLE

Pierre Gilles (Petrus Gyllius in Latin) was born in Albi in 1490. We know little about his youth and early education. Most of what we do know about him comes from his published works and from the writings of others. The books he authored reveal that he was thoroughly steeped in the training of the French humanists. In this Gilles shared in the education and scholarly interests of contemporaries such as François Rabelais, Jacques Lefèvre d'Étaples and Guillaume Budé, who were themselves influenced by Erasmus and the Italian Renaissance humanists. These scholars promoted the arts of science and literature by looking back to antiquity and studying newly discovered, or in many cases rediscovered and edited ancient texts, both pagan and Christian, Greek and Latin. Gilles' own command of these languages was superb, as was his familiarity with the ancient authors who wrote in them.

The young Pierre Gilles was fascinated by the natural sciences. His first published work appeared in 1533 and was the fruit of his investigative work on the study of marine life of the southern French coast and the Adriatic. In an attempt to gain royal notice and, hopefully, royal patronage, Gilles dedicated the work, a book on the nomenclature of fish, to his king, François I. If we are to look at Gilles' entire body of work we might agree with Rabelais, who in his *Gargantua*, claimed that Pierre Gilles made no distinction between "scientific" and other, more literary, studies. Indeed, so vast were Gilles' interests and knowledge that they easily rate on a par with the works of the best humanists of his day. Like his scholarly peers Gilles edited the works of his fellow humanists, composed commentaries of his own, and produced philological materials for the study of antiquity as well. He likewise put his efforts into the collation and publication of secular and religious classical texts. His works include an edition of Elio Antonio de Nebrija's *Dictionary of Place Names* and a *History of King Ferdinand of Aragon* by the great Italian humanist Lorenzo Valla. As testament to his grasp of Greek and Latin are Gilles' additional publications: a *Greek–Latin Lexicon*, a translation of the Greek Father Theodoret's *Commentary on the Twelve Minor Prophets*, and a selection of texts from Aelian, Porphyry, Heliodorus, Oppian and others.

Like other men of learning in his time, Gilles could not afford to live off his published works alone, so he became a tutor to learned aristocrats. Sometime in the early 1520s he was appointed tutor to the young Georges d'Armagnac, one of the great nobles of France. During the course of their forty-year relationship d'Armagnac remained Gilles' loyal patron and friend. One of his most notable acts was to induce Gilles to dedicate his *On the Life and Nature of Animals* to François I in a second attempt to gain royal patronage. This time it worked, for it led to an important assignment that would bring Gilles to the city of Constantinople.

The French king, like most leaders in Western Europe, was intrigued by the Ottoman Empire and its sultan, Suleyman I, with whom he had been attempting to form a political alliance (ultimately successfully) for some time. Embassies from European countries to the Sublime Porte were not unheard of and had long served a myriad of purposes: diplomatic, scientific, intelligence-gathering and establishing goodwill. Each aided in the process of general cultural exchange. Royal embassies, however, were specifically designed to enhance the reputation of the kings who sent them. François, for instance, sent missions to the seats of classical antiquity in the Holy Land, Greece and Asia Minor. It was just such a cultural–diplomatic mission between France and Constantinople that Pierre Gilles and the royal cosmographer André Thevet d'Angouleme joined in 1544. Gilles' mission was clear. He was to search out and purchase ancient manuscripts in Greek and Latin for his king's new library at Fontainebleau (ultimately to become the Bibliothèque Nationale in Paris).

Gilles appears to have remained in Constantinople from 1544 to 1547, during which time he carried out his investigation of the city that would result in what is today his best known work, *The Topography of Constantinople and Its Antiquities*. He was witness to various events in the city, including the 1456 fire that burned down the Grand Bazaar (Kapalı Çarşı) that allowed him subsequently to inspect the ruins of an ancient basilica that had been exposed. The year 1548

3. *Aerial photo of the Grand Bazaar/ Kapalı Çarşı. Photo by Sami Güner.*

found Gilles briefly in the pay of Sultan Suleyman's army, which was marching against Persia and into which he enlisted when promised funds from Paris for the purchase of antique books were not forthcoming. Wintering in Aleppo in 1548 the author met Gabriel d'Aramon, French ambassador to the Sublime Porte, who arranged to have Gilles accompany him to the Holy Land and Egypt. In 1550 the two returned to Constantinople briefly before landing in France that same year. Almost immediately upon reaching France, however, Gilles was traveling once more, this time to Rome to join his patron, Cardinal d'Armagnac. D'Armagnac generously assured his client an income by obtaining for him the absentee priorage of Durenque in Aveyron. Remaining in Rome, Gilles began reworking the notes and other materials he had accumulated during his travels, and was near completion of his book on Constantinople late in 1554. It was at this time, however, that the weary and ageing scholar was struck down by the severe fever that killed him. As we learn from the epitaph on his tomb, he lingered for eleven days before passing away on January 5, 1555. Cardinal d'Armagnac, in his final act of patronage, provided for Gilles' funeral and his tomb, which can still be seen in the church of San Marcello in Rome.[5]

Given that Pierre Gilles died still in toil upon the notes he had written while in Constantinople, we are fortunate indeed that his efforts ever reached the public at all. Our gratitude must go to his nephew, Antoine Gilles, who continued his uncle's work and saw to the final collation and publication of his notes in book form. Ultimately Gilles' travels in and around the Ottoman capital resulted in two separate monographs, both published in Lyons in 1561. The first is entitled *On the Thracian Bosporus*. The second, and by far the more famous of the two, is *The Topography of Constantinople and Its Antiquities*.

The organization of the *Topography* tells us much about how Gilles took on the immense task of reconstructing ancient Constantinople's urban fabric. Organizing it into four books, the author opens in a very modern fashion, much like a modern *Blue Guide*, with an account of the city's physical features, geographical situation and natural resources. Book I takes up the mythological and historical material dealing with the city's origins as a Greek colony, its early growth and its size from antiquity into the sixteenth century. Throughout his monograph Gilles moves across the peninsula and Constantinople's seven hills, progressing from east to west, so that Book II, the largest of the four books, deals with the heart of ancient Constantinople, focusing on Hagia Sophia and surrounding buildings located on the first and second hills. Book III moves eastward, covering the north and central sections of the city, focusing on the third hill. His final book, Book IV, deals primarily with the remaining territory up to the land walls and then makes a jump over the Golden Horn for a brief tour of Galata.

As to the monuments dotting Constantinople's urban landscape, Gilles' approach seems at first deceptively simple and at times redundant. He tells us repeatedly that he has relied on the *Notitia Urbis Constantinopolitinae* as his general guide to exploring the city. The *Notitia* was compiled in the fifth century CE; in essence it is a short list of Constantinople's fourteen wards or regions and the monuments they contained at that time. Gilles utilized it in this way: he would concentrate on a particular ward and then use the *Notitia* to acquire the general layout of that ward and the monuments within it. However, the *Notitia* is only the first tool in Gilles toolbox, for in and of itself this compilation furnishes only minor topographical and no architectural details. Therefore — unless Gilles was fortunate enough to have a well-preserved monument to explore, such as the Aqueduct of Valens — he had to turn to other sources.

The number of other sources Gilles consulted is, in fact, quite impressive. He employed approximately ninety different works to which he refers directly by either title or author. As we might expect in the work of a humanist antiquarian, these include: Xenophon, Strabo, Thucydides, Herodotus, and Livy, for instance. However, Pierre Gilles depended overwhelmingly on a handful of late antique and Byzantine texts. The sources he most carefully scrutinized make an impressive, but by no means comprehensive, list. They are: the *Navigations of the Bosporus* by the second-century CE author Dionysius of Byzantium, the *Notitia*, previously mentioned, and which was compiled in the reign of Theodosius II, the works of the fourth-century churchman and scholar Eusebius of Caesarea, the fifth-century ecclesiastical histories of Socrates and Sozomenos, the sixth-century *New History* of Zosimus, the works of the famous sixth-century historian Procopius of Caesarea, the *Patria of Constantinople* (dated to the ninth and tenth centuries), the Suda Lexicon (compiled about the year 1000), the histories of the twelfth-century writers John Zonaras and George Cedrinus, and finally the *Greek Anthology*[6] (compiled between the tenth and early fourteenth centuries).

One cannot help but wonder where Gilles obtained and read these key late antique and Byzantine texts. Was he in Constantinople? In France? In Rome? In his own book he gives us hints at best. Many of the sources just enumerated could be found in France and most in the Vatican in the sixteenth century; and it should be noted that Gilles settled himself in Rome upon his return from the East and was at work there, collating his notes, when he died in 1555. What is more, Gilles could have examined, in either France or in Rome, other important Byzantine authorities for topographical information — works that either do not appear or are infrequently cited in his *Topography of Constantinople*. For example, Gilles makes only a handful of references to the rich early thirteenth-century *History* of Nicetas Choniates, a text that contains much invaluable material about the city. Even further, he never consulted the *Book of Ceremonies* by

Constantine VII Porphyrogenitus, a work that specifically mentions the most important ancient and medieval monuments and their role in imperial ceremonial. Why didn't he?

More mysterious — and frustrating — are the smaller clues peppering his narrative. For instance, when Gilles discusses the probable location of one of Constantinople's oldest hospitals, the Hospital of Sampson, he tells us that he read in Procopius about the 532 Nike riot and resulting fire that destroyed the ancient hospice: "After I wrote…from an edition of Procopius, I found a hand-written codex of Procopius that stated that the Hospital of Sampson was between the two buildings of Hagia Sophia and Hagia Irene."[7] The impression Gilles gives here is that he read about the famous Nike conflagration in a printed edition of Procopius *before* he traveled to Constantinople, but that he found a *manuscript* of Procopius while in the East, presumably in Constantinople itself. Another piece of evidence from Gilles lends itself to this interpretation. In Book IV of his *Topography* Gilles writes: "… there was a Cynegion [a theater for hunting and animal fights] in Constantinople, according to Procopius, who claims that through the avarice of Justinian the theaters, hippodromes and *cynegia* were in great part neglected."[8] This latter quote from Procopius comes straight out of the *Secret History*, which is now famous for the scurrilous details of the Empress Theodora's wicked past that it contains. Given that the *Secret History* was not known in the West until the seventeenth century, there can be little doubt that Gilles read this work of Procopius, or excerpts from it, in a manuscript he found, we are left to assume, while *in* Constantinople. Yet, he seems completely unaware that he had stumbled upon a previously unknown work of Procopius. Where in Constantinople could he have stumbled upon this rare bit of Procopius?

One possibility is the Sahaflar, or old book market, to the west of today's Grand Bazaar. According to Gilles the book trade there was as lively in his day as it is in ours. Unfortunately for us, even though our traveler visited the Sahaflar, he never claims to have purchased books there. Another possibility is the Greek patriarchal library. It is entirely possible that Gilles could have had access to its collection. But again, here, Gilles is silent. He never tells us anything directly about that resource either. Therefore, the possibility that he could have found Procopius' works in either of these repositories remains just that — a possibility.

In general, we know very little about works of Byzantine authors available to Gilles in Constantinople during his visit. However, two manuscripts have been identified as actually having been in Gilles' own hands, and they contained works by authors previously unknown in the West. The first is the *Navigations of the Bosporus* by Dionysius of Byzantium, from which Gilles quotes extensively (Cod. Palatinus gr. 398)[9]; the other is a medical treatise by the thirteenth-century author Demetrius of Constantinople. Gilles must have purchased the latter for King François since it appears in the 1551 catalogue of the collection of the royal library at Fontainebleau, and it is now in the Bibliothèque Nationale in Paris (Parisinus graecus 2323).[10] Regrettably, these two manuscripts seem to be the only ones directly connected with the "shopping trip" Pierre Gilles was charged with fulfilling.

We should not neglect to consider, however, another major research tool Gilles had at his disposal in his study of ancient Constantinople: the resident population. On this subject Gilles unveils more than a tinge of hostility. Throughout his monograph he cannot resist adding the occasional observation that neither the Greek nor Turkish inhabitants remembered or cared about their city's glorious past. On the very first page of Book II he writes:

> …. Barbarous men have toppled and buried in barbarous buildings these ancient, heroic works of the city's art, using them to embellish their pathetic little dwellings to such an extent that vestiges of ancient foundations remain in only a few places. Add to that the fires and disasters perpetrated by other barbarians, and most recently by the Turks, who in the last century have not ceased utterly destroying the vestiges of the ancient city. Ancient buildings have been so demolished down to their lowest foundations and changed into different forms that not even those who have seen these former things would be able to recognize them. And then there is the feeble foolishness of the Greeks, who seem to have imbibed the entire river of forgetfulness. Not one of them is found who knows or wants to learn where the traces of ancient monuments are. Even their priests do not know of places where churches were destroyed just a few years earlier, and they marvel at those who inquire about such things.

Yet Gilles betrays himself time and again when he admits that he obtained helpful information from one of these so-called oblivious natives. For instance, it was a Turkish resident who aided him in locating the Basilica Cistern, as we shall see in his account of that structure. As for his derogatory comment about the Greeks, one feels compelled to recall the work of a Greek priest, who was associated with the patriarchate in this very period. This was John Malaxos, a contemporary of Gilles, who likewise studied and preserved information on the antiquities of Constantinople. A recent scholar has traced twenty-two surviving manuscripts directly to Malaxos. In them Malaxos preserved antique inscriptions from and descriptions of many of the city's monuments — not unlike Gilles himself.[11]

Gilles' work has passed the tests of time and repeated examination, making his book an essential source on the history of Byzantine Constantinople. Its status as a groundbreaking and amazingly trustworthy document cannot be challenged. Moreover, *The Topography of Constantinople* has an additional facet above and beyond its role as an architectural and historical survey of Constantinople because its author offers his reader the perspective of a traveler. Although his primary interest is always in the city's oldest remains, Gilles cannot help but marvel at the new and grand building projects of the sultans, some of which, like the great complex of the Süleymaniye, were still under construction at the time of his visit. Therefore, although Gilles' work purports to be a study of Constantinople and its *antiquities*, the course of his investigations reveal, in addition, a resplendent and vigorous *Ottoman* city.

NOTE ON TRANSLATION

The following is a modern English translation of the original 1561 Latin edition of Pierre Gilles' *Topography of Constantinople and Its Antiquities in Four Books*. It is intended to replace the only other known English translation made by John Ball, which was published in England in 1729. Ball's translation, although valuable and important for being the first, is incomplete and not without serious errors. The current translation is based solely on Gilles' original 1561 text because his notes, those available to his nephew and editor, Antoine Gilles, have disappeared. My primary goal as translator and editor has been to provide readers, in particular those who do not need or cannot read the original Latin, with a more accurate, complete and annotated English text that they will find accessible, informative and, I trust, enjoyable.

Notes to Introduction

1.   Pierre Gilles, *De topographia Constantinopoleos et de illius antiquitatibus libri quatuor* (Lyon: Guillaume Rovillium, 1561), II.1.

2.   Ronald G. Musto, Introduction to *Pierre Gilles: The Antiquities of Constantinople Based on the Translation by John Ball* (New York: Italica Press, 1988), xv; Fernand Braudel, *The Mediterranean and the Mediterranean World in the Age of Philip II*, 2 vols. (New York: Harper and Row, 1972–73), 410–11, 418–19.

3.   Much has recently been written on Western perceptions of the Turk during the Renaissance. For a summary see Ronald G. Musto, "Just Wars and Evil Empires: Erasmus and the Turks," in *Renaissance Society and Culture: Essays in Honor of Eugene F. Rice, Jr.*, ed. John Monfasani and Ronald G. Musto (New York: Italica Press, 1991), 197–216.

4.   Musto, Introduction, *Pierre Gilles*, xi–xxx; Müller-Wiener, *Bildlexikon*, 16–35, and see the sources on the history of Constantinople on pages 35–38; Mango, *Le développement*, entire.

5.   Jean-Pierre Grélois, "Pierre Gilles" in *Byzance Retrouvée: Érudits et Voyageurs Français XVI-XVIII Siècles* (Paris: Sorbonne, 2001), 30–31; Louis Pascal, "Pierre Gilles," in *Nouvelle Biographie Générale* 20 (Paris: Didot Frères, 1857); E.T. Hamy, "Le Pére de la zoologie française: Pierre Gilles d'Albi," *Revue des Pyrénées* 12 (1900); Musto, Introduction, *Pierre Gilles*, xi–xxx; Cyril Mango, Introduction to *Constantinople and Its Hinterland*, ed. Cyril Mango and Gilbert Dagron (Aldershot: Variorum, 1995).

6.   See, for example, Alan Cameron, "Sir Thomas More and the Greek Anthology," in *Florilegium Columbianum: Essays in Honor of Paul Oskar Kristeller*, ed. Karl-Ludwig Selig and Robert Somerville (New York: Italica Press, 1987), 187–98.

7.   Procopius, *Buildings* I.2.15–17, Bonn ed. III, 183. The probable remains of this hospital and its adjacent martyrium still stand between Hagia Sophia and Hagia Irene just inside the walls of Topkapı Palace. This quote is from Gilles II.8.

8.   Procopius, *Secret History*, 26.8–9, Bonn ed. III, 143–44.

9.   Dionysius Byzantius, *Anaplus Bospori*, ed. R. Güngerich (Berlin: Weidmann, 1958); Dionysius Byzantius, *De Bospori Navigatione. Quae supersunt una cum Supplementis in Geographos Minores Aliiusque eiusdem Argumenti Fragmentis*, ed. Charles Wescher (Paris: E Typographeo Publico, 1874).

10.   Louis Paris, *Essai Historique sur la Bibliothèque du roi* (Paris: Au Bureau du Cabinet Historique, 1856), 21–24.

11.   Peter Schreiner, "John Malaxos (16th century) and His Collection of *Antiquitates Constantinopolitanae*," in *Byzantine Constantinople: Monuments, Topography and Everyday Life*, ed. Nevra Necipoğlu (Leiden: J. Brill, 2001), 203–14.

❧

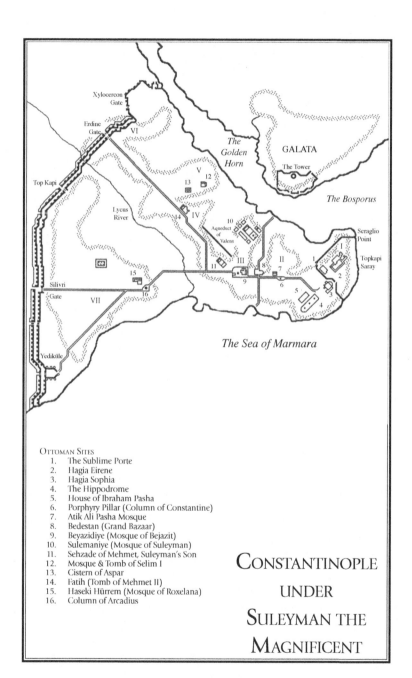

Xylocercon
Gate

Erdine
Gate

VI

The
Golden
Horn

GALATA

The Tower

Top Kapi

Lycus
River

V

12

13

IV

14

10
Aqueduct
of
Valens

The Bosporus

Seraglio
Point

Topkapi
Saray

I

15

16

11

III

8

9

II

7

6

5

1

2

4

Silivri
Gate

VII

Yediküle

The Sea of Marmara

OTTOMAN SITES

1. The Sublime Porte
2. Hagia Eirene
3. Hagia Sophia
4. The Hippodrome
5. House of Ibraham Pasha
6. Porphyry Pillar (Column of Constantine)
7. Atik Ali Pasha Mosque
8. Bedestan (Grand Bazaar)
9. Beyazidiye (Mosque of Bejazit)
10. Sulemaniye (Mosque of Suleyman)
11. Sehzade of Mehmet, Suleyman's Son
12. Mosque & Tomb of Selim I
13. Cistern of Aspar
14. Fatih (Tomb of Mehmet II)
15. Haseki Hürrem (Mosque of Roxelana)
16. Column of Arcadius

CONSTANTINOPLE

UNDER

SULEYMAN THE

MAGNIFICENT

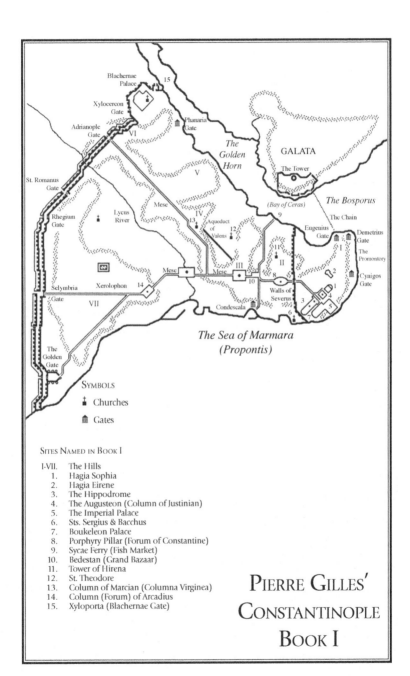

SYMBOLS

🛉 Churches

🏛 Gates

SITES NAMED IN BOOK I

I-VII. The Hills
1. Hagia Sophia
2. Hagia Eirene
3. The Hippodrome
4. The Augusteon (Column of Justinian)
5. The Imperial Palace
6. Sts. Sergius & Bacchus
7. Boukeleon Palace
8. Porphyry Pillar (Forum of Constantine)
9. Sycae Ferry (Fish Market)
10. Bedestan (Grand Bazaar)
11. Tower of Hirena
12. St. Theodore
13. Column of Marcian (Columna Virginea)
14. Column (Forum) of Arcadius
15. Xyloporta (Blachernae Gate)

PIERRE GILLES'
CONSTANTINOPLE
BOOK I

THE TOPOGRAPHY OF CONSTANTINOPLE AND ITS ANTIQUITIES IN FOUR BOOKS

BOOK I

I. THE ORIGINS OF BYZANTIUM AND ITS VARIOUS FORTUNES

Stephanus and Eustathius have recorded that Byzantium was founded by Byzas, son of Ceroessa and Neptune, or by one Byzes, leader of the Megarian fleet who established a colony there.[1] Now, I think this was in fact named after the former Byzas, for if it had been Byzes, we would call the city Byzeum instead of Byzantium. Philostratus (who was a Sophist of Byzantium), in his *Life of Marcus* calls the leader of the Megarian fleet Byzas, when he writes about Marcus, who traced the origins of his family to the old Byzas. Marcus had set out for Megara and was considered dear to the leaders of the Megarian colony.[2] When he consulted Pythian Apollo as to where to establish their city, the oracle responded that they ought to seek a territory across from the land of the blind.[3] This answer indicated the Chalcedonians because earlier, when they were carried there, and when they observed the advantage of the places, they chose inferior places that were not as good.

As for Justin's statement that Byzantium was founded by Pausanius the Spartan, I think that it should be understood in the same vein that some say Sycae, presently called Galata, was first established by the Genoese, and that Constantinople was founded by Constantine, in that they rebuilt or enlarged these places, not that they founded them initially.[4] For when I consider that according to Herodotus, at the time Darius invaded Thrace, the Byzantines and Chalcedonians did not anticipate the arrival of the Phoenician fleet at all; leaving their cities they fell back to the interior shores of the Black Sea, and established the colony of Mesembria there; the Phoenicians burned

Byzantium and Chalcedon. I believe that the Lacadaimonians,[5] led by Pausanius, put a colony there and rebuilt Byzantium, which previously had been either a Megarian colony or the city founded by Byzas, son of Neptune.[6] Eustathius says that the colony of Byzantium was called Antonina after Antonius Bassianus [Caracalla], son of the Caesar Severus. As long as the father lived, it retained this name. Many years afterwards it was called New Rome and Constantinople, and Anthusa or Florentia, or rather Flora by Constantine the Great, as a result of which Priscian called it New Rome, Constantinople.[7]

Indeed, Apollo foretold that those who lived there would be happy, but they experienced fluctuating fortune there. At first, by means of great labor, the colony emerged from struggles with the Thracians, Bithynians and Gallo-Grecians. Indeed, it paid 80 talents a year to the Gauls who dominated most of Asia. By greater exertions it grew but still was frequently vexed not only by external but also by internal affairs. It was governed at times alternately by either aristocrats or populists, and it followed various factions and flourished a long time as a republic. And with Europe and Asia widely dominated by Bithynia, as Philarkos reports in the sixth book of his *History*, the Byzantines dominated the Bithynians just as the Lacadaemonians had the Helots, whose fortune was somewhere between the condition of free people and slaves.[8]

This republic honored the Ptolemaic kings of Egypt so that they paid divine honors to Philadelphus and built a temple to him within sight of their city. And at first they cherished the Roman Empire and opposed the Macedonian king, who was named Pseudo-Philip as a mark of his inferiority.[9] I am not even mentioning the forces against Antiochus, Perseus, Aristonicus and how Antonius was helped in the war against pirates; and how the city repulsed Mithridates' assault and bore the blockade on their necks. At the same time the colony of Byzantium strongly supported Sulla, Lucullus and Pompey when it invaded a place that was convenient for transporting leaders and troops as well as supplies.

Finally it sided with Niger's forces against Severus,[10] and it was deprived of all the dignities of government and subjected to the Perinthians and was despoiled of all dignities and government.[11] The baths, theaters and the strong and high walls that defended the city were demolished. These walls had been built out of square stones rather than stones from Miletus, as Politianos believes.[12] The stone was cut neither in ancient Miletus nor in Miletopolis, because Miletus is too remote. Miletopolis, which lies near the Rhyndacus River, and which I saw in ruins near lake Apolloniatus, retains only its name and has no noteworthy quarries.

The walls of Byzantium were constructed so tightly that their joints seem not to have been put together but to be one piece, as Herodian records. Those who saw ruins of these things and remnants in the era of Herodian were amazed at those who constructed them and those who demolished them.[13] Zonaras quotes Dion as saying that Byzantium had extremely well built walls whose parapet was made with solid, three-foot stones, which were bound by brass ties in so compact a way inside that the entire structure looked like one solid wall.[14]

There were many and great towers with gates set one above another. The land walls were very tall, but the sea walls less so. Two harbors were inside the walls, barricaded by chains. More prominent towers protected the forward corners facing the harbors. While I was without a Greek text of Xenophon I thought one could understand something about one of these ports from a Latin translation that mentions that when Xenophon's soldiers came over to Byzantium from Chrysopolis, and when they had been kept out of Byzantium, they tried to smash the barriers, and they threatened to break down the gates unless the Byzantines willingly opened them. They ran to the sea and leapt from the rising walls within the city near the side of the harbor Chelas, which the Greeks so name because it extends on both sides with curved fortifications, that is, like a pincer of a crab. Later, finding a Greek codex of Xenophon, I saw there was no mention of the harbor, but only the phrase τὼ χηλὼ τοῦ τείχους, that is, "near the foundations of the wall," or rather the projections supporting the wall. If it had read χηλὴ τοῦ λιμένος it would have been referring to an arm or a leg.[15]

Dionysius of Byzantium says the first curve of the Bosporus encloses three harbors.[16] The Byzantines had 500 ships, some of which were *dicrota*, galleys with two banks of oars; some had rudders and pilots at both bow and stern and double crews, so that it was not necessary for them to change directions to go forward and to recede in order to elude the enemy. During Niger's life and after his demise the Byzantines performed miracles during a three-year siege. Not

3

only did they sail about and capture the enemy's ships, but they even pulled the triremes from enemy positions. Divers cut the anchors, and swimming under water with ropes attached to their heels and bound to the rudders, they pulled the ships, which appeared to drift away spontaneously.

The Byzantines were not the first to do this, for the Tyrians, accustomed to collecting conchs and other things like that in deep water, used to cut the anchors, swimming up unseen. When Alexander noticed this he ordered iron chains instead of rope tied to the anchors. When they had used up everything during the siege, the Byzantines even fought back using wood that they pulled down from their homes, and they used rope for their ships made from their women's hair. They sometimes even hurled statues and horses down on their enemies. They were so deprived of anything edible that they ate hides softened in water, and when the hides were consumed they began to act savagely towards each other, eating human flesh! Finally, oppressed by hunger, they unwillingly surrendered their city. The Roman army slaughtered the soldiers and the principal citizens. The entire city was demolished to its foundations, and the walls, whose ostentation used to be such a source of pride, were destroyed. At the same time the theaters, baths and everything of refinement and honor was reduced to the appearance of a village, and it was handed over to the Perinthians. Severus was exceedingly happy with the capture of the city. He took away its liberty and dignity and imposed on it a tribute to the republic, and he confiscated the property of the citizens. He then made Byzantium and its neighborhood a gift for the Perinthians.

Setting out for Byzantium, Severus then saw the citizens coming towards him as suppliants with olive branches, praying for protection and offering excuses for opposing him. He halted the bloodshed, but he kept them subjects of the Perinthians. In spite of this he gave them a theater and portico and took care to oversee the building of a hippodrome. He added baths, which he constructed in the precinct of the Temple of Jupiter, called Zeuxippus. He renovated the Strategium too. Everything Severus started his son Antoninus completed.[17]

II. On the Size of Byzantium

The present residents of Constantinople say that old Byzantium occupied the area of the first hill that is set aside for the sultan's palace

of Topkapı, but it will be clear from the things I will now address that
it had a larger area than this. Recent authors relate that Byzantium
began at the wall of the citadel and stretched all the way to the Tower
of Eugenius and ascended to the Strategium, the Baths of Achilles and
the Urbicion, from where it extended to the Chalkoprateia and the
Miliarium where there was a land gate of the Byzantines. Then it ran
to the Pillars of Zonarius and after a descent, on up to the Acropolis
by way of the Mangana and Baths of Arcadius.[18]

I would put my faith in all these more recent authors, not that
their trustworthiness is more evident to me in many other instances
but because of Eustathius, who writes that the Athenians used
Byzantium, a small city, for storing their treasury.[19] But Zosimus,
a more ancient historian, describes Byzantium in this way. It was
situated, he says, on a hill that occupied part of the isthmus, forward
where the bay called the Golden Horn and the Propontis [Marmara
Sea] come together. At the end of the portico Emperor Severus built
a gate after he had calmed his anger at the people of Byzantium for
supporting his enemy Niger. The wall of Byzantium ran from the
western part of the city to the Temple of Venus and to the sea opposite
Chrysopolis; likewise from the north it descended to the harbor
called Neorium on to the opposite sea, which lies in the region of the
outlet through which ship traffic passes to the Euxine or Black Sea.[20]
This, Zosimus says, was the ancient area of the city; but Dionysius,
who is a more ancient writer than Zosimus, since his account was
written before the destruction by Severus, tells us that the circuit of
Byzantium was forty stadia,[21] a much larger area than others would
have it.[22] Herodian says that in the time of Severus Byzantium was
the greatest city in all of Thrace.[23]

III. The Rebuilding of Constantinople and Its Size

Zonaras writes that Constantine the Great, wanting to build a
city named after himself, initially selected Sardicus, a territory in
Asia. Then he chose the Sigeum promontory and finally Chalcedon
and Byzantium.[24] George Cedrinus says Constantine first chose
Thessalonica and lived there two years. Since that locale pleased him,
he built wonderful temples, baths and aqueducts until, interrupted
or frustrated by plague, he left this site. Zonaras writes further that
he continued on to Chalcedon, which had been overthrown by the

Persians of Bithynia.[25] While Constantine was starting to rebuild it, eagles showed him where Constantinople should be built. They often snatched the architects' small stones and carried them to Byzantium.[26] Zonaras does not mention the stones but claims instead that they were ropes.[27] But it seems this is a legend taken from Dionysius of Byzantium who says that Byzas, the founder of Byzantium, was a little way off from his ultimate destination; he would have built Byzantium at a place called Semystra, situated at the entrance of the Cydarus and Barbysa rivers, had not a crow portended to him that Byzantium should be founded there by stealing a bit of the sacrifice from the middle of the flames and carrying it to the promontory of the Bosporus.[28]

Constantine does not seem to me to have been as oblivious as the ancient Chalcedonians, whose blindness was repeatedly noted in all kinds of literary records. Any reasonably intelligent person can see that Byzantium was a much more suitable home for the Roman Empire than Chalcedon! The far more ancient authorities were more perceptive. Among these better authorities are Sozomen of Salamis and Zosimus, who wrote his history in the time of Theodosius the Younger [Theodosius II]. They do not even mention Sardica, Thessalonica or Chalcedon. They say that Constantine considered building a city equal to his own name in degree and equal to Rome in dignity, and that he found a suitable place between ancient Ilium and the Hellespont and that he laid the foundations and even raised part of the wall to some height. Parts of this wall can be seen today on the Sigeum promontory, which Pliny called Aiantium because the sepulcher of Ajax was located there overlooking the outermost point of the straits of the Hellespont.[29] Here, it is said, there was a ship landing, and the Achaeans pitched their tents here while at war with Troy. Later Byzantium seemed a more suitable place to Constantine. Three hundred and sixty-two years after the reign of Augustus, Constantine rebuilt it, enlarged it and surrounded it with excellent walls. By imperial edict, which was engraved on a stone column publicly displayed in the Strategium near his own equestrian statue, he ordered that it be called New Rome, Constantinople.[30]

Because Constantine determined that the number of indigenous citizens was not sufficient for the size of the city, he erected scattered houses near the public squares, which he presented as residences to senators and other elites that he had brought with him from Rome and other nations. He built forums for the beautification of the city; he constructed others for its business. He built the Hippodrome, along with temples, fountains, porticos and a Senate, which he intended to have a dignity equal to what the senators of Rome had. He also built himself a royal residence not much inferior to the Imperial Palace in Rome. Eventually, eager to make it similar in design and equal to Rome itself, he brought it to such a state of greatness that, according to Sozomen, Constantinople was greater in multitudes of people and luxuries than Rome.[31]

Cunapius [sic] of Sardis, no base writer and although biased against Constantine, nevertheless describes the extraordinary greatness of Constantinople as follows. Constantinople, he says, formerly called Byzantium, granted the Athenians of long ago the privilege of importing grain, which they were used to transporting in large amounts. But at present neither the vast number of commercial grain ships from Egypt, nor the imports from all of Asia, Syria, Phoenicia and many other countries are able to support Constantinople or satisfy the people whom Constantine brought to the city of Byzantium from other cities that he had depopulated.[32] Moreover Zosimus, although otherwise unfriendly towards Constantine on account of his religion, nevertheless allows that Constantine enlarged Constantinople to the size of the greatest city and says that the city was enclosed by walls cutting off the isthmus from sea to sea 15 stadia beyond the walls of old Byzantium.[33]

But however large Constantine might have increased its area, succeeding emperors increased it further still and, because of the hordes flowing in for military service or trade or other business, they enclosed the city in walls far greater than the Constantinian ones. His successors allowed the inhabitants to build houses so near each other that they lived closely packed even in the market places and travelers moved along at some peril because of the crowds of men and animals. Hence it came about that no small part of the sea surrounding the city was dried up. In addition, with pilings driven into the sea and houses put on them, the city was made large enough to hold the most people possible.[34] So Zosimus discusses the great size of this city as it stood in the time of either Arcadius or Theodosius.[35]

Agathias writes that in Justinian's time building had been so uninterrupted, constant and close together that one could rarely get a view of the sky that was open to daylight and free on all sides. One could only see the sky by looking straight up.[36] We can get an idea of the large size of Constantinople before Justinian's time from an ancient description of the city by an unknown, but apparently reliable, author.[37] He says that the length of the city in a direct line from the Porta Aurea to the seashore was 14,075 feet and the width was 6,150 feet.[38] It is not clear in Procopius that the Blachernae was enclosed within the walls during the reign of Justinian,[39] although before his time the city had been enlarged by Theodosius the Younger [Theodosius II]. As Zonaras and others record, he had given this piece of business to Cyrus, prefect of the city.[40] This Cyrus constructed a land wall over the ground from sea to sea in sixty days with great and swift diligence. The people of the city, happy with this work, and amazed at the speed with which it was completed, proclaimed aloud with one voice in the Theater, in the presence of Emperor Theodosius, that "Constantine founded this city, but Cyrus renewed it!" Because of this, envy and suspicion grew against Cyrus, so by the command of Theodosius he was tonsured against his will, and then he was made bishop of Smyrna.[41] Inscriptions written for a Constantine on the gates called Xylocerum and Rhegium refer to him with these words:

On the gate Xylocerum in Byzantium:

Θεωδόσιος τόδε τεῖχος ἄναξ καὶ ὕπαρχος ἑῷας
Κωνσταντῖνος ἔτευξαν ἐν ἤμασιν ἐξήκοντα.[42]
In sixty days Emperor Theodosius
And Constantinus, Prefect of the East, built these walls.

On the Rhegium Gate in Byzantium:

Ἤμασιν ἐξήκοντα φιλοσκήπτρῳ βασιληνι
Κωνσταντῖνος ὕπαρχος ἐδείματο τεῖχει τεῖχος.[43]
In sixty days Constantine the Eparch added wall to wall
For the scepter-loving emperor.

As to what moved Constantine to call Byzantium "New Rome" or "Queen of the Roman Empire," Sozomen and others relate that one night God appeared to Constantine in a dream and delivered an oracle telling him that he should build a city worthy of Constantine's name at Byzantium.[44] Others say that just as when Julius Caesar wished to avoid the plots against him and thought it wise to move to Alexandria or Ilium, carrying the wealth of the empire along with him, so too Constantine sensed that he was drifting into disfavor with the Senate and the Roman people. He therefore emptied the city of Rome and moved first to Troy then later to Byzantium.

Zosimus, who hated the Christian name, asserts cowardice as an especially impious cause for Constantine's move. Constantine, he says, had murdered Crispus and was guilty of other flagrant crimes, so he requested expiation for these crimes from the priests. The response he received from them was that his crimes were so severe that he could not atone for such wickedness. But a certain Egyptian, who came from Iberia to Rome, told Constantine that he could obtain expiation for all of his crimes if he would follow the Christian belief that men contaminated by evil and crime could obtain remission of all their sins immediately upon repenting for them. Constantine had no problem believing this report and abandoned the national religion. He was made one of the Christians whom the Egyptian told him about. Constantine was afraid when the time came for him to go up the Capitoline Hill with his army, as customary, and carry out the traditional rites of his own pagan religion, and did not attend because he had been warned not to attend by a vision sent to him by the Egyptian.[45] His refusal of the holy sacrifice angered the Senate and excited the antagonism of the whole populace of Rome against him. On account of this, unable to bear all these execrations, he sought out a city similar to Rome where he could set up his palace and seat of government. He found a place between the Troad and old Ilium suitable for building a city; he laid the foundations for the royal palace and raised part of the city's wall. But then, regretting this locale, Constantine abandoned the incomplete work and approached Byzantium, admiring the situation of the city. He judged it to be especially suitable for establishing the residence of the emperor.[46] So says Zosimus, a follower of Julian the Apostate and an avid enemy of Constantine on account of his religion. On account of his views I cannot give credence to the crimes he assigned to this fictitious Constantine. Such things were quite far from the mind of Constantine, who was a man of the greatest piety and civility.

I could attempt to demonstrate this fully if it would not pose such a great digression from the present history. In fact, both Sozomen and Evagrius have adequately refuted these malicious claims.[47] In terms of these crimes I say that I disagree entirely with Zosimus, but as far as his description of the size and extent of the city goes, I am compelled to agree; for although he is Constantine's enemy, he is forced to credit him with building such a large, great and beautiful city. I am even more inclined to credit his history because he lived many years closer to the time of Constantine than our present monks. In the little, unreliable books they have composed about Constantinople these monks write that Constantine erected a wall from the tower of Eugenius, which was the border of old Byzantium, to the church of St. Anthony, from the precincts named for the Mother of God called Rabdon, up to the Exacionion, and that after a mile it ran up to the old gates of the church of St. John the Baptist, going further to the cistern of Bonus, from where it stretched to the Armation and thence back around to St. Anthony's again. I might accept this description if I had not noticed that the authors of these things are frequently untruthful, so that I think it wise to pass over them. I find it to be a genuine mistake that they place the church of St. John the Baptist *inside* the Constantinian walls, when for many years after Constantine's death it stood outside the city. I will take up many other errors below.

IV. THE FORM, AREA, LENGTH AND BREADTH OF PRESENT-DAY CONSTANTINOPLE

Constantinople is washed on three sides by the sea. To the north is an inlet called the Horn, where the Bosporus pushes in towards Europe. On the east it is bounded by the outer edge of the Bosporus, on the south by the Propontis, and on the west by the land of Thrace. It is shaped like a triangle; its base runs to the west while the top extends to the east, at least to the beginning of the peninsula, but the sides are unequal. Indeed, should you see the side towards the west, from the corner angle, a gulf lets in a lunate crescent, then after that it proceeds a long ways from the north and it turns to the south. This side really runs southward but allows a bend in this extension, so that were a straight line extended from angle to angle, it would include the large curve of the sea that is at least more than two stades deep in the center. The next side extends northwards to the bay named the Golden Horn in such a way that if you direct a line from one angle to the other angle it would include within the triangle the entire Horn and part of the city of Galata. For this side curves so that its two furthest points form a bow, with two smaller bows in the center. These recede inwards so that the two extreme points of the bow incorporating them do not impede one from looking and making out one point from the other.

It appears, then, that Constantinople is tri-curved instead of triangular in shape, for the sharp angles do not stick out beyond a side nor do they jut inward. The curves indeed do stick out and bend inwards. And so, if these three curves were cut off, however far they may extend from the trunk of the city, the city would be left a rectangle somewhat more than a mile broad and three times more than this in length. And if the Horn, which divides the Bosporus, did not curve toward the solstice east but due east, it would straighten out the longest distance. The city could then be understood as triangular. For the side running along the gulf would almost be straight, and the side on the Propontis would be more straightened out and the angles would be almost equal in degree, but it would still have the shape of sharp angles. Indeed, some would be duller, others sharper, and the sides would not yet have straight lines. Nonetheless we are able to say, as all believe, that the city is a triangle with three corners: the one facing the Propontis and the other bordering continental Thrace are of [roughly] equal length; the third side along the inlet, the Horn, is a mile shorter than the other two.

The city is nearly 13 miles in circumference, but Laonikos Chalkokondyles in his history, which he wrote about the Ottomans, says that Constantinople was 111 stadia in circumference.[48] The length running along the ridge of the promontory forming the six hills is not more than 30 stadia. But if the city were a true triangle it would not exceed nine miles. But if its hilly situation were stretched out into one plateau it would be pulled out to a greater length. Nevertheless, it would not be as large as the populace of Byzantium claim, that is 18 miles. Nor, in any case, would it contain more buildings since it is situated on hills than it would if it were on a level plain, because building is done on a plane [that is, defined by a plumb line] and not perpendicular to the incline of a hill. But this reasoning does not apply to people the way it does to houses, for it is possible that Constantinople could hold more people, since it is situated on hills, than if it were on a plain, but it could not hold more buildings.[49] The bases of people are able to rest on a hill, but not the foundations of homes, whose ground must be level.

The width varies from the east to the middle of the city; it is at least a mile, but no more than a mile and a half in width. Then it gradually separates into two projections, where it is almost as long as it is wide. It is not very different in shape from an eagle stretching its wings and looking at an angle to the left, with its beak positioned on the first hill, where the Royal Palace [Topkapı] is. Its eye is the church of Hagia Sophia. Near the lower back part of its head is the Hippodrome, two hills are on its neck, and the rest of the city occupies its wings and the rest of its body.[50]

V. A General Description of Constantinople

Constantinople occupies a peninsula that has seven hills. Of these hills, the one in the eastern corner of the city rises on the promontory that Pliny called Chrysoceras or "the Golden Horn," and Dionysius of Byzantium called Bosporium.[51] This first hill is divided from the second hill by a wide valley; the single promontory, the Bosporium, contains the other six hills and runs west from the point of the peninsula in the east, with a continuous, slightly convex ridge so that it stretches with six hills along its right side, which overlooks the gulf. The promontory folds inwards with five valleys, but only the third and the fifth valleys go all the way through to the left side of the promontory. But even so, with folds slightly indenting the back of the ridge, it sweeps around almost perfectly smoothly, and on its left side it goes along as one long hill, which does not have separate hills, but rather mounds, where small valleys make slight impressions that are steeper than the mounds themselves. And so the back of the promontory stretches for some way on an uneven plain and with an uneven weight. It curves with two mounds, the first going from the ridge of the first hill. From there it rises gradually to the next bend, which forms on the ridge of the third hill, where there is a slight indentation, as the ridge of the pass between the third and fourth hills comes through.

This promontory, which I said has six hills, has a variety of plains, some are on the top, some at the base, and in either case the plains are not very level. The plain between the first and second hills is 700 paces in length and 200 paces across.[52] Thus, going from the slope of this hill rather smoothly, one arrives at the summit of the second hill, which is somewhat flat for 500 paces, but almost the whole top gradually slopes downhill. The second valley in the ridge is narrow and hardly inclines at all. On the third hill the plateau is more than 600 paces across but is flatter than the place where the third valley arises, which is 600 paces wide. From here one goes up gently to the field sitting on top of the fourth hill, which is no more than 200 paces wide. But on the fifth hill it increases to 700 paces. The ridge is narrower on the hill from where the fifth valley originates; on the sixth hill the continuous ridge rises in altitude again a bit.[53]

Even though it surrounds the entire promontory, the land stretching between the sea and the base of the promontory is not uniform in shape; below the hills it is smaller. At the base of the valleys it is wider by half as much. Going along from the start of the promontory, it opens out 1000 paces near the three valleys. At the base of the hills, though, the promontory is never narrower than 120 paces in width, or an acre, except at the base of hills three and five where it is quite narrow. It stretches over a large area of the fourth valley both in length and width. At the bottom of the sixth hill it gets narrow again, except at the bottom of the two small hills standing behind the first and second hills. One of these small hills runs almost to the sea and the other is not very far from the sea.

But now in order to describe the city's setting more easily, I will describe each of its hills and valleys in turn, which are very pleasant to view. From the ridge of the promontory six hills are born and hang over the cliff. And so just as you could call them brothers, they are situated in order like siblings born in succession so that not one of them blocks the view of the other. As one sails up the bay one can see all of them hanging over the bay on three sides, so that each hill shows both sides. The first of these hills hangs over its eastward base and blocks off the bay. The second and third hills recede more inland to the south. The others look north rolling so gradually that one can see both sides of all of them at once. The first hill sits lower than the second, and the second lower than the third; but the fourth, fifth and sixth hills are higher in some places and lower in others than the third hill. One can determine this by judging their heights against the level of the Aqueduct of Valens. One can see that the first hill is shorter than the third and fourth hills because of the tower on which the water channel of the Aqueduct, which presses out water, is built more than 50 feet high.

In order to clarify all this I will not divide the city's length running from the point of land at the edge of the Bosporus to the walls just short of the surrounding sea, but rather the width spreading from the Propontis to the Golden Horn. The reason behind my dividing Constantinople's breadth into six parts has to do with the promontory's natural setting, which is composed of six hills separated by valleys overlooking the gulf, but not really breaking through to the other side of the promontory. Picking out the seven hills of Rome is not too difficult given that the valleys clearly separate and delineate them, but identifying the hills of Constantinople is rather more challenging since they are united at their summits. Indeed, the part of the promontory generating the hills at the back does not swell out like the front. So I am unable to apply a better description to them than to say that the six hills stretch out from the continuous ridge of a single promontory with valleys in between. Therefore, I shall continue in the following account to describe the right flank of the promontory as I have from the start, namely, in terms of hills and valleys. I will describe the left flank of the promontory as the "back side" of the hills or valleys.

VI. The Layout of the City

The first wide part of the promontory is the front of the peninsula stretching 1000 paces in length to the east, joining the mouth of the Bosporus. Indeed, this part runs down a second part of the promontory with a shore gently curving in an arc so that, from the point where the Bosporus is divided near the edge of the Golden Horn and channel of the outermost opening of the Bosporus, it stretches about four stadia from north to south, and from there a further four stadia more in distance; it turns from the northeast where the sun rises in the summer to the south–southwest where the sun sets in winter, up to the very entrance of the Propontis, which meets with the Bosporus and encircles the front of the promontory to the southwest for two more miles. The bend of the city curves at the bottom of this side of the hill to a coastal plain as wide as it is long, that is, 200 paces. All of the hills rising from this are barely large in size, not exceeding 400 paces in height. On the left side of these hills facing southeast stands the Hippodrome, and on the right side, which faces the northeast, the side of the first hill ends and finishes, on top of which is the Royal Palace [Topkapı Sarayı]. I can say that the entire front is a part of the first hill. It is made continuous with the plain and slope running along equally, and attached to the first hill. But I will discuss each separately, so that each may be understood more clearly.

14

VII. THE FIRST HILL AND PALACE REGION, AND HAGIA SOPHIA AND THE
HIPPODROME

The first hill runs from the northeast to the southwest and initially
opens to a width of 30 paces. Then it widens suddenly and stretches out
just a little less wide than it is long. It starts at the peninsular isthmus,
with its corner forming the tip of the triangle of the city. It juts out
like a sword or a tongue gently sloping into the plain to an area where
the Bosporus divides between its own channel and the area called the
Golden Horn. The whole of the first hill extends out from the others
almost to the mouth of the bay [that is, the Golden Horn] and projects
over the entrance. And like an arm held out, it hides the bay so that
if you drew a line from its tip to the western corner of the city, the
whole bay would be within the line, and you would include the coastal
plain of the town of Galata. Thus, with great assistance from nature,

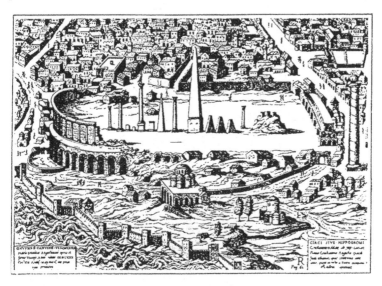

4. *The Hippodrome c. 1450, engraving, Venice, 1600.*

the point of the promontory with the first hill protects the bay from
winds and makes it more of a harbor. The first hill rises with slopes on
all sides except on the neck where the plain is connected to the rest of
the similarly flat back of the promontory, whose slopes look northeast
and rise moderately up to the north. Some mounds are more steeply

sloped, so that in some places they are ascended by stairs. But all the higher places are more than 400 paces high.

The coastal plain wrapping around the base of the hill is uneven. The shore makes the plain on the east broader, swelling in a lunate curve. The part of it that goes north and faces west increases its width where the valley divides the first and second hills. The plain at the summit of the first hill is 700 paces long. This hill is not only defended by nature herself, being bordered on the east by the Bosporus, on the north by the Golden Horn, and on the northwest by a valley, it is also enveloped by the walls of the royal enclosure [Topkapı] by which it is separated from the rest of the city, with many bastions

5. *Plan of Tokapı Palace.*
E. H. Averdi.

16

and towers just as strong as those of the city walls. The gardens of the sultan fill up the bases of the hills and the coastal plain. The palace looks down far and wide on the sea and the plains. The Imperial Palace sits partly on the summit of the hill and partly on the flat top on which the palace areas are completely enclosed. The first area extends about 700 paces in length and is 200 wide. Another squared area follows, separated from the first by walls and gates. It is a quadrangle 200 paces long, surrounded all around by a portico supported by a large variety of marble columns. In the middle of the area plane and cypress trees shade the lawyers, and in the north corner of the court is the Legal Forum that the Turks call *Divan*. On the northeast side the palace of the sultan shines on the north side. On the south side the baths and royal kitchens stand together, with the kitchen's eight arched hemispheric roofs and chimneys standing together. Each one of the domes in this series of chimneys bears a resemblance to a small house. But it's nothing but the glowing chimney roofed on top in the shape of a lantern.[54]

The doors of the first court are situated in the middle of the neck of land on which the ridge of the hill joins with the level area on the flat top of the promontory. These double doors are iron. Open, they stand 20 paces apart, and between them stand guards. Arms, hung in display, shine on either side of the entrance.[55] The jambs and thresholds of the doors are brilliant with shiny marble. A square structure covered with lead sits on top of the vestibule. All the other buildings of the palace are similarly roofed. A passage leads in from the first court through another pair of double doors into the second, inner court. At this second gate, which also bristles with arms, are stationed the door-keepers.[56] This gate has no exterior porch, but a sort of interior one, conveying those departing. It is supported by ten columns of marble of varied types. The paneled ceiling shines with gold and is decorated with Persian work of the most luxurious and detailed colors. At the third gate, through which is the entrance to the royal palace, stand the innermost gatekeepers, the commander of the gatekeepers and the royal bedchamber.[57]

No one enters freely except the household staff of the royal palace. Others are not permitted to enter without permission from the sultan, except while the sultan sits just inside by the doors, so that the royal ministers and ambassadors, when they need to wish the sultan well, pay homage with a kiss on his hand. The sultan sits on a rather

6. *Topkapı Palace. Bab-ı-Hümayün Gate (Imperial Gate, main entrance to palace grounds).*

humble little couch for this, but it is spread magnificently inside a small marble structure, gleaming with gold and silver and precious stones. The structure is surrounded by a portico supported with spiraled columns of rare marble, their capitals and bases entirely gilded.

The palace enclosure has many other gates aside from those I have discussed. But these open only for the sultan and his most trusted ministers. Indeed, I recall counting twelve made entirely of iron. Seven face the city and two, which were used to cart hay into the palace grounds, are closer to the sea. Five more gates are on the sea side: the first is to the north towards the bay; the second, situated on the tip of the hill's point, is fronted by a vestibule having a roof paneled with gold and with Persian paintings, supported by columns of ophitic marble. It looks out on the central flow of the Bosporus. Not far from this gate is a third gate facing Chalcedon and the rising sun. In front of this gate in boathouses there are small boats in which the sultan is accustomed to sail to his hunting grounds or to his gardens. The fourth of these five seaside gates lies to the southeast near ruins of a Christian church. Greeks are accustomed to revere traces of this church, visible in a wall, access to which is very crowded.[58] Past this is a fifth gate where straight beams allow one to see fish entering nets. The sultan's fishermen usually come out here. It has an extremely pleasant view, I might add.

Even though the views from all of Constantinople's hills are very fine, none can compare with the

7. *Topkapı Palace. Bab-üs Selam Gate (Gate of Salutations).*

view you get from the first hill where the sultan resides in extreme comfort. Whether he strolls in his gardens or rests at home, he has before him a complete panorama of the Bosporus and both its shores, which are verdant and lush with the woods of nearby suburbs. On his right hand he can behold the Chalcedonian plain covered with his own gardens, islands crowding the Propontis, and the wooded mountains of Asia. If he looks far into the distance behind him he can see Mt. Olympus covered in snow all year. Closer, he sees the respectable part of the city, the church of Hagia Sophia and the Hippodrome. If he turns his gaze to the left he can see the city's seven hills and the plains of Thrace stretching far and wide. He can look in every direction and wherever he turns he views vessels, some sailing from the Hellespont or the Black Sea and others returning to his ports from all the coasts of the Propontis, while still others sail up and down the Golden Horn. At any given moment he sees an infinite multitude of small boats passing back and forth. And if he glances below, the sultan has the pleasurable prospect of three sides of the first hill covered with flowers, trees and plants of all sorts.

The view is not limited to the extremely pleasant royal complex but even includes all the hillsides of the gardens, in which there are many vistas, and indeed all three sides of the hill stand out as a viewpoint. Should he desire to have a view closer to the sea, at the center of the

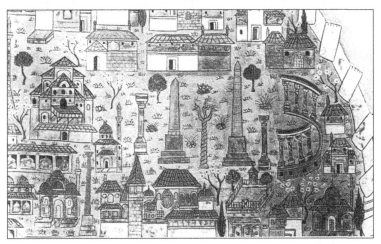

8. *Matrakçı Nasuh's view of the Hippodrome. MW Archive.*

19

shore sloping to the point where, as I said, the Bosporus is divided into two parts, the royal portico gleams with marble and columns. It has a beautiful and extremely pleasant appearance, where refreshing breezes blow all through the summer, and one can see into the branches extending everywhere as if the portico were hidden in netting. Hence, like another Gyges, seen by no one, he can see all who sail their boats so near that he can make out their faces. And should the sultan ever tire of his servants' companionship he can amuse himself in the silly

9. *Hippodrome, Palace of Ibrahim Pasha.*

humor of free men outside who struggle, pushing their oars and poles on the rocks on the shore line to work against the strong Bosporus current that is more rapid than the Rhone's.

Outside the royal enclosure of Topkapı stands the church of Hagia Sophia, about 70 paces from the gate of the royal enclosure [that is, the first court of Topkapı]. It sits on the neck of the first hill on a projection overlooking the garden in the first valley. From here there is an ascent by stone steps to the gate of the royal grounds and the church of Hagia Sophia, which has a slope from the southeast so gradual that it joins up with the summit subtly and widely with the plain below it. In short, all the slopes from the Imperial Palace enclosure to the Hippodrome are moderate and easy. To the southwest of Hagia Sophia a field over of 700 paces long stretches to the end of the Hippodrome. The length of the Hippodrome is more than two stadia and its width is one stade; it stands perfectly level but this is due not so much to its natural setting as to human labor. Its center stretches toward the Propontis and is bound by hills that slope gently to the east, more steeply to the west, falling off to a great depth, from the Propontis; indeed, it looks not so steep and precipitous, as it appears as if its height were straightened to a perpendicular height of about 50 feet.[59] The entire façade [or Sphendone] of the Hippodrome, built on arches, rises above the floor of the Hippodrome and affords a fabulous view of the Propontis, so that not only boat traffic but even leaping dolphins are visible. The stairs on the north side of the Hippodrome existed there until a few years ago when they were taken out by Abraham Bassa [Ibrahim Pasha] while he was building his own residence.[60] Between the Hippodrome and Propontis lies a field, which widens to 400 paces across, where the church of Sergius and Bacchus also stands. I will address this monument below. Beneath the Hippodrome, to the south, is the Porta Leonis or Gate of Leo, which stands outside the city upon the ruins of the palace of Leo Macellus. Its windows of ancient workmanship still remain in the walls. This palace was built on a hill adjacent to the sea about 100 paces high .

VIII. The First Valley

From the highest plain of the promontory on which, as I stated, are the church of Hagia Sophia and the Hippodrome, one climbs to the ridge of the second hill, ascending 1000 feet up to the Porphyry Column erected on top of the second hill. The second hill is bordered on the east by the first valley, which separates the first and second hills. It rises at the plain of Hagia Sophia and continues on from south to north. This valley is shaped just like a compass opened with straightened legs, one leg runs to the east while the other runs to the north. Down its middle runs the wall of the royal complex that separates Topkapı from the rest of the city. The lowest plain on the promontory stretches in length and width into this valley so far that from the bay to Hagia Sophia one may walk almost 1000 paces without going uphill or down. At first the sea plain opens out into 500 paces of flat ground. Then it winds into the valley and rises a bit for 300 paces. Although it declines gently, it is easier to determine the incline by observing running water than by walking on it. The plain starts out rather wide and not very steep but grows deeper after it pulls into two little valleys near Hagia Sophia.

Although the valley is 400 paces long, it inclines gently and is very narrow so that the public road takes up its flat bottom.

IX. The Second Hill

The ridge of the promontory swells up a little and the two valleys adjacent to it form the second hill. The first valley on the east separates the first and second hill, and the other valley to the west distinguishes the second and third hills. It is bordered on the north by a coastal flatland. The moderately sloped backbone of the promontory runs from south to north for a distance of 1000 paces and is 400 paces wide. The different widths of the valleys cause the width of the entire hill to vary. The valleys that rim its border at the top increase it where they are narrow. But at the base of the hill they open out and make the hill narrower and increase the length of its rise to two places where it overlooks the bay. Here it falls to a different height with a tripartite cliff.[61] The slope facing southeast is carried up evenly and smoothly from the lowest part of the valley to the top of the hill to the height of around 1000 paces. Then as the valley broadens the slope diminishes, but it is steeper, with two small valleys that the large valley sends down more precipitously, but not for more than 100 paces.

The altitudes of the different cliffs projecting over the bay can best be measured by looking at the different heights of the five public thoroughfares that run from the ridge to the base of the hill. The first of these roads rises to 500 paces, 200 of which from the foot of the hill are very steep and the remaining 300 are flat. The second road is 600 paces high, the first paces rising gently through a small valley floor, and the next 100 paces being steep so that one must use steps to climb it; the other 400 paces run gradually to the hill's summit which is 60 paces wide. From the summit the ridge of this second hill extends 150 paces to the south to the street leading from the church of Hagia Sophia to the Porphyry Column.

The other three public routes leading from the bottom of the hill ascend gradually for the initial 100 paces, but the next 200 paces are very steep so that the way is eased by switchbacks and turns; the last 500 paces that take you up to the plain on top of the hill are of moderate incline. From the sides of the cliffs, which I said bordered on the bay, however, two small hills, one to the north and one to the east, stick out from the face of the cliffs overlooking the bay. Both lean towards each other and form a single, gentle slope 80 paces high, which is bordered on the east by a steep little hill. For this reason most of this hill look east, and the western side of the hill has various degrees of incline. Its slopes touch the lowest plain of the valley and are steep and almost straight up from the foot of the hill to its center, and from its center to the summit they rise just a small amount. Indeed the slopes at the top of the valley do not exceed 200 paces high. But they have different inclines, for the cliffs seem lower as the valley gets higher. In fact all the smaller cliffs of this hill have two kinds of decline from the point of a hill's length, one sloping from the sides of this length — the ones sinking this way face east and west, as ones falling the other way sink north.[62] Essentially all sides of this hill even in the steepest places are not more than a stadia high but in other places they descend with a gentle slope. The bases are drawn out gradually into a plain and the high slopes almost make the top of the hill a kind of plateau. The coastal plain between the bay and hill is narrowest at the north base of the hill and spreads out a distance of 300 paces, but it suddenly widens again to 500 paces between the two small hills and runs into the valleys more wide than it is long.

I now come to the left side the promontory. Behind the second and third hills stand two smaller hills overlooking the Propontis, and between three hillsides a valley runs down like a roof-tile — not slightly inclined as they are on a roof but rather very steep. There are hills in the center of each valley: the eastern hill as well as the western one draws up to more than 200 paces in height. Between these hills there is a small valley, barely curved. Below it is a walled harbor located on the coastal plain that extends to the front of the Hippodrome. The mouth of this harbor is 300 paces across. From the Golden Horn to the Propontis the width of the hill stretches two miles.

X. The Second Valley, which Divides the Second Hill from the Third

The valley dividing the second and third hills begins at the ridge of the promontory and ends in the plain running along the sea. It contains the fish market and ferry landing to Sycae. From the plain on the sea to the mouth of the valley a plain spreads out 400 paces wide and is so level that water is just able to run downhill from the valley into the bay. At the opening of the valley it spans 200 paces and begins to narrow gradually up to the middle of the valley, where it compresses to a width of 50 paces. From this point on it is no wider than the public street. It is similar to a roof-tile gently inclined at about the angle it has on the roof of a building. It is more than 600 paces long, 300 feet of which run level and the last 200 at more of a decline. It ascends gently to a place on the promontory where the ridge of the second hill joins the ridge of the third hill. The wide street that faces Galata runs through the lowest part of this valley. Both sides of this avenue are lined with stalls and shops roofed with shingles but with openings letting light into small windows.

The Galata merchants go up to the forum that the Turks call the Bedesten. It lies in part at the yoke of the valley and in part on a slope of the third hill. In the year 1546 the Bedesten was razed by fire except for two merchants' halls roofed with brick that were locked up each night as were their iron doors and windows. After the fire I was allowed access to observe the area of the forum laid out with straight and criss-crossed streets. I discovered it lay so flat that it was only slightly inclined from west to east and from south to north. I noted that the perimeter of the burnt forum–market was more than five stadia. On its highest part lying to the west, or sunset, I saw a fountain decorated with 45 marble columns supporting a brick roof. Because of the fire I could now see the old merchants' hall, which I could not see before because of the crowd of stalls and workshops in the way. But now, stripped of neighboring shops, I had a look around it. I noted two additions joined to the merchants' hall like wings. Each wing was divided into sixty arched rooms topped with lead roofs, the same kind they use for their shops and ateliers. The innermost rooms of these shops are always locked and safe behind an iron door. The merchants' hall itself, girded by these additions, stands on eight piers, and has fifteen domes, roofed in brickwork and covered in lead.

Twelve pillars built of squared stones support the new merchants' hall, and four arches weigh on each pillar, supporting twenty domes roofed with lead. The wing additions, with their sixty vaulted-roof taverns and shops, stand around this area. There are over 220 more warehouses within the merchants' hall that are constructed in this way: around the merchants' hall's walls and piers, broad platforms run where the sitting merchants display their wares, which they produce from wooden chests with compartments. Behind the merchants the chests are set up, standing on their own against the walls, not fixed to the walls, but closed by folding doors.[63]

XI. The Third Hill

Two valleys border the sides of the third hill, the one stretching east divides it from the second hill and the other, western one separates it from the fourth hill. The ridge of this hill extends more than 1000 paces in length from the top of the promontory. From the south towards the bay in the north it is of almost equal height, whereas the ridge of the second hill falls from the height of the promontory and drops towards the north to the low coastal plain. The summit of the third hill continues beyond the ridge of the promontory in a large, wide plain; at the base it runs 300 paces further north, swelling to the ridge of the promontory. The plain at the top of the hill varies. Extending to the ridge of the promontory, it opens roughly 800 paces in every direction, with the enclosures of the women's quarters [the Harem] occupying part of it. On the part of the plain to the east are situated the merchants' forum or Bedesten, a building for travelers, the poor or ill and the tomb [türbe] of Sultan Bayezit.[64] The south side is an open area around which are shops. There are bookstores on the rest of the plain turning to the north, a plain that is both natural and manmade. The buildings here occupy a platform supported by the foundations of the buildings that Sultan Suleyman now prepares for his own tomb, a building for travelers, the poor or ill and a sumptuous religious edifice for the Islamic religion.[65] This hill descends on three sides that swell into three minor hills. On its east flank, where the Tower of Hirena stands, a small hill sticks out into the second valley. The long projection on the back of this hill on the summit, jutting a long way towards the bay, forms another minor hill facing north. A hillock going west protrudes into the third valley where the church of St. Theodore is. It runs from the center of the ridge of the third hill towards the coastal flatland. Two sides of this hill slope downwards in a double descent, one in a straight manner and the other obliquely slanted. After it has gone a distance of 1300 paces the eastern flank of the third hill eases up gradually in its slope, which makes the side more level close to the top, but nearer the plain the descent is more of a struggle, and steeper.

The slopes coming down the ridge of the hill into the valley are varied. The highest of them, towering over a deeper valley, is raised to an altitude of 500 paces, the first 300 paces of which are extremely steep and the next 200 paces only half as steep, certainly not steeper than tiled roofs. The other slopes of this hill change gradually on their way into the valley, diminishing as the valley gets higher. The slopes of the western side are like those on the eastern side. The north face of the hill has slopes with several heights: a small hill projecting from the point of the ridge of this hill is 500 paces high, the lower 300 paces of which fall away so sharply that the buildings standing on them are all on pilings underneath; the upper 200 paces are sloped, but gently and gradually, like the back end of a horse's buttocks sloping up to the horse's back. The remaining slopes of this side, where it is drawn in closer by the coastal plain, are drawn out a long way from themselves by a diagonal slope running down the side of the hill, extending east. The coastal plain, between the base of the hill and the bay where, as I said, the hill comes down from the pointed tip of the bigger hill, is not more than 200 paces wide, but at the foot of the other parts of the hill it gradually broadens toward the entrance of the valleys.

When I first arrived in Constantinople the women's quarters of the Grand Seraglio, which is located on the back side of this hill, were just under 6000 paces in circumference; but now Sultan Suleyman's building for travelers, the poor or ill encroaches on it, taking up the cemetery that accounted for at least half of the area of the women's enclosure. The left side of the promontory, facing to the south and the Propontis behind the third hill sticks out with two smaller hills; from the one that is closer to the east, the promontory curves around gradually to the west to the other hill, which is set a bit above the base of the promontory. At this hill the side of the six-hilled promontory suddenly allows in the hindmost indent from the third valley that starts to turn north. The left side of the third hill, therefore, has two slopes: the one to the south is 600 paces high and the other, running south-southwest, is 700 paces high. But at the west end it is far shorter.

The plain that sits between the rear of the southern side of the third hill and the shore of the Propontis is never less than 300 paces or more than 700 paces across. The plain of a valley closing in the base of the hill to the west separates the seventh hill from the six-hilled promontory. This area extends from the plain on the shores of the Propontis to the [land] walls of the city not bordered by the sea. It is almost perfectly level and is consistently 500 paces across. The three hills I have discussed may accurately be called the Promontory of the Bosporus for they extend over the sea in such as way that whether one sails into Constantinople from the Black Sea or from the Propontis they can be seen from very far away, prominent over the waves of the Bosporus. The third valley appears to separate the other three hills, which stand further away from the sea and into the continent than these do. I put six hills on the promontory of the Bosporus because they stand in a row near the bay and are linked together by their summits and sides. The plain, which spreads out onto the ridge of the third hill, gradually descends to a plain overlooking the third valley, which is 620 paces long and the same number wide.

XII. THE THIRD VALLEY

The third valley lies between the third and fourth hills and appears to be a double-valley because in its center it rises in altitude, which makes it unclear as to whether it belongs to the valley or the promontory. That this rise is part of the valley seems clear, however, from the height of the arches of the Aqueduct of Valens that run from one side of the valley to the other. And it may seem to be part of the ridge of the promontory due to the valley's furthest parts which fall to the right and left, on opposite sides, far from the middle of the valley. The right side has a broad plain at its opening, which is 300 paces wide and contracts gradually to 200 paces of level plain 500 paces long. Though at the bottom the level is consistent, its sides are not raised to the same heights. Where the valley is deepest, one side rises quite high while the other side goes up three times higher. From this plain you easily ascend by steps to the ridge in the middle of the valley to the ridge of the Promontory — a flat place with a slight depression between the third and fourth hills — which is 600 paces broad, except for a small part through which the middle of the valley seems to penetrate the promontory, where it is not more than 400 paces wide.

Across this valley or ridge of the promontory the arches of an aqueduct run from the fourth hill to the third by a direct route. The level of the arches of the aqueduct is equal to the height of the hills, which is evident in that however much the ridge of the promontory sinks, the arches are still equal in height, and though flat they rise with unequal lengths. They are very high at the crest of the valley, which is a plain of level ground, but not nearly so high on the slopes of the hills. Indeed, for 800 paces they are straightened out to the same altitude, but the remaining arches are shorter, where the slopes of either hill rise up. From the ridge of this valley or, if you will, promontory, the left side of the valley declines gently, curved for 700 paces to a plain, which separates the promontory from the seventh hill, proceeding to the Propontis. From the Golden Horn to the Marmara the width of the city, running through the third valley, stretches more than ten stadia.

XIII. THE FOURTH HILL

On the fourth hill one can see the Tomb of Sultan Mehmet (he who captured Constantinople), along with a temple of the Muslim faith, as well as buildings for travelers, the poor and ill and baths. It is bordered by two valleys, the ridge of the promontory and the shore of the Golden Horn, and is more than 3600 paces in circumference. Its length from its top to the bay to the north stretches more than 1000 paces, and its width from east to west is at least 800 paces. Proceeding in a square-shape from the summit to the bay, the hill seems to end in two unequal projections, one of which runs to the north along a continuous ridge sloped on each side, the other, facing east, sinks in such a way that it seems to lie as a kind of step to the other projection. Indeed, a plain runs out on the upper part of this hill, from which an ascent opens out like a step to a lower part of the other. It proceeds to the west forming a small valley. The east side of this hill is surrounded by a valley on the east, separating it from the third hill by the coastal plain on the north that skirts the bay, and partially by a valley on the west, which isolates it from the fifth hill, and in part by the continuous ridge of the promontory that ascends so gently from the top of the fourth hill to the summit of the fifth hill that one can only make out the uneven nature of the ridge with sharp eyes rather than slowed steps.

These hills are so united that no incline is perceptible between them. The continuous plain covering the back of the fourth hill is under 800 paces long and less than 200 paces wide, but when you get to the fifth hill the plain increases to a width of 700 paces. Even though the fourth hill is equal in height to the other six hills on the promontory, its ascent is as easy going straight up as it is going up at angles, because it is pulled out a long ways, gently sloped, sinking on three hill sides. The first of these descends for the entire length of the hill from the southwest to the north more than 1000 paces, 200 of which rise up from the sea and are somewhat steep. But the remainder are so gentle that they are mounted by a nearly level path, though the last 100 paces that lead up to the top of the hill tower more steeply over the rest. The diagonal descent defining the width of the hill is two-sided; one side falls west and the other stands towards the east. Nevertheless the whole incline together originates in the valley dividing the third and fourth hills.

From the highest portion of this valley the slope ascends 200 paces. Below the summit is another incline of 500 paces, 100 of which, surging from the base, are raised on a steep incline. The level of the aqueduct reveals the height of the remaining, gently sloped distance. From the bottom plain of this valley the slopes rise 400 paces, but in a way that you ascend the first 180 by a steep slope, then one may walk 200 more paces gently sloped and almost flat. From here one goes to the middle part of this side, which is more imposing, 100 paces wide and elevated from the bottom of the hill to the top, 800 paces high. From here one descends 200 paces to the west to the lowest part of the valley that separates the fourth from the fifth hill. The whole valley is narrow, but it is about 1400 paces long. The first 200 paces along the shore of the Golden Horn are level but it is unclear whether they belong to the valley or the shore. For this valley is bounded in such a way by two hills that the fourth hill is hemmed in by the plain on the shore, which is 200 paces across but the fifth hill nearly touches the shore. The next 800 paces are nearly flat but slightly inclined; the remaining 400 paces, which broaden to the top of the promontory, are very steep.

The plain along the shore, almost perfectly level, passes between the Horn and the fourth hill and is of a varying width. The part of the plain that stretches to the curve or horn of the hill looking southwest is 400 paces across, but the part that stretches to the north point of the hill is 200 paces across. In essence the fourth hill is situated so that when one sails in the Golden Horn one would assume it to be a higher portion of the third valley, because the ridge of this hill extends so far to the south, and its slopes lie low and nearly flat for some distance, whereas the ridge of the fifth hill, which rises to the same altitude, projects far beyond the fourth hill to the north. The southward declines on the rear side of the third hill are very gentle and pleasant all the way to the plain of the valley that sets apart the promontory from the seventh hill. The back of this hill projects in a southerly direction and is removed from the third valley on both sides, so that one may call the back part of the hill the south side. The southern portion of the third hill just past a small hill in the third valley is somewhat contracted near a building for travelers, the poor or ill built by Sultan Mehmet, but the rear of the fifth hill beneath the Columna Virginea is even narrower.

XIV. The Fifth Hill

The lowest levels of the fifth hill, on the slopes of which stands the tomb of Sultan Selim, touch the Golden Horn and close off two valleys, one to the east, the other to the west. The distance around the base is about 4000 paces. The top of this hill extends so far northwards towards the Golden Horn, and the side of the fourth hill is so low towards the north, that the fourth hill seems to be more a kind of valley lying between the third and fifth hills. The fifth hill does not sit on the ridge of the promontory as the other hills do but goes out at an even height beyond the slopes of the entire promontory. It is drawn north just as the fourth hill is and falls on three sides. One faces north. How steep and upright it is can be gathered from the fact that although it is almost as high as the top ridge of the fourth hill, which has a descent over 1000 paces long, the highest summit of this hill recedes from the perpendicular of its base less than any other hill does. For the ascent is only 300 paces long through a little valley formed by two mounds that touch the shore of the bay.

After walking these 300 paces one finds stone steps built into the substructure of the leveled area above, by which one ascends to a building for travelers, the poor or ill built by Sultan Selim. This side of the hill, which looks north, swells out with four hills that sink into three small valleys and that start from the summit of the hill and interrupt the plain on the shore, which is so narrow that two of them reach the wall of the city that stands on the shore. The two small hills leave a plain 100 paces wide. The plain along the shore is never narrower than it is at the base of this hill since its width never goes over 100 paces for a stretch of 1000 paces and in some places is only 50 wide. Two of these four hills are so extremely precipitous that the buildings look as if they are on supports that are themselves about to fall. It is even possible to see the cliff face has been cut into, to facilitate the switchbacks of the streets. The other two are less abrupt and fall less precipitously, and even the valleys that border them are not so steep. The eastern face of this is 1400 paces long and 200 direct paces high. The western side sinks down from different altitudes, just as the valley sinks. In the flat plain where it is deepest, one side rises to an altitude of 500 steep paces in one place and in another slopes for 300 easy paces that are almost flat.

The southward side of the peninsula lies to the rear of the fifth hill and terminates in the valley plain that separates the six-hilled promontory from the seventh hill. At some points it inclines for a shorter distance, at others it inclines more gradually, swelling out into a big hill that looks out over the fifth valley and the valley that separates the seventh hill and the promontory. The backside of the fifth hill also bends itself into a little valley that originates from the brow of the promontory where not too long ago the Columna Virginea stood. From here the slope of the promontory towers slightly over the top of the gently curved plain on the fifth hill, which is never narrower than 600 paces across and at one place is more than 700 paces across. However, past the ridge of this hill it extends far and wide and joins the plain on the fourth hill and the plain of the rest of the promontory, proceeding up to the land-bound wall of the city. It continues 2000 paces in length with only a small dip where the ridge looks over the fifth valley.

XV. The Fifth Valley

The fifth valley, which divides the fifth and sixth hills, originates north from the bay and heads south. It is as long as the promontory is wide, that is to say, approximately 1200 paces. The first 800 paces proceed from the shore of the bay with no dips or hills. The entrance to the valley is initially 400 paces across but then imperceptibly tightens to 200. For the first 600 paces it never becomes narrower than 200 paces across. Further along it is raised up for 500 paces. At the top the ridge of the valley the back of the promontory is located, spreading out onto a plain 200 paces wide. From this summit the left side of the promontory and valley gently slopes downhill for 500 paces where it runs into the valley that divides the sixth hill of the promontory from the seventh hill. The fifth valley seems to cut right through the back of the promontory. One can observe this by looking at the right- and left-hand slopes of the two hills, which rise around it, for a very gentle incline runs from the ridge of this valley to the summits of both hills.

XVI. The Sixth Hill

The sixth hill is as long as the promontory is wide, and the promontory expands over this hill to a width of 2400 paces. The walls of the city extend north over the back of the hill as far as the shore. The ridge of this hill sinks down on two slopes within the city. Outside the walls the ground is level and joins up with the continent through a suburban plain. At its widest the hill is no more than 800 paces across and at its narrowest about 400 paces wide. Three slopes run downhill from the summit; the one on the left side of the promontory gently slopes toward the south and west, the one on the right runs towards the north and the Golden Horn, elevated for a distance of 1500 paces. This slope terminates by forming two small hills divided by a little valley. There is an aqueduct at the base of the smaller hill that sits closest to the land-bound walls of the city. When I first came to Byzantium, between this hill and the bay there stood that sacred church called the Blachernae, made famous in the writings of many historians.[66] At the base of this hill, which sits above the Blachernae church, water brought into the city from outside flows through arched subterranean passages and leaps into a marble basin with a continuous flow.[67] The eastern side of the hill is as long as the hill itself but does not have the same downward grade throughout, for the varying depths of the valley cause changes in it. Where the valley is sunk into a level plain the slope rises up for 600 paces. Where it is not so high it is no more than 500 paces, and it is the least steep where it is not raised more than 400 paces in altitude. Not only does this face of the hill slope down eastward but even as it sinks east it gradually falls on its right side to the north and on the left to the region of the sky in the south between due south and west. The plain along the shore lies between the base of the sixth hill and the Golden Horn and its most narrow section is about 800 paces across. Indeed, this is the former site of the noble church of the Blachernae and also of the Blachernae Triclinium. Further on the plain widens, winding into the fifth valley.

XVII. The Valley that Divides the Sixth Hill from the Seventh Hill

The valley dividing the seventh and sixth hills stands out gently curved and runs a distance of about 4000 paces in length, if you include the coastal plain. But if you exclude that plain and begin to measure at the bend of the seventh hill, then the valley is not more than 3300 paces long. Its plain widens at one point to 600 paces across and constricts to 500 paces at another point. No dips or rises can be felt when walking on it, but with keen eyes it can gradually be seen to stretch as far long as it is wide. It rises so gradually that the incline of the valley, which is very much like a roof tile flat on its back, would not be noticed except by one who took pains to perceive it. The sides of the third and fifth valleys and the lowest outcroppings on the fifth and sixth hills fall into this valley. It is full of agreeable gardens and fields, where the soldiers sometimes practice their mock-fighting. A small stream, which is frequently dry in the summer, courses through its center.

XVIII. The Seventh Hill

The seventh hill is called the Xerolophos, on the back of which stands the Column of Arcadius. The hill is encompassed by a circumference of about 12,000 paces, and it contains more than a third of the city. The other two-thirds lie within the area of the promontory that is enclosed by a periphery of more than 20,000 paces. Understand these "paces" as strides I usually make while actually walking around — and this goes for all of my previous mentioning of paces. I do not presume that my paces correspond with standardized Roman paces due to the circuitous paths and different types of paces that vary depending on the incline or decline of a slope. Again, consider how the peoples of this rude nation get in the way, with their confrontations more violent than an onslaught of bulls.

This seventh hill makes the third corner of the city whereby Constantinople is thought to be a triangle. Its two faces fall gently on two sides; one of which runs into the valley that separates the seventh hill from the six-hilled promontory and is of the same length as the valley itself. Its slope is easy but is 500 paces to the top. The other slope falls towards the Propontis in part to the southeast and in part to the south with a mild and varied decline, at first 500 paces to the top, then less — 400, 300, 100 or even 50 paces — at which point it reaches the third corner of the city, where a large plain runs out all the way to the sea. Between the sea and the slopes just mentioned runs a coastal plain that varies in width. It is narrowest at the corner of the city, then becomes wider due to the curvature of one of its sides, a sort of flat valley. Where the plain runs from the sea towards the slopes it is 400 paces wide, then further back it narrows to 50 paces across then finally it widens to only 100 paces. Finally, for a length of 1000 paces, the plain is over 400 paces across. The back of this hill evens out into a long, broad plain. The hill is closed off to the west by the land walls. On its summit lies a cistern called Mocisia that has been utterly stripped of its columns and vaults. Walls built of squared stone still stand around, but the site, measuring 970 paces in circumference, is only maintained for the gardens laid out in it.

So far I have concerned myself with the topography of Constantinople. I have tried to lay it before the eyes as a sort of outline, so that where the fourteen regions of the city lie will be more easily understood. I trust I have not dwelt too long on this topic, since no description of a city can be shorter than one informed by the sensation of the eyes, and nothing is sharper or swifter than that. For although Constantinople is raised on high like a spectacle to be viewed from every side, nevertheless you will have read this description of the individual parts of the city far faster than you would have swept over the whole city with a bird's eyes, or than you would have crossed over it on foot.

XIX. CONCERNING THE WALLS OF THE CITY

In some places the walls of Constantinople have been constructed with squared stone, in other places with rough stone and in many places with alternating courses of stone and brick. The land walls are double, guarded by a ditch, and are 25 paces deep when fortified on either side by walls; then on the inner side the other wall rises somewhat above the moat with closely packed battlements. The space between the walls is 18 feet. The inner walls are very high and more than 20 feet thick. Two-hundred-fifty towers are set in a series along it. They have stone steps to the top. The outer walls are not more than half as large but have the same number of closely packed towers. For the purpose of fortification the space between the moat and the exterior wall is higher than the moat on the other side. Likewise the space between the two walls is higher than the space just mentioned.

The neighboring countryside outside the walls is free of buildings. It is both hilly and flat so that the fields stretch out a long way, and from the tops of the walls there is a distant view everywhere one turns. It is clear that Constantinople could be made extremely secure. The walls along the sea are not as high as the land walls and they are of plainer construction but very thick and heavily fortified with towers. On the bay of the Golden Horn they are about 50 easy paces from the shore, as I wrote before in the description of the Bosporus. The sides at the opening of the Bosporus and the Propontis are not set back from the shore, but the shore is right at the base of the walls, except for where there are stairs, where they allow a space between the stairs and the wall. Zonaras says that Emperor[68] Theophilus repaired the sea walls of the city, which were falling apart from age and the action of waves and other effects. He even built these walls to a higher level than they were before.[69] The sea walls that exist today were rebuilt by Theophilus, as is indicated by the name of Theophilus carved in large letters on many parts of the wall. The Emperor Nicephorus was oppressive to the Byzantines because he imposed a tax for the aging walls. The tax called the Diceraton was exacted. We are able to gather from the *New Constitutions* of Justinian that there had been old and new walls in his time. For he decrees a greater tax on bier-bearers and those assisting a funeral who carry a corpse past the new walls of the city.[70] What we gather from this is that in the time of Justinian there were walls built by Constantine and the new walls, constructed by Theodosius II.

I have already described at the start of this book the walls that existed when the republic of the ancient Byzantines flourished. We can learn from Herodian, who recorded that Byzantium was encircled by a very mighty wall built of huge stones squared with such joints that no one would have thought it to be composed but that it was all of one rock.[71] It is possible to gather this from Pausanias, who tells us in his fourth book: "I never saw the walls of Babylon or of Memnon nor ever knew of anyone who had seen them. The walls of Byzantium and Rhodes are thought to be incredibly formidable, but the walls that guard Peloponnesian Messene are stronger even than these."[72]

Some historians have it that the Athenians stored their treasury at Byzantium in Thrace because it was extremely well protected. But whether or not those walls, which the author of the *Ancient Description of the Wards* calls double-walls, are the same as we see today at Constantinople I leave others to decide.[73] I shall only say that the walls that the *Ancient Description* describes do not seem to be complete, because it locates the church of the Holy Apostles in a ward near the city walls and says the fourteenth ward is outside the city walls. This is inside the city walls today, either entirely or at least the greatest part of it.[74] Furthermore, Theodosius II, who ruled before Justinian, does not locate the Blachernae inside the walls, which I know from Procopius were outside the city in the time of Justinian. Now they are inside the walls as are the Seven Towers, which weren't before. Likewise the church that that illustrious Studios built, further in than the towers, was not inside the city then, but it is now.[75]

XX. The Gates of Constantinople and the Seven Towers of Ancient Byzantium

There are six gates in the land walls, one below the palace named after Constantine, another named the Adrianople Gate, and a third on the brow of the seventh hill. In addition there is the Golden Gate or Porta Aurea, the Gate of Selymbria or Rhegium and the Gate of the Seven Towers. On the side of the city by the Golden Horn stands the Gate of Blachernae, today called Xyloporta, near the third corner of the city. The following gates are the Cynigos or Porta Palatina, Phanaria, Agia, Porta Jubalica, Farinaria, Lignaria, Seminaria, Piscaria, the gate of the Neorium, and the Gate of Demetrius, which is located on the tip of the first hill. There are five gates situated on the Propontis side, each having piers out to the sea by which the port is accessible to sea traffic, except the gates to the royal precinct of Topkapı, the first of which is the Stercoraria, the second the Leonina, and the third the Condescala; two more lie at the foot of the seventh hill.

Those that have drawn the most notice of historians are the Cynigos Gate, then the gates of Rhegium and the gate of Xyloclerum, the Porta

Aurea, the Myriandros, the Condescala and the Carsiana. In ancient Byzantium there was once a Thracian Gate. Dion records that the seven towers ran from the Thracian Gate to the sea. George Cedrinus says that they extended north, that is, toward the Bay of Ceras.[76] If anyone said anything inside the first of these towers, or threw a stone, the sound echoed immediately by some mechanism, and passed on the sound to the second tower for repeating, and so the voice went on to all of the rest, so that one did not distort the other sound, but each one received the full sound. Pliny attributes the same phenomenon to Cyzicus. He says that in the same city near the Thracian Gate there are seven towers that multiply the received voices with numerous repetitions. The name given to this miracle by the Greeks is "Echo." However, I have never come across any reference to the Thracian Gates in any history but Pliny's, but I judge it to have been a gate of Cyzicus named from the Port of Cyzicus called the Thracian Port.[77] In fact, Apollonius in the first book of his *Argonautiks* tells of the Thracian Port that existed in Cyzicus, that is Thrace, which is mentioned as follows:

...λυσάμενοι Ίρεῆς ἐκ πείσματα Πέτρης,
ἤρεσαν ἐς λιμένα Θρηίκιον,....[78]
...slipping their hawsers from the sacred rock
they rowed on to the Thrakian Harbor....[79]

Plutarch, in his *Life of Lucullus*, states quite clearly that there was a street near Cyzicus named the Thracian.[80] Not only more modern authors on Byzantium, but even Dion and Xenophon say likewise; the latter writes that the Byzantines let Alcibiades in through open doors called the Thracian Gates.[81]

XXI. The Long Walls

The suburban farmland of Constantinople was enclosed in long walls two days journey in length from the Euxinus or Black Sea to Selymbria on the shore of the Propontis, 40,000 paces from the city and 20 Roman feet wide.[82] Emperor Anastasius built them to impede Bulgarians and Scythians, and these walls were often taken by barbarians and damaged in many places, but Justinian repaired them. So that defensive soldiers could guard the walls more easily, Justinian blocked up openings from one tower to the other, except for a single one; he left only one stairway open, which allowed a single turret to be held even against enemy forces between the walls. Evagrius, the compiler of sacred history, has it that Anastasius raised the long walls 280 stadia away from Constantinople. From one side to the other, 420 stadia in length, they reached the sea on both sides so as to form a sort of channel, making Constantinople a small island instead of a peninsula, protecting those wanting to pass from the Black Sea to the Propontis, and blocking incursions of barbarians from the Euxinus, from Colchis, from Maeotis and from the Caucasus into Europe.[83]

10. Theodosian Walls. General view to the north of the Golden Gate.

NOTES TO BOOK I

1. Eustathius quotes Stephanus of Byzantium. Eustathius of Thessalonika, *Commentarii ad Homeri Iliadem Pertinentes,* ed. M. Van der Valk, (Leiden: J. Brill, 1979), III. 3, 66.6f.; Stephanos Byzantinii, *A Geographical Lexicon on Ancient Cities, Peoples, Tribes and Toponyms* (Chicago: Ares, 1992), 215.15, pp. 189–90. Archaeological evidence on the site of the ancient Acropolis indicates the presence of human settlements dating back to c.5,000 BCE. See M. Özdoğan, "Istanbul in Prehistory," in *Istanbul, World City, Habitat II* (Istanbul: Türkiye Ekonomik ve Toplumsal Tarih Vakfi, 1996), 88–101.

2. Philostratus, *Lives of the Sophists,* trans. W.C. Wright, LCL, 104–5.

3. Strabo, *Geography,* 7.6.2.

4. Marcus Junian Justin, *Epitome of the Philippic History of Pompeius Trogus,* trans. J.C. Yardley (Oxford: Oxford University Press, 1997), 9.1. See also Janin, *CPByz2,* 13; Charles Du Cange, *Constantinopolis christiana, seu descriptio urbis Constantinopolitanae* (Paris, 1680; Reprint, Brussels, 1964), I.16.

5. Spartans.

6. In 477 BCE the Spartan general Pausanius rescued the city from Persian control (under which it had struggled from 512–477 BCE). During the Peloponnesian War of 431–404 the city was allied alternately with Sparta and Athens. In 409 Athens gained control of Byzantium and built Chrysopolis on the Asian shore (modern Üsküdar). See Strabo, *Geography,* 7.6.2. Herodotus, *History,* trans. A.D. Godley. 4 vols. LCL, 6.33.

7. I suspect Gilles read this reference in John Lydus, *Ioannis Laurentii Lydi Liber de mensibus,* ed. Richard Wünsch (Leipzig: Teubner, 1898), 4.25, 50, 51; Janin, *CPByz2,* 16; Müller-Wiener, *Bildlexikon,* 16–26.

8. Müller-Wiener, *Bildlexikon,* 16–19.

9. Byzantium withstood a lengthy siege by Phillip II in 341–40 BCE.

10. By 129 BCE Byzantium was under the control of the Roman Empire, when the Roman province of Asia was set up. Here Gilles is speaking of events that occurred in the later Roman Empire; in the late second century CE civil war was raging between Pescennius Niger and Septimius Severus for control of the Roman Empire. Severus defeated Niger in 194, and the Byzantines paid dearly for their alliance with his rival.

11. Perinthos is modern Marmara Ereğlisi; Pliny, *Natural History,* trans. H. Rackham, 10 vols. LCL, 4.47; Cyril Mango, "The Shoreline of Constantinople in the Fourth Century," in *Byzantine Constantinople: Monuments, Topography and Everyday Life,* ed. Nevra Necipoğlu, (Leiden: J. Brill, 2001), 22.

12. Müller-Wiener, *Bildlexikon,* 18–19.

13. Herodian, *Histories,* trans. C.R. Whittaker, 2 vols. LCL 3.1.4–7.

14. Zonaras, *Epitomae historiarum*, XIII.3, Bonn ed. III, 15-16. Actually Zonaras has Severus saying that the walls were built in such a way with finished stones that the wall looked to be all of a piece.

15. Xenophon, *Hellenika*, I.1.22.

16. Dionysius Byzantius, *Anaplus Bospori*, ed. Güngerich, 5, ll. 10ff.

17. Gilles is still quoting from Dionysios Byzantius here.

18. *Patria CP*, ed. Preger, I, 141.

19. Eustathius of Thessalonika, *Commentarii ad Homeri*, IV.908.20

20. Zosimus, *New History*, II.39: Ridley's translation runs:

> Formerly it [the city] had a gate at the end of the portico built by the emperor Severus [note: this was when he was reconciled to the Byzantines after being angry with them for harboring his enemy Niger] and the wall used to run down from the western side of the hill to the Temple of Aphrodite and the sea opposite Chrysopolis. On the northern side of the hill the wall ran down to the harbor called Neorion (the Docks) and thence to the sea which lies opposite the channel through which one enters the Black Sea. The length of this narrow channel leading into the sea is about three hundred stades. This then was the extent of the old city.

21. A stade, or furlong, is 125 paces, 625 Roman feet or 606¾ English feet: Lewis, *Elementary Latin Dictionary* (Oxford: Oxford University Press, 1992), 804.

22. Van Millingen, *Walls*, 12-13; Dionysius Byzantius, *Anaplus Bospori*, ed. Güngerich, 3, ll. 7-9.

23. Herodian, *Histories*, 3.I.4-7; Janin, *CPByz2*, 13.

24. Zonaras, *Epitomae historiarum*, XIII.3, Bonn ed. III, 13–18.

25. Ibid.

26. Cedrinus, *Historiarum compendium*, Bonn ed. I, 495–96.

27. Zonaras, *Epitomae historiarum*, XIII.3, Bonn ed. III, 13–14.

28. Dionysius Byzantius, *Anaplus Bospori*, ed. Güngerich, 12, ll. 1–17 and 13, ll. 1–4.

29. Pliny, *Natural History*, V.124-125. See also Strabo, *Geography*, I.13.

30. Sozomen, *Ecclesiastical History*, II.3; Theophanes, *The Chronicle of Theophanes Confessor, Byzantine and Near Eastern History AD 284–813*, trans. and ed. Cyril Mango and Rogers Scott (Oxford: Clarendon Press, 1997), 46. Zosimos: see notes 33ff. below.

31. Sozomen, *Ecclesiastical History*, II.3.

32. Eunapius Sardianus, *Lives of the Philosophers*, trans. W.C. Wright (Cambridge MA: Harvard University Press, 1952), Sopater, 382–83.

33. Zosimus, *New History*, II.30 (p. 37). Ridley translates as: "To make the city much larger, he [Constantine] surrounded it with a wall fifteen stades beyond the old one, cutting off the whole isthmus from sea to sea."

34. Zosimus, *New History*, II.35 (p. 39). Ridley translates this passage as:

> The size of Constantinople was increased until it was by far the greatest city, with the result that many of the succeeding emperors chose to live there and attracted an unnecessarily large population which came from all over the world — soldiers and officials, traders and other professions. Therefore, they have surrounded it with new walls much more extensive than those of Constantine and allowed the buildings to be so close to each other that the inhabitants, whether at home or in the streets, are crowded for room and it is dangerous to walk about because of the great number of men and beasts. And a lot of the sea around has been turned into land by sinking piles and building houses on them, which by themselves are enough to fill a large city.

35. Zosimus does not mention either of these emperors specifically at the spot where Gilles quotes from him, but Zosimus' text implies that the results of Constantine's initial expansion occurred at a later time.

36. Agathias, *Histories*, V.3.9. Gilles' Latin here is difficult to translate.

37. This is Gilles' first reference to the *Notitia urbis Constantinopolitanae*, a Latin text dated to about 425 CE and which he includes in Book IV. Throughout this work Gilles refers to this text as the *Ancient Description of the Wards of the City*. In my translation I have retained his title for this work. *Notitia urbis Constantinopolitanae*, ed O. Seeck, *Notitia Dignitatum* (Berlin: Weidmann, 1876).

38. *Notitia urbis CP*, 243.

39. On the Blachernae, see Procopius, *Buildings* I.3.3, Bonn ed. III, 184; *ODB*, 293. The Blachernae area in the northwestern corner of Constantinople was not originally inside the Theodosian Walls but stood a short distance outside them. The area was still outside the walls during the Avar siege of the 620s, so Gilles is mistaken here.

40. Zonaras, *Epitomae historiarum*, XIII.22, Bonn ed. III, 106.

41. Ibid.

42. This inscription was in situ and visible in Gilles' day. See also Van Millingen, *Walls*, 47.

43. This inscription was also in situ and visible in Gilles' time. See also Van Millingen, *Walls*, 47.

44. Sozomen, *Ecclesiastical History*, II.3.

45. This and the previous sentences are very difficult to translate accurately due to Gilles' convoluted Latin.

46. Zosimus, *New History,* II.29-30 (pp. 36–37). Ridley translates:

Without any consideration for natural law he [Constantine] killed his son, Crispus, on suspicion of having had intercourse with this stepmother Fausta. And when Constantine's mother, Helena, was saddened by this atrocity and was inconsolable at the young man's death, Constantine as if to comfort her, applied a remedy worse than disease: he ordered a bath to be overheated, and shut Fausta up in it until she was dead. Since he was himself aware of his guilt and of his disregard for oaths as well, he approached the priests seeking absolution, but they said that there was no kind of purge known which could absolve him of such impieties. A certain Egyptian, who had come from Spain to Rome and was intimate with the ladies of the court, met Constantine and assured him that the Christian religion was able to absolve him from guilt and that it promised every wicked man who was converted to it immediate release from all sin. Constantine readily believed what he was told and, abandoning his ancestral religion, embraced the one which the Egyptian offered him. He began his impiety by doubting divination; for since many of its predictions about his successes had been fulfilled, he was afraid that people inquiring about the future might hear prophecies about his misfortunes. For this reason he applied himself to the abolition of divination. When an ancient festival fell due and it was necessary for the army to go up to the Capitol to carry out the rites, for fear of the soldiers he took part in the festival, but when the Egyptian sent him an apparition which unrestrainedly abused the rite of ascending to the Capitol, he stood aloof from the holy worship and thus incurred the hatred of the senate and people. Unable to endure the curses of almost everyone, he sought out a city as a counterbalance to Rome, where he had to build a palace. When he found a place in the Troad between Sigeum and old Ilium suitable for constructing a city, he laid foundations and built part of the wall which can still be seen to this day as you sail towards the Hellespont, but he changed his mind and, leaving the work unfinished, went to Byzantium. The site of the city pleased him and he resolved to enlarge it as much as possible to make it a home fit for an emperor....

Note: Gilles gives *Troad* instead of *Sigeum.*

47. Sozomen, *Ecclesiastical History,* books I and II on the history and glorious deeds of Constantine I; Evagrius, *Ecclesiastical History,* III.41 per Pauline Allen, ed., *Evagrius Scholasticus, the Church Historian* (Louvain: Spicilegium Sacrum Lovaniense, 1981), 63 and esp. 160–61.

48. Laonikos Chalkokondyles, *Historia,* VIII, Bonn ed., 388–89.

49. This and the previous three sentences closely echo Polybius' *Histories,* IX.26.6, in which Polybius discusses the computation of the size of cities: "Most people

suppose that cities set upon broken and hilly ground can contain more houses than those set upon flat ground. This is not so, as the walls of houses are not built at right angles to the slope, but to the flat ground at the foot on which the hill itself rests." Polybius, *The Histories,* trans. W.R. Paton, 6 vols. LCL, 9.26.6. Gilles does not credit Polybius here in any way, but it seems undeniable that he drew directly from this text. I thank Patrick Myers for pointing this out to me.

50.   This is Gilles' well-known passage in which he appears to have been the first to notice that the shape of the promontory resembles the silhouette of an eagle's head. It also illustrates that Gilles was possessed of some literary artistry.

51.   Dionysius Byzantius, *Anaplus Bospori,* ed. Güngerich, 3 line 2. Pliny, *Natural History,* IX.51.

52.   See I.xviii (p. 33 above) on what Gilles means when he uses the term feet/paces to discuss the terrain as opposed to when he cites measurements from ancient sources.

53.   Gilles seems to be describing different kinds of plains: the plateaus on the hills themselves and the ones running as valleys between the hills.

54.   *Ortum aestium* = north; *latere brumali* = south. The terms Gilles uses to deliniate points of direction seem to follow Pliny, *Natural History,* II.47. I thank Patrick Myers for pointing out this connection.

55.   Presumably Gilles means the Imperial Gate or *Bab-ı Hümayün* opposite the northeast corner of Hagia Sophia.

56.   It follows then that this must be the gate to the second court, the Gate of Salutations (*Bab-üs Selam*) better known as the *Orta Kapı* or Middle Gate.

57.   From the description that follows this can only be the Gate of Felicity (*Bab-üs Saadet*), which is indeed the true entry into the most strictly private areas of the palace. At the time of the sultans' accession and on other holidays and special occasions they sat enthroned before this gate to receive officials, etc.

58.   Gilles seems to be speaking of the ruins of the church of Christ Philanthropos. See Majeska, *Russian Travelers,* 374.

59.   It would seem that Gilles is talking about the Sphendone's substructure, which is still to be seen above Sergius and Bacchus overlooking the Marmara.

60.   Gilles can only be referring to Ibrahim Pasha, grand vezir to Sultan Suleyman from 1534 to 1536 and whose palace (now the home of the Museum of Turkish and Islamic Art) still stands on the west side of the Hippodrome.

61.   Gilles' Latin is very difficult to translate here.

62.   Again the Latin here is very hard to decipher.

63.   Gilles is describing the temporary exterior stalls of merchants one still frequently sees in the Kapalı Çarşı and throughout the traditional markets of modern Turkey.

64. The tomb is that of Bayezit II. The türbe of Yıldırım Bayezit I is in Bursa.

65. The Sulemaniye Camii complex, one of Koca Mimar Sinan's masterpieces, was under construction at the time of Gilles' visit. In reference to certain Ottoman buildings Gilles often employs the Greek term *"xenodochium,"* which is a building for travelers or the poor. It could also mean a hospice or hospital. Gilles is not specific about the uses of the Ottoman buildings to which he applies the term. I have therefore opted to translate *xenodochium* when it is used in an Ottoman context, as "a building for travelers, the poor or ill" unless the specific use of the building is known.

66. The 1561 edition of Gilles' Latin text has problematic punctuation in this section and others.

67. These "subterranean passages" sound like they might be the multistoried substructures underneath the Blachernae site, substructures that are now called "the dungeons of Anemas," a name intended to attract tourists rather than follow history.

68. Gilles is not always consistent in his use of the title "emperor," for sometimes he calls a Byzantine emperor or Ottoman sultan *"imperator"* and at other times he uses *"rex."* I have translated *"rex"* as "emperor" or "sultan" when the term is applied to a known ruler of the Byzantine or Ottoman Empire respectively.

69. Zonaras, *Epitomae historiarum,* XV.27, Bonn ed. III, 364.

70. Justinian, *Corpus iuris civilis,* ed. Mommsen and Kruger, Vol. 1 (1902), 11.7, and Vol. 2 (1889), 47.6; also, the *Codex Justinianus* I.2.4 mentions the "Parabalanoi" or "Paraboloi" responsible for burial of the dead.

71. Herodian, *Histories,* 3.1.4–7.

72. Pausanias, *Description of Greece,* trans. W.H.S. Jones, 5 vols. LCL, IV.31.

73. *Notitia urbis CP,* 242.

74. *Notitia urbis CP,* 238, 242 and 240–41.

75. Gilles does not seem to be quoting from Procopius directly here as respects the Studion and Seven Towers of Byzantium, but making a deduction based on an earlier quote that the Blachernae was inside the walls of the city in Justinian's time, *Buildings,* I.3.3.

76. Dio Cassius, *Historia romana,* LXXXIV.14,5; H. Delehaye, *Synaxarium Ecclesiae Constantinopolitane* (Brussels, 1902), 753, 754; Janin, *CPByz2,* 14 and 30; Cedrinus, *Historiarum compendium,* Bonn ed. I, 442. This quote from Dio Cassius is also in Zonaras, *Epitomae historiarum,* XIII.3, Bonn ed. III, 17. Note that neither Cedrinus nor Zonaras name the Ceras directly in these references.

77. Pliny, *Natural History,* IV.40–46.

78. From I, ll. 1109-10 of the *Argonautica*, ed. Herman Frankel. *Scriptorum Classicorum Bibliotheca Oxoniensis* (Oxford: Oxford University Press, 1961), 47.

79. Translation from Peter Green, *Argonautika: The Story of Jason and the Quest for the Golden Fleece* (Berkeley, University of California Press, 1997), 72–73.

80. Plutarch, *Lives*, trans. Bernadette Perin, LCL, Lucullus, c. 17.

81. Janin, *CPByz2*, 14–15; Xenophon, *Anabasis*, trans. C.L. Brownson, 4 vols. LCL 1, 24; Dio Cassius, *Historia romana*, trans. Earnest Cary, LCL, LXXXIV.14.5.

82. Gilles is discussing not the land walls of Constantinople, which are certainly not two days journey in length, but the long walls of Thrace. See James Crow and Alessandra Ricci, "Investigating the Hinterland of Constantinople. Interim Report on the Anastasian Long Wall (Thrace, Turkey)," *JRA* 10 (1997): 235–62.

83. Evagrius, *Ecclesiastical History*, III.38 per Allen, 157–58. Earlier in her edition of Evagrius, Allen states that Anastasius was not the originator, but the rebuilder of the Long Walls of Thrace. See Allen, 88.

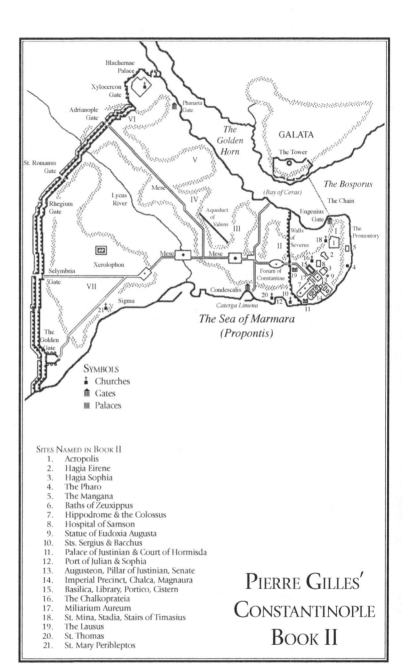

Blachernae
Palace
Xylocercon
Gate
Adrianople
Gate
VI
Phanaria
Gate
St. Romanus
Gate
Rhegium
Gate
Lycus
River
Mese
V
IV
The
Golden
Horn
(Bay of Ceras)
GALATA
The Tower
The Bosporus
The Chain
Aqueduct
of
Valens
III
Eugenius
Gate
Walls
of
Severus
II
18
I
The
Promontory
5
Selymbria
Gate
Xerolophon
VII
Sigma
21
Mese
Mese
Mese
Forum of
Constantine
Condescalis
Caterga Limena
20
7
19 17
15
16
8
3
9
10
12
11
2
4
The
Golden
Gate

The Sea of Marmara
(Propontis)

SYMBOLS
Churches
Gates
Palaces

SITES NAMED IN BOOK II
1. Acropolis
2. Hagia Eirene
3. Hagia Sophia
4. The Pharo
5. The Mangana
6. Baths of Zeuxippus
7. Hippodrome & the Colossus
8. Hospital of Samson
9. Statue of Eudoxia Augusta
10. Sts. Sergius & Bacchus
11. Palace of Justinian & Court of Hormisda
12. Port of Julian & Sophia
13. Augusteon, Pillar of Justinian, Senate
14. Imperial Precinct, Chalca, Magnaura
15. Basilica, Library, Portico, Cistern
16. The Chalkoprateia
17. Miliarium Aureum
18. St. Mina, Stadia, Stairs of Timasius
19. The Lausus
20. St. Thomas
21. St. Mary Peribleptos

PIERRE GILLES'
CONSTANTINOPLE
BOOK II

BOOK II

I. The Buildings and Monuments of Ancient Byzantium and of Constantinople, the New Rome

After describing the shape of the city, explaining its size and disclosing the natural situation of the seven hills, there remains the task of addressing what buildings and monuments Constantinople once had and currently possesses, and into how many regions it was divided when it was called New Rome. Indeed, it is divided into the same number as ancient Rome. In fact when I discovered these 1000-year-old divisions written by an author more noble than well known[1]; I hoped I was on the verge of identifying the ancient city with ease. But barbarous men have toppled and buried in barbarous buildings these ancient, heroic works of the city's art, using them to embellish their pathetic little dwellings to such an extent that vestiges of ancient foundations remain in only a few places. Add to that the fires and disasters perpetrated by other barbarians, and most recently by the Turks, who in the last century have not ceased utterly destroying the vestiges of the ancient city. Ancient buildings have been so demolished down to their lowest foundations and changed into different forms that not even those who have seen these former things would be able to recognize them. And then there is the feeble foolishness of the Greeks, who seem to have imbibed the entire river of forgetfulness.[2] Not one of them can be found who knows or wants to learn where the traces of ancient monuments are. Even their priests do not know of places where churches were destroyed just a few years earlier, and they marvel at those who inquire about such things.

However, so that I would not waste away in idleness while I waited for funds from the king for the purchase of an old, expensive book, I made an effort to discover, by whatever evidence I did have, a very large number of ancient monuments. In describing the ancient monuments I will proceed according to the same order of the hills

47

that I used in describing the situation of those hills, and sometimes I will use the order of the fourteen regions into which the city was once divided.

II. The Monuments of the First Hill and the First Ward of the City

Pliny sometimes calls the first hill Chrysoceras, "Golden Horn," and other times Auri Cornu, "Horn of Gold."[3] But, as I asserted in the book that I wrote on the Thracian Bosporus, Dionysius of Byzantium is wrong when he calls it the Bosporus Promontory.[4] He says there are two stories in circulation about the Promontory we call the Bosporus: some say a cow, stung by a horse-fly and brought to this place, crossed over the middle passage. Others report more incredibly that Io, daughter of Inachus[5], crossed from here to Asia.[6] Dionysius of Byzantium, while mentioning a place called Semystra, says that Byzantium was almost founded in Semystra by the leaders of the colony, were it not for the raven, which, having stolen a piece of the sacrificial meat from the fire, carried it to the promontory of the Bosporus. The Greeks followed this sign and established Byzantium on the Bosporus promontory.[7]

Dionysius of Byzantium also mentions elsewhere a promontory called Metopus. He specifies an area called Ostreodum as Metopus. This place, he says, is opposite the first hill of Constantinople. Indeed it looks directly at the promontory of the Bosporus.[8] Dionysius continues on to say that a bit above the Bosporus promontory there was once an altar to Minerva or Athena Ecbasia, also called Egressoria, because the leaders of the colony marching out from here immediately fought as if for their own homeland.[9] As for this name Ecbasia, we might also use the name Ecbateria, by which Diana was also called and worshipped in Siphnus, Hesychius says.[10]

Dionysius adds that the ancient Temple of Neptune stood on the Bosporus promontory, and that below the temple in the plain stood stadiums, sporting places and race courses for youths.[11] Finally at the base of the promontory of the Bosporus stood a bay called Ceras,[12] which had three ports protected by towers and defensive walls, upon which the Acropolis of Byzantium stood, which Xenophon mentions. He wrote when the soldiers, over whom he was leader, entered Byzantium by force. Some of the citizens, fearing every extremity, as if the city had been captured, fled to the adjacent promontory, and others took to the sea, and many sailed around in a fishing boat and went up to the citadel. From here they summoned help from Chalcedon. For not only was the Acropolis of the ancient Byzantines located on the first hill, but even that of the emperors of Constantinople, whom writers report had stretched a chain from the Acropolis to the Galata castle to prevent enemies from getting into the port. Even now the Turkish sultans, kings of the Turks, have on this promontory a citadel, which is surrounded by great walls far and wide, enclosing the sultan's gardens.

In old Byzantium there was a field called Thrace particularly well-suited for stretching a battle-line over the whole length of the city since it was flat and void of houses. Upon this plain Xenophon assembled his Greek army into military order. This place was near the Thracian Gate, according to Xenophon in Book I of his *Hellenica*, ...ἀνοίξαντες τὰς πύλας τὰς ἐπὶ τὸ Θράκιον καλουμένας....[13] And in Book VII of his work about the expedition of Cyrus he mentions a place near Byzantium where he prepared his army for battle, τὸ δὲ χωρίον ὅιον κάλλιστον ἐκταξάασθαι ἐστὶ τὸ Θράκιον καχούμενον, ἐρημον οἴκων καὶ πεδίνον....[14] I noted earlier that Dionysius claims that Byzantium's seven towers ran from the Thracian Gate to the sea.[15] George Cedrinus holds that they stretched to the northern sea, that is, to the bay called the Horn.[16] Herodotus writes that an altar to Diana Orthosia and a temple of Bacchus stood in ancient Byzantium. He records that Darius, observing this place, returned to the sea near the bridge and above the Bosporus erected two pillars of bright stone, carving Assyrian letters on one and Greek on the other. Later the Byzantines moved them into their city near the altar of Diana Orthosia. The one stone with Assyrian letters was then taken away and deposited near the Byzantines' Temple of Bacchus.[17] Laurentius takes *Orthosia* to mean *Erecta*, but I say *Erectoria* or *Erectrix* are better, π.. το.. ἐπιρτώμι τας ...θεὸς: by raising up and supporting, she brings help not only to [those women] giving birth but even to fugitives.[18] I take this meaning from, among other authors, Plutarch in his *De fluminibus* [*On Rivers*].

Plutarch says that Teuthras, king of the Mysians, and his pack of spearmen pursued a wild boar, which fled into the temple of Diana Orthosia as a suppliant. As they all thundered into the temple it cried out in a human voice: "King, may you pity one protected by a goddess!" Hearing this, Teuthras became furious and killed the animal. Resenting this insult, Diana restored the boar to life and caused the king, who rashly killed it, to go insane. Unable to bear his illness, the king was compelled to wander in the mountains. When his mother Lysippa learned of this, she ran to the woods with the prophet Polydius, by whom she had been informed. She appeased the goddess with sacrifices. When Lysippa saw that her son was restored to sanity she built an altar to Diana Orthosia and commissioned the fashioning of a boar of gold with a man's head.[19]

Until Severus destroyed Byzantium both the boar and the altar were in the first valley of the first hill. After Constantine rebuilt the city and called it New Rome, it was divided into fourteen regions. The first hill was included in the First Ward, which contained the house of the Augusta Placidia and also the house of the most noble Marina and the Baths of Arcadius. I learned this from the ancient division of the city into wards, though I admit I cannot be sure in which part of the city the First Ward began, nor can I find any answer in the remains of ancient buildings, which are now completely destroyed.[20]

However, this much can be gleaned from Procopius, who records that "when one sails from the Propontis to the eastern part of the city there lies the public bath built by Arcadius and in this location Justinian constructed a court stretching to the city, bordered by a calm sea, so that one walking in its gardens was able talk with the sailors, because the sea was so near.[21] The court was very beautiful and had a fantastic view; it was extremely pleasant for those on whom gentle winds blew. There were columns with decoration and the finest marble, with which the entire surface of the court was covered. Its extreme shininess blazed like the sun. It was also decorated with many bronze statues and marble statues sculpted with extreme care. It made a lovely picture, filled with great dignity. You would think it was the work of the Athenian Phidias or of Lysippus the Sicyonian or Praxiteles. In the same place a statue of the Empress Theodora was placed on a tall porphyry column from the city, so that it could express thanks for the courtyard granted to her. The column is beautiful, but the empress is even more beautiful. Her grace exceeds human ability to describe in speech or express by an image."[22]

Based upon what Procopius says, I must say that the column currently standing on the slope of the seventh region, facing southeast, is not the one set up by Theodora, as some hold. It is not porphyry, and it is too far away from the court. Moreover, judging from the citation of Procopius just given, you should understand that the First Ward encompassed the projection of the first hill that is bordered on three sides by the sea.

I have noticed in the works of many historians and even in Suidas the Grammarian that the statue of Arcadia, second wife of Emperor Zeno, stood in the Baths of Arcadius near the region called Bathra because of the stairs.[23] Likewise there were two statues of Verina, wife of Leo the Great, one in the north part of the city near the church of St. Agathonicus, past the steps that lie near the Bath of Arcadius. The other statue is in the area of the city where the church of St. Barbara is located.[24] The first statue was put up during Leo's lifetime, the second after his death, because, once Zeno had fled from his family, he crowned his own brother Basiliscus. I come to the opinion that part of the Second Ward was enclosed inside the palace grounds on the basis of the layout of the wards. I also base this opinion on the terrain, which the *Ancient Description* reports that after the level part of the hill rises imperceptibly it suddenly falls to the sea with steep cliffs. I believe that these cliffs are right where the sultan's kitchens and royal baths of Topkapı now stand. If they were elsewhere, that precipice has been graded by human hand.

Within the royal enclosure today is the church commonly referred to as the Little Hagia Sophia. Some of the oldest residents claim it is the church of St. Irene, which Socrates says was constructed by Constantine the Great.[25] I think this is the same church that residents of the Second Ward call the Old Church. I also have cause to believe, based upon the position of the churches and Baths of Zeuxippus inside this ward, that another part of the Second Ward stood outside the palace. For Zonaras and other historians say that the church that was once called the Great Church was later called the church of Hagia Sophia which, as everyone knows, stood outside the palace.[26] And I have reason to believe that the Palace of Maximinus once stood in the royal enclosure. This fact was made famous by the verses of poets, as I gather from the following poetic inscription, which was made by Cyrus, a former consul and noble of Rome:

Δεῖματο Μαξιμίνος νεοπηγεὸς ἔνδοθι 'Ρωμης,
αὐταῖς ἠϊώνεσσι θεμείλια καρτερὰ πήξας.
ἀγλαίη δέ μοι ἀμφὶς²⁷ ἀπειρεσὶη τετάνυσται.
τῇ, καὶ τῇ, καὶ ὄπισθεν ἔχω πτόλιν ἀλλὰ καὶ ἄντηι
πάνθ ὁρόω γαίης βιθυνηίδος, ἀγλαὰ ἔργα.
ἡμετέροις δ ὑπένερθεν ἐρισθενέεσσι θεμέθλοις
πόντος ἁλὸς προχοῆσι²⁸ κυλίνδεται εἰς ἅλα δὶαν,
τόσσον ἐπιψαύων ὁπόσον χθονὸς ἄκρα διῆναι.
πολλάκι δ ἐξ ἐμέθεν τις ἑόν μέγα θυμὸν ἰάνθη,
βαιὸν ὑπερκύψας, ἐπεὶ εἴσιδεν ἄλλοθεν ἄλλα,
δένδρεα, δώματα, νῆας, ἅλα, πτόλιν, ἠέρα, γαῖαν.²⁹

Maximinus built me in the newly constructed Rome,
fixing my secure foundations actually on the beach.
Infinite beauty extends itself around me. To the right, left
and behind me lies the city, but facing me I see all the
beauties of the Bithynian coast. At the foot of my most
strong foundations the salt current rolls to the lovely sea,
just touching the land in front of me enough to wet its
edge. Often a man leaning out from me slightly has greatly
rejoiced in his heart, seeing in all directions different
things: trees, houses, ships, sea, sky and earth[30]

III. HAGIA SOPHIA

Recent Greek authors say that the church of Hagia Sophia was
first built by Emperor Constantius, son of Constantine the Great,
with a wooden roof, not a vaulted one of brick. It was burnt down
by the Arians, stirred to revolt, in the age of Theodosius the Great
during the Second Council of the Church. Theodosius covered it
with cylindrical vaults, but then the same writers say it was burned
down a second time during the reign of Justinian. But Sozomen,
an ancient and trustworthy author, records that during the reign of
Theodosius II an uprising broke out over the expulsion of Patriarch
John Chrysostom, and suddenly fire engulfed the church, started
by those who wanted to burn the church and also the followers of
Chrysostom shut up inside it.[31] Procopius maintains that it was
first burnt down in Justinian's reign and that Justinian rebuilt the
building that stands there today.[32] But he does not say if it sits on
the same ground. That seems doubtful on the basis of an unknown

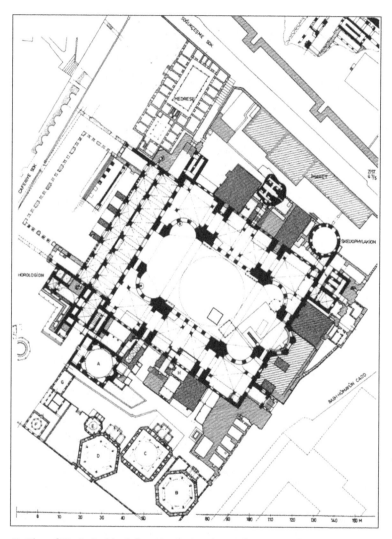

11. Plan of Hagia Sophia. Robert Van Nice, Saint Sophia in Istanbul: An Architectural Survey *(Washington DC, 1966).*

writer who preserves the names of those from whom Justinian was to have bought homes for the purpose of establishing its foundation. *The Ancient Description of the City,* which was compiled before Justinian's day, would locate the church in another place; this author

53

puts the Great Church and the Old Church in the Second Ward and the Augusteon in the Fourth Region, but as I will demonstrate, the Augusteon stood next to the church of Hagia Sophia.[33] Zonaras says that Justinian constructed a much larger church on its foundations, but it is not certain that Justinian bought up the neighboring houses in order to make his church larger.[34] For although the Great Church and Augusteon were in different regions, there was nothing preventing them from standing next to each other.

So then, Justinian rebuilt and decorated Hagia Sophia and adorned it with all kinds of metals. He constructed the walls and the roof with bricks and stone and bound it together with iron in many places, and so it would not experience another fire, avoided the use of wooden beams entirely.[35] Nevertheless, even though it has survived unscathed by fire to this very day, it has undergone a number of accidents ever since Justinian rebuilt it. Before its completion the eastern arch placed such enormous stress on the piers[36] that it would certainly have collapsed had not the architect quickly finished it so that its completed curve pressed down less heavily on the supporting piers. The two arches to the north and south put out such pressure that the columns thrust out the lower structures touching the lowest curve of the arches, and some small stones were pushed outwards as though they were twigs. It appeared that the structure was going to be ruined, had it not been for the genius of the architects, whereby the highest parts, laboring with the weight, were hastily demolished and restored a little later when the wetness of the structure dried out.

At last Justinian completed this church at great expense and labor, and it endured unharmed for several years until it was hit by an earthquake in Justinian's lifetime. Agathias wrote about this earthquake saying that the dome was thrown down and the emperor rebuilt it stronger and higher than before, although Anthemius, the first architect, had died.[37] But when they examined the original form Isidorus the Younger and other architects detected the defect, yet left the eastern and western arches in place. In fact, they slightly increased the north and west arches, whose structure had pulled the curve of the arch down in the middle. They made them visibly larger, so that the entire structure appeared more harmonious and balanced, and so that spectators could see the equal dimensions of the sides defined by a dome and how the architects had pulled together such a vast space within an enclosure, and how they pulled in a small portion of the oval shape so that the form was balanced everywhere. Above the arches, positioned as they were, the architects placed a dome of great height in the center that was balanced on all sides but steeper and straightened out more to a point to make it stronger against any motion.[38]

Zonaras writes that when the Great Church was finished and consecrated an earthquake caused the great dome's eastern part to fall and smash the altar, but that it was rebuilt by Justinian twenty feet higher than the first one.[39] George Cedrinus also says in the time of Justinian the dome of the Great Church was in difficulty and developed cracks from frequent earthquakes. He relates that an earthquake threw the eastern part of the dome onto the ciborium, holy altar and ambo.[40] He says also that Justinian raised other piers, which raised the dome twenty feet higher than it had been, and on the exterior he built staircases next to the four interior piers, whose walls were like buttresses that gradually ascended from the ground to the roof with many switchbacks, and sustained the piers and arches.[41] Other more obscure authors say that because of this earthquake the dome of Hagia Sophia collapsed but not the arches supporting it and that when the emperor rebuilt it he made it 25 feet *lower* that it was before.[42]

I would endorse this version if these same historians wrote that the church continued to be hit by other earthquakes and was rebuilt at the lower height. For Evagrius says that Justinian built it so high that from the inside one could, from the ground, barely see the top, and that from the summit one would not dare to look down.[43] Most likely he only restored it to its original height. Cedrinus holds that the Emperor Basil ordered that the great western arch of Hagia Sophia be repaired and buttressed after it was seriously damaged by an earthquake and threatened to collapse.[44] Nicephorus rails against the Empress Anna who, during the reign of the tyrant Catacosmus, plundered the treasury of the Hagia Sophia. He also asserts that tyranny and religious factions ruined the structure of Hagia Sophia without any earthquake. For, he adds, during one very clear night at midnight one of the four arches collapsed and brought down with it the eastern part of the dome that supported it, destroying the altar and the decorative images below, the sacred columns and the central galleries. He continues, saying that many people at the time felt that if the Emperor Andronicus had not added buttresses to the eastern end of the building, the destruction would have been far greater and irreversible.

Evagrius wrote that the length of Hagia Sophia was 190 feet from the conch of the apse where the sacrament is performed to the main door opposite, and from north to south it is 115 feet wide, and from the floor to the top of the ceiling it is 180 feet high.[45] It was too dangerous for me to measure the east–west length myself so I had to have the measurements made for me by a Turk who reported that the church was 213 feet wide and 240 feet long and from the pavement to the highest curve of the arches was 142 feet high. The man never measured up to the dome, but if he had he would have found his measurements to be but little different from those of Evagrius. For other features of Hagia Sophia one may look to Procopius, Agathias, Paulus Florus and Evagrius.[46] As for the building's present state, in the next chapter I will offer as much as I was permitted to discover.

12. Hagia Sophia. View of southwest side.

IV. DESCRIPTION OF HAGIA SOPHIA AS IT APPEARS TODAY

The walls and vaults of the church are constructed of baked brick. The surface of the interior walls shine, being covered with different

13. Hagia Sophia. View of Apse.

kinds of excellent inlaid marble. As it unites the highest force
of nature and the minds of the spectators, the vaults shine with
stones and golden glass tiles [mosaic tesserae] even in the eyes
of the barbarians, since it has been erected with the highest art.
This vaulted roof is supported by eight piers, the four largest and
highest being the ones that bear the four arches that support the
dome. Two of these, namely the north and south arches, have at
the lowest foundation, a wall, curved and full of small windows,[47]
supported by two rows of columns standing one above the other.
The lower row has eight columns, resting on the floor, and the higher
row has six columns supporting a fine wall that stretches below
the bottom curve of the arch. The eastern and western arches have
no structures beneath them but are free of walls and columns so
that by their absence the church is made larger. For the end parts
of these arches join at the base of their curves and project out
beyond the pillars into the quarter parts of the dome.[48] They rest
on four other arches supported by piers that not only hold up the
four great arches but each of them also supports two small arches,
one of which runs the length of, and the other across the width of,
the church. With these arches the church is stretched out a long

way and greatly widened. For on the east and west the quarter part of the dome connects to the dome in such a way that it seems to have the same ceiling inside the church, although indeed outside it seems separated. The dome seems more ornate, rising above the two quarter parts of the dome.

The breadth of the church extends beyond the piers, arches and columns, and walls on the north and south sides, making, as it were, six inner courts: the three upper and lower galleries.[49] These are covered with a variety of marble, roofed over with finely gilded mosaics and decorated with figures.[50] Hence, indeed, two arches spring from single piers, stretching out the length of the church, so that each of their curves comes to rest on the wall that itself rests outside on the larger piers, over which four arches hang over both sides of the wall. Two of these arches hold up the roof of the three lower galleries and the other two support the roof of the three upper galleries whose sides rest partly upon the walls, partly on arches, and partly on columns. Therefore, if we regard only the interior of the church, as it is enclosed by its piers and columns, we find that it has an oval shape, but if we regard the entire space without the piers it is a perfect square. The upper and lower galleries, like wings, have been attached in such a way that, as one proceeds from the floor, it is squared to the lower curve of the upper galleries, and from there between eight piers it pulls into an oval shape up to the curves of the four arches that support the dome.

The form of the galleries on each side is this: on three sides they are square, and the fourth side that looks into the building follows the shape of the church, which the position of the columns and piers makes oval. The ceilings of the galleries rest on arches and columns. I will describe three of them; the rest are all the same. I will begin with those three in the upper gallery on the north side of the building. The first of these is in a corner facing east and north. The two sides start at the wall of the church and end at the arch. In the center of each side there are three square columns measuring 5 feet 9 inches in circumference and indeed these form window frames. These pillars support three more square pillars that are a shade of white, verging on blue-gray.

The side facing the church interior has six columns of green marble that stand beneath the arch that supports a fourth part of the eastern dome and whose shafts measure 7 feet 8 inches.

The intercolumniations of these measure a little under 7 feet and 11 inches in width and are supported with four-foot high marble railings so that when one leans on these one has a complete view of the upper and lower portions of the church. The side that separates the first and second galleries runs from the exterior wall north to the main pillar that supports the dome and is 44 feet long, of which part includes the piers and part an arch that rises from behind the pier and supports the dome. The open space on the ground between the first and second gallery is 20 feet wide, and the piers and the wall that rise as a wing up to the ceiling of the dome occupy the rest of the width of 24 feet. The outer edges of the vault of the second gallery are supported by walls and arches at each end. In the center four bluish-white columns support it, and they measure 7 feet around.

The second, or middle, gallery is square in shape and two sides are supported partly by walls and partly by arches. One end of these arches rises up in back of the two large piers that support the dome, and the other end sits on pillars that rise up from the inward part of the walls that help support the very large pillars.

The outer side of this second or middle gallery has, instead of walls, eight square columns that are 6 feet in circumference. In the middle of these columns stands a larger pillar that acts as a window frame between each of the columns. Above them are more pillars that also act as window frames for the upper windows. These windows, both above and below, number 16 and allow a lot of light into this middle gallery. The side of this gallery facing the interior of the church is ornamented with six columns of green marble. Their intercolumniations have the same small walls as in the first gallery.[51] The center of the chamber is supported by columns, somewhere between white and blue-gray, arranged in a square, two of which are not far from the exterior wall. The other two are close to the inner wall, which is decorated with six columns. From the middle gallery one moves on to the third gallery through an exit that is as wide as the one from the first to the second gallery. The third is very much like the first in its length, its windows with columns as window frames. Four piers support the ceiling and the interior-facing side has six green columns. Indeed, between the two piers that hold up a quarter of the western part of the dome there are four green marble columns, and between these, in pairs that join together, are six little ionic columns.

At the church's western entrance are two porticos instead of a vestibule, and the lower portico lies at the same level as the church itself. The upper one leads to the women's gallery. Both run along the width of the church and are 28 feet wide. The portico above lies on top of the lower portico between the piers that support a quarter part of the western dome and the windows. Both inside and outside it is supported by eight pillars, which have between them windows in both the upper and lower galleries that emit a lot of light. Nothing separates this portico from the women's gallery except the pillars that hold up the ceiling of the portico, for the floor of the portico lies at the same level as the floor of the galleries. The interior of the lower portico is double and enclosed within walls that are faced with a wonderful selection of marbles, and its vault is covered with figures done with ornamental mosaic of gilded stones. On the east side of the portico there are nine doors that open into the church, and on the western end one may exit through five folding brass doors into a portico with a pair of exits to an outer portico that stands outside.

Through these one continues into a court where several springs perpetually flow. There is a descent to these waters with many steps from the plaza. Entrances into the church are located at the ends of the porticos. There is one on the north side and another on the south with six double doors. All of these doors were once made of brass but today only three are still bronze, and these have been made with extraordinary workmanship. Hagia Sophia also has two double doors on the eastern end. There are some more doors in the sides that are now never opened. The interior of the church is full of light due to the numerous windows all around. The high wall that stands between the four high arches and the dome is circular in shape and lets in light through its 40 windows. The small tympana walls beneath the arches are lit up by 26 windows, and the middle galleries have 32. The individual galleries on the east have more than 20 windows. I will not mention here the windows in the two western and four lower galleries or those in the two semi-domes or those in the sanctuary of the building, which used to be open but now admit only religious leaders. I also pass over in silence the upper portico, which lets in bright light. I have not enumerated the windows in these parts because there are so many of them. The main entrance to Hagia Sophia is on the western end. It is level, unlike the Roman Pantheon, which used to be entered going up five steps, and which now is entered by going down five steps. One gets to the top of the church by way of four sets of winding stairways, not circular staircases that curve like a cockle-shell, as Cedrinus would have it, but with more square, linear turnings.[52] These stairways ascend gently with five turnings. They are made of large marble slabs. Each of the five turnings is 19½ feet high and five feet across. Above them are more winding staircases that lead to the top of the church — not by a gentle incline, but in broken steps. One must use these to ascend to the upper galleries and porticos, and the upper parts of the church.

Now, if one should compare what I have written about the church to what Procopius and Agathias record, one may see that Justinian's building has not been as diminished as the citizens of Constantinople have said before, asserting that the church was originally much larger in size and that parts of it have been dismantled by barbarians and that only one-tenth of the original structure remains today. This tale would have the ring of truth if they were including the houses of the kings, priests and senators built around the church that have been destroyed by barbarians and fire. But I am sure they are quite mistaken about Justinian's Hagia Sophia, because I saw parts of this church that Procopius described still in situ excepting one portico. For Procopius says that the church had two porticos, one at each end, but there is only one on the western side.[53] Very likely an earthquake destroyed the other one, and in its place a mass of square stones was put up as a steep buttress to support the east end of the building.[54] Indeed I do not think it is so tall because of the earthquake that first hit it. Nevertheless it is almost as tall as Evagrius says it is. And after the earthquake it was enlarged by the addition of four walls to buttress the piers stressed by earthquakes and the weight of the dome. These walls are over 20 feet long and 8 feet wide and rise to the top of the main piers and, according to the terms of architecture, look to be wings on the church or rather ἐρείσματα — that is "solid supports" — by which the northern and southern sides are completely surrounded and reinforced.[55] Both ends of the church still stand, extending beyond the eight piers and disappearing into quarter parts of the dome and bringing themselves out from above as a crescent moon curves its horns. The lower rooms or galleries, for the men, the upper galleries for the women, still exist with their walls and piers, covered with an infinite variety of outstanding marble. And the entire ceiling remains, covered with golden tiles, not done in that style of mosaic work now so utterly debased, but in that old, now lost, style. The mosaics are extraordinarily clear even today, except for intermittent gaps made by those who opposed the use of images.

Essentially the whole structure of Hagia Sophia can still be seen, since nothing is removable except for a bit of the metal decoration of which there remains an abundance throughout the building. The part of the building that was once pure and holy and only used by priests still exists, although nothing remains of the gems that embellished it, for they have been plundered as the wartime spoils of many nations. Hagia Sophia has been robbed not only of that incomparable altar that Justinian remade after the destruction of the first dome with silver, gold and every sort of wood and precious stones that the sea and earth produce, it has also been robbed of countless gifts with which Constantinopolitan emperors, popes, princes adorned it. Even women adorned it. For instance, Sozomen writes that, along with other women, Pulcheria, daughter of Arcadius and sister to Theodosius II, gave the sacred church of Constantinople an extremely beautiful and amazing spectacle: an altar made of gold and precious stones.[56] The Islamic priests have neither been deprived of taxes, by the enormity of which the mosque has been enriched, nor have they lost the 1100 shops or the ateliers that are taxable, and they own many things situated within the most beautiful forums of Constantinople.[57]

V. The Statues Found near Hagia Sophia

Suidas, whom I cite as a first-rate grammarian, records that on the side of the church of Hagia Sophia more than 70 statues of Greek gods were found as well as statues of the twelve signs of the zodiac and 80 statues of Christian rulers that Justinian distributed throughout the city when the Great Church was built.[58] I could list the names of the statues of these gods from an unreliable author who wrote the *Patria* of Constantinople except that in many areas I had detected that he was not telling the truth.[59]

VI. The Pharos on the Ceres Promontory and the Mangana

Ammianus Marcellinus wrote that there was a rather tall lighthouse as a beacon for ships called Pharos or lighthouse built near the Ceras promontory.[60] It is not possible to assign it more correctly to any other location than near the church of Hagia Sophia. For from that spot it would have been possible to shine a rather helpful and far-reaching light for those who sailed from the Bosporus and Propontis. Dionysius refers to the Ceras Promontory as the Bosporus

Promontory and says that Io, the daughter of Inachus, was driven to cross from here over to Asia as the result of Juno's anger.[61] Mangana is the place so called where they stored their weapons of war, and it was within the royal enclosure or near it, next to the shore of the Bosporus. Emperor Constantine Monomachus constructed a large and splendid monastery in the name of the great martyr St. George that is called Mangana.[62] Alexius Comnenus, when he suffered from gout, was transported to the Great Palace that stands on the east side of the city, but when the doctors saw that the air in the palace was not healthy he was transferred to the Mangana Palace.[63]

VII. THE BATHS OF ZEUXIPPUS AND ITS STATUES

The Baths of Zeuxippus were named after Jove Zeuxippus and were built, Cedrinus says, in this god's precinct.[64] Eusebius appears to confirm this. He records that people supposed that a certain bath in the area of Hagia Sophia was named after the painted images of Zeuxes, of which the bath of the Byzantines had very many.[65] I learned this not only from the ancient description of the city, which locates the Baths of Zeuxippus and Hagia Sophia in the same region, but also from the fact that the conflagration of Justinian's time consumed Hagia Sophia and buildings in the vicinity, including, as Procopius says, the Baths of Zeuxippus and the entrance to the Imperial Palace that is called the Chalke.[66] And Zonaras records that the Emperor Severus connected it to the Hippodrome and built it within the precinct of Jupiter.[67] Leontius, a more ancient and authoritative witness, does not join it to the Hippodrome, but has it standing nearby, according to the verses inscribed on a house situated between the Baths of Zeuxippus and the Hippodrome:

Ἐν μὲν τῇ Ζεύξιππον ἔχω πέλας, ἡδὺ λοετρόν,[68]
ἐκ δ ἑτέρης ἵππων χῶρον ἀεθλοφόρων.
Τούς ῥα θηησάμενος καὶ τῷδ ἔνι χρῶτα λοέσσας
δεῦρο καὶ ἄμπφευσον δαιτὶ παρ ἡμετέρῃ
καὶ κε πάλιν σταδίοις ποτὶ δείελον ὥριος ἔλθοις,
ἐγγύθεν ἐγγὺς ἴων γείτονος ἐκ θαλάμου.[69]

On the one side I have close by me the Zeuxippus, a pleasant bath, and on the other the race-course. After seeing the races at the latter and taking a bath at the former, come and rest at my hospitable table. Then in the afternoon you will be in plenty of time for the other races, reaching the course from your room quite near at hand.[70]

Cedrinus says that there were many thought-provoking and splendid works of marble and stone and bronze statues of men of antiquity who lacked nothing but breath, so accurately have they been reproduced. There was Homer focusing his mind and concentrating. He was joining his hands below his chest and his beard flowed simply, with his hair thinning the same way on both sides of his bald spot, and his face hardened with old age and thought, and his nose was ordinary-looking. His eyes, covered with eyelids, just as the legend of him says, held only darkness before them. A pallium was draped over his tunic and a bronze strap was wrapped around his feet. Other bronze statues had been made of all the supreme wise men — poets, orators, and courageous heroes famous for strength. But works of marble had also been carefully carved by an ancient technique that made them seem to breathe. Fire destroyed them all.

Among these were statues of Deiphopus, Aeschines, Demosthenes, Aristotle, Euripides, Hesiod, Theocritus, Simonides, Anaximenes, Chalcas, Pyrrhus, Amynione, Sappho, Apollo, Venus, Chrysa, Julius Caesar, Plato, Hermaphroditus, Herinna, Terpander, Pericles, Pythagoras, Stesichorus, Democritus, Hercules, Aurora, Aeneas, Creusa, Helenus, Andromachus, Menelaus, Helen, Ulysses, Hecuba, Cassandra, Polyxena, Ajax, Paris, Oenoa, Milos, Dares, Entellus, Charidemus, Melampus, Panthous, Demogeron, Isocrates, Amphiarus, Sarpedon, Achilles, Mercury, Apuleis, Diana, Pherecydes, Heraclitus, Cratinus, Menander, Amphitryton, Thucydides, Herodotus, Pindar, Xenophon, Alcmaeon, Pompey and Virgil.[71] There were many other statues there that have been mentioned in the poetry of Christodoros of Thebes or, as others hold, Christophoros of Coptos in Egypt, which, if it were not such a lengthy work I would quote it.[72] It should be sufficient just to dip our fingers in the fountain.

Near the Baths of Zeuxippus there was a smaller bath that Leontius celebrated in these lines:

Μὴ νεμέσα, Ζεύξιππε, παραντελλοντι λοετρῷ
καὶ μεγάλην παρ' Ἅμαξαν Ἐρωτύλος ἡδὺ φαείνει.[73]
Do not resent, Zeuxippus, this bath rising next to you
For even the small star Erotylus shines sweetly by the great star.

Nothing is left of the Baths of Zeuxippus nor of any of the other beautiful baths, but we possess many inscriptions about them, such as the well-known one by Agathias where Venus was. There is also a verse by Paul Silentiarius concerning another bath called Didymum where both sexes once bathed, and a third bath described in an epigram of Leontius Scholasticus.[74] And there was another bath called Cupido described by Marianus Scholasticus. But all of these have either perished or have been so altered by the Muslims that one can not make them all out.[75]

14. *Hospital of Samson and Hagia Irene. DAI 66/189.*

VIII. The Xenodochon or Hospital of Samson and the Xenodochon of Eubulus

Procopius says that there once was a hospital for the relief of the poor and sick. A certain pious man, Sampson by name, built it in better times. But it did not escape the fire that seditious people started and by which it was burnt down along with the church of Hagia Sophia.[76] Justinian[77] rebuilt this with a beauty more worthy of the structure and enlarged it with many apartments and then provided a great annual endowment so that he could help more of those afflicted. But he was not content with this gift he made to God and so with his Empress Theodora he built next to it two more hospitals on the same site where the houses of Isidorus and Arcadius formerly stood.[78] This much Procopius records, and from it I deduce that the Hospital of Sampson that perished in the conflagration was not far from the Great Church of Hagia Sophia. I also read in a history by an unreliable writer that it stood near Hagia Sophia.[79] Zonaras supports my view for he writes similarly that a fire, started by a rebellious faction, burned down the Great Church, Hagia Irene, the Hospital of Eubulus, the Chalke, the Baths of Severus called

Zeuxippus, and many other structures.[80] George Cedrinus says the same thing concerning that conflagration. He says that a large portion of the city and the churches of Hagia Sophia and Hagia Irene, and the Hospitals of Sampson and Eubulus including their sick tenants, and also the vestibule of the Basilica, the Augusteon, the Chalke, and two porticos as far as the forum, the Octagon and the Baths of Zeuxippus were all destroyed in the flames.[81] After I wrote the above from an edition of Procopius, I found a hand-written codex of Procopius that stated that the Hospital of Sampson was between the two buildings of Hagia Sophia and Hagia Irene.[82]

IX. The Statue of Empress Eudoxia, for Which John Chrysostomos Was Exiled

The writers of sacred history, Socrates and Sozomen, record that a silver statue of the Augusta Eudoxia was erected on top of a column of porphyry on the south side of Hagia Sophia with a wide street between the two. It rose in front of the great curia [the Senate House]. The populace often applauded the statue and public spectacles of dancers and mimes regularly acted in front of it, according to the custom that had become firmly entrenched of revering imperial images. John Chrysostom viewed this as contrary to the Christian faith and at a public gathering he condemned those who did this in any way. Eudoxia, thinking her power threatened by these things, had Chrysostom sent into exile. I could add here that the Miliarium and the Basilica were near the church of Hagia Sophia, except now I prefer to follow the order of the region, rather than the proximity of buildings.[83]

X. On the Part of the City Contained within the Third Ward

It can be determined that the Third Ward was once where today there is the Hippodrome, the Palace of Ibrahim Pasha, the Gate of Leo and the port that the common people of Byzantium call the Caterga Limena, the Port of the Triremes. The ridge up to the second hill to the Forum of Constantine was also in it. I discerned this not only from their arrangement but also from the description [of the wards] that declares that the Third Ward is level at its upper part, with a space opened out for quite a distance. But at the furthest part it slopes steeply to the sea. It encompasses the Tribunal of Constantine's Forum, the Circus

Maximus,[84] the Palace of Pulcheria Augusta, the New Port, and the semicircular portico that is called the Sigma by the Greeks because of its similarity to that letter's shape.

XI. The Hippodrome and Its Obelisk, Columns and Statues

Recent historians, such as Zonaras and others, say that Severus built the Hippodrome due to his reconciliation with the Byzantines.[85] Zosimus, a more ancient historian, writes that Constantine the Great completed the Hippodrome and adorned it with every beautiful refinement. He says that Constantine made the Temple of Castor

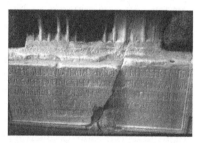
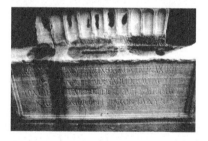

Clockwise from right: 15. Hippodrome. So-called Obelisk of Theodosius (Obelisk of Thutmose III on Theodosian base), general view. 16. Hippodrome. Obelisk of Theodosius. Detail of east side of base with Latin inscription. 17. Hippodrome. Obelisk of Theodosius. Detail of west side of base with Greek inscription.

and Pollux part of it, and that it was possible to see their statues in his time, that is, in the time of Theodosius II, in the porticos of the Hippodrome.[86] In the middle of the circus that the Greeks call the Hippodrome, stands an obelisk made from the stone of Thebes, but which the *Ancient Description of the Wards of the City* neglects to mention, though it does mention the square obelisk of Theban stone in the Fifth Ward.[87] I would think that this obelisk was toppled by an earthquake and then brought by Theodosius to the Hippodrome after the *Ancient Description* was published. Besides these things, the author mentioned many of Theodosius' works, except he passes over some things in his descriptions of the regions that he later mentioned in his general description of the city.[88] It is possible that Constantinople had very many obelisks.[89] The one that the *Ancient Description* puts in the Fifth Region no longer exists. I saw two others still extant when I first came to Byzantium. One is in the Circus Maximus.[90] The other is inside the walls of Topkapı Palace on the north face of the first hill. This latter one, of squared Theban stone, had been set up near the house of the royal glass-makers. But a little later it was toppled. When it was carried outside the walls I saw it lying 35 feet long, and each of its sides was, if I remember correctly,[91] 6 feet wide, making the entire circumference 24 feet. Antonius Priolus, a Venetian nobleman, bought it, and it is going to be exported to Venice and erected in the forum of St. Stephen's.

The other obelisk remains to this day in the middle of the Hippodrome, as a turning point, and it stands on four bronze cubes each 1½ feet high and sustained on a base and stylobate.[92] Two steps rise up from the bottom of the stylobate, the lowermost being one foot high and one foot wide, the uppermost being two feet high and projecting beyond the stylobate four feet, four fingers in width. The steps are not attached to the stylobate but are adjacent and built around like a platform, clearly visible from the pavement. Above, each side of the stylobate, which is 12 feet across on each side, rises 4 feet 8 fingers high and extends beyond the next base up by 1½ feet. Except for these four feet six fingers, a foot-high length of the stylobate does not extend past the base, for from the summit of all four sides of the stylobate fluting is conspicuous. It is 1 foot 13 fingers high and all made of the same piece of stone as the stylobate. For the stylobate sends up its uppermost part not only 1½ feet narrower than its lowest part, but also its corners are mutilated. Yet where the four corners are damaged there are four squared stones of red Theban marble each one 1½ feet high. And as for all of the fluting on the stylobate, which is between the four red marble corner stones and the top of the pedestal, all of this supports the base, which is 7 feet 13 fingers high and extends 1½ feet past the bottom of the obelisk's shaft to a width of 9 feet 9 fingers.

The whole base is carved, as is the pedestal, which has all of its sides carved with towering figures. On the north face there are relief sculptures carved in two registers; the lower row containing 18 figures and two machines. Groups of four men operate each machine by means of iron levers, and around each ropes are wound in order to drag the prone obelisk. In the same register the obelisk has been carved in the upright position, as it now appears. There are also three figures: the Constantinopolitans say one represents the master, the second the assistant, whom the master struggles to reprimand for erecting the obelisk in his absence. But he is held back by the intervention of the third figure. In the upper row there are also two erecting machines working with the lower ones to raise the obelisk. Each one is again accompanied by four men who wind strong ropes that are well represented by conspicuous bulges in the stone. But if the size of the stylobate was able to capture the means by which the obelisk was raised, I am sure it would have sculpted on it such a

Hippodrome. Obelisk of Theodosius. 18. Detail of south side of base with circus race. 19. Detail of north side of base with scene of erection of the obelisk.

thing as Marcellinus describes.[93] He says that nothing remained but the raising of the obelisk, which was scarcely, or not even scarcely, hoped to be accomplished but for the long thick ropes attached to the towering beams that constitute a sort of forest of machines. The ropes created an appearance of lots of threads and huge, long ropes blocking out the sky with their extreme density. Bound by these, the obelisk was pulled up little by little with great difficulty through the empty air. And with many thousands of men hanging on the ropes for a long time, turning ratchets on wheels like millstones, it was finally settled in the middle of the *cavea*.[94]

I see that Byzantine engineers could move this obelisk safely to another site, and there are those who could do the same today. I think this way judging from the column situated on the back of the fifth hill of Constantinople, which is just a little smaller than the Hippodrome obelisk. I saw this removed from its base and placed on the ground in this way: Around the shaft but at some distance away from it large poles were erected close together in a square, fixed in the ground equidistant from one another. These poles were taller than the column itself. Across the tops of the poles beams were set and securely fastened. Closely packed pulleys were attached to these beams through which ran strong ropes that stretched from the bottom of the column to the top where they were fastened to it very closely with a dense cluster of ropes. These ropes touched each other, and the perpendicular ones crossed the transverse ones, just like warps with crossing woofs, making it look like a work of weaving. Outside the square of beams it looked like a square tower. Many levers had been set up all around and were operated by countless strong youths pulling on strong ropes until they removed the column from its stylobate and laid it prone on the ground. They then placed it on sturdy carts having wheels bound with thick iron, and safely delivered it to the third hill and erected it at the Mosque of Sultan Suleyman as decoration.[95]

Even now, carved on the west side of the stylobate of the Hippodrome obelisk, is the epigram:

Κίονα τετράπλευρον ἀεὶ χθόνι κείμενον ἄχθος
Μούνος ἀναστάσαι Θευδόσιος Βασιλεὺς
Τολμήσασ Πρόκλῳ ἐπεκέκλετο καὶ τόσος ἔστη
Κίων ἠελίοις ἐν τριάκοντα δύο.[96]

A four-sided column, a burden lying continuously on the ground
Only Emperor Theodosius daring to stand it up
Called on Proclus, and such an enormous column stood in 32 days.

On the eastern side of the pedestal was the following inscription in Latin, somewhat deteriorated, but as far as I could make it out, it reads:

DIFFICILIS QUONDAM DOMINIS PARERE SERENIS
IUSSUS, ET EXTINCTIS PALMAM PORTARE TYRRANIS,
OMNIA THEODOSIO CEDUNT SUBOLIQUE PERENNI
TER DENIS SIC VICTUS EGO DUOBUSQUE DIEBUS
SUB IUDICE PROCLO SUPERAS [SUBLIMAS?] ELATUS AD AURAS. [97]

20. *Hippodrome. Obelisk of Theodosius. Detail of east side of base showing imperial party in kathisma.*

Difficult for fair lords once to fashion
Being bid to bring the palm of victory from fallen kings
Yet all things yield to Theodosius, son of eternity
And so in 32 days I was bested
And was raised into the lofty air at the bidding of Proclus.

On the south face there are two registers of sculpture, the lower has four chariots carved on it, two of these pulled by a pair of horses and two pulled by four horses and each having a driver. In the upper register there are two equestrian figures, three on foot, three figures wearing togas, two obelisks and four columns arranged in a square and holding up architraves.

On the north side of the base four rows have been carved which bear 35 figures dressed in togas. On the west side two registers stand out, the lower having nine figures in supplication offering gifts to the emperor who stands in the register above surrounded by 16 figures. The south face has two registers. In the lowest ten figures dressed in togas have been represented in a solicitous posture, and in the upper register there are 20 figures in togas except that four of these are with shields. On the east face, on its lower side, there are three registers. The bottom register has 16 figures of men and women dancing and playing

21. Hippodrome. Colossus. General view from the west.

musical instruments, and above them are two more registers in which only heads have been depicted, which I take to be spectators. The top register has 20 figures, six of which are separated from the others by columns; the center figure holds a wreathe in his hand. On top of the pedestal there are four bronze cubes arranged in a square pattern, by which the obelisk is supported. The obelisk is 6 feet wide at the base and is carved with Egyptian hieroglyphics from base to summit.[98]

22. Hippodrome. Colossus. Detail view of east side of base with inscription.

XII. On the Structure of the Colossus

In the center of the Hippodrome the Colossus still exists, constructed out of square stones. An ignorant person has informed us that it was once faced with marble. In fact, an inscription on its base testifies that it was covered with bronze plates bound to the core with iron, as is obvious not only by the holes in the shaft but by the holes in the base where the iron ties were affixed and reinforced with molten lead. It has suffered the effects of barbarian greed, and its bronze plates have been pillaged. Only its interior stones are visible. Before this the Rhodian Colossus was similarly endangered when, during the reign of Constans the descendent of Heraclius, the Agarenes dismantled it 1300 years after it had been built. Then it was bought by a certain Jew of Emesa, and its bronze was carried away by 900 camels.

On the base of the Colossus of Constantinople the following verses are inscribed:

Τό τετράπλευρον θαὖμα τῶν μεταρσίων
Χρόνῳ φθαρὲν νῦν Κωνσταντῖνος δεσπότης
οὗ Ρωμανὸς παῖς δόξα τῆς σκηπτουχίας
Κρεῖττον νεουργεῖ τῆς παλαὶ θεωρίας.
Ὁ γὰρ κολοσσὸς θάμβος ἦν ἐντῇ Ῥόδῳ
Καὶ χαλκὸς οὗτως θάμβος ἐστὶν ἐνθάδε.[99]

The four sides of this amazing and towering monument,
Destroyed by time, Constantine now emperor,
Glorious Roman son, the scepter-bearer.
Renewed to a better appearance than of old.
For the Colossus was an amazing thing in Rhodes,
And this bronze [monument] is amazing here.

There are three steps at its base, the first on the earth is 2 feet high, the second is 1 foot and 2 fingers and the third is the same. The base is a square piece of marble 7 feet 3 fingers tall. Each side is 10 feet 9 inches across. This Colossus is taller than the Obelisk.

On a holiday celebrating the circumcision of the prince of Boldania I watched as a very experienced show-off climbed to the top and came back down safely. Right away another, less experienced man made the same attempt to reach the summit, but the altitude so blinded him that, having no hope of descending properly, he jumped as far away from the Colossus as he could lest he land on the base of the Colossus. He fell so straight to the ground that he died instantly, with his feet fixed deep in the ground.

XIII. The Columns of the Hippodrome

In a straight row down the middle of the Hippodrome within the line of obelisks stand seven columns. One is made of Arabian marble and measures 17 feet 8 fingers in circumference. On top of this the statue of Hercules was put up by Ibrahim Pasha, using spoils he had taken in Hungary. But after his death, the statue was pulled down by the Turks, the hostile enemies of statuary and even greater enemies of the whole art of Vitruvius than of Hercules. Hercules had not only wandered the world, vanquishing monsters while alive, but had even carried the dead here and there, escaping so many calamities, until at last he was overcome. It was these Turks who vanquished Hercules

23. Hippodrome. Serpent Column. Bottom half with base.

with the proposition of the thirteenth labor, rather than those who first overcame him a long time ago. Likewise they had burned a Hercules made of wood, as the impious Diagoras did. Entering an inn and wanting wood with which to cook his lentils, he [Diagoras] found a beautiful, artfully made wooden Hercules and cut it up and built a fire, saying these words: O Hercules! He who underwent twelve labors, Go on! Suffer a thirteenth labor! Now you will cook lentils![100]

There stands in the same row another bronze column, not striated with grooves recalling the folds in a matron's gown, but twisted around with the coils of three snakes, winding around each other, not aiming directly for the sky but twisted like knotted muscles. They stand out so much that they resemble huge ropes. They terminate in a top with three heads arranged in a triangular pattern on top of the brawny shaft. The people of Constantinople devise many explanations for the reason that this column had been put up, but these are all nonsense because they are ignorant of the histories of their elders. Amongst these elders, Zosimus wrote that Constantine the Great erected in the Hippodrome the Tripod of Apollo from Delphi upon which Apollo had been placed.[101] Sozomen of Salamis adds that Constantine not only erected the Delphic Tripod in the Hippodrome but also the famous Tripod that Pausanius the Spartan dedicated along with the cities of Greece to Delphic Apollo after the Persian War.[102] Eusebius states more clearly that Constantine put up the Sminthian Apollo in some region of Constantinople but erected the Pythian Tripod in the Hippodrome, around which a serpent was wound in coils, from which it seems likely to me that that this was the same tripod that was erected on top of this three-headed bronze column.[103]

For so it was, according to Herodotus, who relates that from one-tenth of the portion of the spoils seized from the Persians, a golden tripod was made in Delphi and put on top of a bronze, three-headed serpent. He says too that when the Persians were defeated at Plataea, a golden tripod, discovered there near an altar, was returned to the Delphic god. It rested on three entwined snakes made of bronze.[104] Likewise are those mistaken who believe that this column was plated in gold that was taken as spoils by the Turks, since it was relieved of its gold long before the Turks captured Constantinople, as is clear from Pausanias. He says that the golden tripod supported on the bronze snakes was a communal offering of the Greeks from the battle of Plataea. The bronze of this gift remained in his day but the gold was stolen by Phocean generals.[105]

Five other columns stand in the same row with the obelisk, Colossus and bronze column along the middle of the Hippodrome. When I first came to Byzantium there was still standing in front of the Hippodrome, looking out on the Propontis, a row of seventeen white marble columns with spirals and architraves arranged in order and going around the southwest side of the Hippodrome. Their stylobate was 2 feet 10 fingers tall and was supported by arched substructures that were level with the inside plain of the Hippodrome, and about 50 feet high on the outside. They were on top of a small wall from which two steps or square plinths projected; the lowest of these is not formed from a single stone and is 1 foot, 1 finger high. The upper step is 1 foot 6 fingers high and extends 8 fingers past the stylobate. The steps' individual sides are 8 feet 9 fingers. The stylobate measured 5 feet 7 fingers wide on each side. The lowermost projections for the convex moldings and other parts were 6½ fingers high, and the uppermost projections for the coronides measured the same. The plinth of the coils is 11 fingers thick, the lower ring of the cornice molding is 7½ fingers thick, the scotia 4 fingers, the upper ring of convex molding is 6 fingers, and the stone supporting the shaft of the column is 5 fingers high. The shafts are 3 feet 5 fingers in diameter and 28 feet high.

These column shafts now lie on the ground. They were dismantled, along with their bases and capitals, for the construction of Sultan Suleyman's buildng for travelers, the poor or ill. I have lamented, not so much that they lie cast upon the ground, but because some of them have been cut up to pave a bath, and because the capitals, which had been sculpted according to the rules of ancient architecture, have been altered into small-sized pieces or have been hollowed out into mill-house mortars. The architraves' coils have been cut to build walls. The distance between the shafts of the columns was 11 feet — a dangerous arrangement as I noticed that the architrave had been fractured, due to the great intercolumniation. The capitals had all been carved in all styles of the Corinthian order and the trabeation marvelously adorned except for the echinos, which had not been carved. Rings of iron had been attached to the architrave from which curtains had been suspended.

Above this row of columns there was another row of columns that even stood for some time after the Ottomans captured the city. Before the Gauls and Venetians captured Constantinople there existed in the Hippodrome many other bronze and stone horses. There were four gilded horses of such surprising artistic workmanship that they equal the ones that stand today on the vestibule of St. Mark's in Venice. Some say they were transported there from Constantinople. I will not discuss here the numerous statues of princes and emperors that were erected in the circus, among which was the statue of Emperor Justinian celebrated in popular poetry. I will pass over also the other statues of eunuchs, who were often highly esteemed by the emperors of Constantinople. Among these was the statue of Plato the Eunuch, a royal chamber attendant who was burned at the stake in the reign of Basiliscus, although Suidas testifies that there was an inscription on the breast of this statue, which read as follows: "may whoever removes this statue to another location be hanged."[106] Nevertheless it was removed from the church of Procopius, when that was being rebuilt, and taken to the Hippodrome.[107]

I do not have time to discuss the countless statues of the boxers, wrestlers and charioteers that once stood in the Hippodrome, of which nothing remains except their memory in a poem of 300 verses. It mentions some charioteers but the memory of most has been extinguished. For instance, that most excellent charioteer — a fragment of stones notifies me of his existence lest he should perish utterly. I saw it in Byzantium, with this inscription: Θομᾶς Ἡνίοχος, Thomas the Charioteer. This is probably the same Thomas mentioned in a letter written by the Emperor Theodoric to Faustus, who had been put in charge of Rome, which says:

> For the arrival of Thomas the charioteer from eastern regions, our consideration has bestowed the annual gift of money to be continued

as long as we are fully satisfied by his skill and life. But since he is said to have obtained absolute first place, and because his own will has chosen to favor the seat of our power, leaving his own country behind, let us determine to have him compensated with a substantial monthly payment so that we do not give up this man, whom we know to have chosen the supremacy of Italy. Because of his many victories he has received the acclaim of many people and has been borne up by favor with the people more often than by his chariot. He has been very inclined to support the people, and those whom he has saddened he has tried to make happy again, overcoming agitators by skill at one time, at another time going beyond the speed of horses. He was so often victorious that some people thought he was a doer of evil, a sorcerer, but among such victories it seems to be a great honor to have reached such a level of crime. It is not necessary to assign to magic the perversion of those who are not able to assign success to real merit, spectacle driving out very important traditions, letting in trivial disputes, a draining of honesty, an unwatering fountain of quarrels, and what the past held as sacred, posterity has turned into something difficult to hold.[108]

From these words of Theodoric we can gather that this Thomas, who perhaps had departed from Byzantium on account of conflicts between the factions, was also in danger in Rome because of the discord between parties pulled apart by different colors and by conflicting pursuits. These partisan conflicts afflicted not only Rome but even afflicted Constantinople quite gravely. And by these conflicts, not only citizens but also great emperors frequently fell into the most serious crises of power. Now the circus of Constantinople bakes in the sun, stripped of all its ornamentation.

That it is now being finished-off has struck me with grief as I watch it happen. This grief was increased by the commemoration on a coin of Belisarius I happened to have in my hand. After defeating the king of the Vandals, he was first given an official triumph in the Hippodrome and then he was put in great danger because of his extreme virtue. On one side of the coin had been stamped Justinian as he welcomed the triumphant Belisarius, and on the other side was a portrait of Belisarius with the inscription: GLORIA ROMANORUM BELISARIUS, Belisarius the Glory of the Romans.

Procopius records that in the Hippodrome there was an entrance called the Cochlea because it proceeded with a circular descent. He also writes that there was a certain entrance called "the Dead." Procopius also says that there was a Venetia Gate in the Hippodrome named for the Blue faction that always sat there, and from this fact we might infer that there was a Prasina Gate for the Greens and other gates for other colors. The factions did not mix but watched in groups segregated off by gates.[109]

24. *Sts. Sergius and Bacchus. DAI 66/165.*
25. *Plan, Alexander Van Millingen,*
Byzantine Churches in Constantinople
(London, 1912).

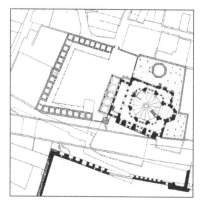

XIV. The Church of Bacchus, the Court of Hormisdas and the Palace of Justinian

The Imperial Palace and house of Justinian, in which he resided before he became emperor, stood between the Hippodrome and the Propontis, as one perceives from the church of Sts. Sergius and Bacchus, which presently sits on the plain between the Hippodrome and Propontis, concerning which Procopius wrote:

Justinian built a church dedicated to Sts. Peter and Paul near the Imperial Palace that was formerly called Hormisdas. For he made this a private house for himself, and made it so that it seemed to be a sumptuous palace with a graceful structure. After he was made emperor he joined this house to the other royal properties, whereupon he then sensibly constructed another church to two famous saints, Sergius and Bacchus. These churches of Sts. Sergius and Bacchus and Sts. Peter and Paul are no way inferior to each other in beauty or in size or any other feature. Both simply out-do the brilliance of the sun with the shine of their polished stone surfaces. Each is similarly filled with an abundance of gold and is embellished by gifts. In only one way are they different, for the length of one runs straight and the columns

26. *Sts. Sergius and Bacchus. Interior elevation. DAI 68/111.*

of the other are arranged in a semi-circle for the most part. Thus indeed both seem wonderful and serve as a conspicuous ornament to the entire city and especially to the Imperial Palace.

Procopius goes on a little to say that Justinian remodeled the house named after Hormisdas near the palace, making it into a more illustrious structure. He also connected it to the Imperial Palace.[110] I think that this Hormisdas, whom Procopius calls a prince, was son of the Persian king, as Marcellinus wrote about Constantius, son of Constantine, in the context of giants, when Constantius had come to Rome, casting his thoughts about, all hope of building such giant things lost.[111] Marcellinus writes that Constantius declared he wanted to copy the only horse of Trajan on the Forum of Trajan; Hormisdas responded, "You shoud first build a stable like Rome."[112]

George Cedrinus offers further information about how close the house of Justinian was to the church of Bacchus. He says that Justinian built the church of Sts. Sergius and Bacchus, which is near the palace in the direction of the shore, and he built another church near it as well. Because this church had been the house of Justinian he expended all his money — until he became emperor — in building the two churches and establishing a monastery that he populated with men of superior learning.[113] Today nothing is left of the church of Sts. Peter and Paul, but the church of Sts. Sergius and Bacchus still stands. Although the Turks own the building and its income, it is still known by its ancient name. Its shape is a hemispherical rotunda of brick supported on eight piers between which are two rows of columns of the Ionic order. In the lower row are 16 columns standing on the floor. Six of these are green marble and ten are white marble with red veining. The upper row has 18 columns, eight of which are green and ten are white with red veining like the others. An *echinos* decorates the capitals on the columns of the lower row and the rest of these capitals are covered with foliage. The volutes of the columns in the upper row project from the four corners of their capitals, and *echini* stick out from the side. The rest of the capitals are covered with finely-carved foliage. The epistyles on top of the capitals of the lower row are beautifully sculpted. Greek verses were carved by Zoophoros in large letters around the entire circuit of the building. The tops of the piers are embellished with the vine foliage and intermittent grape clusters, indicating that this building was dedicated to Bacchus.[114]

XV. THE HARBOR OF JULIAN AND SOPHIA AND THE PORTICO CALLED THE SIGMA, AND THE PALACE OF SOPHIA

The Port of Julian stood near the church of Sergius and Bacchus, as stated in the account of the conflagration that broke out in the reign of Leo the Great, which, wrote Evagrius, began on the city's north side and consumed everything in its path from the port called the Bosporus to the ancient Temple of Apollo and on the south side of the city from the port of Julian to houses in the area of the Temple of Concord.[115] Zonaras, in describing the same fire, explains the port of Julian was near the church of Sergius and Bacchus, and he reports that it struck the north from the Bosporus to the church of St. John Calybites[116] and in the south from the church of St. Thomas to the church of the great martyrs Sergius and Bacchus.[117] The church of St. Thomas was located near the Temple of Concord. Zonaras begins to narrate the southern side of the fire, from west to east, contrary to Evagrius, who goes from east to west.[118] Cedrinus says the same fire went around the city from the sea in the north to the area of the church of Sts. Sergius and Bacchus by the sea in the south.[119] Emperor Anastasius fortified the Port of Julian with reinforcement and a mass of stones. That it was later called the Port of Sophia, George Cedrinus demonstrates; he writes that at the Port of Julian, Justin, uncle of Justinian, constructed a palace, and he had this port dredged and ordered that statues of himself and of his wife Sophia be erected there. He changed the name of the port and called it Sophia.[120] An epigram on the statue of Justin at this port ran:

Τοῦτο παρ᾽ ἀιγιαλοῖσιν ἐγὼ Θηέοδωρος ὕπαρχος
Στῆσα φαεινὸν ἄγαλμα᾽ Ιουστίνῳ βασιληῖ,
Ὄφρα καὶ ἐν λιμένεσσι ἐὴν πετάσειε γαλήνην.[121]

Here by the shore, I, Theodore the Eparch
Put this up as a great honor to the Emperor Justin
So that he may also spread peace in the harbor.

Procopius writes that the church of the martyr Thecla was near
a port of the city called Julian. Indeed, recent historians relate that
from this port Belisarius set sail in the war against the Vandals.[122]
But upon what basis they make this assertion I cannot tell unless
it is based on the words of Procopius, who wrote that Justinian
ordered that the general's ship be brought down to the shore near
the Imperial Palace. Then Epiphanius, bishop of the city, offered a
prayer of blessing for the fleet, and in this way Belisarius with his
wife Antonina set sail. Now, there *were* royal palaces near this port,
but there were also royal palaces on the port-filled gulf, which stood
a little distance away from the house of Belisarius. Suidas says that
Anastasius strengthened the Julian port. Zonaras adds that Justin
built some palaces and named them Sophia after his wife Sophia,
whom he deeply loved.[123] Many believe that these palaces stood
near the Port of Sophia, but reason and the authority of learned
men persuade me not to agree. For Zonaras, among other writers,
states that Justin built the palaces of Sophia on the other side of
the city.[124] The much more ancient writer Agathias Scholasticus,
who lived at the time when the palaces of Sophia were constructed,
inscribed these epigrams, from which one can see that they were
not near the Propontis, which was adjacent to the Port of Sophia,
but on the other side of the city, near the Bosporus, where the land
is divided into two parts:

Εἰς παλάτια σοφιανων ἀγάθιου σχολάσζικου
Ὁππόθι τεμνομένης χθονὸς ἄνδιχα ποντοον ἀνοίγει
πλαγκτὸς ἁλικλύστων πορθμος ἐπ' ἠϊόνων
χρύσεα συλλέκτρῳ τάδ' ἀνάσση
τῇ πολυκυδίστῃ θεῖος ἄναξ Σοφίη
ἄξιον ὦ 'Ρώμην μεγαλοκρατές, ἀντία σεῖο
κάλλος ἀπ' Εὐροώπης δέρκεαι εἰς 'Ασίην.[125]

Agathias Scholasticus on the palaces of Sophia:
Where the land is split in two
By the wandering channel whose coast
Opens the way to the sea,
The Divine Emperor built these golden palaces
For his wife the glorious Empress Sophia.

Powerful Rome looks across from Europe
To Asia's worthy beauty.

The codex of Zonaras reads δέρκεται.[126] One can easily see from
these verses that the Palace of Sophia was not only near the Bosporus
but outside the city walls, which both the *History* of Cedrinus and
many other historians confirm. They tell of the bitter winter during
the reign of Leo Copronymus, when the Bosporus was frozen so
hard that whoever desired to go from the Palace of Sophia to the
city or from Chrysopolis to the church of St. Mamas or to go over
to Galata on the Bosporus might cross on the ice as if on dry land
without any danger at all.[127] I gather from this and from the other
sources that the Sophian palaces were across the Bosporus, on the
opposite side from the city.

Now it seems to me that the Port of Sophia, previously called
the Port of Julian, was the same as the new port that the *Ancient
Description of the Wards* puts in the same ward as the Hippodrome.[128]
But whether it is called the New or the Julian Port or the Port of
Sophia, today it is now completely built up with landfill. But if it
was the port that stands on the west side of St. Bacchus, it is now
almost completely in ruins and surrounded by walls, though part of
it remains as a pool where women wash their linens. The residents
say they have seen sunken triremes here. The residents now call it
Caterga Limena, or the Port of the Triremes. It may have been the
port that exists on the east of St. Bacchus near the city gate called
the Porta Leonis, which is named after a stone lion near it or the
Emperor Leo, who, the Constantinopolitans say, had a palace
there. Nicephorus, a more recent historian, says that when the
emperor of Constantinople was besieged by the Latins he ordered
that many artisans assemble in the Morion, which was around the
Hippodrome. I could not tell where the place called the Pyctacia
was in Constantinople. But this I noticed in Cedrinus and in other
recent historians, that there was a column in the place called the
Pyctacia [Pittakia] that bore upon it a statue of Leo, husband of
the Empress Verina. Some record that his sister Euphemia erected
this near her own house, where Leo was in the habit of visiting his
wise and chaste sister every seventh day.[129] All those affected by
wrongs placed their petitions in the Pyctacia on the steps of the
column, which the servants collected and gave to the emperor. He
immediately gave a response to each one. Guillaume Budé says

that *pyctia*, or *pyctacia*[130] were briefs, which the Gauls commonly call borderellos, but I think it's possible to call them letters of petition.[131] For a *pyctium* is book, and a *pyctacion* is a booklet. Today the Greeks commonly call their letters *pyctacia*.

I read in an anonymous history that Eudoxia put her own statue in solid silver on a high column in a place called the Pyctacium.[132] If the author is correct, then I interpret this to be the same statue that was near Hagia Sophia, near where Eudoxia's statue stood, as I indicated before. A small book, the *Patria* of Constantinople, relates that Constantine the Great built the church of St. Euphemia near the Hippodrome, which afterwards the Iconoclast Constantine Copronymus converted into an armory and threw the relics of St. Euphemia into the sea.[133] Suidas

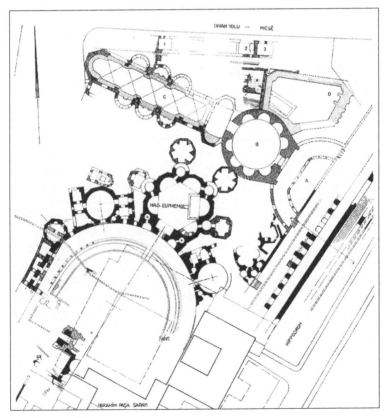

27. *Plan of St. Euphemia and the Palace of Lausos. From R. Duyuran.*

writes that a statue of Euphemia, who was the wife of Justin of Thrace, was put up in the church of St. Euphemia that she herself constructed.[134]

Some recent historians of Constantinople say that in the time of Emperor Basil a massive earthquake destroyed the church of St. Polyclete and killed all who were inside it and, from that time forward, it was called the Sigma.[135] I think, however, that the Sigma took its name from the portico of the same name long before this earthquake, because it was built in the shape of the letter sigma, and the *Ancient Description of the Wards* locates it in the same ward with the Hippodrome.[136] George Cedrinus mentions this place.[137] He says that Emperor Michael was seized in his monastic attire from the Studion Monastery by the populace. They then dragged him through the forum by his feet and, leading him past the Peribleptos Monastery to the place called Sigma, they put out both of his eyes. The same Cedrinus says that Emperor Basil the Macedonian built from its foundations a church to the Virgin Mary called the Sigma.[138] The eunuch Chrysaphius Zomas erected a statue of Theodosius II in a place called Sigma.[139] And some writers say that Constantine the Great built a church to St. Stephen near a place called Sigma.[140] But the Sigma here must be in some different spot in the city from that place that I mentioned in the Third Ward, and should be written with an "e," as in "segma," because, as I just said, the collapse of St. Polyclete due to an earthquake crushed to death all who were inside it.[141]

XVI. The Fourth Ward

The *Ancient Description of the Wards* declares that the Fourth Ward extended, with hills rising on the right and left, from the Miliarium Aureum to a valley plain 200 paces long.[142] If the Miliarium Aureum still remained or if the Constantinopolitans had remembered it, it might be easily observed that the Fourth Ward encompassed the first valley and the ridge of the hill above the valley. From this we are able to deduce where it is, or if any vestiges exist of the Augusteon, the Basilica, the Nymphaeum or of buildings that are said to be in this region. Since no ruins are visible today, initially I was unsure if the valley that the Fourth Ward contains was the same valley that I described as being the first, not because it has hills rising up on the right and the left and goes up to a plain, but because this happens to other valleys.[143] Then later, after I learned from the writings of others where the monuments that once stood in this ward were located, I easily discovered that the Fourth Ward stood in the first valley and on its sides and ridge in the vicinity of Hagia Sophia, as you will learn from reading what I have written below.

XVII. THE FORUM AUGUSTEON; THE COLUMNS OF THEODOSIUS AND JUSTINIAN; THE SENATE

Procopius declares that the forum that the people of Constantinople called the Augusteon stood in front of the Imperial Palace and was surrounded by columns. But now not only is its name forgotten, but

28. Aya Sofya Meydanı. Square in front of Hagia Sophia (formerly the Augusteon).

the forum no longer even exists, having been almost completely built over.[144] Recently the Imperial Palace has been destroyed. However the Augusteon was where there is now a water fountain not far from Hagia Sophia's western corner. I discovered this from the stylobate of a column of Justinian, which until recently remained but has been taken down by the Turks. Procopius says that Justinian put this in the Forum Augusteon, and Zonaras says he put it in front of Hagia Sophia.[145] Suidas adds that when he built Hagia Sophia, Justinian cleared the courtyard and paved it with marble and that where he erected his own column was called the

Forum Augusteon.[146] Procopius says that there was a forum that was across from the Senate that was called the Augusteon by the Byzantines. Here no fewer than seven stones are joined together to form a quadrangle and are all set on a base. Each one of these is made smaller and drawn back further than the one below so that each projection or retraction of the stones is made into a step and seat for men.

I decided to include this description of the stylobate from Procopius rather freely, as it does not appear in his edited books. Next Procopius adds that on the uppermost of these seven stones was a column not made of a single stone, he says, but composed of many huge stones that were covered in bronze tablets and crowns, which both supported and decorated them. The sheets of bronze are weaker than pure gold but were only a little less than silver in worth. At the summit of the column was a large bronze statue of a horse that faced eastward and that gave a dignified appearance, for he looked like he was walking and wanting to go beyond its pedestal. His front left hoof was raised as if he were about to tread on the ground. His other front hoof was resting on the stone, and he contracted his hind legs as if he was eager to go.

On top of the horse was a bronze statue of the emperor, like a colossus, dressed in armor like Achilles, wearing sandals and protected by heroic chest-armor and a shining helmet. He looked to the east. I assume he was undertaking an expedition against the Persians. He held a globe in his left hand by which the artist signified that the entire earth was obedient to him. He had neither a sword nor a spear, but emanating from the top of the globe was a cross, by which his imperial rule and victories in war were attained. He held out his right hand to the east with his fingers

29. Drawing of the equestrian statue of Justinian I.

straightened. He thus ordered the barbarian nations of the east to keep themselves at home and not to come forward any further.[147] On the kind of helmet Justinian wore, Tzetzes has this to say in his *Historiarum variarum*: The Persians usually wore a tiara on the head, he says, and after their victories the Romans put the crown of the conquerors on their heads. The statue of Justinian on top of the column wears a tiara, or "tipha" of the equestrian sort.[148] Cedrinus, adding to Procopius, says that Justinian held the globe in a silver hand.[149] Zonaras records that in the seventeenth year of his reign Justinian erected this column in the place where another column of Theodosius the Great once stood, which bore a silver statue made by his son Arcadius, and it weighed 7400 pounds. Justinian dismantled this column and silver statue and took the silver and then erected his own column and statue. With the huge amount of lead that he took from it, he brought water into the city.[150] Would that it were the case that the barbarians avenged the wrongs done by Justinian against Theodosius because they became learned from the law books that Justinian destroyed whenever they were found, and because they converted the badly organized laws into orderly legal briefs. For the barbarians despoiled the column of Justinian of all its bronze clothing, the horse and statue, and for some years it remained a bare column. Finally, thirty years ago the entire column was toppled down to the stylobate, which a year ago I saw cut out at its foundation. From the foundation water came up through water pipes to a large basin. Now in place of the stylobate a bigger shelter has been built for the water and the pipes have been enlarged.

The equestrian statue of Justinian had been on top of the column that stood here and that had been kept a long time inside the compound of the royal palace of Topkapı. I recently saw it carried into the melting houses where the Turks cast their weapons of war. Among the fragments were the leg of Justinian, which was taller than a man, and his nose, which was over nine inches long. I was not able to measure the horse's legs that lay on the ground but secretly measured one of the hoofs and found it to be nine inches tall.

Recent historians and even the grammarian Suidas claim that this forum was called the Augusteon because on October 15 the *curatores* and *sebastophori* danced in honor of Augustus in the public market place; or else it was because statues of Constantine the Great and his mother Helena were erected here inside its arched galleries.[151]

Zosimus, a more ancient historian than Procopius, says that Constantine built a circular forum at the place where the terrestrial door of the Byzantines had been before. It was surrounded, he says, with double porticos, one on top of the other. It also had two arches of Proconnesian marble facing each other through which you might proceed to the Portico of Severus and exit the ancient city.[152] This is the same forum designated as the Augusteon by an author of the city's history who says that Constantine built a forum in a circular manner to be like the ocean.[153]

The same Zosimus records in another place that the Byzantines' greatest forum was surrounded by four porticos. In it Constantine erected two statues, one at each end of one of the porticos, to which many steps lead up. At one end was the statue of Rhea, the mother of the gods, which the Argonauts sailing with Jason placed on Mount Didymus, towering over the city of Cyzicus. But they say that it was mutilated out of neglect in matters of worship of the gods. When both of the lions were taken away the position of her hands was also changed. For the hands, which used to hold back the two lions, were changed into a gesture of supplication. Rhea is looking upon and adorning the city.[154] At the other end of the portico was the statue of the Fortune of Rome erected by Constantine.[155] Suidas puts the statue of Fortune in a niche in the Miliarium.[156] If this statue were set up here by Constantine, I would conclude that both the markets mentioned by Zosimus are one and the same. But to me they seem to be two different forums, because Zosimus tells us in one place that Constantine built a forum bounded by two porticos; and he says a little further on that another was bordered by four porticos. Perhaps he means the porticos of Severus and of Constantine from each of which it was possible to exit to the other.

Procopius says that on the east side of the Augusteon forum Justinian constructed a Senate House in which the Roman senators used to convene and celebrate the annual festival of the in-coming year. Six columns stand in front of the Senate, two of which support the center of its west wall and the other four stand a little further out. The columns are of white marble, and I think they must be the largest in the world. The columns make a portico that even goes around the roof on the rotunda; the upper parts of the upper portico are all equally ornamented elegantly with marble columns and with a multitude of statues.[157] I believe that Justinian did not build *this* Senate but rebuilt an older Senate House, which was burnt down in the fire that burnt down Hagia Sophia and the Baths of Zeuxippus. For Sozomen says that Constantine the Great constructed the great Consilium, which is called the Senate and which he wanted to have the same dignity, organization and the feast of Calends, as the Senate in ancient Rome. He discloses the location of the Senate, writing that the silver statue of Empress Eudoxia stood on a porphyry column to the south of Hagia Sophia, above the high platform across from the great Senate House.[158] Socrates claims it was neither close to, nor far from, Hagia Sophia but past the broad street in the middle that separates the two, as Suidas mentions.[159] He says that the statue of Eudoxia, wife of Theodosius, stood in the Palace Tribunal.[160] The *Ancient Description of the Wards*

30. *Drawing of 1870 of the Boukoleon Palace. C.G. Curtis and M.A. Walker,* Restes de la Reine des Villes *(Constantinople 1891).*

puts the Senate, the Basilica and the Tribunal with porphyry stairs in the same ward.[161] Sozomen also locates the Senate House clearly, saying that during the riot that resulted from the expulsion of John Chrysostom, fire spread everywhere and burned the Great Church as well as the entire walkway, and the very great Senate House, which stood to the south of them.[162] Some remains of the Senate walls still stand by the south corner of Hagia Sophia, past the road that runs from the imperial enclosure to the Forum of Constantine.[163]

XVIII. The Imperial Palace, the Basilica, the Palace of Constantine and the Chalke Gate

Procopius writes that not far from the Augusteon was the Imperial Palace. We know its nature the same way, as they say, that we know a lion from his claws. Those about to read these things will see. Procopius says that the vestibule of this palace, which they called the Chalke, is such: four straight, high walls arranged in a square are lifted into the sky from their corners, a certain building rises up and is stretched out by stones carefully worked. This building rises up with a wall from the ground to the top, not interfering with the beauty of the spot but even adding to its harmoniousness. On top of these sit eight arches supporting a central roof that is curved to a rounded height. The ceiling is beautifully done. The entire ceiling is not done with wax-covered paintings but glitters with small stones, decorated with all types of colors depicting images of men and other things. Procopius described what had been depicted: scenes of war and battles, the capture of many cities in Italy and Africa, Emperor Justinian conquering with his general Belisarius, and the general returning to the emperor with his high-spirited army, booty, kings, kingdoms and other things that are precious to mortals. In the center stand the Emperor Justinian and Empress Theodora, looking happy and celebrating the victories over the king of the Vandals and the king of the Goths, and the captives being brought to them. The whole Senate is represented standing around them and celebrating, for the stones depict their expressions, in which happiness and cheerfulness blossom. For all are being honored with the emperor, and they laugh, enjoying divine honors.[164]

As Papinius in his *Sylvae* calls the Basilica of Paulus the Palace of Paulus, so the palace that Procopius calls Βασιλείον was called both the Basilica and the Imperial Palace.[165] I gather this from Cedrinus, who describes the fire in the time of Justinian that burnt the vestibule of the Basilica, the Augusteon, and the bronze roof on the Palace of Constantine the Great, which from that time to this day is called the Chalke because it was adorned with gilded bronze sheets.[166] What Cedrinus calls the Basilica, Procopius calls τὰ Βασιλεῖα in his book *De Aedificii Justiniani* when he tells of the conflagration just mentioned above. He says that the fire consumed the vestibules "of the emperor's place," τῶν βασιλείων, also called the Chalke. Procopius adds further concerning the Persian war and Hagia Sophia and the Baths of Zeuxippus, καὶ τῆς βασιλείου αὐλῆς, τὰ ἐκ τῶν προπυλαίων, "of the emperor's court, the things outside the main gate," all the way to the palace of Martis.[167] He says a little further on that the emperor ordered Belisarius to the place called the Chalke and the vestibules situated there, from which it seems that Procopius distinguishes the vestibule of the royal grounds from the Chalke, although first he calls the vestibule the Chalke Palace.[168]

For my part, I think that the residence of the emperor was initially called the Basilica, and later there were great buildings in which merchants assembled, also called basilicas. The imperial residence was called Βασιλείον or Basileion, and then finally the Palace, to distinguish the Basilica from the imperial residence. Nevertheless, it was either part of the Palace or close to it, as is seen in the *Ancient Description of the Wards*, which puts the Augusteon and the Basilica in the same ward.[169] But since this work mentions neither palace nor courts in its commemoration of this region's locations, but only the Basilica, it seems to suggest that the Basilica was, in fact, the Imperial Palace. But whether or not the Basilica was inside or outside of the palace, accounts of the fires show that it was clearly close to the Palace because both were consumed by the fire since they were so close together. And the rules of architecture prescribe that a basilica be placed near forums such as the one I have mentioned that is near the palace. A basilica should also be set up in the warmest place possible so that the merchants can conduct their business in the winter without suffering from the bad weather. Julius Pollux agrees when he says that the Stadia, the Hippodrome, the Senate, the Forum, the Imperial Court, the Imperial Portico and the Tribunal ought to be near the Theater.[170] George Cedrinus says that Aetherius was the architect who built the beautiful Chalke building upon the order of the wife of the wise Emperor Anastasius. An inscription once written on it proves this, which I will add in Greek so it is more clearly understood:

Εἰς τὸν οἶκον τὸν ἐπιλεγόμενον χαλκὸν ἐν τῷ παλατίῳ,
ἴκτισε Ἀναστάσιος βασιλεύς.

Οἶκος Ἀναστασίοιο τυραννοφόνου βασιλῆος
Μοῦνος ὑπερτέλλω τανυπείροχος ἄστεσι γαίης,
Θαῦμα φέρων πάντεσσιν ἐπεὶ χοσμήτορες ἔργων
ὕψος ὁμου μῆκός τε καὶ ἄπλετον εὖρος ἰδόντες
ἀσκεπὲς ἐφράσσάντο πελώριον ἔργον ἐᾶσαι.
ἀλλὰ πολυκμήτοιο λαχὼν πρεσβήϊα τέχνης
Αἰθέριος πολυιδρις ἔμην τεχνήσατο μορφήν,
ἀχράντῳ βασιλῆι φέρων πρωτάγρια μόχθων,
ἔνθεν ἀπειρέσιον μέγεθος περὶ παντὶ τιταίνων,
Αὠσονὶης νίκησα βοώμενα θαυματα γαίης.
Εἶξον ἀρειοτέροισι, χάρις καπετωλίδος αὐλῆς,
εἰ καὶ χαλκείων ὀρόφων ἀμαρύγματα τέμπεις
κρύψον ἀμετρητων μεγάρων στεινούμενον αυλαῖς
Πέργαμε, φαιδρὸν ἄγαλμα τεόν, Ῥουφίνιον ἄλσος
ὑηδὲ τανυπλεύροισιν ἀρησότα, Κὠζικε, πέτροις
Ἀδριανοῦ βασιλὴος ἀμεμφέα νηὸν ἀείσεις.
Οὔ μοι Πυραμίδες ἰκέλη κρίσις, οὐδὲ Κολοσσοῦ,
Οὐδὲ Φάρου μεγάλην μοῦνος δ ὑπερέδραμον αἴγηλι
αὐτὸς ἐμὸς σκπτοῦχος Ἰσαυροφόνον μετὰ νίκην
χρυσοφαές με τέλεσσεν ἐδέθλιον Ἠριγενείης,
πάντη τετραπόρων ἀνέμων πεπετασμένον αὔραιφς.[171]

Upon the house called the Chalke of the Imperial Palace,
I am the House of Anastasius the tyranicide emperor
And I alone surpass by far all the cities of the world,
A source of wonder to all. The architects,
On seeing my height, length and immense
Breadth were inclined to leave the vast pile unroofed.
But cunning Aetherius, possessed of preeminence in this
Laborious art, devised my form and offered
To the stainless emperor the first fruit of his toils.
So, stretching my enormous bulk on all sides
I excel the celebrated wonders of the Ausonian land.
Yield to thy betters, graceful hall of the Capitol,
Even though thy brazen roof radiates glitter.

Hide, Pergamus, thy gay ornament, the grove of
Rufinus, narrow beside the endless expanse of these palatial halls.
Neither wilt though, Cyzicus, sing of Hadrian's perfect temple
Founded on the long cliff. The Pyramids stand no
Competition with me, nor the Colossus, nor
The Pharos; single-handed I have surpassed a whole big legion.
My emperor himself, after his victorious annihilation
Of the Isaurians, completed me, the shrine of Dawn,
Resplendent with gold, fronting on all sides
The breezes of the four winds.[172]

Some recent historians say that Constantine the Great first built the palace of the Chalke. I might disagree except that I was persuaded by the verisimilitude that I believe Constantine had tried to achieve to those gilded bronze Capitoline tiles of ancient Rome, which itself had a bronze-roofed forum. I never could find out who removed the tiles from the Chalke, but it is not unlikely that the fire destroyed them. Procopius writes that Genseric plundered half of the gilded bronze and gold tiles that covered the Roman Capitol and that Constantine III, nephew of Heraclius, carried away the silver plates that decorated the Pantheon.[173]

On the southwest side of Hagia Sophia, a short distance from where the pipes of an aqueduct emerge from a shelter, in the place where I said the column of Justinian was in the Forum Augusteon, seven Corinthian columns still stand. On the shaft of one there is carved the name of Constantine the Great. There is also his sign that was seen in the sky and the words: ἐν τούτω νίκα, "in this conquer."[174] The bases and bottom parts of them are buried in the ground a depth of six feet, which I discovered when I happened upon the foundations of some walls that were being put between the columns. I could not see the plinth of the base at all because it was buried, but I saw the lower torus,[175] which was seven fingers high and eight wide. The base without the plinth was two feet 9 fingers high; the bottom heel of the shaft was nine fingers wide. Each column is 30 feet 6 fingers tall. In fact, the whole column with base and capital is about 46½ feet high. I measured the bottom of the shaft just above its base at 19 feet in circumference. The columns stand 20 feet 10 fingers from one to the other.[176] The residents of Constantinople say that these columns had stood inside the Palace of Constantine, but others say that they used to support a bridge that lead from the Palace to Hagia Sophia.[177] But there is no truth in either of these stories, for it is clear, as I mentioned before, that they stood in the Augusteon. So I think that they supported the arches of the porticos that held the statues of Constantine the Great, his mother Helena and others.

From what I have written, one may imagine the excellence of the imperial buildings. And we learn this from Zosimus too, who says that Constantine erected palaces in Constantinople that were scarcely inferior to those in Rome.[178] Eusebius, who cites him, says that Constantine not only brightened New Rome with ornaments, but even decorated the best places in the royal buildings and saw to it that a symbol of the cross, made with various precious stones and decorated with much gold, should be wrought into the middle of golden ceilings — thinking that it would be a protection for his rule.[179] From St. Jerome we are able to understand how greatly Constantine decorated New Rome with palaces. He stripped nearly every city of its decorations and rare items in order to embellish his New Rome.[180] Eusebius also mentions statues of the Muses that Constantine placed in his palace.[181] Sozomen writes that, with the order of Constantine, all the ancient temples and all the bronze statues in his domain were to be taken away; indeed wooden items were burned and they had brought well-worked bronzes from everywhere to Constantinople. He says that these statues stood along public streets and in the Hippodrome and the Palace in his day.[182]

Not only Constantine the Great but also many other emperors of Constantinople ransacked the entire world in order to decorate New Rome, among whom was Constantine III, Heraclius' nephew, who despoiled ancient Rome of all its bronze and marble statues and sent off all the expensive temple furnishings in ships prepared for this purpose. Thus one man took away more in a mere seven days than the barbarians did in 250 years. That is how many years there were from the first decline of the empire until that foul depredation. Jordanes, not an altogether inferior author of the *Getick History*, says that the Emperor Zeno adopted Theoderic, prefect of Byzantium, and made him consul and honored him with an equestrian statue erected in front of the Imperial Palace.[183] In his *Historiarum variarum* Tzetzes says that in his time even the head of Apollo, made by Phidias to resemble the sun, was still in the Imperial Palace.[184] Suidas says that the statue of Pulcheria, the daughter of Arcadius, was put in the Chalke near the portico, and that

the statue of Ariadne, Zeno's first consort, and Zeno's own statues were
erected in the royal Chalke Gate, and there existed two others standing
on their feet on top of a small column with eulogies by the philosopher
Secundus carved on them.[185]
A history, familiar to the residents of Constantinople but
otherwise unknown, reports that Justinian put up seven statues
of his family members on the left side of the Chalke, some in
bronze and some in marble, and that he also erected two horses
in a niche on the front vault of the Chalke, and also some gilded
heads of women resembling Medusa. It mentions things that I pass
over because the history is so little known.[186] Suidas says that the
statues of Eudoxia and her husband the Emperor Theodosius, and
of Marcian and Constantine stood in the Tribunal of the Palace,
where the dancing of the two parties used to take place, until the
time of Heraclius.[187]

XIX. The Basilica and Its Surroundings

The Basilica, which I discussed earlier, stood in the Forum
Augusteon and had four arches, as is clear from the following
inscriptions that were upon them:

Εἰς ἀψῖδα ἐν τῇ βασιλικῇ ἐν Βυζαντίῳ
Τετραπόροις ἀψῖσι πόλιν Θεόδωρος ἐγείρας
Ἄξιός ἐστι πόλιν καὶ τέτρατον ἡνιοχεῦσαι.[188]

On the vault of the Basilica in Byzantium:
Theodore, who increased the city with four porticos,
Is worthy to rule the city a fourth time.

Εἰς ἕτερον μέρος τῆς αὐτῆς Βασιλικῆς
Ἔπρεπέ σοι, Θεόδωρε, Τύχης εὐκίονα νηὸν
Ἔργου κοσμῆσαι θαύματι τοσσατίου
Δῶρά τε κυδήεντα πορεῖν χρυσάσπιδι Ῥώμη
ἥ σ᾽ ὕπατον τεῦξεν καὶ τρισέπαρχον ὁρᾷ.[189]

On another part of this Basilica:
It is fitting for you, Theodore to decorate a well-columned temple of
    Fortune
By such marvelous work
And to bestow spendid gifts on Rome of the golden shield,
Which saw that you, three times prefect, were made consul.

Calliades of the imperial Byzantine army put up statues of Byzas and Phidalia in the Basilica bearing these inscriptions:

Τὸν κρατορὸν Βυζανα καὶ ἱμερτὴν Φιδάλειαν
εἰν ἑνὶ κοσψήσας ἄνθετο Καλλιάδης. [190]
Calliades set up Byzas and Phidaleia
Arraying them in a single group.

Εἰς Φεδίαλειαν
Ἱμερτή Φιδάλεια δάμαρ Βύζαντος ἐτύχθην
Εἰμὶ δὲ Βουπάλεως δῶρον ἀεθλοσύνης. [191]
And on the statue of Phidalia:
I happen to be the lovely Phidalia, wife of Byzas,
And I am of Bupalus, gift of a struggle. [192]

Pliny lists, among other makers of statues, Anthermus of Chios, and his sons Biopalus and Anthermus. Dionysius of Byzantium writes that Byzas, after whom Byzantium was named, was the spouse of Phidalia, after whom the Bosporus port Phidalia was named, which I discuss at greater length in my work, *The Thracian Bosporus*.[193] Suidas the Grammarian and recent writers claim that in the Basilica, behind the Miliarium Aureum, there stood a gold-covered statue of a man, and there was also the Exammon of Emperor Heraclius and a kneeling statue of Julian the Tyrant. Terbelis, it is said, preached in the same location. And here, on the orders of Severus, stood the statue of a huge elephant for the following reason: An elephant was kept with many keepers, and nearby a money-changer practiced his art of weighing. When his house had been damaged the money-changer threatened to kill the keeper unless he controlled the elephant. When the man scorned the threats the money-changer murdered him and threw his body to the elephant as food. The elephant became incensed and killed the money-changer in turn. Severus, having learned of this incident, made sacrifices to the elephant and ordered that he and his keeper be depicted in bronze and erected there.[194] Also in this location, as Suidas says, there was the statue of Hercules, which was worshipped. Many sacrifices were made to it, and later it was transported to the Hippodrome in the time of the Consul Julian. Originally it was carried down with ten statues brought from ancient Rome partly by land and partly by sea. If this is the same Hercules that Ibrahim Pasha took from Hungary to Byzantium and put in the Hippodrome, Hercules wandered the world no less when he was dead than when he was alive.[195] Suidas

records that in the Imperial Portico there stood the equestrian statues
of Trajan, Theodosius, Valentinian, Gibbus and Firmilianus the Fool.[196]
Many other statues not only of emperors but of eunuchs were there.
Among them was the famous statue of Eutropius who was in charge of
the bedroom of Arcadius. His power, demonstrated by gilded statues
erected to him and by the rather splendid houses built all over the city,
incited a nation of eunuchs to such a degree that even young men with
the first down on their cheeks were willingly made eunuchs, hoping
that they might be like Eutropius.[197]

The Basilica was close to the Miliarium Aureum and the Augusteon
as was the Horologion, which Justinian had made. George Cedrinus
locates it in the Miliarium, but others in the Forum Augusteon, and
others in the Basilica, as the following epigram shows:

Εἰς βάσιν τοῦ ὡρολογίου τοῦ εἰς τὴν ἁψίδα
τὴν κειμένην εἰς τὴν βασιλικήν.
Δῶρον Ἰουστίνου τυραννοφόνου Βασιλῆος
καὶ Σοφίης ἀλόχου, φέγγος ἐλευθερίης
Ὡράων σκοπίαζε σοφὸν σημάντορα χαλκόν
αὐτῆς ἐκ μονάδος μέχρι δυωδεκάδος,
ὄντινα συληθέντα Δίκης θρόνον ἡνιοχεύων
εὗρεν Ἰουλιανὸς χερσὶν ἀδωροδόχοις.[198]

On the base of the Horologion above the vault of the Basilica:
Look at this gift of Emperor Justin the Tyrannicide,
And of his wife Sophia. Look, light of Freedom,
At the bronze indicator of the hours from one to twelve,
Which Julian, governing the seat of justice, recovered
When it had been stolen, and replaced with incorruptible hands.

XX. The Library and Gate of the Basilica, and the Basilica Cistern

Zonaras says that the Imperial Palace was in the area of the Basilica,
near the bronze workshops, and that many books of foreign wisdom
and of rather noble and divine doctrine were kept in it. This residence
was, in better times, for the schools of an outstanding teacher whom
they called "Oeconomicus." He had twelve teachers living in his house
with him, all endowed with the utmost refinement of reasoning.
Food was provided for them at public expense. Those who were most
dedicated to the reasoning of wisdom went to them, and even kings
consulted them as advisors about things that should be done.[199]

During the reign of Basiliscus there was a great fire in Constantinople that started at and burnt down the bronze workshops and their excellent neighborhood. It reduced buildings to ashes along with the place called the Basilica, which held a library of 600,000 books. Included among its other marvels was the coil of a snake that was 120 feet in length and was inscribed in golden letters with Homer's *Iliad* and *Odyssey*. Malchus, the Byzantine Sophist, wrote a history from the reign of Constantine to Anastasius in which he deplores in an earnest and tragic way the burning of the public library and of the statues of the Forum Augusteon.[200]

George Cedrinus writes about the same library. At the cistern called the Basilica, he says, the palace was full of dignity, in which, by an old ordinance, the master instructor lived with twelve students, very serious in speech and lifestyle, knowledgeable in every discipline of reasoning, endowed with a quickness and grandeur of nature, especially those practicing divine philosophy [theology], about whom it seemed impious for even kings to speak without wisdom. The fire occurred in Constantinople while Basiliscus ruled. It destroyed the most flourishing part of the city. Starting from the bronze workshops it destroyed both porticos and the entire Basilica neighborhood in which there was a library with 600,000 books. Among them was the coil of a snake 120 feet long on which the *Iliad* and *Odyssey* of Homer were written in gold letters. In this library there were even histories of the deeds of famous heroes.[201] Years after the burning of this library, when Emperor Leo Conon was unable to bring the wise men of the Basilica over to the opinion of his sect, he set them on fire along with the Palace Basilica and the library. After the second fire it was furnished with beautiful books.[202]

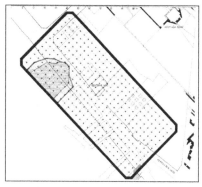

31. *Plan of the Basilica Cistern/Yerbatan Sarayı. E. Unger, E. Mamboury, T. Wiegand.*

The basilicas of Rome were dedicated to courts, councils and business; in Constantinople they were dedicated to book storage and schools of letters, as is evident from what I have previously said as well as from the following inscription:

Εἰς τὴν βασιλικὴν τῶν παιδευτηρίων ἐν Βυζαντίῳ
Χῶρος ἐγὼ θεσμοῖσιν ἀνειμένος ἐνθτάδε πηγή...
Ἄφθονος Αὐσονίων ἐκκέχυται νομίμων.
Ἡ πᾶσιν τέτατται μὲν ἀεινάος, ἠϊθέοις δὲ
Ἐνθάδ ἀγειρομένοις πάντα δίδωσι ῥόον.[203]

Upon the Basilica of the schools in Byzantium:
I am a place dedicated to the study of the laws.
Here flows the abundant spring of Roman laws
Which flows out continually for all
And gives its current to the youths gathered here.

The area that contained the library, recent writers say, was octagon-shaped and there were roofed porticos and a place where the master of teachers met with his followers.[204] George Cedrinus says that the fire in the time of Justinian burnt the great church, the Hospital of Sampson, the vestibule of the Basilica, the Augusteon, the Chalke, the two long porticos up to Constantine's Forum and the Octagon, and the Baths of Zeuxippus.[205] From this I suspect there must have been two Octagons close together, because, if the Octagon that Cedrinus mentions had been the same one that housed the library, he would not have neglected to add that the library was also burnt in the time of Justinian.[206] I think that the area where the library stood was quadrangular and its courtyard is the one surrounded by columns arranged in a square that Procopius mentions.[207] Zonaras does not discuss the Basilica that housed the library, but says that it was near the Chalkoprateia, that is the bronze-smithing district.[208]

Cedrinus calls the Basilica "Cisterna,"[209] which some people claim was constructed by Constantine the Great. But this is incorrect, as I learned from Procopius. He records that near the Imperial Portico, where the orators used to make their cases there was a courtyard of great length and width surrounded with columns set in a quadrangular shape, built with a stone, not an earthen surface, and hollowed out by Emperor Justinian to a great depth for containing water in the summer. Filled in winter by underground pipes running from the aqueducts, it would supplement them when the water was low.[210] Menander, nicknamed Protector, says that he was not happy to enter into legal disputes, nor to stroll in the Imperial Portico, nor to reconcile men's minds with an effusion of speech.[211] Agathias ridiculed Uranius of Syria who practiced as a doctor even though he was completely ignorant of the discipline of Aristotle. Nevertheless he was loud and insolent and used to make himself a nuisance in the Imperial Portico, among other places. This same Agathias says that Uranius used to occupy himself in the royal porticos contemplating books of all legal cases and of business from sunrise to sunset, from which we are able to discern that the Imperial Portico and Basilica Cistern were in the same location.[212] The Imperial Portico no longer remains but the cistern is intact. Because of the negligence of the citizens this structure was not known, but being found by me, a foreigner, it came to the notice of many.

Houses built over the Basilica Cistern make it hard to detect. I found out that many neighbors did not know that a cistern was under their houses even though every day they drank water from wells penetrating into the cistern between their buildings. At length I came upon a house in which there was a stairway down into it. I boarded a small boat, in which the householder, holding lit torches, rowed me back and forth through the columns, as if through a forest, which stood quite deep in water. I passed over everything there while he focused on catching fish, with which the cistern abounds. He caught some with his spear by the torchlight. A bit of light appears through the intermittent opening of the wells, like air holes, in which the fish gather. The cistern is 336 feet long, 182 feet wide and 224 Roman paces in circumference. The roof, arches, and walls are all brickwork covered with plaster, which is not at all decayed by time. The roof is supported by 336 marble columns. The space of the intercolumniation is 12 feet. Each column is more than 40 feet 9 inches high. They stand lengthwise in twelve rows, twenty-eight to a row.

In some places the capitals have been decorated in the Corinthian style, while others are unfinished. Over the abacus above the capital of each column a large stone has been placed that appears to function as another larger abacus to support the four arches above. Many wells penetrate into this, from which water is drawn up from the cistern. In the winter time it is filled by the aqueduct. I saw it being filled in the winter; a steady flow fell from a large pipe into the cistern with a loud noise until the columns were submerged in water up to the middle of their capitals. This cistern lies to the west side of Hagia Sophia a distance of 80 Roman paces away.

XXI. The Chalkoprateia

The Chalkoprateia, which we can translate as the place where bronze works were executed, stood near the Basilica, as is clear from the things just said. George Cedrinus states that Theodosius II built the church of the Chalkoprateia and dedicated it to the Virgin Mary.[213] Others add that Theodosius II expelled from there the Jews, who had their residences in the Chalkoprateia from the time of Constantine the Great. They also say he had built the church to the Virgin Mother-of-God there, which was later damaged in an earthquake and rebuilt by Justin the Curopalatos.[214] But Zonaras takes a different view. He says that when Theodosius the Great marched into the territories of the west, the Jews came to an understanding with Honoratus, prefect of the city, and they got permission from him to erect a synagogue in the Chalkoprateia. Enraged at this action, the populace burnt the synagogue to the ground. When Theodosius learned of this fire he imposed a punishment on those who did this and gave the Jews permission to construct another synagogue. St. Ambrose, bishop of Milan, pointed out to Theodosius the injustice in permitting the Jews to have a synagogue in the very heart of the Queen of Cities. With the advice of Ambrose Theodosius cancelled the punishment and forbade the Jews from having a synagogue within the Queen of Cities.[215]

Today there are no bronze shops, as they have been moved to another spot in the city, but I was told by some residents that not many years ago the bronze smiths still worked near the Chalkoprateia. While giving the circuit of ancient Byzantium, the anonymous writer of the *History of Constantinople* states that the Chalkoprateia was not far from the Miliarium.[216] Other writers claim that it was near Hagia Sophia.[217] From all this we can see that the Hippodrome, Senate, Imperial Palace, Imperial Portico and Basilica were all in the same area, according to architectural principle. Strabo says that part of the palace of Alexandria had been a museum, which had a portico and exedra and a great hall in which resided men engaged in disciplines.[218]

XXII. The Gates Situated between the Palace and Forum of Constantine, and the Palace Called Lampterum

The fires have left a record that besides the Imperial Portico, which was near the Library, other porticos stood not far from it that ran from the Palace to the Forum of Constantine. Procopius records that the first of the fires during Justinian's reign burnt the Palace and Hagia Sophia and also the great porticos all the way to the Forum of Constantine.[219] Of this same fire Cedrinus says that the Chalke, Hagia Sophia, the Augusteon and two porticos to the Forum of Constantine were consumed.[220] Afterwards, the fire in the reign of Basiliscus started at the Chalkoprateia and consumed the surrounding porticos and other buildings in the vicinity, the Basilica that held the library, both porticos between the palaces, and finally all the beautiful ornaments of the Lausus.[221]

32. Drawing/plan of Arch of Theodosius in the Forum Tauri. Naumann, Müller-Wiener.

These porticos were frequently burnt down and frequently rebuilt, first by Justinian, later by others, and lastly by Domninus, according to a recent historian who records: "when the city was captured by the Gauls and Venetians, the covered porticos of Domninus, which ran along both sides of the street and stretched from the Miliarium to the Forum of Constantine were burned down."[222] There are some who say that in the time of Constantine the Great Eubulus erected four porticos, each one doubled, covered and extending from the Palace to the land walls of the city, one pair of which ran as far as the church of St. Anthony at the edge of the city, and the other pair ran from the Daphne and the Port of Sophia to the church called Rabdon. The other double portico stretched from the Chalke and Miliarium to the Forum of Constantine and the Taurus and the Bronze Bull. All of the porticos were paved with marble and ornamented with countless statues.[223] Even though these accounts are by unknown writers whom I have detected stating falsehoods on many other occasions, nevertheless they seem to be accurate here, since it is agreed among more authoritative historians that Constantine despoiled every city in order to decorate New Rome. And it is clear from the *Ancient Description of the Wards* that Constantinople had fifty-two public porticos, five of which stood in the Fourth Ward, in which also stood the Basilica, the Imperial Portico and the one named after Fanio.[224]

The *Ancient Description of the Wards* also mentions four large porticos in the Sixth Ward, and one to the right of the Forum of Constantine to the Forum of Theodosius. It adds that the Seventh Ward had extensive porticos, and in the Eighth Ward, in fact, was a portico to the left of the Taurus and five more larger porticos; there were two rather large porticos in the Ninth Ward, six large porticos in the Tenth Ward, and the Fourth Ward had eleven large porticos.[225] From this it appears likely that there were many porticos from the Chalke to the land walls. However I cannot affirm that they continued past the Taurus.

XXIII. THE MILIARIUM AUREUM AND ITS STATUES, AND THE FORTUNA OF THE CITY AND HER STATUE

The Miliarium Aureum was a golden column from which the main roads to all the gates proceeded. Pliny says the the Miliarium of Rome was at the head of the Forum in Rome, but whether in fact the

33. *Fragment of Milion.*

Miliarium of Constantinople was similar to the Miliarium of Rome, none of the Greeks in all their writings have said a thing, not even knowing its name, unless they altered it to *Milion*. They mention that some statues were placed in its vaulted structure. It seems to me, nonetheless, that it was probably similar to that in Rome, and was situated in the same place in New Rome, which emulated ancient Rome as much as it could. So we are able to assert with some authority that it had been in the forum or near the forum. The *Ancient Description of the Wards* places it in the region with the Forum Augusteon and Basilica, whose vicinity is understood from the fire that Zonaras says the rioting mob started at the Miliarium in the reign of Justinian. Procopius claims that this fire burnt Hagia Sophia, the Baths of Zeuxippus, the Vestibule of the Imperial Palace and the great Portico to the Forum of Constantine.[226] Those writers who record the deeds of Alexius Comnenus say that at sunrise Alexius' army, under the General Sabatius, marched out of the Great Palace and into the church of St. John the Theologian, and having ascended to the top part of the church, their voices poured out full of outrageous abuse. A battle started at about three o'clock, and those who were fighting from the roof of the Miliarium and the top of the church of St. John the Theologian injured people crowding the Forum.[227]

The residents of Constantinople say that the church of St. John the Theologian is where the lions of the sultan are now kept, in the area near the Hippodrome and the Forum Cupedinis, formerly called the Forum Augusteon, situated near Hagia Sophia. From this it appears the Miliarium was near the Forum. But why repeat a more remote source, when Suidas, close by, explains as follows:

In the Basilica, he says, behind the Miliarium there was a realistic statue of a man, gilded, and also statues of an elephant and his keeper had been set up.[228] Others more clearly state that these statues were positioned behind the Basilica near the Miliarium. Suidas adds that the statue of Theodosius was in the Miliarium and that when Theodosius erected it he distributed much corn.[229] From the equestrian statue of Theodosius, which no longer exists, the following verses remain:

Ἔκθορες ἀντολίηθε φαεοφόρος ἥλιος ἄλλος
Θευδόσιε, θνητοῖσι, πολοῦ μέσον ἠπιόθυμε,
Ὠκεανὸν παρὰ ποσσὶν ἔχων μετ᾽ ἀπείρονα γαῖαν,
Πάντοθεν αἰγήλεις κεκορυθμένος ἀγλαὸν ἵππον
Ῥηϊδιώς μεγάθυμε, καὶ ἐσσύμενον κατερύκων.[230]

O Theodosius, you rise from the east like another sun,
Hurling your rays upon mortals, and you, so gentle,
Having Ocean and the endless land below your feet,
Helmeted in your shining helmet,
You easily rein in your handsome, eager steed.

Suidas adds that the statues of Sophia, wife of Justin of Thrace, of his daughter Arabia and his niece Helena, and also the equestrian statues of Arcadius and his son Theodosius had all been in the Miliarium near the statue of Theodosius the Great.[231] Cedrinus writes that two statues were set on top of the Miliarium, one of Constantine the Great and the other of his mother Helena, having a cross between them. Behind these was the equestrian statue of Trajan, and near him a similar equestrian statue of Aelius Hadrianus.[232] Suidas talks similarly about the statues of Constantine and Helena with a cross between them on the top of the Miliarium having this inscription: UNA SANCTA ET DUO CELERES CURSORES, or "one holy cross and two swift messengers." The same Suidas puts in the vault of the Forum Augusteon these same statues of Constantine and Helena with the cross and this inscription, from which it is clear that the Forum, the Miliarium and the Basilica were in the same vicinity. So not only do different writers put the same things in different locations, but sometimes even the same author does so! Furthermore, Suidas says in the Miliarium there was a chariot pulled by four tawny horses from ancient times, sustained by two pillars in this place, where Constantine was received with the auspicious acclamations of his army after he conquered Azotium, where Byzas, founder of Byzantium, was lauded.

The chariot of the Sun bearing a statuette that was fashioned at Constantine's orders was transferred into the Hippodrome. This statue was the Fortune of the city, whose carving Constantine had seen to and which, with a cross on her head, was put up in the Senate during major festivals and on the anniversary of the founding of the city. Julian the Apostate buried it in the same location in which Arius suffered a hideous death not far from the Senate.[233] This is also where pious Theodosius ordered the statues of Arius, Macedonius, Sabellius and Eunomius, fashioned in marble, be seated on the ground as a mark of their faithlessness in order to be soiled with excrement and to receive the abuses of the populace.[234] Others say that the statue of the Fortune of the city was brought by Constantine the Great from Rome and put on the vault of the palace. Zosimus says that Constantine erected the Fortune of Rome in part of one of the four porticos that bordered the Great Forum.[235]

It is very likely that the Constantinopolitans held a festival in Fortune's honor, just as she used to be celebrated in ancient Rome, with both natives and foreigners, and in the same temple and on the same day that the Parilia used to be celebrated. Socrates reports that as Julian was making public sacrifice to the Fortune of Constantinople in the Basilica where the statue of Fortune was erected, Mares, bishop of Chalcedon, was led to this place by the hand since he was old and had difficulty with his eyes. He attacked the emperor with many reproaches, calling him an impious deserter from the Christian religion. Julian avenged the reproaches with his own words, calling him blind. He said: "Now, will your Galilean God cure you?" (He used to call Christ "the Galilean.") So Mares responded to Julian without hesitating, "I give thanks to God who has taken sight away from me," he said, "so that I cannot see your character lapsed into apostasy." Julian responded nothing to this.[236]

Zonaras and some ancient historians before him state that in the time of Emperor Anastasius there was a statue of Fortune, fashioned in bronze, that stood with one foot in a bronze ship and was set up in a certain part of the city. When the image of this bronze ship had deteriorated, either with age or else from malevolent design, certain parts of it were broken off and taken away. It came to pass that ships stopped putting ashore at the port of Byzantium, for when coming near the city, a violent storm kept them from entering the harbor, and if the long-boats were rowed into the port of the city carrying a cargo, it was immediately consumed because of the scarcity at the time. While this went on for some time, the government officials desperately needed to find the cause of the problem. Then, when there was suspicion that the theft of the ship-statue's bronze was responsible, and when this was reported to the city officials, these men found the pieces of the bronze ship, which were diligently sought out, and they put them back and fixed them up. And so, to know if the damage to the ship of Fortune was the cause that prevented ships from putting in, they again removed parts of the bronze ship, and once again ships were driven back by the force of the winds. So they had special concern for that ship, and they repaired it.[237]

Eunapius of Sardis wrote in his volume of the *Lives of the Philosophers and Sophists* that in the reign of Constantine the populace assigned another cause to this difficulty of navigation to Byzantium. He says that it just so happened that the geographical situation of Byzantium made sailing into the city difficult unless the wind blew from the south directly and, when this failed to happen often, the populace, suffering from famine and angry at Constantine, gathered in the theater. The prefect of the Imperial Palace, holding a grudge against Soprater the Philosopher, dragged him before Constantine and denounced him with these words: "Soprater, whom you honor, has stopped the winds with an excess of wisdom, for which even you yourself praise him and cause him to sit on the royal throne." Hearing this, Constantine was persuaded and ordered Soprater killed by the axe.[238]

XXIV. The Temple of Neptune, Church of St. Mina [St. Menas], the Stadia, the Pier of Timasius

It seems to me I ought not neglect to mention the church of St. Mina,[239] since it illustrates in what part of city the Fourth Ward stood. This ward contained the Basilica, Augusteon and church of St. Mina. The history of an unknown author says that Byzas once constructed a temple of Neptune near the sea on the Acropolis, where in his day he says the church of St. Mina the Martyr stood. But he is inconsistent here, for he claims that the church of St. Mina used to be the Temple of Jupiter and that its marble arches were supported by two great columns.[240] So, from this inconstant author I can deduce nothing conclusive, except that it seems more likely to me that the church of St. Mina was in parts of the Acropolis where the Temple of Neptune once existed. According to Dionysius of Byzantium, a very ancient writer, an altar to Minerva Egressoria and a temple of Neptune were erected a bit above the Bosporus promontory, and below the Temple of Neptune inside the walls were the Stadia and Gymnasia, as I amply demonstrated in my *Thracian Bosporus*.[241] So I am supported by the memories of men now living, who say that inside the palace grounds, formerly called the Acropolis, stood the noble church of St. Mina.[242] The *Ancient Description of the Wards of the City* says that the church of St. Mina stood in the same ward as did the Stadia and Pier of Timasius.[243] Procopius writes that at the place next to the sea called the Stadium, because people used to engage in certain contests there, Emperor Justinian and Empress Theodora constructed large hospice buildings.[244]

XXV. The Lausus and Its Statues: Cnidean Venus, Samian Juno, Lindian Minerva, Winged Cupid, Olympian Jupiter, Saturn, Unicorns, Tigers, Vultures, Camel-Leopards; and of the Cistern of the Hospital Called Philoxenos, and the Chrysotriclinium

The Lausus is a place in the city celebrated by many writers, some of whom record that it was the house of the patrician Lausus, who held many offices during the reign of Arcadius, son of Theodosius the Great.[245] They say that it was a house embellished with many remarkable monuments.[246] There still exists a book entitled *Lausaicus*, which was written by Heraclidas, bishop of Cappadocia, and dedicated to Lausus. These sources do not reveal in which part of the city the Lausus was, but I gather that it was between the Imperial Palace and the Forum of Constantine, based on what Zonaras and Cedrinus say about the fire in the time of Emperor Leo destroying buildings on the north side of the city from the port of the Bosporus to the church of St. John Calybites, and on the south side from the church of the Apostle Thomas to the church of Sts. Sergius and Bacchus, and that it burnt the center of the city from the Lausus to the Taurus.[247] In describing the same fire, in the place where the others say that the conflagration destroyed all the buildings in the center of the city from the Lausus to the Taurus, Evagrius says the fire burned from the Forum of Constantine to the Taurus.[248]

From this account it is clear that the Lausus was in the vicinity of the Forum of Constantine. But Cedrinus, who wrote of the fire in the reign of Basil, says that the Lausus was to the east between the Palace and Forum of Constantine, and that this fire destroyed the most beautiful part of the city, the Chalkoprateia, and also the portico and all the buildings it contained, and the Basilica in which, as I mentioned, stood the famous Library and all the beautiful ornaments of the Lausus to the Forum of Constantine. For, Cedrinus says, there were many statues in the Lausus, among which the most excellent was the statue of Minerva Lindia,[249] which was four cubits long and made out of emerald by the sculptors Scyllis and Dipoenus. It was once given by Sesostris, pharaoh of Egypt, to wise Cleobulus, tyrant of Lindia, and from this the place is called Laousus, because Minerva is named Laossos.[250] Theophrastus says that the Egyptian commentaries mention a king of Babylon who made a present to the emperor of an emerald four cubits long and three cubits wide.[251] If King Sesostris, Scyllis and Dipoenus lived at the same time, I expect that the story of the emerald Minerva should be found in Pliny's text. Yet Dipoenus and Scyllis were famous as the foremost marble sculptors, born on the island of Crete during the rule of Medes before Cyrus came to reign in Persia, that is, around the fifteenth Olympiad. They fashioned the likenesses of Apollo, Diana, Hercules and one of Minerva that was later struck by lightning. Pliny records that Ambracia, Argos and Cleone were full of works by Dipoenus, but he does not mention Minerva Lindia.[252]

Besides these Cedrinus adds that in the Lausus was the statue of Venus of Cnidos, celebrated in the writing of every mortal, made of white marble and covering with a hand only that part of the body that is treated with special modesty, a work of Praxiteles. And there was Juno of Samos, a work of Lysippus and Bupulus, and a winged Cupid holding arrows, brought there from Myndus, and there was Phidias' ivory Jupiter, which Pericles put in the temple at Olympia, and another statue by Lysippus presumed to be of Saturn, which was bald in back with hair combed forward. There were unicorns, tigers, camel-leopards, bull elephants, and vultures.[253] In the book by Cedrinus it reads *Taurelephas*, but more correctly it should be *Taurelaphos*, which I learned from the ancient and noble writer Cosmas Indicopleustes, who gives *Taurelaphos*, that is, bull-deer.[254] The unknown author of the *Patria* says that in the Lausus in his era there were stone eagles,[255] which I believe only in so far that there was something there in his time. I am justified in doubting this source and asserting that those were not eagles, which Cedrinus calls vultures, for a very large number of things written in this source are far less corroborated by others. Cedrinus writes that there were various buildings in parts of the Lausus and some hospices. There was also the famous Philoxenon, which supplemented the water supply. Some say the Philoxenon cistern was built by Philoxenos. I myself think it was filled with earth by Heraclius and stood between the Triclinium and the Lausiacum.[256] Menander Protector writes that the Macedonian emperor cleaned many of the cisterns that Emperor Heraclius had filled up with dirt. It seems that if the emperor ordered the cleaning of that cistern between the Triclinium and Lausiacum, among other cisterns, then it seems to be the same cistern that lies underground on the north side of the Palace of Ibrahim Pasha, which has a roof held up by 424 marble columns, that is, 212 columns supporting the same number of columns on top. I measured one of the columns, since they all looked to be about the same size, and found it to be 6 feet 9 inches around.[257]

Another cistern exists on the west side of the same palace with arches resting on 32 Corinthian columns standing in four rows, each row containing eight columns whose shafts are 12 feet 9 fingers in circumference.[258] As for the Triclinium, between which and the Lausus the Philoxenon Cistern was located, I suspect it is the same that Zonaras writes that Justinian III built in the Imperial Palace and called Justinian after himself.[259] Cedrinus claims that Emperor Tiberius refurbished more decoratively the Chrysotriclinium built by Justinian.[260] Leo V mentions the western door of the Chrysotriclinium when he predicted to Andronicus, who was bent on tyranny, that the severed head of Andronicus was going to be brought to Leo in the Hippodrome via the western door of the Chrysotriclinium.[261] Historians who lived before the fall of Constantinople often mention the Chrysotriclinium, and all the citizens knew the name and location of the Chrysotriclinium, but now there is no one who knows or cares to know. Rather one does not notice, and one has contempt for all the other things that have to do with education.[262]

PIERRE GILLES' CONSTANTINOPLE ❦

NOTES TO BOOK II

1. *Notitia urbis CP*, ed. O. Seeck.

2. Gilles is alluding to the mythological river Lethe.

3. Pliny, *Natural History*, IX.51.

4. Gilles refers here to his treatise *On the Thracian Bosporus*, which was first published posthumously as *De Bosporo Thracio libri tres* (Lyon: Guillaume Rovillium, 1561), I.iv and I.v.

5. Io had been transformed into a cow, or *"bos."*

6. Dionysius Byzantius, *Anaplus Bospori, De Bospori Navigatione. Quae Supersunt una cum Supplementis in Geographos Minores Aliisque Eiusdem Argumentii Fragmentis,* ed. Charles Wescher (Paris: E. Typographeo Publico, 1874) 5, ll. 9f.; Dionysius Byzantius, *Anaplus Bospori,* ed. Güngerich, 4, ll. 10f.

7. Dionysius Byzantius, *Anaplus Bospori,* ed. Wescher, 12, ll. 5f.; Dionysius Byzantius, *Anaplus Bospori,* ed. Güngerich, 12 and 13.

8. Dionysius Byzantius, *Anaplus Bospori,* ed. Wescher, notes on page 53; Dionysius Byzantius, *Anaplus Bospori,* ed. Güngerich, 33, ll. 2–5.

9. Dionysius Byzantius, *Anaplus Bospori,* ed. Wescher, 5, line 17 and notes on bottom of page and notes pages 37 and 44; Dionysius Byzantius, *Anaplus Bospori,* ed. Güngerich, 4, ll. 19–20.

10. Dionysius Byzantius, *Anaplus Bospori,* ed. Güngerich, 4, ll. 19–20; 5, ll. 1–5; Hesychius quoted in Lilius Gregorius Gyraldus, *Historiae Deorum Gentilium* (Basel: Oporinus, 1548), Syntagma XII, p. 501.

11. Dionysius Byzantius, *Anaplus Bospori,* ed. Wescher, 6, ll. 1–9, and page 37 notes; Dionysius Byzantius, *Anaplus Bospori,* ed. Güngerich, 5, ll. 1–9.

12. Dionysius Byzantius, *Anaplus Bospori,* ed. Güngerich, 5, ll. 8–9.

13. See Teubner edition of Xenophon's *Hellenika*, Book I, 3, line 20.

14. Gilles says these lines are from the *Expeditio Cyri*, but in fact they appear to come from the *Anabasis: Xenophon, Anabasis,* trans. C.L. Brownson, 4 vols. LCL, VII.1.24.

15. Dionysius Byzantius, *Anaplus Bospori,* ed. Güngerich, 3, line 17f.

16. Cedrinus, *Historiarum compendium,* Bonn ed. I.442, line 10f.

17. Herodotus, *History,* trans. A.D. Godley, LCL, IV.87.

18. The Greek text in Gilles' 1561 edition is poorly imprinted and partly illegible.

19. I expect Gilles is refering to Artemis Throsia, who had a cult at Larissa in Greece. See *OCD,* 184; Plutarch, *Plutarchi libellus de fluviis,* ed. Rudolf Hercher (Leipzig: Weidmann, 1851), 21.4. Plutarch refers to Diana (Artemis) Orthosia in his *Lives,* Theseus 31.2–32.1.

112

20. *Notitia urbis CP*, 230.

21. Procopius, *Buildings*, I.11.3, Bonn ed. III, 207.

22. Procopius, *Buildings*, esp. I.11, Bonn ed. III, 205f. See also I.10, 201f.

23. Suda, *Lexikon*, Vol. I, 360.14.; Janin, *CPByz2*, 217; 311–12.

24. Majeska, *Russian Travelers*, 387f.

25. Socrates Scholasticus, *Ecclesiastica Historia*, Vols 1, 2 and 3, ed. Robert Hussey (Hildesheim-New York: Olms Verlag, 1992), Book I.16.103.

26. Indeed, Zonaras seems to call Hagia Sophia "The Great Church" consistently until XVI.10, *Epitomae historiarum*, Bonn ed. III, 434–35; Socrates, *Eccl. Hist.* II.16; Janin, *Églises*, 471f.

27. Gilles has ἀμφοῖς.

28. Gilles seems to have προχυήσι.

29. *Greek Anthology (Anthologia Graeca)*, trans. W.P. Paton, 5 vols. LCL, IX.808

30. *Greek Anthology*, IX.808. I have used Paton's translation here.

31. Sozomen, *Eccl. Hist.*, VIII.20–22, esp. 22 on the resulting fire.

32. Procopius' famous description of Hagia Sophia is in *Buildings*, I.1.20–78, Bonn ed. III, 170f.

33. *Notitia urbis CP*, 231

34. Zonaras, *Epitomae historiarum*, XIV.6, Bonn ed. III, 156–57; Janin, *Églises*, 471f.

35. Wooden beams are, in fact, present and visible in Hagia Sophia, particularly in the gallery level.

36. *Pila, -ae* (f) can be translated as both "pillar" and "pier."

37. Agathias, *Histories*, V.6–9; Averil Cameron, *Agathias* (Oxford: Clarendon Press, 1970), 80, 85 and Appendix C.

38. Agathias, *Histories*, V.9.

39. Zonaras, *Epitomae historiarum*, XIV.9, Bonn ed. III, 170–71

40. Cedrinus, *Historiarum compendium*, PG 121, col. 737; Mainstone, *Hagia Sophia*, 213; Theophanes says practically the same thing, as does Malalas, see Mango, "Byzantine Writers on the Fabric of Hagia Sophia," in *Hagia Sophia from Justinian to the Present*, ed. Cakmak and Mark (Cambridge: Cambridge University Press, 1992), 51–52.

41. Cedrinus, *Historiarum compendium*, Bonn ed. I. Bekker (1838), I:676–77; Mango, "Byzantine Writers," 52. Mango's translation: "He [Justinian] also made outside the church the four spiral ramps opposite the interior piers. These he planted in the ground and raised as far as the dome so as to buttress the arches. At the same time he made the altar table, an incomparable work...."

42. Cedrinus, *Historiarum compendium*, PG 121.737; Mainstone, *Hagia Sophia*, 217; 90–91. Note that Cedrinus' text reads (per Mainstone): "Seeing [the damage] the emperor [Justinian] erected new piers to support the dome, which was made more than 20 feet higher than the previous structure. Outside the church he also erected, from the ground up to the dome, four spiral stair towers opposite the interior piers to buttress the arches and vaults." Gilles, however, does not say which other authors he is quoting who claim that Justinian rebuilt the dome lower, not higher, as Cedrinus states. But it is interesting that Zonaras has it that the dome was rebuilt 25 feet higher. See Zonaras, *Epitoma historiarum*, ed. T. Buttner-Wobst, CSHB (Bonn: Weber, 1897), 3:170–71. Theophanes and Malalas both have it that the second dome was built higher than the first, with Theophanes, *The Chronicle of Theophanes*, 341, giving the figure of 25 feet and Malalas giving the figure at 20 feet and then later at 30 feet. See Mango, "Byzantine Writers," 52. The figure of 25 feet is the same, so maybe Gilles misread one of his "more obscure" sources. Gilles does not say which source claimed the second dome was 25 feet lower than the first.

43. Evagrius, *Ecclesiastical History*, IV.31 ed. Allen, 197–98; idem, ed. J. Bidez and L. Parmentier (London: Methuen, 1898), 180–81, English translation in Mango, *Art of the Byzantine Empire 312–1453. Sources and Documents* (Toronto: University of Toronto Press, 1986), 79–80.

44. This comes from the *Vita Basilii* (c.950), ed. I. Bekker, in *Theophanes Continuatus* (Bonn ed. 1838), 321; Mango, "Byzantine Writers," 53–54; Mainstone, *Hagia Sophia*, 98 on evidence that in about 869 Basil I undertook some reconstruction as referred to by inscription.

45. Evagrius, *Ecclesiastical History*, IV.31 ed. Allen, 197–98.

46. Gilles has already quoted from both Agathias and Evagrius, among others, above. He quotes extensively from Procopius, *Buildings*, 1.1.22–78 below. See Agathias, *Histories*, 5.9.1–3; and Mango, "Byzantine Writers."

47. Gilles is talking here of the north and south tympana.

48. Gilles is describing the pendentives.

49. Hagia Sophia has only two gallery levels, the ground floor and second floor, but on the second floor the galleries do run along three sides of the building: north, south, west. On the ground floor the western side of the church has no gallery but an inner and outer narthex.

50. Surely Gilles cannot be talking of human figures since Hagia Sophia at this time was being used as a mosque. Probably he refers to the Justinianic mosaics that are comprised of floral and geometrical motifs.

51. The "small walls" are clearly the balustrades running between the columns of the galleries.

52. Cedrinus, *Historiarum compendium*, PG, 121.737; Mainstone, *Hagia Sophia*, 217.

53. Procopius, *Buildings*, I.1, Bonn ed. III, 173–81; Janin, *Églises* (1963), 471f.

54. Gilles is aware that the buttressing on the eastern end of Hagia Sophia is later — much of it is Ottoman, as he seems to hint here (accurately).

55. He means buttresses.

56. Sozomen, *Eccl. Hist.*, IX.1.

57. The Latin in this last sentence is unclear to me.

58. Suda, *Lexikon*, IV, 400–401.

59. *PatriaCP*, II, 96; III, 201–2.

60. Ammianus Marcellinus, *Rerum gestarum libri qui supersunt*, ed. W. Seyfarth, 2 vols. (Leipzig: B.G. Teubner, 1978), XXII.8.8. See also Ammianus Marcellinus, ed. John C. Rolfe, vol. 2, LCL, 219. Rolfe's translation and Latin read, respectively: "...and the promontory Ceras, which bears a tower built high and giving light to ships...": "et promuntorium Ceras praelucentem navibus vehens constructam celsius turrim...." Nowhere does Marcellinus use the word *pharos*, but he clearly means a lighthouse.

61. Dionysius Byzantius, *Anaplus Bospori*, ed. Güngerich, 4, ll. 13–17.

62. Anna Comnena, *Alexiad*, trans. Elizabeth Dawes (London: Kegan Paul, 1928), 80.

63. Ibid., 422.

64. Cedrinus, *Historiarum compendium*, Bonn ed. I.442; 647–48; Janin, *CPByz2*, 222–24. Apparently it was Hesychius of Miletus who said the bath was located near the Temple of Zeus Hippios.

65. For sources see Janin, *CPByz2*, 222; see also Müller-Wiener, *Bildlexikon*, 18–19 and 22, 48, 51.

66. Procopius, *Buildings*, I.10, Bonn ed. III, 202.

67. Or rather the Baths of Zeus Hippios, see Zonaras, *Epitomae historiarum*, XIV.6, Bonn ed. III, 154–55.

68. Gilles has λοεθρόμ.

69. Gilles has θανάτου; *Anthol. Graec.* IX, n. 650. Leontios Scholastikos.

70. *Greek Anthology*, IX.650. I have used Paton's translation here.

71. Cedrinus, *Historiarum compendium*, Bonn ed. I, 647–48; Janin, *CPByz2*, 223.

72. Gilles means the Egyptian Christodorus, whose account of the collection of statues in the Zeuxippon is preserved in his poem that is in *Anthol. Palat.* Book II. See also Mango, "Antique Statuary and the Byzantine Beholder," *DOP* 17 (1963): 57ff., and S. Casson and D. Talbot-Rice, *Second Report upon*

the Excavations Carried out in and near the Hippodrome of Constantinople in 1928 on Behalf of the British Academy (London: Oxford University Press, 1929), 18ff.

73. *Anthol. Graec.* IX, n. 614. Leontios Scholastikos.

74. *Anthol Palat.* IX, n. 624, ed. Dübner, II, 125.

75. On the myriad epigrams having to do with the baths of Constantinople that Gilles is alluding to here, see *Anthol. Palat.*, IX, ed. Dübner, II, 126–27 and 132; Janin, *CPByz2*, 224.

76. Procopius, *Buildings*, I.2.15–17, Bonn ed. III, 183.

77. I think Gilles must mean Justinian I although his text actually reads "Julian."

78. Procopius, *Buildings*, I.2.15–17, Bonn ed. III, 183.

79. Gilles possibly obtained some information on the Hospital of Sampson from a version of the *Patria CP.* See ed. Preger, III, 235 and footnote for line 3, and 254.

80. Zonaras, *Epitomae historiarum*, XIV.6, Bonn ed. III, 153–54.

81. Janin, *CPByz2*, 35–36; Schneider, "Brände in Konstantinopel," *BZ*, 41 (1941): 382–403; Cedrinus mentions the Eubulus Hospital, Bonn ed. I, 647; the *Chronicon Paschale* mentions the location of this hospital after the 532 fire near Hagia Irene in Bonn ed. I, 622.

82. Procopius, *Buildings*, I.2.15–17, Bonn ed. III, 183. The probable remains of this hospital and its adjacent martyrium still stand between Hagia Sophia and Hagia Irene just inside the walls of Topkapı Palace. The identification of these remains may not be entirely secure.

83. Socrates, *Eccl. History*, VI.15–18; Sozomen, *Eccl. Hist.*, VIII.20–22.

84. Gilles means the Hippodrome.

85. Zonaras, *Annalium* XII.9, Bonn ed. II, 548–49 and *Epitomae historiarum*, XIII.3, Bonn ed. III, 15, 18–19.

86. Zosimus, *New History*, II.31 (p. 38). Ridley translates as: "He decorated the hippodrome most beautifully, incorporating the temple of the Dioscuri in it; their statues are still to be seen standing in the porticos of the hippodrome."

87. *Notitia urbis CP*, 233.

88. *Notitia urbis CP*, 241–42.

89. Or at least more than one. See Majeska, *Russian Travelers*, 252–53 and especially Mango, "Columns of Justinian and His Successors," *Studies on Constantinople* (Aldershot: Variorum 1993), Appendix, X:17f.

90. Gilles means the Hippodrome.

91. One senses that Gilles wrote his notes down at a later point in time; apparently he did not write down the measurements when he was on the

spot in this case, and now he is forced to estimate the measurements from memory.

92.   The Obelisk of Thutmose on the Theodosian base probably was not located on the end or turning point of the spina. Many believe it marked the center of the spina, but, as Mango points out, there is no way to be sure without further excavating the site of the Hippodrome in order to determine its true length. See Mango, "Columns of Justinian," Appendix X.

93.   Ammianus Marcellinus' description of the erection of an obelisk that Gilles quotes below is not about the obelisk in Constantinople, but the one set up in the Circus Maximus in 357 CE by Constantius II. This obelisk is now in the area of the Lateran in Rome. But Gilles is wise to quote its method of erection since the second obelisk obtained by Constantius II (or, originally, Constantine I) was destined for Constantinople. See Mango, "Columns of Justinian," 18.

94.   Ammianus Marcellinus, *Rerum gestarum libri*, ed. John C. Rolfe, LCL, XVII, 4, 15, 324–27. The Loeb translation runs:

> After this there remained only the raising, which it was thought could be accomplished only with great difficulty, perhaps not at all. But it was done in the following manner: to tall beams which were brought and raised on end (so that you could see a very grove of derricks) were fastened long and heavy ropes in the likeness of a manifold web hiding the sky with their excessive numbers. To these was attached that veritable mountain engraved over with written characters [i.e. the obelisk], and it was gradually drawn up on high through the empty air, and after hanging for a long time, while many thousand men turned wheels resembling millstones, it was finally placed in the middle of the circus.

95.   In this passage Gilles confusingly calls the obelisk he witnessed being lowered to the ground a "column." He could, in fact, be referring to one of the enormous porphyry columns reused and still to be seen in the Mosque of Suleyman, which was under construction at the time of his visit.

96.   I have rendered the Greek here as close as possible to how it appears on the inscription itself, still in situ, and not how it appears in Gilles' first edition. See also, Janin, *CPByz2*, 190.

97.   Gilles has the last line of this inscription wrong. On the monument it actually reads: IUDICES SUB PROCLOS [SUBLIMES — presumably the word here, but this portion of the inscription is now damaged] ELATUS AD AURAS. Janin, *CPByz2*, 190.

98.   It seems that Gilles has a pattern of describing things from bottom to top.

99. This inscription remains visible today on the monument. See also: Janin, *CPByz2*, 192–93.

100. Possibly this is a reference to Diagoras of Melos, the mythic poet who was reknowned for his atheisim. See *OCD*, 461. On the monuments of the Hippodrome see Sarah Guberti Bassett, "Antiquities in the Hippodrome of Constantinople," *DOP* 45 (1991): 90–91 and footnotes 35f.

101. Zosimus, *New History*, II.31(p. 38). Ridley translation: "He [Constantine] even placed somewhere in the hippodrome the tripod of Delphic Apollo, which had on it the very image of Apollo."

102. Sozomen, *Eccl. Hist.*, II.5, p. 67, col. 945.

103. Eusebius, *Vita Constantini*, 3.54, ed. Winkelmann (1975).

104. Herodotus, *History*, 9.81; Pausanias, *Description of Greece*, trans. W.H.S. Jones, vols. I–V, LCL X.13.9; Bassett, "Antiquities in the Hippodrome," 90.

105. Herodotus, *History*, 9.81; Pausanias, *Description of Greece*, X.13.9; Bassett, "Antiquities in the Hippodrome," 90.

106. *Parastaseis Syntomoi Chronikae* in *Scriptores Originum Constantinopolitarum*, ed. Theodor Preger (Leipzig: B.G. Teubner, 1901), 25; Janin, *CPByz2*, 414.

107. Janin, *Églises*, 458f.

108. Cassiodorus, *Variae*, ed. Theodore Mommsen, 3 vols. MGH (Berlin: Weidmann, 1894), III.li.1; this is an excellent example of Gilles going directly to the sources to provide information on the ancient charioteers from the *Greek Anthology* as well as Theodoric's letter. Gilles' rendition of this letter however involves some very strange Latin that is difficult to translate.

109. Procopius, *Persian Wars*, I.24.1–2, Bonn ed. I, 128 and 119. On Belisarius' triumph see *Vandal Wars*, II.8.9, Bonn ed. I, 445. The *Paschal Chron.* also mentions the Cochlia, *Chron. Paasch*, Bonn ed I, 569; Janin, *CPByz2*, 183f.

110. On these churches in Procopius, see *Buildings*, I.4.3–8, Bonn ed. III, 186f.; Janin, *Ésglises*, 466–70.

111. This Latin is difficult to make out.

112. Ammianus Marcellinus, *Rerum gestarum libri*, XVI.10.15–16, pp. 250–51.

113. Cedrinus, *Historiarum compendium*, Bonn ed. I, 642–43; Alexander Van Millingen, *Byzantine Churches in Constantinople* (London: Macmillan, 1912), 62f; Janin, *Églises*, 466–70; J. Ebersolt and A. Theirs, *Les Églises de Constantinople* (Paris: E. Leroux, 1913), 23f.

114. Gilles is wrong, of course, in reading the vine and grape motifs in the sculptural decoration as indication of the church's dedication to the pagan Bacchus. The church was, in fact, dedicated to two military saints, Sergius and Bacchus,

martyred in the persecutions of the Early Christian period. Majeska, *Russian Travelers,* 265.

115. Fire of September 2–6, 465. Evagrius, *Ecclesiastical History,* II.13, ed. Allen, 111.

116. On John Calybites, see Janin, *Églises,* 270–71; Majeska, *Russian Travelers,* 154, footnotes.

117. Zonaras, *Epitomae historiarum,* XIV.1, Bonn ed. III, 124.

118. Evagrius, II.13, per Allen, 111.

119. Cedrinus, *Historiarum compendium,* Bonn ed. I, 609–11; Zonaras, *Epitomae historiarum,* XIV.1, Bonn ed. III, 124.

120. Cedrinus, *Historiarum compendium,* Bonn ed. I, 685–88; Janin, *CPByz2,* 231f and 134 and 427.

121. *Anthol. Graeca.* XVI, n. 64. Anonymous.

122. Procopius, *Buildings,* I.4.28; Bonn ed. III, 190.

123. Suda, *Lexikon,* II, 187; Janin, *CPByz2,* 231; Zonaras, *Epitomae historiarum,* XIV.10, Bonn ed. III, 174–75.

124. Zonaras, *Epitomae historiarum,* XIV.10, Bonn ed. III, 174–75.

125. *Anthol. Graeca.* IX, n. 657. Marianos Scholastikos. These verses were wrongly attributed to Agathias by Zonaras. See Averil Cameron, *Agathias,* 13; and idem., "Notes on the Sophiae, the Sophianae and the Harbor of Sophia," *Byzantion* 37 (1967): 15–16.

126. Zonaras, *Epitomae historiarum,* XIV.10, Bonn ed. III, 175.

127. Gilles is refering to Constantine V Copronymous "Name of Dung" and not Leo. Cedrinus, *Historiarum compendium,* Bonn ed. II, 11–12. This reference to the frozen Bosporus in 764 under Constantine V Copronymus is also in Theophanes, *The Chronicle of Theophanes,* 670–71. For Cedrinus on St. Mamas, see Bonn ed. I, 707 and Bonn ed. II, 25. For Agathias on the Palace of Sophia, see Cameron, *Agathias,* 13. The epigrams by Marianos Scholastikos were wrongly attributed to Agathias by Zonaras. See also Cameron, "Notes on the Sophiae," 15–16; Van Millingen, *Walls,* 181.

128. *Notitia urbis CP,* 232.

129. Cedrinus, *Historiarum compendium,* Bonn ed. I, 563–64 and 679; Janin, *CPByz2,* 76; *PatriaCP,* I, 166 (pseudo–Codinus).

130. The text of Gilles' first edition reads *pyctacia* twice with no difference in spelling.

131. Janin, *CPByz2,* 413 on Pittakia.

132. *Patria CP,* II, 168 states that Eudoxia's statue was erected in the Tribunal; this comes just after the section in *PatriaCP* on the Pittakia.

133. *Patria CP,* III.9, 216–17.

134. *Paras. Synt. Chron.*, ed. Preger, 37

135. *Patria CP*, III, 272–73

136. *Notitia urbis CP*, 232.

137. Cedrinus, *Historiarum compendium*, Bonn ed. II, 238, 540; Janin, *Églises*, 424–26.

138. Cedrinus, *Historiarum compendium*, Bonn ed. II, 238, 540; Janin, *Églises*, 424–26; On the church of the Mother of God of the Sigma, see Magdalino, *Constantinople Médievale*, 26 and note 55 on that page; *PatriaCP*, III, 182, *Scriptores*, 172–73.

139. *PatriaCP*, II, 182.

140. *PatriaCP*, III, 280–81.

141. Does Gilles mean "Zeugma?," see Majeska, *Russian Travelers*, 351–52 on the church of St. Stephen at Zeugma (there were also churches to St. Stephen the Protomartyr in the palace, Mangana and Constantinianae). See Majeska, *Russian Travelers*, 302f.

142. *Notitia urbis CP*, 232–33.

143. I am not sure of Gilles' meaning here.

144. Procopius on the Augusteon. See *Buildings*, I.10, Bonn ed. III, 202; and I.2.1–12.

145. Zonaras says Justinian's statue was in the vestibule, προαυλιω, of Hagia Sophia: Zonaras, *Epitomae historiarum*, XIV.6, Bonn ed. III, 157.

146. Suda, *Lexikon*, II, 644.

147. Procopius, *Buildings*, I.2.1–12.

148. Ioannes Tzetzes, *Historiae*, VIII.295–305 (Naples: Libreria scientifica editrice, 1968), 310. Also see *Historiarum variarum chiliades*, ed. T. Kiessling (Leipzig: F.C.G. Vogel, 1826), 293; Mango, "Justinian's Equestrian Statue," published as Letter to the Editor, *AB* 61 (1959): 4–5, who translates what Tzetzes does say as this: "The tiara was a Persian headdress. Later, our emperors, in their victories, placed on their heads the tiara or toupha, such as the one worn by Justinian's equestrian statue, on top of the column."

149. Cedrinus, *Historiarum compendium*, Bonn ed. I, 556

150. Zonaras, *Epitomae historiarum*, XIV.6, Bonn ed. III, 157; also Zonaras, ed. Teubner, III, 274; Janin, *CPByz2*, 74–75.

151. Suda, *Lexikon* I, 410–11.

152. Zosimus, *New History*, II.30 (p. 37), Ridley translation: "Constantine built a circular forum where the gate used to be and surrounded it with double-roofed porticos. He set up two huge arches of Proconnesian marble opposite each other, through which one could enter the portico of Severus or go out of the old city."

153. *Patria CP,* ed. Preger, II, 174 and III, 218.

154. There are punctuation problems with this and the prior sentence. It is unclear if the former sentence ends after *"est"* or after *"ornans"* but the meaning is clear: that the statue of Fortuna is looking upon and honoring the city of Constantinople.

155. Zosimus, *New History,* II.31 (p. 38); Ridley translates:

> There was in Byzantium a huge forum consisting of four porticos [the Tetrastoon, in other words], and at the end of one of them, which has numerous steps leading up to it, he built two temples. Statues were set up in them, in one Rhea, mother of the gods [Zosimus' aside: The statue which the Argonauts had set up on mount Didymus overlooking the city of Cyzicus, but they say he damaged it through his disregard for religion, by taking away the lions on each side and changing the arrangement of the hands; for whereas previously she was apparently restraining lions, now she seemed to be praying and looking to the city as if guarding it], and in the other, the statue of Fortuna Romae.

156. Suda, *Lexikon,* III, 395.

157. See Procopius, *Buildings,* I.10.6–9.

158. Sozomen, *Eccl. Hist.,* VIII.20 and 22

159. Socrates, *Eccl. Hist.,* VI.18.711, ed. Hussey. On the Basilica of the Senate in the Suda, see Suda, *Lexikon* I, 459 and footnote below; Janin, *CPByz2,* 155f.

160. Suda, *Lexikon* III, 220.

161. *Notitia urbis CP,* 233.

162. Sozomen, *Eccl. Hist.,* VIII.22

163. The road he means is the Mese.

164. Procopius on the Chalke, see Procopius, *Buildings,* I.10.12–20. See too Mango, *Brazen House,* 32f.

165. Statius P. Papinius (Publius Papinius), *Silvae,* trans. J.H. Mozley, 2 vols. LCL, I.i.30–36; Procopius, *Buildings,* I.10, Bonn ed. III, 202.

166. Cedrinus, *Historiarum compendium,* I, 656–57, and 563; Mango, *Brazen House,* 21–26.

167. Procopius, *Buildings,* I.10, Bonn ed. III, 202 which includes mention of the residence of Martis; see also Procopius, *Persian Wars,* I.24.9, Bonn ed. I, 127.

168. Procopius, *Persian Wars,* I.24.44–50, Bonn ed. I, 126–27.

169. *Notitia urbis CP,* 232.

170. Müller-Wiener, *Bildlexikon,* 229–37; Julius Pollux, *Pollucis Onomasticon,* ed. Eric Bethe, 3 vols. (Leipzig: B.G. Teubner, 1900–1937); Vitruvius, *Ten Books on Architecture,* 5.1.3–4.

171. *Anthol. Palat.* IX.656. See also Cedrinus, *Historiarum compendium*, Bonn ed. I, 563; and Mango, *Brazen House*, 26.

172. Translation of Greek here from Mango, *Brazen House*, 26. And he rightly points out that the text is not clear as to whether Anastasius built the Chalke anew or restored it, see *Brazen House*, 27.

173. Procopius, *Vandal Wars*, II.8.9, III.5.1–9, III.9.5, Bonn ed, I, 332, 445.

174. Gilles is referring, of course, to the famous CHI-RHO symbol that Constantine reportedly saw in the sky on the eve of the Battle of the Milvian Bridge and in which sign he did conquer. See Eusebius.

175. The concave molding on the base of the lowest drum.

176. He means the intercolumniation.

177. Mango, *Brazen House*, 87–92, on the raised portico leading from the Chalke to the Holy Well in Hagia Sophia.

178. Zosimus, *New History,* II.31 (p. 38); Ridley translates: "When he [Constantine] had thus enlarged the original city, he built a palace scarcely inferior to the one in Rome."

179. Eusebius, *Vita Constantini*, 3.48 and 3.49, ed. Winkelmann (1975).

180. St. Jerome, *Dedicatur Constantinopolis omnium paene urbium nuditate* in *Chronicon*, ed. Fotheringham (London: H. Milford, 1923), 314. On the multitude of antique statuary in the Byzantine capital see also C. Mango, "Antique Statuary and the Byzantine Beholder," 53–76.

181. Eusebius, *Vita Constantini*, 3.54.2, ed. Winkelmann (1975).

182. Sozomen, *Eccl. Hist.*, II.5

183. Jordanes, *The Gothic History,* intro. & commentary by Charles C. Mierow (New York: Barnes & Noble, 1960), 56.289.

184. Tzetzes, *Historiae*, VIII.330–33, ed. Leone, 312.

185. Suda, *Lexikon*, IV, 183; *Parastaseis*, ed. Preger, 70; *Patria CP,* ed. Preger, II, 165; Mango, *Brazen House*, 99–100; Janin, *CPByz2,* 111

186. Gilles conceivably could mean Papias, one of the authors mentioned in the *Parastaseis*, but he is being extremely vague. See *Parastaseis*, ed. Preger, 38, 51–52, 70. With modern translation see now *Constantinople in the Early Eighth Century: The Parastaseis Syntomoi Chronikai*, trans. Averil Cameron and Judith Herrin (Leiden: E.J. Brill, 1984), 95, 121–23, 158; *Patria CP,* ed. Preger, II, 164–66, 196–97; III, 218–19. See Janin, *CPByz2,* 112 for more sources.

187. *Patria CP,* ed. Preger, II, 218 and Mango, *Brazen House*, 34 on Heraclius turning the Chalke into a prison.

188. *Anthol. Palat.*, IX.696, ed. Dübner, II, 142; Janin, *CPByz2,* 158.

189. *Anthol. Palat.*, IX.697; ed. Dübner, II, 142; Janin, *CPByz2,* 158.

190. *Anthol. Graec.* XVI, n. 66. Anonymous.

191. *Anthol. Graec.* XVI, n. 67. Anonymous.

192. Mango, "Antique Statuary," 60. *PatriaCP,* I, 20f. Apparently when this statue was taken down the ground on that spot shook until St. Sabas managed to still the earthquake.

193. Dionysius Byzantius, *Anaplus Bospori,* ed. Wescher, 24, line 19 notes; Dionysius Byzantius, *Anaplus Bospori,* ed Güngerich, 12, ll. 3–14. Gilles, *Bosporo Thracio,* II.viii. Pliny, *Natural History,* 36.4.11.

194. Suda, *Lexikon,* I, 459; *Patria CP,* ed. Preger, II, 171–72.

195. Suda, *Lexikon,* I, 459–60; On this statue of Hercules, see Sarah Guberti Basset, "Antiquites of Hippodrome of Constantinople," *DOP* 45 (1991): 90.

196. Suda, *Lexikon,* IV, 740.

197. Suda, *Lexikon,* II, 476 on Eutropius.

198. *Anthol. Palat.,* IX.779; Janin, *CPByz2,* 159; see also Cedrinus, *Historiarum compendium,* Bonn ed. I, 616; *Patria CP,* ed. Preger, 179 and 218; and Janin, *CPByz2,* 157f.

199. Zonaras, *Epitomae historiarum,* XIV.2, Bonn ed. III, 128–33; Janin, *CP-Byz2,* 161

200. Zonaras, *Epitomae historiarum,* XIV.2, Bonn ed. III, 128–33; esp. 131 where it is Zonaras who also quotes Malchus.

201. Cedrinus, *Historiarum compendium,* Bonn ed. I, 616.

202. Cedrinus, *Historiarum compendium,* Bonn ed. II, 25; see Janin, *CPByz2,* 163.

203. *Anthol. Palat.,* IX.660, ed. Dübner. II, 135; Janin, *CPByz2,* 164.

204. *Patria CP,* ed. Preger, III, 226.

205. Cedrinus, *Historiarum compendium,* Bonn ed. I, 647.

206. Cedrinus, *Historiarum compendium,* Bonn ed. I, 647; Janin, *CPByz2,* 161.

207. Procopius, *Buildings,* I.11, Bonn ed. III, 206.

208. Zonaras, *Epitomae historiarum,* XIV.2, Bonn ed. III, 128–33.

209. Cedrinus, *Historiarum compendium,* Bonn ed. I, 616.

210. Procopius, *Buildings,* I.11.13–14, Bonn ed. III, 206f.

211. Müller-Wiener, *Bildlexikon,* 283–85; Janin, *CPByz2,* 206–7; *OBD,* 1338; Marlia Mango, "The Porticoed Street at Constantinople," in Necipoğlu BC, 29–51.

212. Agathias, *Histories,* II.29; Cameron, *Agathias,* 104f.

213. Cedrinus, *Historiarum compendium,* Bonn ed. I, 616; Janin, *CPByz2,* 328; Jonathan Bardill, "The Palace of Lausus and Nearby Monuments in Constantinople: A Topographical Study," *American Journal of Archaeology* 101

(1997): 74 says: "The church of the Theotokos in the Chalkoprateia (Copper Market)... is possibly to be ascribed to Verina (ca. 457–484) rather than to Pulcheria (ca. 414–453)...".

214. *Patria CP*, III.32, ed. Preger, 226–27.

215. Zonaras, *Epitomae historiarum*, XIII.18, Bonn ed., 87–89.

216. *Patria CP*, ed. Preger, I, 141.

217. Is Gilles refering to Cedrinus here? See Cedrinus, *Historiarum compendium*, Bonn ed. I, 616.

218. Strabo, *Geography*, XVII.1.8.

219. Procopius, *Buildings*, I.1.20–22, Bonn ed. III, 173 on Nike fire; *Persian Wars*, I.24.9–12.

220. Cedrinus, *Historiarum compendium*, Bonn ed. I, 647.

221. Cedrinus, *Historiarum compendium*, Bonn ed. I, 647 and 616.

222. This is a rare example of Gilles' consulting the thirtheenth-century historian Niketas Choniates, *Nicetae Choniatae historia*, CSHB (Bonn), 555 and, in a modern translation, *O City of Byzantium: Annals of Niketas Choniates*, trans. Harry J. Magoulias (Detroit: Wayne State University Press, 1984), 303–4.

223. *Patria CP*, I, ed. Preger, 148–49.

224. *Notitia urbis CP*, 232–33.

225. *Notitia urbis CP*, 234–38 and 232–33; *Anthol. Palat.* XVI.65; ed. Dübner, II, 539.

226. *Notitia urbis CP*, 232; Procopius, *Buildings*, I.1, Bonn ed. III, 173; Zonaras, *Epitomae historiarum*, XIV.6, Bonn ed. III, 153–54.

227. This account appears in the *History of Niketas Choniates* and records the conflict of May 2, 1182, which Mango translates and discusses at length in his *Brazen House*, 94–96f. See *Nicetae Choniatae historia*, CSHB (Bonn), 306–9.

228. Suda, *Lexikon*, I, 459.

229. Suda, *Lexikon*, III, 395.

230. *Anthol. Palat.*, XVI.65, ed. Dübner, II, 539; Janin, *CPByz2*, 64–68.

231. Suda, *Lexikon*, III, 395.

232. Cedrinus, *Historiarum compendium*, Bonn ed. I, 564, 650; Janin, *CPByz2*, 392.

233. All of this on the Milion comes from the Suda, *Lexikon*, III, 395.

234. On the blasphemy of Eunomius and Arius see, Suda, *Lexikon*, II, 459 and III, 246, but it is not clear that Gilles has taken this information on their statues from this source. I was unable to find such a reference in the Suda. I

suspect Gilles used the *Patria Constantinopoleos*. See *Patria CP*, II.43, ed. Preger, 173. See also: *Parast. Synt. Chron.*, 39, ed. Preger, 43–44 and Theophanes, *The Chronicle of Theophanes*, 105.

235. Zosimus, *New History*, II.31, 38.

236. Socrates, *Eccl. Hist.*, III.11–12, 416–22, ed. Hussey.

237. Zonaras, *Epitomae historiarum*, XIV.4, Bonn ed., III, 141–42.

238. Eunapius, *Lives of the Philosophers*, LCL, "Sopater," 382–85.

239. This can only be the church of St. Menas near the Acropolis mentioned in the *Patria CP*, III.2, ed. Preger, 214–15, and in the *Parastaseis Syntomoi Chronikai*, 24, ed. Preger, 34. See also Janin, *Églises*, 345ff; Delehaye, "L'Invention des réliques de S. Menas à Constantinople," *AB* 29 (1910): 1–34.

240. *Patria CP*, I, ed. Preger, 140–41.

241. Dionysius Byzantius, *Anaplus Bospori*, ed Güngerich, 4 ll. 19–20; 5 ll. 1–9; Gilles, *Bosporo Thracio* (1561), II.ii and I.ii.

242. Gilles, *Bosporo Thracio* (1561), II.ii and I.ii; see also III.v on other temples.

243. *Notitia urbis CP*, 233; Van Millingen, citing Codinus and Cantacuzenos, says this pier, "so named after Timasius, a celebrated general in the reign of Arcadius, was in the Fourth Region, and must therefore have been a pier near the Gate of Eugenius," Van Millingen, *Walls*, 228.

244. Procopius, *Buildings*, I.11.27, Bonn ed. III, 208.

245. Lausus, says Mango, was "*praepositus sacri cubiculi* in the reign of Theodosius II (406–450)," not Arcadius. Mango, "Antique Statuary," 58.

246. *Patria CP*, ed. Preger, II, 170.

247. Cedrinus, *Historiarum compendium*, Bonn ed. I, 564; Zonaras, *Epitomae historiarum*, XIV.1, Bonn ed., 124–25. This fire occurred in 475 per Mango, "Antique Statuary," 58. On the Lausus statues, see also Mango, "The Literary Evidence," in C. Mango, M. Vickers and E.D. Francis, "The Palace of Lausus at Constantinople and Its Collection of Ancient Statues," *Journal of the History of Collections* 4 (1992): 91; *Patria CP* II.26; and Jonathan Bardill, "The Palace of Lausus and Nearby Monuments in Constantinople."

248. Evagrius, *Ecclesiastical History*, II.13, ed. Allen, 111.

249. Zosimus also mentions this statue as well as those of the Muses in the Senate that were destroyed in the fire of 404. See Zosimus, *New History*, V.24, 246f.

250. Cedrinus, *Historiarum compendium*, Bonn ed. I, 610, 616; Janin, *CPByz2*, 379.

251. The reference is to Pliny, *Natural History*, 37.19.2.

252. Idem, 36.4.9.

253. Cedrinus, *Historiarum compendium*, Bonn ed. I, 10, 616.

254. Cosmas Indicopleustes, XI.3, ed. Wanda Wolska-Conus, *Topographie Chrétienne* I–III (Paris: Éditions du Cerf, 1973), III:318–19.

255. *Patria CP*, II.36, ed. Preger, 170.

256. Cedrinus, *Historiarum compendium*, ed. Bekker, I, 564; and see translation in Mango, Vickers and Francis, "The Palace of Lausus," 91; Bardill, "Palace of Lausus," 67f.

257. This reference appears to come from Cedrinus, *Historiarum compendium*, ed. Bekker, II, 241.

258. Gilles identifies what is known today as the Binbirdirek cistern as that of Philoxenos, as many scholars have done since. Jonathan Bardill, however, questions this identification. See Bardill, "The Palace of Lausus," 69f.

259. Gilles is in error here in attributing the Triclinium called "Justinianos" to Justinian III; it should read "Justinian II" here. Furthermore, I do not believe his source here is Zonaras, but is actually the *Patria CP*, III.257, ed. Preger.

260. Cedrinus, *Historiarum compendium*, Bonn ed. I, 690, line 6f.

261. The Σχυλα was the passage connecting the Hippodrome to the Great Palace. See Cedrinus, *Historiarum compendium*, Bonn ed. II, 171; *De ceremoniis aulae byzantinae*, ed. J. Reiske (Bonn: Weber, 1829–40), 190; Janin, *CPByz2*, 108, 116 and 119.

262. *PatriaCP*, III.126, ed. Preger, 256; Janin, *CPByz2*, 108, 116–19.

❧ ❧

❧

34. *Constantinople. From Hartmann* Schedel, Nuremberg Chronicle. *Nuremberg: Anton Koberger, 1493.*

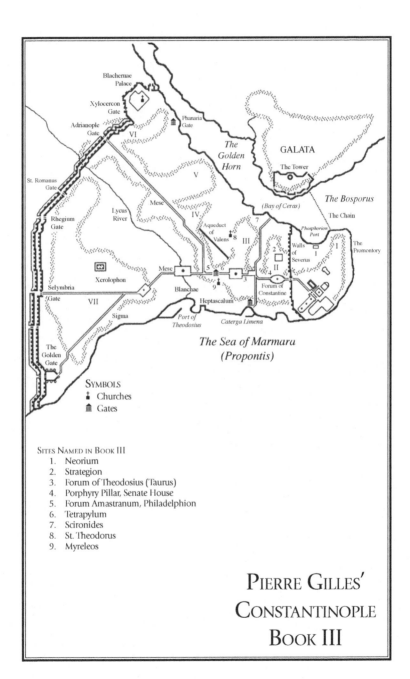

Blachernae
Palace

Xylocercon
Gate

Adrianople
Gate

VI

Phanaria
Gate

*The
Golden
Horn*

GALATA

The Tower

St. Romanus
Gate

V

(Bay of Ceras)

The Bosporus

Rhegium
Gate

Lycus
River

Mese

IV

The Chain

7

Aqueduct
of
Valens

8

III

*Phosphorion
Port*

I

*The
Promontory*

Selymbria
Gate

Xerolophon

VII

Mese

Blanchae

5

6

9

3

2

1

Walls
of
Severus

II

Forum of
Constantine

4

Heptascalum

Sigma

*Port of
Theodosius*

Caterga Limena

*The Sea of Marmara
(Propontis)*

The
Golden
Gate

SYMBOLS

‡ Churches
🏛 Gates

SITES NAMED IN BOOK III

1. Neorium
2. Strategion
3. Forum of Theodosius (Taurus)
4. Porphyry Pillar, Senate House
5. Forum Amastranum, Philadelphion
6. Tetrapylum
7. Scironides
8. St. Theodorus
9. Myreleos

PIERRE GILLES'
CONSTANTINOPLE
BOOK III

BOOK III

I. THE FEATURES OF THE FIFTH WARD AND THE SECOND HILL; THE NAVALIUM/
NEORIUM; THE PORT CALLED THE BOSPORUS, THE STRATEGIUM, AND THE FORUM
OF THEODOSIUS

I did not gather from the *Ancient Description of the Wards of the City* that
the Fifth Ward was on the north face of the second hill and the plain
at its base and that it ran downhill from the ridge of the promontory
to the Golden Horn alongside the Fourth Ward. It does mention,
however, that not a small portion of it rested on slopes and had
stretched out into a plain in places. For this description blends together
other wards of the city. Neither could I learn from the buildings of this
ward, which are said to have been contained in this ward, of which
no vestige remains, nor from the memory of men. But a light dawned
on me from the Phosphorio, or the Port of the Bosporio as it is called,
and from the docks of Chalcedon, which I began to understand do not
have that name because they sit in that part of city that faces Chalcedon
and the east. Indeed, they do not face there, but rather northward.
Likewise the Bosphorian Port is not named after the Bosporus, but
from the usual distortion of the Byzantines who mispronounce it as
the Bosporium when they should call it the Phosphorium, according
to the testimonies of Stephanus and Eustathius, who mention the
Phosphorium being the Port of Byzantium, which got its name the
following way.

When Philip of Macedon was besieging Byzantium and while his
soldiers were tunneling underground to get into the city, Hecate, called
Phosphora,[1] brought light to the citizens and revealed the trap.[2] And
so, freed of the siege in this manner, they called it the Phosphorium.
But although they shed some light as to why the same port is called
by two names — Bosporium and Phosphorium — they say nothing
of its situation, whether it was located in the southern, northern or
eastern part of the city. But from the Pier of Chalcedon, which the
Ancient Description puts in the region of the Bosporium Port, we are

able to estimate that it was a port in the north of the city, not the east, even though it sits across from Chalcedon.[3] For the rapid current of the Bosporus straight makes sailing from Chalcedon to those parts of Constantinople in the east and south difficult, but quite easy to northern parts, as those clearly understand who know the rapidity of the Bosporus and see that those navigating between Chalcedon and Byzantium sail their ships to the north part of the city or depart from there. Furthermore, the *Ancient Description of the Wards* says nothing about a pier across from Chalcedon. If it did put one there it would have put it in the First Ward or the Second to the east across from Chalcedon, or in the Third Ward lying to the south, in which the Neorium was, as I stated above.

But what is the use of dwelling on this subject further, seeing as I can offer the names and brief testimonies of important writers who will clearly illustrate that the Bosporium Port and the Pier of Chalcedon stood in the north part of the city. First I cite Dionysius Byzantius, who places the Temple of Tellus just outside the walls of Byzantium just above the bay of the Bosporus, and who places the temples of Ceres and Proserpina a little above this temple.[4] He does not name the Phosphoron but gives κόρην,[5] that is, virgin, as Proserpina is sometimes called. That we are able to deduce from the location of the site that he meant Hecate, whose tripod Cedrinus places in the Strategium[6] where the Temple of Proserpina had also been, it seems from Dionysius Byzantius' description, not far from the Strategium. But Evagrius writes more clearly when he says that there was a fire during the reign of Leo in the northern part of the city where the Neorium stood. This fire progressed from the Port of the Bosporus to the ancient Temple of Apollo in the south part, and from the Port of Julian to the Temple Omonoae, that is, of Concord, and in the center part from the Forum of Constantine to the Taurus.[7] Zonaras says that this fire progressed from the north sea to the south sea of the city, which ran along from the Bosporus to the church of John Calybites, and in the south from the church of St. Thomas the Apostle to the church of Sts. Sergius and Bacchus, and in the center of the city from the Lausus to the Taurus.[8] George Cedrinus says that this fire started at the Neorium, that is at the dockyard, and proceeded to the same church of John Calybites.[9]

From these sources I deduce that the Neorium and the Bosporium Port were in the same vicinity, even though the description in the *Ancient Description of the Wards* puts the Bosporium Port in the Fifth Ward and the Neorium in the Sixth Ward.[10] For since these wards joined and ran together from the ridge of the hill to the sea, there is no reason why the Bosporus Port could not have been near the Neorium. For in describing ancient Byzantium the ancient historian Zosimus gives the very spot of the Neorium in Byzantium, when he says that it was situated on a hill, occupying part of the isthmus that the Propontis and bay called Ceras bordered. And he adds that the wall of Byzantium progressed over a hill from the western part of the city to the Temple of Venus and the sea across from Chrysopolis, and on the north part of the city it descended equally to the port that is called the Neorium,[11] because it is near the gate that the Greeks call the Oreiam, mistakenly meaning "of Neorius" or something like that, I suppose. Today, between the sea and the Porta Oria, is a place that the Turks call Siphont because the Jews dwell there. It is a large, open seaside forum that appears to be adjacent to the Pier of Chalcedon, or the Scutarica, from whence daily are crossings to Scutarieum, or Scutaricum, formerly called Chrysopolis, a shopping district and port of Chalcedon.[12]

Near the Pier of Chalcedon are ferries to Galata, formerly called the Sycenus, which the *Ancient Description of the Wards* locates near the Neorium and Bosporion, the site of which has scarcely altered due to the granaries once there that have now been moved to another place, or due to the expansion of the enclosure of the Sultan's Palace, or because first the Neorium was constructed but afterwards was filled up with earth.[13] For it is very likely that during the period when Philip of Macedon made the underground passage there was no port in existence, which the Byzantines would later call the Phosphorion, because the streaming of water would have made it impossible. But then the port called the Phosphorion was built in another location. So it is said of the Neorium, which they claim was enclosed by Constantine, in which there was a market related to sea-trade. Later in the reign of Justin it was transferred to the Port of Julian. Some writers state that Emperor Leontius [Leo], who ruled after Justin, dredged the Neorium Port. Others add that an enormous bronze cow had been set up in the lagoon of the Neorium. It is said to have resembled a bronze bull in the Eleventh Ward, which some modern writers say cried out once a year, and then bad things happened to the city.[14] I think this story was pilfered from Callimachus and Pindar, who have written that on the mountain called Artabyris in Rhodes there existed bronze oxen that used to cry out whenever calamities were impending for Rhodes.[15]

It is thus clear from this evidence that a Neorium had been built, which now no longer exists. Therefore, given an understanding of the Bosporian Port and the Pier of Chalcedon, we know that the Fifth Ward was on the side of the second hill and on the plain below it; here too were the Baths of Honorius, the Prytaneum, the Baths of Eudoxia, the Granaries of Valentinian and of Constantius, the Theban Obelisk, the Bosporian Harbor, the Pier of Chalcedon, the Theodosian Cistern and the Strategium, in which was the Forum of Theodosius. Those describing the circuit of ancient Byzantium say its walls began at the Acropolis, continued on to the Tower of Eugenius, and then ascended to the Strategium and Baths of Achilles, which Justinian mentions in his *Constitutions* concerning aqueducts, when he says:

> The lead water-pipes bringing water to the Baths which are called Achilles, which we know to have been made by the magnificence of your foresight, are in the same condition as those set up by Theodosius and Valentinian; likewise the pipes called to mind are only for the baths and Nymphaeae that your eminence considers worthy. We wish to serve, with permission of your sublimeness being granted, with your agents, and go around without fear to houses and suburban baths to investigate whether there is any deception or hiding of water against the public interest.[16]

I already cited from the *History* of Socrates the law in which Constantine the Great ordered that Constantinople be called the New Rome. This law was inscribed on a public column in the Strategium near his own equestrian statue.[17] From the *Ancient Description of the Wards* I discovered that the city had three forums named after Theodosius: in the Fifth Ward one named the Theodosiacum, which I mentioned, another had been in the Strategium in the Seventh Ward, called the Theodosium, and a third in the Twelfth, which was called the Theodosiacum.[18] The latter two were marketplaces, and the first was the Forum Praetorium, as we can conjecture from the same description of these wards, which says that it was in the Strategium, which the Latins called the Praetorium and which later was called

Praetorium even by the Greeks to distinguish it from the other of the same name. It seems likely to me, but I am not quite certain, that this Theodosiacum Forum was that great Praetorium that was made more beautiful by Emperor Justin and by the work of Domninus. It is evident from the verses of Paul Silentiarius, which I quote below so that it might be clearer, that the term *praetorium* was common usage for the Greeks, as were many other Latin words:

'Εν τῷ μεγάλῳ Πραιτωρίῳ καλλοωπισθέντι
Κώσμον Ἰουστῖνος Βασιλεὼς ῥυπυωντα καθήρας
καὶ τὰ μέγιστα Δίκης ἠγλάϊσεν τεμένη
σοῖς δὲ πόνοις Δομνῖνε κατηρφέα νύκτα διώκεις
ἐκ Θέμιδος μεγάρων ἐκ βιοτῆς μερόπων.[19]

O the Great Praetorion, made beautiful:
Emperor Justin, who cleansed the impure world,
Embellished the great precincts of Justice.
And you, Domninus, through your efforts,
You chased dark night from the shrine of Themis
And from the life of men.

II. The Sixth Ward and the Ancient Buildings on the Second Hill

I would not have learned that the Sixth Ward was in the north part of the city, rather than in the south, either from the Column of Constantine

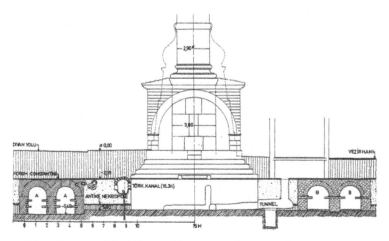

35. *Plan of the base of the Column of Constantine. Ernest Mamboury.*

that still exists to this day or from the Forum of Constantine, or from the *Ancient Description,* although it tells of the Porphyry Column of Constantine. And although it briefly describes the Sixth Ward as ending in a short plain with the remainder on an incline, it added that it went as far as the pier from the Forum of Constantine and that the pier stretched to the crossing to Sycae.[20] The Sycae crossing was so called from the place once named Syca, but now it is called Galata or Pera, as I will describe further regarding the Thirteenth Ward. The Sixth Ward joined up with the Fifth Ward as I indicated a little earlier about the area of the Neorium, the Pier of Chalcedon, the crossing and the Bosporian Port. After I had identified Syca, I understood that the Neorium was near the sea plain at the base of the second hill, and that the Sycae crossing was situated where the Galata ferry is today, and that the Porphyry Column now extant is the same that the *Ancient Description* mentions in the Sixth Ward. But how close the Senate was to the column and the Forum of Constantine I was not able to determine from the *Ancient Description,* although it does put the Senate in the Sixth Ward.[21] In fact, a little later I will clarify from other writers that the Senate was in the north part of the Forum of Constantine. Furthermore, this ward was, in part, on the back of the second hill, where the Porphyry Column is seen today, as were the poultry market, which the Turks call *Tavuk Pazar,* and the cloth-dyers shops, and the Palace of Aenobarbus, admiral of the Turkish fleet, and the Mosque of Ali Pasha. Part of the Sixth Ward is in the second valley on its right side and part on a coastal plain spreading below this valley and at the foot of the second hill, which is primarily inhabited by Jews.

III. The Porphyry Column, the Forum of Constantine, and the Palladium

Those who have written about the deeds of Constantine the Great say that he transported from Rome the "well-turned" Porphyry Column, that is, polished and encircled with laurel rings, which the *Description of the Wards of the City* calls the purple one from Rome. The story goes that it was set up in the forum called the Placoton because it was paved with large, smooth stones that the Greeks call *placae.*[22] They also say that a marvelous bronze statue, remarkable both for its artistry and magnitude, was erected on top of this column. It was made by the ancient art with the highest skill so that it appeared to breathe. The historians of Constantine say that it was formerly the statue of Apollo of Troy but that the emperor dedicated it in his own name and ordered that some of the nails, which were used to pin Christ to the redeeming cross, be attached to the head of the statue. And upon the statue the following inscription was carved:

Σύ, Χριστέ, κόσμου κοίρανος καὶ δεσπότης,
Σοὶ νῦν προσηῦζα τήνδε σὴν δούλην
Πόλιν, καὶ σκῆπτρα τάδε καὶ τὸ
Τῆς Ῥώμης κράτος. Φύλαττε ταύτην,
Σῶζέ τ᾽ ἐκ πάσης Βλάβης.[23]

You, Christ, are the Creator and Lord the World.
To You I have offered this city that is yours
And also offered the scepter and power of Rome.
Guard the city and save it from all harm.

Cedrinus says the twelve baskets famous from holy scripture were placed underneath the base of the column.[24] This Porphyry Column has no internal staircase but is solid, therefore the antiquarian Fulvius is wrong in saying there was one. Zonaras says that in his time the statue of Constantine was standing on top of the column, and during the reign of Alexius Comnenus in the springtime, when other structures were toppled by a powerful windstorm, the statue of Constantine the Great was blown off of the summit of the Porphyry Column and destroyed, and that the fragments broken from it killed several passers-by.[25] The author of the *Deeds of Alexius Comnenus* adds that the statue was not only knocked off by lightening but that three of its rings were as well. Which ones these were will presently be explained from the things I will soon add.[26]

This column still exists on the summit of the second hill, somewhat damaged, not by the ages, although it is quite ancient, so much as by fires, earthquakes and storms. For it no longer has its statue, or even in fact the three "zones," that is to say its uppermost spondyls or drums, which led historians to say this is the "cycloteris" column, as if it were distinguished by its circular elements. Stripped by a tempest of winds in the time of Alexius Comnenus, it was heightened in place of the lost spondyls with the addition of a polished construction placed on top, of the same thickness and size as the rest of the shaft. The column is set up on top of a square marble pedestal that is eleven feet nine fingers across on each face and eighteen feet high. A Doric coil of purple marble stands on a plinth, with an upper and lower tore and a scotia in between. Upon the coil is the shaft of the column, 33 feet in perimeter.[27] The shaft is not of a single stone, but of eight stones or spondyls each joined with a single wreath, belt, convex molding or laurel band encircling the seams of the stone joints, none of which appeared when it was intact and covered with the bulging rings.[28]

And so it looks like a single stone since its joints, covered entirely with separate bands of intertwining vines and leaves, cannot be seen. And if it had not been damaged from the beginning it would appear to be made of a single stone, as claimed not only by the common people but by some historians who falsely assert that this column was constructed from one piece of stone. They also ridicule those who do not believe it to be one stone as fools who have been deceived by the bronze bands that encircle it. They also say that the bands were added only for ornamental reasons. Now the bronze bands no longer exist, but a few iron hoops have been bound around the column, which has been damaged by fires.

After a violent windstorm had thrown down some drums, a spondylus of many stones was built on top, on whose summit was inscribed in Greek the name of the emperor who added the decorative structure on top after the statue of Constantine had been toppled. This column had a resemblance to those columns that Athenaeus describes in these sentences:

> In Egypt columns polished and round were erected of various drums, some black and some white, set in alternation. Their capitals were made similarly round, encircled with garlands carved all around, not fluted as in Greek work, nor encircled by rough foliage, except for lotuses and the fruits of young palms, and occasionally sculpted with many kinds of flowers. In fact, this large vessel, below its base, which projects above the spondyl, has the same sort of joint as the capital, distinguished by flowers and foliage. In this manner the Egyptians construct columns and build walls with sides of alternating black and white stones.[29]

In addition to this account by Athenaeus, I have observed the Egyptians, Syrians and Persians building their walls in alternating arrangements of colors, the richest of which are of stones or tiles with a variety of natural colors, the mediocre adorned with art and various paintings. Some say that these sculpted bands foretold happy years for Constantine, and many victories; but I believe they represent laurel wreaths, which are sacred to Apollo. For this ancient column had supported a colossal statue of Apollo, and Constantine attributed the column and the statue to himself either by reason of his victories, or because he was drawn to Apollo so that, after destroying other statues of the gods, he had the statue of the Delphic Apollo and the Tripod erected in the Hippodrome, as is stated by that famous Belgaen orator who recited a panegyric to Constantine. He said:

> Constantine, when you turned aside to the precinct of Apollo, the most beautiful in all the world, I believe you saw your Apollo offering you his crowns, each of which foretold thirty years, this being the length of a human generation, which should be for you beyond old age,[30] and I know that you recognized yourself in the appearance of this, for whom the songs of the prophets sing, god deserving to rule over the entire world. I know that now it has come to pass at last, for you are, like that Apollo, young, cheerful, salubrious and a most handsome emperor.[31]

If the Turk whom I employed to climb the pedestal had followed my directions — while I was posing as mere tourist — and held his measuring rod steady, I would have discovered from a notch cut in it that the bottom drum was nine feet and four digits high, and the convex molding at the base of the column projected six digits and was a foot and a half wide in all, so that each drum was nine feet ten fingers high. The height of all the eight drums was therefore about eighty-six feet and nine fingers. The whole column was made even taller by the abacus placed on the uppermost drum and by a coil and by the stylobate itself with its four marble steps at the bottom. The lowest of these steps is a foot and six digits high; the second is the same height; the third and fourth are each a foot and a half high. It is not possible to tell from any of the literature the location of this column or rather colossus (since it held upon it the statue of Constantine), as it was not formerly named, and Zonaras and other recent historians say it was in the Forum Placoton.

Since neither Procopius nor any others of those times mention this, I initially questioned whether this was the same as the Forum of Constantine, since it seemed likely to me that Constantine set up his statue on a column in his forum, as Trajan set up his statue on the Cochlea in the forum with his name.[32] But then later Socrates, historian of *The Dissensions amongst the Christians*, showed me that the

Forum Placoton was the same as the Forum of Constantine. He writes that when Arius came near the Forum of Constantine, in which the Porphyry Column was located, he perished by means of the violent spilling of his stomach.[33] But it is more clearly evident that the Placoton was what was called the Forum of Constantine, from the Palladium of Minerva, which Zonaras says Constantine transported from Troy to the Forum Lacoton, and Procopius says to the Forum of Constantine.[34] Procopius says that the Maleventi brought Diomedes to meet Aeneas when he was coming from Troy, and in response to the oracle gave him the image of Minerva [Palladium] that he had formerly brought from Troy with Ulysses, when they both set out to discover in that place how Ilium might be captured by the Greeks. They add that when Diomedes became ill, he consulted the oracle about the outcome of the disease. He was told he would never be free from sickness unless he gave that statue to a Trojan man.[35]

Yet, Procopius adds, the Romans say they don't know where this likeness of Minerva was. They indicate that it might be an image made from sculpted stone, which today stands in the Temple of Fortune in front of the statue of Minerva, in the eastern part of the temple. This image, which I said is sculpted in stone, has a warlike stance, wielding a spear just like in battle, wearing an oblong costume, which does not look like Minerva as she is portrayed by the Greeks, but the Egyptians. The people of Byzantium assert that Constantine ordered this statue buried underground in the Forum of Constantine.[36]

From the terms used by Zonaras and Procopius it is clear that the Placoton and Forum of Constantine are the same. This should be kept in mind, for without this information four regions and the fires of the city cannot be clearly understood. For the third region contains the Tribunal of the Forum of Constantine. The sixth extends from the Forum of Constantine containing the Column of Constantine to the pier at Sycae. The seventh extends from the right side of the Column of Constantine to the Forum of Theodosius with continuous porticos. The eighth region contains part of the Forum of Constantine. Fires ignited during the time of Justinian and Basil came as far as the Forum of Constantine. Under Leo buildings burned in a fire from the Forum of Constantine up to the Taurus.

In fact, not long ago I recall some men filled with curiosity who once asked me if I knew where Constantine obtained that

Palladium; I responded that I did not know. For Zonaras holds that it was brought from Troy. How can this be possible since Troy was destroyed so many ages ago that Strabo himself struggled with many maps to track it down? What about the fact that it was removed by Diomedes and Ulysses? For who was able to take it from ancient Rome so burned by fire so many times, especially since, as Procopius says, the Romans themselves were ignorant of where it was. Nevertheless, Latin authors say that it was presented as a gift from Diomedes to Aeneas. It was in Lavinium and later transferred to Rome to the Temple of Vesta. The Greeks disagree. Among these Pausanias, writing in the time of Hadrian, says that it was the most sacred of all things on the citadel of Minerva in Athens, and that ever since it fell from the sky it was dedicated on the Acropolis by general agreement of all the priests.[37]

There has been some controversy about whether it was fashioned of wood or bronze, and whether it was a statue or an image of Minerva on a shield. Some have written it was like the shield at Rome. But Dion and Diodorus think differently, writing that it was a wooden statue three cubits high that fell from the sky into Pessinus, a city of Phrygia, holding a spear in her right hand and a distaff and spindle in her left.[38] It seems likely to have been a statue, given that it has the name "Pallas," whose statue, wherever it was, was called the Palladium. Procopius testifies that the statue of Minerva that the Romans point out in the Temple of Minerva is not how the Greeks sculpt her. He says that she is a stone statue bearing the likeness of a warrior brandishing a spear. But even the Greeks say this statue holds a spear to symbolize strength and a round metal shield because it symbolizes wisdom, repelling dangers; and she is helmeted because the height of wisdom is unseen. She holds an olive branch that provides a source of light and has on her breast the Gorgon symbolizing quick thinking. At chest level Minerva has depicted on her aegis Gorgon and the Owl. The Owl indicated the depths of thought, for wisdom understands all that is dark and hidden.[39]

But I have said more than necessary for present purposes about the Palladium. Perhaps I have done this so that I might give notes on the Palladium like pieces of a puzzle. And I recommend to those who want to travel among the barbarians after me that they first come to Constantinople, and that they dig up the Palladium that

Constantine buried in the earth so that they can repel dangers, hardships and unimaginable crises. For I myself neglected to dig it up and to carry it with me, and I fell into all sorts of dangerous incidents. If I had been shielded by it then, just as I avoided other problems, I would have been admitted into Minerva's citadel, from which the Turks drove me when I had spent a long time in Athens, desiring to inspect the Temple of Minerva more closely. This still exists, with a Doric peristyle of 48 columns. But joking aside, I did not entirely lack the same divine Minerva who fell from heaven and who was deemed wise in her native land. She roused me, picked me up and restored me not only when I was once in danger in her temple, called Sophia, but very often when I was far away among the barbarians, abject and utterly despondent.

IV. The Senate, the Nymphaeum, Statues in the Forum of Constantine, the Philadelphion, the Museum, the Labarum, the Suparum; the Death of Arius; the Temples of Tellus, Ceres, Persephone, Juno and Pluto

36. *Statue of the Tetrarchs, Venice. Archive DAI Rom.*

The Ancient Description of the Wards of the City places the Porphyry Column and the Senate in the same ward and the Nymphaeum in the Fifth Ward.[40] How close they stood to each other it does not explain, but that they stood not far distant from each other I was able to learn in no other way than from the fire during the reign of Leo. This was caused by his wife Verina, and, say Zonaras and Cedrinus, it consumed the great house called the Senate situated in the north part of the Forum of Constantine. It was decorated with bronze statues and porphyry marble ornaments. In it was the gate of Ephesian Diana, the gift of Trajan from the spoils of the Scythian campaigns. It represented the wars of the Giants, a lightening-bolt of Jupiter, a Neptune with Trident and an Apollo with quiver and arrows. In the lower register of the gate were images of Giants attacking dragons, throwing large

37. Reconstruction drawing of columns with Tetrarchic sculptures from the Philadeiphion. Archive DAI Rom.

rocks, and glowering with murderous eyes. In this Senate House the principal men and citizens convened to give and take council, and the emperor himself came in when he took possession of the consular vestments.[41]

The same writers testify to a building of magnificence and splendor that was consumed by the fire at this time. It was situated in the area of the Senate, near the Senate House, and was called the Nymphaeum, because those getting married, whose homes were not large enough for crowds, celebrated in this house. And they also say that in the western part of this forum was located the statue of Minerva of Lyndus, who wore a helmet and had the Gorgonian monster and a neck woven around with snakes; for this is how the ancients depicted Minerva.[42] Cedrinus says that in the eastern part of the forum was the statue of Amphitrite, one of the sirens, wearing crab claws on the sides of her head.[43] An anonymous author asserts that the Sirens were in this same part of the forum, which some people called Seahorses, and three of these were extant in his day and located in the suburb of St Mamas.[44]

In the north part of the Forum of Constantine situated on the top of a tall column was the very large cross that Constantine the Great saw in the sky. Everyone corroborates this. Although he does not name what forum it was in, when Eusebius describes its being set up, he says that it was in an area in the middle of the city. On the example of ancient Rome the same was erected in New Rome. The same Eusebius states that this cross was set up in all the royal buildings and in all the important places in Constantinople, just as Constantine saw it in the sky. Sozomen of Salamis writes about this symbol, saying that Constantine changed the most honorable war standard, called the Labarum by the Romans, which was carried before the emperor and which was consecrated by law to be revered by the army.[45]

I believe that Constantine suddenly changed this most famous emblem of the Roman Empire into the sign of Christ so that by the habit of having it in sight and venerating it, they would grow unaccustomed to the rites of their fathers and become subject to his authority. About this Prudentius says: "'Christ' was represented on the purple Labarum with gems on gold, 'Christ' was written as an the insignia of their shields, and the cross blazed forth fixed atop their standards."[46] Eusebius says of the time of Constantine that he saw with his own eyes this arranged in this form. He says that, being very tall, it had a spear with a crossbar transfixed at the top, so it was made in the form of a cross. In the uppermost part was a wreath of precious stones cunningly worked in gold, on which the first two letters of the life-saving name of Christ were marked, which the circle of the wreath enclosed, with *rho* in the center and the letter that the Greeks call *chi* [X] marked on that. From the top cross points that divided the spear a banner was affixed.[47]

From this description by Eusebius it is possible to tell what the Labarum is, what the Syparum is, and which is the part of the Labarum that Eusebius said hangs from the cross-bar of the cross, as can be gathered from Tertullian. Long before Eusebius and Constantine, he said that the Labarum bore a similarity to the cross in these terms:

> Then if any of you think we render superstitious adoration to the cross, in that adoration he is sharer with you. If you offer homage to a piece of wood at all, it matters little what it is like when the subsance is the same: it is of no consequence the form, if you have the very body of the god. And yet how far does the Athenian Pallas differ from the stock of the cross, or the Pharian Ceres as she is put up uncarved to sale, a mere rough stake and piece of shapeless wood? Every stake fixed in an upright position is a portion of the cross; we render our adoration, if you will have it so, to a god entire and complete. But you also worship victories, for in your trophies the cross is the heart of the trophy. The camp religion of the Romans is all through a worship of the standards, setting the standards above all gods. Well, those images decking out the standards are ornaments of crosses. All those hangings of your standards and banners are robes of crosses. I praise your zeal: you would not consecrate crosses unclothed and unadorned.[48]

Arnobius, or rather I should say Minutius Felix,[49] said the same things. He said, "we neither worship nor desire crosses; indeed you, who consecrate gods of wood, adore wooden crosses perhaps as parts of your gods. For your very standards, as well as your banners and the standard-bearing Labara of your camp, what else are they but gilded and ornate crosses? Your victorious trophies not only imitate the appearance of a simple cross, but also that appearance of a man affixed to it."[50]

From this it is clear that the Sypara were banners that were suspended from the Labara, that is, from the military and victory standards that the Romans carved onto the triumphal arches of their emperors. Labara and banners are carved elsewhere, such as on the Spiral Column of Trajan, where there are squared things, like the sails of ships, which we can call Sypara. In short, all the insignia of the Roman army and of all the trophies that are seen sculpted at Rome bear an image of a cross. Seneca says that the Sypara, or rather the Supara, are distinctive banners of the Alexandrine navy, by which he may mean the Suparum of the Sun, which not all ships fly at sea.[51] Lucan says *"supara"* for sails; others say that the suparum, or rather the syparum is a linen garment of maidens, concerning which Affranius writes: "I am not a maiden, if I am not covered by a suparum."[52] I pass over the fact that this custom does not appear in Festus and Donatus, who write that the syparium is a stage covering that mimes and professional actors use to conceal the stage that is set before the audience.[53] And later ages used these syparia as curtains, concerning which the Satiric Poet observed, "When my strength is exhausted, Damasippe, you have put my voice on the syparum."[54] Apuleius says, "when the curtain is raised and the syparia folded up, the stage is ready."[55] Seneca says that words are far greater than the tragic costume and the sypara, which are grand and praised above the tragic loftiness.[56] And so we are able to speak of the Sypara's crosses and banners on account of the highest excellence of these authors.

Anyone may rightfully say to me that I have gone on a little longer than my purpose calls for, and I admit it. But what would I do unless I paused a little bit, confined in such a closeness of ruins in New Rome? Even when that city flourished, free citizens were unable to look up at the sky through this density. Indeed, while I walk about I can see what not a single native resident was able to show me, and so I will respond, either to expand on the scarcity of evidence or for the purpose of recovering my breath, to those who think that the apparition of the cross to Constantine was an invention of the monks.

It seems to me that there is no miracle that has been attested to so much in the records of literature and verified by eyewitnesses. Eusebius, who lived in those times, claims the cross was seen not only by Constantine himself but also by his entire army in the middle of the day, and not only the Christian men of those times but even those unbelieving men who cursed the Christian faith professed to have seen it. So famous was this affair that the Romans bore witness in their triumphal arch, which they dedicated to Constantine[57] who conquered Maxentius through divine inspiration. But they had been supporters of Maxentius until won over to the Christian religion at that point.[58] And yet on the Arch of Constantine they did not alter the figure of the cross, but they took care that it was sculpted as Trajan and

Severus and other emperors seem to have carried out for them, as can be seen from ancient monuments still extant in Rome.

I suspect that Nazarius was a Christian, more on account of his Christian daughter the virgin Euphemia than from the panegyric that he recited on behalf of Constantine, where he says:

It was the talk of all the Gauls that those divinely sent were seen. And although heavenly things are not usually seen by the eyes of men, because a substance simple, delicate and uncompounded in nature eludes our rude and cloudy vision, yet these, your auxiliary troops, allowing themselves to be seen and heard, testify to your worthiness. They flee from contact with mortal appearance. But what sorts of thing are these apparitions said to have been? Of what bodily strength and of what size of limbs? Of what swiftness of will? They were ablaze in an awesome way with shimmering shields, and the terrible light of their celestial armor blazed forth. For they came on so that they seemed your [soldiers]. This is what they said. They spread this news among those listening: "We seek Constantine. We go with Constantine as an ally." Divine beings certainly have reason to boast, and ambition for honor has touched heavenly beings too. Flying through heaven, divinely sent, they boast that they fought for you.[59]

I pass over the rest about this host.

Certain authors write that the place in which Constantine erected this grand cross was on top of a gilded column that was in the Philadelphion, the college of those studying the Muse, which was near the Porphyry Column, as the epigram inscribed on it indicates:

Ἐν τῷ πορφυρῷ κίονι τὸ ὄν εἰς τὸ Φιλαδέλφιον.
Εὔνους μὲν Βασιλεῖ Μουσήλιος ἔργα βοῶσιν
δημόσια σθεναρὴν πράγματα πίστιν ἔχει.
Μουσεῖον Ῥώμη δ ἐχαρίσσατο καὶ βασιλῆος
εἰκόνα θεσπεσίην ἐντὸς ἔγραψε δόμων.
Τιμὴν μουσοπόλοις, πόλεως χάριν ἐλπίδα κούρων,
ὅπλα δὲ τῆς ἀρετῆς, κρήματα τοῖς ἀγαθοῖς.
Ταῦτα λόγοις ἀνέθηκεν ἑκὼν Μουσήλιος ἔργα
Πιστεύων καθαρῶς, ὡς θεός ἐσὶ Λόγος.[60]

On the Porphyry Column in the Philadelphion:
Muselius is a well-disposed supporter of the emperor.
His public works proclaim it beyond a doubt.
He gave Rome a Museum, with a marvelous image of the

Emperor within. This Museum is an honor
To poets and an ornament to the city,
The hope of youths, the spur to virtue and the wealth of men.
Muselius gladly dedicated these works to words,
In a steadfast belief that God is the Word.

Julian, prefect of the city, set up a gilded statue of Anastasius in front of the House of the Muses, notable for its verses, which although ingenious and many, nevertheless do not say in what part of the city this House of the Muses was. It was reported to Emperor Manuel that in the western part of the Forum of Constantine above the arch there had been standing, since ancient times, statues of women made of bronze, one Roman, the other Hungarian. The Roman leaned out from her base, and the Hungarian stood upright on her base. The emperor, very much moved by this announcement, sent workmen who reset the Roman and demolished the Hungarian, supposing that with alteration of the statues, the affairs of Rome would be improved.[61]

In the same forum, among statues of other celebrated men, there was the statue of Longinus, prefect of the city, on which was carved these verses by Arabius Scholasticus:

Νεῖλος, Περσὶς, Ἴβηρ, Σώλυμοι, Θύσις,
Ἀρμενίς, Ἰνδοί,
καὶ κόλχοι σκοπέλων ἐγγύθι καυκασίων,
καὶ πεδία ζείοντα πολυσπερέων Ἀγαρηνῶν
Λογγίνου ταχινῶν μάρτυρες εἰσι πόνων
ὡς δὲ ταχὺς βασιλῆϊ διάκτορος ἦεν ὁδεύων,
καὶ ταχὺς εἰρήνην ὤπασε κευθομένην.[62]

The Nile, Persia, Iberia, the Lycians, the West,
Armenia, the Indians, and the Colchians
Near the peaks of the Caucasus,
And the boiling plains of the scattered Arabians,
They witness the swiftly completed efforts of Longinus,
And his traveling, a swift minister of the emperor.
And he was swift in giving peace that had been in hiding.

I will pass over Themistius the Philosopher, whom Valentinian made prefect of Constantinople, and whom Valens' writings had honored more than any other statue, having a precinct of the city near the Forum of Constantine. Socrates tells the story of the demise of Arius, leader of the Arians. He says that Arius, after having spoken before Constantine the Great, left the Royal Palace, escorted by the attendants of Eusebius, and he proceeded through the center of the city, seen by all. Later, when he came near the Forum of Constantine, where the Porphyry Column is, his conscience was so thoroughly terrified by some fear that he needed to move his bowels. He asked if there was a private place nearby, learned that there was a latrine behind the Forum of Constantine, and he went to it. He urgently needed to pass gas. Suddenly, with the violent unloading of his bowels, his intestine fell out, and next there was a great flowing of blood, and with the blood came out his intestinal membrane, liver and spleen; and he perished immediately. Socrates adds that in his own time this latrine was still behind the Forum of Constantine and the meat market in the portico.[63] But today, of these things that were said to be in the Forum of Constantine, nothing remains except the Porphyry Column. For the forum has been built over, so that near the Porphyry Column a building for travelers, the poor or ill has been built, and near this a mosque built by Ali Pasha. The very large entrance porch is of marble, decorated with six shining columns, four of white marble and two of Thebaic marble, whose lowest shafts have a perimeter of 7 feet 4 inches around. Although they are very tall columns, they have double bases, the lowest of marble and the uppermost in bronze, as is most commonly done by the Turks, who learned this, and many more things, from the Greeks who customarily augmented columns with a coil of bronze.

A little way along the road near this building is a school for those professing Islamic theology. This presently has a square atrium surrounded by a portico sustained by 18 columns, partly green and partly white. A little below the mosque of Ali Pasha is another religious building placed by the Turks on the highest point of the second valley, with a marble porch having six glistening columns, two of porphyry, two white with various bluish-gray waves, and two of dark green marble with white spots. From the things that I described before on the second hill, one can clearly discern part of the Third Ward, which contained the Tribunal of the Forum of Constantine, and almost the whole of the Fifth and Sixth Wards.

Moreover, on part of the slope of the second hill and on part of the coastal plain situated below it, Dionysius of Byzantium places the temples of Tellus, Ceres, Proserpina, Juno and Pluto. The Temple of Tellus, above the bay outside the walls of ancient Byzantium, is not roofed, signifying the free power of ancient Tellus, and it is enclosed by walls of polished stone. Beyond the Temple of Tellus he says there were the paired temples of Ceres and Proserpina, in which were many paintings, remarkable relics of the former age, and statues of a sophisticated skill that was not inferior to these paintings, all exquisitely fashioned. The two temples of Juno and Pluto stood where the sea recedes or goes away, but of these nothing remained in his day, except their names. The Persians burned down the Temple of Juno during the expedition of Darius against the Scythians in revenge for the things the Byzantines were blamed for, namely struggling against King Darius. When Philip of Macedon was besieging Byzantium, lacking material, he destroyed the Temple of Pluto. But the names of these temples remain in human memory.

The Temple of Pluto was called Acra, and the Temple of Juno was called the Bronze, that is, the Junonian Acra, and here at the beginning and end of the year youths slaughtered sacrificial victims. It seems more likely that these acrae were on a slope of the second hill instead of on the plain of the sea at the base of the hill where one sees this maritime plain in which there is no acra. Hence Dionysius says that the acrae of Pluto and of Juno were ἀπόβασιν τῆς θαλάττης, "a landing on the sea."[64] The acrae on this part of the hill were in contact with the sea by a port; and the base of the hill adjoined a shipyard on the seaside plain. The wings of the port formed headlands. Otherwise, the acrae are to be interpreted as the seaports. But my treatise on the Bosporus has more on this.[65]

V. The Seventh Ward

Before I entered upon the subject at hand I thought that it would be easy to determine the situation of the Seventh Ward from the *Ancient Description of the Wards*, which said that this ward, in comparison with the Sixth Ward above, was flatter, and yet as respects its outermost edges, it ran to the sea in a decline. But who would know it from this description when other regions of the city also run down to the sea in slopes at their outermost edge?[66] For the author of the *Ancient Description of the Wards* adds that this ward extended from the right-hand side of the Column of Constantine to the Forum of Theodosius with a long, continuous portico, and its other side extended in the same manner all the way to the sea and inclined toward the sea and led down to it.[67]

It has three churches: Irene, Anastasius and St. Paul. It proceeds inland to the Column of Theodosius all the way to the summit, accessible by stairs, and to part of the same forum, of which now nothing remains. Nor do our contemporaries remember where it had been located. Nor is anything left that was said to have been in this region. At first it seemed unclear to me which part was on the right of the column. Indeed, Titus Livius did not free me from doubt concerning this, writing that Romulus determined the wards from east to west, so that things on the right faced south, those on the left faced north. This region would therefore be situated to the south, nonetheless I may show that it was located in the north.[68]

Nor have geographers helped me, for those who look to the northern region where they seek the altitude of the pole have the east on their right. Varro, following the argument of astrologers in marking out the horizon, has shed not a little light for me, when he established the four parts of the sky; the east is to the left, the west to the right, the south in front and the north behind.[69] By Varro's divisions I concluded that the Seventh Ward was to the west of the column, but I was not certain whether the *Ancient Description of the Wards* followed Romulus' division of the sky or the divisions of astrologers. And so I was in doubt until at last, after making a great investigation, I discovered where the Column of Theodosius was, and I found some remains of the churches of Anastasius and Irene. By this I learned that the Seventh Ward ran from the summit of the ridge of the promontory to the bay. The *Ancient Description* would have been more clear if it had described that, for one going from east to west, the Seventh Ward extended on the right-hand side from the Column of Constantine to the Forum of Theodosius with continuous porticos.

This region contained the places where today there is the largest forum of the entire city, which the Turks call the Bedesten. Here all the costly goods customarily sold by the merchants are kept, just as in the times of the Christian emperors they were in the house called the Lampterum. That this was located somewhere else than where today there is a Turkish forum, I conclude from the fire that began at the Miliarium Aureum in the reign of Justinian. Cedrinus says it consumed a great part of the city and the Great Church and its Carthophilacium, and two porticos all the way to the Forum of Constantine, and also the Octagon and Baths of Severus called the

149

Zeuxippus, and at the same time the famous building called the Lampterum, as it was the practice to burn lamps there at night time. The Lampterum had a wooden roof, in which were stored the most valuable goods of the merchants, such as silks, cloth interwoven with gold and other valuables. In fact, all of the beautiful ornaments of the city that remained after that earlier great conflagration were burned by this fire.[70]

I would have written *"Lampteras"* as *"Lucernas"* in Latin, except I judged that proper names ought not to be translated into another language, and anyway Titus Livy adopts the word "Lamptera." He says that, "the city of Phocaea is located at the far end of a bay of the sea and is oblong-shaped; it is surrounded by a wall 2500 paces long and becomes more narrow at each of the ends, similar to a wedge-shape. The people themselves call it "Lampter." There it is 1200 paces wide, and from it a tongue of land extends out into the sea like a marker, almost through the middle of the bay; where it connects with the narrow entrance it makes two very safe ports running in opposite directions. They call the one to the south the Nausthamos,[71] because it holds many ships; the other is near the Lamptera itself."[72] And so it seems most likely to me that the Massilien colonists, descended from the Phoceans, called the lake situated on the coast of the province of Narbonensis the Lamptera, which Pliny's published text calls Lampterum.[73]

VI. The Taurus, Forum of Theodosius, Spiral Column of Theodosius, the Tetrapylum, the Pyramid of the Winds, the Statues of Arcadius and Honorius, the Churches of Irene and Anastasia, and the Scyronides Rocks

When I considered that I was not able to find the Seventh Ward easily, the Taurus also seemed hard to find, which I was unable to learn of without knowing where the spiral Column of Theodosius was. Likewise, without the Taurus the Eighth Ward could not be known. With eagerness I investigated the vestiges of these things. Since for a long time the Column of Theodosius had been inland, I searched all of the streets up to the summit. I finally learned from some old men that the Column of Theodosius was located on the back of the ridge containing a plain joined to the third hill and stretching northwest near the new baths that Sultan Bayezit built. This is the same Bayezit who, more than forty years before I came to Byzantium, destroyed this column so that he could build his baths more easily. Above this bath towards the north is a wide street having bookstalls and an ancient cistern. To the north is the enclosure of the Sultans' Harem. Indeed the street widens out to the east into a great area in which the furthest eastern part is the Tomb of Sultan Bayezit with a mosque and building for travelers, the poor or ill.

Cedrinus says that this Column of Theodosius was in every way like the one Arcadius erected, which still exists today on the Xerolophon[74] hill. We will describe this in its own place. Zonaras says the Column in the Taurus was erected by Theodosius the Great as a monument, with the well-fought battles Theodosius made against the Scythians and barbarians depicted on it. It had a passage inside leading to the top, and a statue of Theodosius himself set up on top, which was toppled by an earthquake in the year that ancient Rome was captured. Emperor Anastasius melted down many works fashioned of bronze, among which was the statue of Constantine the Great, and remade one with his own name and inscription — a gilded bronze equestrian statue that he put on top of the same column in the Taurus where the statue of Theodosius the Great formerly stood.[75] From this we know that the Taurus was where the Column of Theodosius was, and with this being known we know that the Seventh Ward was on the ridge of the third hill and the slopes of the same, and that it had continuous porticos from the Column of Constantine to the Forum of Theodosius, which was in the Seventh Ward. Yet it is still not clear how near it was to the Column of Theodosius. However, it is possible to deduce that it was close, not only from the example of the Forum of Trajan Hispanus, who had a similar column in the center of the forum of his own name in Rome, as Theodosius Hispanus afterwards erected in New Rome, but also from what we can learn from Evagrius, who relates that the fire under Leo consumed the buildings from the Forum of Constantine all the way to the Forum Tauri.[76]

An old Constantinopolitan man told me that in his day the Forum Tauri existed where I said the Column of Theodosius was, overgrown with trees no less than the Hippodrome was at that time. Because there were robbers in that place, the Sultan Mehmet, who captured the city, gave it to those who were willing to build on it. In fact, part of the Forum of Theodosius was occupied by the Forum Pistorium or was in the vicinity, as I deducted from Zonaras, who relates that Emperor Nicephorus Phocas went from his palace at the

Golden Fountain. Near the Golden Gate, returning to his estate, he encountered insults from the people at the Forum τῶν ἀρτοπολίων [Forum Artopoleion] all the way to the Column of Constantine.[77] An anonymous author says that the Taurus was near a column near the Forum τῶν ἀρτοπολίων,[78] in a courtyard paved in stone. In the same place there were four gates in a square building, and four porticos, which was called the Tetrapylum, but he says it was once called the Quatrivium. George Cedrinus locates the Tetrapylum not far off from the Forum Tauri when he relates that the fire during the reign of Leo burned down two great holy buildings in the Taurus, ornamented with all kinds of stones, one of which was not far from the Tetrapylum and the other overlooked the Forum Tauri. The same author, speaking of another fire under Leo, says that it consumed everything in its path from the Bronze Tetrapylum to a church, which he does not name.[79]

The *Ancient Description of the Wards of the City* says that Constantinople had a gilded Tetrapylum, but he does not write in which ward it was, and I do not know whether the city had two Tetrapyla, one gold and one bronze, or whether it had merely one, which was made first of gold. Then later, with the gold stripped off, only the bronze remained.[80] John the Rhetorician, as he is cited by Evagrius, says that in the time of Emperor Zeno a distinguished senator named Mamianus built some beautiful royal porticos at Constantinople. He adorned and decorated these with renowned splendor, and between two porticos he constructed a Tetrapylum as a sort of enclosure, ornamented with columns and bronze material. And in his time the porticos retained a royal name, carrying on the decorativeness of the earlier work of Proconnesian marble scattered on the ground, but not retaining the distinctive structure. But not even a vestige of the Tetrapylum remained.[81] An anonymous author says that in the Tetrapylum there was a small room above the columns where relatives and the queen of the dead emperor received news of his death and were concealed inside in the shrouds of the dead until the sixth hour of the day. Then meeting the dead man, they took him out and accompanied him as far as the church of the Holy Apostles, where customarily they lay their emperors to rest.[82] It seems to me that the Tetrapylum was once the Temple of Janus Quadrifons not far from the Capitol of Constantinople, and it was decorated, as formerly in Rome, with four doors representing the four seasons of the year. For Janus is called upon by those about to depart, and so all transitional passageways are sacred to Janus, and the doors of temples are called Janae. Some have written that in the Forum Pistorium there was a Tetrasceles. George Cedrinus records that the Tetrasceles was a four-sided machine, which indicated the δῆριν, or force, of the winds. He says that Theodosius the Great erected this in the shape of a pyramid ornamented with animals, plants, fruits and gilded garlands bearing gold objects similar to Punic apples, and with putti, some of which were laughing amongst themselves. Some of the uppermost putti sported with those below, and others danced. It had youths blowing into bronze trumpets. Set on the top of the pyramid a moving bronze statue indicated the direction of the winds.[83] The statues of Arcadius and Honorius were near the Column of Theodosius, the statue of their father Arcadius in an eastern niche and the statue of Honorius in a western niche.[84]

Socrates, the popular author of *The History of the Christian People*, claims that from the aqueduct that Valens introduced into the city and constructed out of the ruins of Chalcedon, Clearchus, prefect of the city, built a great cistern (ὑδρεῖον) that was in the forum called, at that time, the Forum of Theodosius. In everyday speech it was said to have been liberal and abundant with water, on account of which

Hagia Irene. 38. View from southeast. 39. View from the northeast.

the people held a joyous festival. Socrates calls it ὑδρεῖον, that is, "cistern" or "lake."[85] Zonaras and Cedrinus call it the Nymphaeum, because they likewise say that the prefect of the city built it using material from the Aqueduct of Valens in the Taurus, and that they held a great celebration there and all the people took part.[86] From all this we understand that what Socrates calls the Forum of Theodosius, Zonaras and Cedrinus call Taurum, and that therefore the Forum Tauri and Forum of Theodosius are the same.[87] And the Nymphaeum of the Forum Tauri is different from the Nymphaeum situated near the Forum of Constantine in the area of the Senate. As we saw before, the great house in this place was so called because those whose homes did not have space for a crowd celebrated weddings in it. But it is likely that this Nymphaeum of the Forum Tauri had been the lake or fishpond or cistern that was similar to the one that had been within the walls of the Royal Harem. This occupied part of the Forum of Theodosius. Into it the Aqueduct of Valens penetrated, and from it there are many watersheds, as on the sides of the third hill, especially inside the enclosure of the Royal Harem.

It appears from the *Ancient Description of the Wards* that the Carosian Baths, named after Carosa, daughter of Emperor Valens, were on the third hill, but on what part it does not explain. Nor am I able to determine whether they had disappeared down to their foundations or whether there are bath buildings built on their foundations. We see large structures built by the Turks, partly on the ridge of the third hill and partly on its sides.[88] The *Ancient Description of the Wards* places the churches of Irene and Anastasia in this Seventh Ward, but in what part it does not indicate, nor can it be determined from the remains.[89] In which part of the third hill the church of Irene was located can be determined now from a history. It says that when the city was captured by the Franks and Venetians a fire started at the Synagogue of the Saracens in the part of the city that inclines toward the sea, bordering the north near the church of Hagia Irene.[90]

I first learned from some old men who knew of it that this church was inside the enclosure of the Royal Harem. Later I noticed a high tower outside the women's enclosure, situated on the side of the third hill facing southeast, a square building, now commonly called Hyrene, but I don't know whether this is because of the church of St. Irene or because of the Empress Irene.[91] There were, I have learned from literary records, three churches of Irene in Constantinople; the first was called the ancient Irene, which Socrates says was built by Constantine the Great and was near Hagia Sophia, as we showed earlier.[92] The second, which I just now say is set on the third hill, the *Ancient Description of the Wards* puts in the Seventh Ward; and the third church of Irene Procopius locates, saying that Justinian had built it at the mouth of the Golden Horn and it was called the church of Irene the Martyr.[93] However, some say the church of Anastasia was in that place where there is a new bedesten, that is, a new merchants' hall; others say where there is still a cistern supported by many marble columns, located between the merchants' halls of the forum and Sultan Bayezit's tomb and his building for travelers, the poor or ill.

Sozomen records that when Gregory came from Nazianzus to Constantinople he made a speech in a building that lovers of his speeches constructed, which later emperors made extremely famous for its architecture and size, and they called it Anastasia.[94] It was called this perhaps because those very things that had been established by the Council of Nicea and lay half dead were once again renewed in Constantinople, and revived a second time in this church by the speeches of Gregory Nazianzus; or perhaps because, as he says, when there was a crowd of people assembled in this church, a pregnant woman fell from the upper portico and died immediately, but was revived by the combined prayers of the entire congregation, and so the church is called St. Anastasia.[95] From these words of Sozomen it is clear that recent writers err saying this church is named in memory of a Roman St. Anastasia. The *Description of the Wards* simply mentions a church Anastasia, which I believe it to be one of two that existed. Cedrinus writes that they were very large and decorated with all kinds of stone and were burned in the fire that started in the reign of Leo, one not far from the Tetrapylum, the other next to the Forum Tauri.[96]

When I wrote *On the Thracian Bosporus* I showed that on the lowest slopes of the third hill, facing north, there are situated the Scironides Rocks, so called by the leaders from Megara and Corinth who established the colony of Byzantium. They are named on account of their difficult position, which they share with the Scironides Rocks between the Isthmus of Corinth and Megara.[97] And so indeed I will say what the pre-eminence of the third hill contained. On its ridge is the tomb of Sultan Bayezit with its building for travelers, the poor or ill and a large mosque, which he built to resemble Hagia Sophia. Vaulted in brick work and roofed in lead, it has a roomy porch, paved with white marble, and encircled by four porticos, which are held up by brilliant columns of the most exquisite marble. In the center water gushes forth high into the air and then falls into a great bowl that emits water leaping from many small fountains. The building with the porch is encircled on three sides by a great area, enclosed partly by walls and in part by a building for travelers, the poor or ill. The fourth side is bordered by a garden, in the center of which is the tomb of Sultan Bayezit, a small building bearing a similarity to the middle of a cylinder.

In addition, on the ridge of the third hill are the palaces of the Royal Harem enclosed by a high wall, which I wandered around for more than two miles after coming to Byzantium. Sultan Suleyman recently has occupied the center part with enormous substructures for his future tomb and a building for travelers, the poor or ill, which are now being constructed out of bright marble collected from many regions of the Turkish Empire. You may see thrown on the ground infinite kinds of marble, not only those recently taken out from the stone quarry, but countless others for many ages wandering through different buildings of the rulers not only of Byzantium but of all of Greece and even of Egypt.

In the Seventh Ward I saw three ancient cisterns that the *Ancient Description of the City* does not mention: one in the Forum Tauri and a second between the tomb of Sultan Bayezit and the Bedesten Forum, which are both supported by marble columns. The third is on the third hill on a cliff facing to the north. Of this there still remain six Corinthian columns made of Arabian marble, wonderfully tall and solid. Underneath the stylobate of the columns is a tile water pipe from which water is directed into a brick cistern that is vaulted in brick as well. Twenty brick pillars support it. Above the cistern was once the site of a church of the Christian religion, which the Turkish sultans dismantled. They adorned their own buildings with its reworked stones.

On the side of this same hill extending to the west stands a mosque that has a porch held up by twelve columns, of which six are Arabian marble. A little above this mosque is another mosque that was once a church dedicated to St. Theodore, decorated with columns. But in fact it is not the same one that Procopius says Justinian built in front of the city walls in a place called Rhessium.[98] Another building, which was once Christian and is now a mosque, stands between the enclosure of the Harem and the tomb that Sultan Suleyman erected for his son Mehmet, covered with a layer of different kinds of marble.

VII. THE EIGHTH WARD AND BACK OF THE THIRD HILL

I did not discover from the *Ancient Description of the Wards of the City* that the Eighth Ward was on the third hill facing south. It says that the Eighth Ward on the side of the Taurus, nowhere near the sea, was a space narrow rather than a wide in comparison to its length. And so from this description I do not know whether it extended toward the north or to the south. But I do recognize the Eighth Ward, which it says contained part of the Forum of Constantine and a portico to the left as far as the Taurus. I already knew that the Seventh Ward contained the right portico from the Porphyry Column to the Forum of Theodosius.[99] From this I learned that part of the promontory stretching from sea to sea between the Porphyry Column and the Taurus was divided along the ridge into a northern and a southern side by the porticos on the right. I also learned that the Seventh Ward was divided from the Eighth by the continuous portico running from the Porphyry Column to the Taurus, and that it contained the right portico. The Eighth Ward contained the left portico. Nothing at all of these porticos remains today, but at least the street is wide that runs across the middle of the ridge of the promontory from Hagia Sophia to the Land Walls.[100]

This ward likewise contains the Capitol and the Basilica of Theodosius, both of which were probably near the Forum of Theodosius and his column, as we can learn from Zonaras and George Cedrinus. They say that a fire, started in the reign of Leo, consumed the great and extremely famous house in the Taurus used by the counselors and the emperor. It was for convening together to consult on business to be undertaken, and it was used by the emperor as consul, presiding over the council. These authors add that it had twelve assorted columns made of Trojan marble, 25 feet tall, which supported a roof with four arches. They also add that the house was approximately 240 feet long and 140 feet wide. This house was the Basilica of Theodosius, or the Capitol.[101] From these facts, which I have said before, it is possible to judge what these buildings were after the fire. I gather that they lost their original names after being rebuilt since recent writers claim that the palace and building for travelers, the poor or ill were in the Taurus. Even the old people of Constantinople do not disagree with these writers, testifying that even in living memory near the mint, in the vicinity of the Forum of Theodosius, there was a great palace. Some say it was the palace of Sultan Mehmet, who began living in Constantinople before he constructed the huge enclosure of the palace located on the first hill. They say that the Turkish sultans have decorated their buildings from its ruins. The building for travelers, the poor or ill, or rather church that was to the south and west of the Taurus, I saw dismantled and its columns transferred to the building for travelers, the poor or ill that Sultan Suleyman constructed in memory of his son Charus.[102] Let the Greek priests judge whether this was the church of St Paul that was contained in the Seventh Ward. I was never able to find one of them from whom I could learn about it.

VIII. The Ninth Ward, the Temple of Concord, the Granaries of Alexandria and Theodosius, the Baths of Anastasia, the House of Craterus, the Modius, the Temple of the Sun and the Moon

The Ninth Ward was on the back of the third hill, partly on the slopes lying underneath the ridge, on which I said the Taurus was, partly falling away below the crest, where we can see part of the aqueduct to the east and the mosque that, as I said before, Sultan Suleyman had dedicated to his son. It was partly on the Propontic coastal plain stretching to the Gardens of Blancha, where the Portus Theodosiacus formerly was. I learned from other writers, but especially from the *Ancient Description*, that the Ninth Ward is entirely on an incline and bends down towards the south, terminating at the shores of the sea,[103] but I also learned this from the Eighth Ward. It is bounded on the side of the Taurus nowhere near the sea, so I conclude that the Eighth Ward occupied the plain on the ridge, where I indicated the Taurus was, but did not occupy the slopes falling below the plain. And so I also conclude that the Ninth Ward is partly under the Eighth Ward on the hillside below the plain, from the part that extends from the Taurus to the south and the shore of the Propontis, and partly situated on the two slopes descending with a double incline, one from the Taurus to the southwest, the other from the buildings of the Janissaries to the south. Where this ward may be may also be discerned from the Temple of Concord. But the *Ancient Description* does not say in which part of this ward the Temple of Concord and the Granaries of Alexandria and Theodosius were, or what the Ninth Ward contained. However through reason and from the testimony of other writers we are able find out.

Evagrius indicates where the Temple of Concord (which the *Description of the Wards* calls ὁμόνοιαν)[104] is when he describes the fire that started during the reign of Leo in the north part of the city, raging along from the Port of the Bosporus all the way to the ancient Temple of Apollo. In fact, it raged on the south side of the city from the Port of Julian as far as the houses situated not far from the Temple of Concord. In the center of the city the fire extended from the Forum of Constantine to the Taurus, and the fire stretched five stadia through the length of the city.[105] From this we can see that the fire was in that part of the Ninth Ward imagined along a straight line from the Forum Tauri to the shore of the Propontis. This would be clearly understood by anyone who walks the five stadia from the Forum of Constantine to the Forum Tauri, puts down a mark there, and then continues from the Port of Julian west, across the coastal plain five stadia, puts another mark there, and then compares it to the other mark fixed in the Taurus. Then one would not be far off from the traces of the Temple of Concord, which is not extant today. Also no longer extant is the church of St. Thomas the Apostle, which was near the Temple of Concord, as is evident from what I wrote before concerning the Port of Julian. The

40. *Bodrum Camii/Church of the Myrelaion. Photo by Kuzey Taffalı.*

Granary of Theodosius was not far from the Port of Theodosius, once situated in gardens that are now named after Blanchae. This seems probable due to the rules of architecture, which prescribe that a granary be placed near a port. There were none in either the Eighth Ward or the Ninth, but part of the Twelfth Ward is in the vicinity of the Ninth Ward, where the Port of Theodosius is. In fact, it is also obvious that Theodosius would have embellished the Port of Theodosius with a granary and the forum called by the same name. But I will discuss the Port of Theodosius further below.

Above the outermost eastern part of the gardens called the Blanchae, which once contained the Port of Theodosius, a slope projects to the north, where there is the church commonly called the Myrelaion.[106] It has a cistern inside, which has brick vaulting sustained by approximately 60 marble columns, where there was once a granary, which Suidas incorrectly calls *horeium*. He says that the statue of Maimus, who led his army against the Scythians, stood in the so-called Horeium in front of the house of Craterus, which is now the Myrelaion, and near the Bronze Hands and near the bronze Modius.[107] Indeed, the Modius was a legal measure by which all corn was measured out and sold. By a law not to be broken by anyone Emperor Valentinian had established that twelve modii may be sold for a nomisma. A certain sailor not following this law was punished with the loss of his right hand. Because of this the Bronze Hands were set up here, and the bronze Modius was set up by Valentinian in the niche of the Amastrianum between the two Bronze Hands. Others say that in the law Valentinian decreed that the modius be sold not by ruler but in dry measure, and that anyone who broke the law should have his hands cut off.[108]

George Cedrinus says that there were places called Amastrianum after a poor man whose homeland was Amastrum, who went to Constantinople out of poverty or from infamy, because all murderers and evildoers pay for their crimes in that place that had earned a most odious name for cursing the Paphlagonians. Cedrinus also writes that in the same place there was a great Temple of the Sun and Moon. It had a work by Phidalia: the Sun in a white chariot and the Moon as a bride being brought on a four-horse team to her husband. Below, next to the foundation and seated on a throne, was the statue of a scepter-bearing figure instructing the populace to obey their rules; and in the same place on the ground was a statue of Jupiter in white marble, reclining on a couch, the work of Phidias. Previously the house was named the Craterum, after Craterus the Sophist. His desk was in it, as was celebrated by the verses of Julian of Egypt.[109]

In addition the Ninth Ward contained the Baths of Anastasia, which Marcellinus says were named after Constantine's sister Anastasia.[110] Sozomen says that Marcian the Grammarian instructed Emperor Valens' two daughters, Anastasia and Carosa, and that the baths named after them existed in Constantinople in his day.[111]

IX. The Third Valley and the Tenth Ward of the City; the Residence of Placidia and Palace of Placidia; the Aqueduct of Valens; the Baths of Constantine; the Nymphaeum

From the *Ancient Description of the City* it is clear that the Tenth Ward inclined to the north and was situated in the third valley. Its eastern side was also on the promontory towering above the third valley, through which the aqueduct runs from the west to the east with many arches above the ground. These become vaulted structures underground.[112] The *Ancient Description* says that the Ninth Ward is entirely inclined towards the south. It turns, continuing to the edge of the seashore. The Tenth Ward on the other side of the city is divided from the Ninth Ward by a great broad way as if cut in half by a river. It is more flat in this district except near the sea. Its terrain is uneven along its length and does not get any shorter in width. It contains the church of St. Acatius, the Baths of Constantine, the palace of Placidia Augusta, the greater Nymphaeum and many others, of which nothing remains. Nor could I find traces no matter how long and diligently I searched.[113] I was not able to learn from anyone living in which part of the Tenth Ward these buildings were, but at least I gathered some things from deceased authors.

From these sources I discovered an error in the manuscript of the *Ancient Description of the Wards* where its says that the Tenth Ward contained the Baths of Constantine, which never were in Constantinople. But there were, at least, the Baths of Constantius, which Sozomen of Salamis mentions when speaking of those who fled from Constantinople because they supported John Chrysostom. He says, "sensing the hysteria of the populace, they left the Great Church the following day and celebrated Holy Communion in the public bath, exceedingly spacious for the great crowd, named after Emperor Constantius."[114] Suidas says that in the time of Theodosius II Helladius

Alexandrinus wrote an *ekphrasis* on the Baths of Constantine.[115] Socrates claims that Emperor Valens ordered the walls of Chalcedon dismantled and the stones transported to Constantinople to build a public bath that was called the Constantius Baths. He adds that on one of the stones that were transported a prophecy was carved that was hidden ever since ancient times, then was discovered, foretelling that when there would be abundant water in the city then a wall would certainly be used for a bath. Numberless barbarian nations would invade Roman territory, perpetrating many evils, but in the end they themselves would perish. Socrates gives the prophecy as follows:

Ἀλλ ὅτε δὴ νύμφαι δροσερὴν κατὰ ἄστυ χορείην
τερπόμεναι στήσωνται εὐστεφέας κατ ἀγυιὰς,
Καὶ τεῖχος λουτροῖο πολύστονον ἔσσεται ἄλκαρ.
Δὴ τοτε μυρία φῦλα πολυσπερέων ἀνθρώπων,
Ἄγρια μαρμαίροντα, κακὴν ἐπιειμένα ἀλκὴν,
Ἴστρου καλλιρόοιο πόρον διαβάντα σὺν αἰχμῃ (?),
καὶ ξκυθικὴν ὁ λέσει χώρην καὶ Μυσηΐδα γαῖυν,
Θρηϊκίης δ ἐπιβάντα σὺν ἐλπίσι μαινομένῃσιν,
Αὐτοῦ κεν βιότοιο τέλος, καὶ πότμον ἐμπίσποι.

When delicate virgins shall dance in circles
Around the public cistern and decorate
Its great interior with flowers, and when
The streets are perfumed with sweet smells and adorned
With garlands and when the waters shall flood over the top,
And a stone basin fashioned to receive them,
A great army in shining armor,
Of a wild and belligerent race, shall come from a great distance
And cross the silver currents of the Danube,
And Scythia and the boundless territory of Maesia
Will be razed by their victorious sword,
And all of Thrace will dread the arrival of this event.[116]

Zonaras and Cedrinus both record this same prediction, but where Socrates writes δροσερήν they write ἴερην, and other wordings are different, for example λουτροῖσι for λουτροίο and ἄγρα μαργαίροντα for ἄγρια μαρμαίροντα and κιμμεριόιο for καλλιρόοιο.[117] Socrates interprets the prophecy as follows. He says this prediction later came to pass: when Valens constructed an aqueduct, which supplied abundant water to the city, the barbarian nations invaded the lands of the Romans. This

41. Aqueduct of Valens, view from north, looking southeast.

prophecy can be interpreted in another way, for after Valens introduced the aqueduct into the city, Clearchus, prefect of the city, constructed a large ὑδρεῖον (cistern) in the forum now called the Forum of Theodosius. In the voice of the people this is celebrated as abundant water in the place where the city celebrates a joyous festival. And this was predicted by the prophecy, "...χορείην τερπόμεναι στησίωνται εὐστεφέας κατ᾽ ἀγυιας..." But a second thing came to pass a little later in accordance with a second prophecy: when the wall of Chalcedon was being dismantled for Byzantium, the Nicomedians, Niceans and Bithynians implored Emperor Valens to stop destroying the wall. The emperor, angered, barely acknowledged their entreaties, and so that he might absolve himself from an oath obliging him not to demolish it, he ordered that at the same time the Chalcedonian wall was demolished, they fill it in with other long stones. Today one can see that in certain parts of the wall a cheap construction had been built by Valens on the huge and wonderful blocks.[118] Zonaras and Cedrinus likewise say that in order to punish the Chalcedonians for sheltering his enemy Procopius, Valens had the stones from the ruins of the Chalcedonian walls transported over for the aqueduct building, which Zonaras calls the Valens, but Cedrinus sometimes calls it the Aqueduct of Valens and sometimes the Valentinian. It brought copious amounts of water into the city, not only for other uses but also for the baths, including the one that the prefect of the city made in the Taurus called the Nymphaeum, worthy of the magnitude of the city.[119] And when an annual feast was declared, he invited the whole populace to the banquet. Not long afterwards (as the prediction said) the barbarians invaded Thrace, after which they were annihilated.[120]

The Valentinian Aqueduct still exists with towering arches, from the slopes of the fourth hill to the slopes of the third hill, continuing through the Tenth Ward. I would have been surprised that the *Ancient Description of the Wards of the City* does not mention it, since it mentions the Valentinian Granaries, except I am aware that it also neglects to mention a great number of monuments that existed at that time.[121] In the reign of Constantine Iconomachus, son of Leo, in the 759th year from the human birth of Christ, there was such a drought that the dew did not even fall from the sky, and the cisterns, baths and fountains of Constantinople, which had flowed continuously before, dried up. When Emperor Constantine saw this he set about repairing the Valentinian Aqueduct, which had remained sound up to the time of Heraclius, when it was cut by the Avars. He rebuilt it with workers summoned from diverse places. From Asia and Pontus a thousand builders and two hundred workers of white stone, from Greece five hundred brick-makers, from Thrace five thousand workers and haulers, and two hundred tile-workers. Over all of these he put executive managers and foremen and a single patrician. When the work was completed the water entered the city, coursing through the territory of the Ninth and Tenth Wards.[122]

In fact, many aqueducts course underground through the ridges of six hills, and one, the Aqueduct of Valens, is above ground. Those who have written of the deeds of Emperor Andronicus say that it went through the Great Forum, carrying sweet and pure water. Emperor Andronicus repaired it, enlarged it, and added to it the river they call the Hydrales. At its source he built a tower and a palace where he relaxed in summer, and he brought water from the same river into the place in the city that they call Blachernae. But Isaac, his successor, destroyed the tower out of hatred for Andronicus.[123]

Procopius says that Justinian restored the dilapidated church of Acacius, surrounding it on all sides with white columns. With similar marble he covered the floor of the building and dressed the church in dazzling white stone so that the entire church appeared to be covered in snow. Two porticos were adjacent to the church, one of which, surrounded by columns, led to the forum. Now the previous description is not in the edited text of Procopius' writings, and so I gladly add it here.[124] George Cedrinus says that the church of Acacius was in a place called the Heptascalum [Seven Steps], other writers say the church of St. Acacius was in a place called the Scala, but no one today knows where it was.[125] But whoever desires to make diligent inquiry after this little note, he should look for the Great Palace, which historians call the Caria from the nut tree that was in this area, from which they say the martyr Acacius perished by hanging. Later a shrine was consecrated to him, which some think had been situated in the Neorium because they have read in the writings of a good many authors that the image of Acacius, fashioned from gilded glass beads, was placed in a church located in the Neorium.[126] But this is a different Acacius, whom not only the historians but even Suidas the Grammarian identify as bishop of Constantinople in the reign of Leo Macellus, who was so very ambitious that many people put up images of Acacius in the churches while he was still alive. From that time on he was called Doxomanes.[127]

A little while ago we saw that the Palace of Placidia was in the First Ward. So see if it should be correctly read as being in the Tenth Ward, or whether it should be read as the Palace of Placilla or as Placidae. For Agathias mentions the palaces of Placidae, or Placidi, in these verses in an inscription:

εἰς εἰκόνα ἀνατεθεῖσαν ἐν τοῖς Πλακιδιάς ὑπὸ τῶν τοῦ νέου σκρινίου.
Θωμᾶν, παμβασιλῆος ἀμεμφέα κηδεμονῆα,
ἄνθεσαν οἱ τὸ νέον τάγμα μετερχόμενοι,
θεσπεσίης ἄγχιστα συνωρίδος, ὄφρα καὶ αὐτῇ
εἰκόνι χῶρον ἔχῃ γείτονα κοιρανιής
αὐτὸς γὰρ ζαθέοιο θρόνους ὕψωσε μελάθρου,
πλοῦτον ἀεξήσας, ἀλλὰ μετὶ εὐσεβίης.[128]

Upon an image in the Palaces of Placidia, set up by the new men of the
  chancery:
The men entering the new position dedicated
Thomas, the blameless guardian of the all-powerful Emperor,
Near the royal couple, so through Thomas's image
He may be in proximity to sovereignty. For he raised the thrones of the
  sacred palace

By increasing the wealth, but with piety too.
The work is gratefully given, for what can the stilus give
If not the memory owed to good men?

Past the Scironides Rocks, which I said before were on the north side of the third hill, Dionysius of Byzantium says the seashore of the third valley and fourth hill was a long coastal plain no worse than any of the best for catching fish, for the water is especially deep and still near the mouth of the sea. This place was once called Cycla because the Greeks had trapped the barbarians here. And here there was also an altar to Minerva Dissipatoria, in reference to the routing of the trapped barbarians. Beyond Cycla is the bay of Melias, like the other well suited for fishing. It is concealed by the towering summits of the promontory and by rocks on each side.[129] Today there is no bay left in this valley for it has been obliterated by time and built over. This is evident not only from the bay of the Melias stream, but also from Strabo, where he says this bay was called the Horn because it was branched into many recesses like the horn of a deer.[130] But none of these inlets remain today, except very few.

Zosimus, who wrote his history in the time of Arcadius and Honorius, testifies that in his day there were such multitudes of people crowded into Constantinople that not only did the emperors extend the walls beyond the Constantinian walls, but they also covered a large portion of the sea surrounding the city with pilings driven in and buildings placed on top of these posts. What and how much sea from the time of Arcadius and Honorius it was possible to cover can be seen from how many and how great are the ruins of the city extending into the sea.[131] Dionysius says that at the end of the bay of Melias was a place called Κῆπος [Garden], from the soil there being so exceptionally suited for growing plants.[132] Beyond this garden is a place called Apsasius, which we have mentioned in relation to the Bosporus.[133]

❧

Notes to Book III

1. "Light-bringing."

2. Stephanos Byzantinii, *A Geographical Lexicon,* 177–79; Müller-Wiener, *Bildlexikon,* 57–58.

3. *Notitia urbis CP,* 233–34.

4. Dionysius Byzantius, *Anaplus Bospori,* ed. Güngerich, 5 ll. 15–19; 6 ll. 1–5.

5. Dionysius Byzantius, *Anaplus Bospori,* ed. Güngerich, 6, l. 3.

6. Cedrinus, *Historiarum compendium,* Bonn ed. I, 563; Janin, *CPByz2,* 432; Cedrinus also says there was a mounted statue of Constantine holding a cross in the Strategion.

7. Evagrius, *Ecclesiastical History,* II.13, ed. Allen, 111.

8. Zonaras, *Epitomae historiarum,* XIV.1, Bonn ed., 124–25.

9. Cedrinus, *Historiarum compendium,* Bonn ed. I, 610.

10. On John Calybites, see: Janin, *Églises,* 270–71. See Majeska, *Russian Travelers,* 154, footnotes; on the ports in Wards V and VI, see *PatriaCP,* 232–34.

11. Zosimus, *New History,* II.30 (p. 37).

12. Chrysopolis/Scutari is modern Üsküdar.

13. *Notitia urbis CP,* 234.

14. *PatriaCP,* II, 180; II, 188; II, 196; III, 271.

15. Gilles means Mt. Attaviros, the highest peak on the island of Rhodes. See J. Sandys, *Pindar's Odes,* (New York: Macmillan, 1924), xxv.

16. Justinian I, *Corpus iuris civilis,* ed. T. Mommsen, P. Kruger, et al. (Berlin: Weidmann, 1899–1902; 2nd ed. Hildesheim: Weidmann, 1928–29), *Codex Iustinianus,* 11.43.6.

17. Socrates, *Hist. Eccles.*, I.16.102–3.

18. *Notitia urbis CP,* 233, 235, 239.

19. *Anthol. Palat.*, IX.658; Fr. Dubner, II, 134–35; Janin, *CPByz2,* 167–68.

20. *Notitia urbis CP,* 234.

21. Ibid.

22. On the Porphyry Column of Constantine, its statue, chapel and history, see Mango, *Studies on Constantinople,* I–IV. As for sources on column that Gilles does not site directly, it appears he could have used Anna Comnena's *Alexiad,* ed. Leib, 3 vols. (Paris: Les Belles Lettres, 1937, 1967), III, 66–67; Cedrinus, *Historiarum compendium,* I, 656; *PatriaCP,* 174; Zonaras, *Epitomae historiarum,* XIII.3, Bonn ed., III, 18.

23. Janin, *CPByz2,* 83.

24. Cedrinus, *Historiarum compendium,* Bonn ed. I, 564–65.

25. Zonaras, *Epitomae historiarum,* XIII.3, Bonn ed., 18; As Mango, again, points out, Gilles seems to have obtained this tale from Glycas (Bonn ed., 617) and so may have had a this quote from Glycas before him when writing of the column.

See Mango, "Constantinopolitana," *Studies*, II:312; Michael Glycas, *Annales*, ed. Immanuel Bekker, CSHB (Bonn: Weber, 1836), 617.

26. Anna Comnena, *Alexiad*, XII.4,5, ed. Leib III:66f; *Alexiad*, trans. Elizabeth Dawes (London: Kegan Paul, 1928), 309; but Anna Comnena does not appear to state that any drums were damaged, just the statue. Nor does she mention any victims. Mango, *Studies*, II:312 believes Gilles may have been citing Glycas (Bonn ed., 617) or Attaliates (Bonn ed., 310) and mistranslated the Greek. See also Zonaras, *Epitomae historiarum*, XIII.3.27 and XVIII.26.21–22, Bonn ed. III, 18, 755 and *PatriaCP*, II, 138. It appears to me that Gilles may have gotten the story of the statue's demise from a variety of sources and conflated them. There is no way to tell for sure if he used Glycas, whom he does not cite by name. When Gilles uses a source for which he knows the author he often but not always gives the name.

27. See Mango, *Studies*, II:307. The pedestal of the column, from excavations, is only 3.8 meters wide.

28. As Mango has repeatedly pointed out, Gilles is (unusually) in error here for there are seven, not eight, porphyry drums. See Mango, *Studies*, II:310f.

29. Athenaeus, *Deipnosophistae*, trans. Charles Burton Gulick, LCL, 7 vols. (1967), 2, v. 205–6.

30. The Latin contains a reference here to Pylian of Pylos, that is Nestor, who in Homer was several generations old. See *Iliad* I, line 247f. I thank Patrick Myers for pointing out this reference to me.

31. This quote comes from the Anonymous Panegyric on Constantine, the *Panegyrici Latini* VII (6), trans. Mark Vermes in Samuel N.C. Lieu and Dominic Montserrat, eds., *From Constantine to Julian: Pagan and Byzantine Views* (London: Routledge, 1996), 76–91; this quote, 90. My translation.

32. Zonaras, *Epitomae historiarum*, XIII.3, Bonn ed, III, 18; Procopius on Forum of Constantine, *Buildings*, Bonn ed. III, 190.

33. Socrates, *Hist. Eccles.*, I.38, 169–72. Despite what Gilles writes, Socrates here does not use the term τό Πλακωτόν for the Forum of Constantine, but writes: ἀγορᾶς Κωνσταντίνου. But the term doubtless applies to the flat space of the forum or flat paving stones therein, see Janin, *CPByz2*, 62–63.

34. Zonaras, *Epitomae historiarum*, XIII.3, Bonn ed. III, 18; Procopius, *Buildings*, I.5, Bonn ed. III, 190.

35. Procopius, *Gothic Wars*, V.15.9–14, Bonn ed. II, 78.

36. Ibid.

37. Pausanias, *Description of Greece*, I.24.5–7, I.28.9, II.23.5; idem, *Gothic Wars*, V.15.9–14.

38. Pessinus (modern Balıhisar) was a key center for the cult of Phrygian Cybele. Livy records that her sacred stone was taken to Rome. Livy, *Histories*, 29.10.4; *OCD*, 1148; Diodorus Siculus, *Bibliotheca historica*, trans. C.H. Oldfather, LCL, XIII.90.4.

39. Procopius, *Gothic Wars,* V.15.9–14, Bonn ed. II, 78; Gilles seems to be discussing the great statue of Athena outside the Senate House on the Forum of Constantine that was destroyed by a mob that feared the statue was beckoning to crusaders threatening the city. See Mango, "Antique Statuary," 62–63; and R.J.H. Jenkins, "The Bronze Athena at Byzantium," *Journal of Hellenic Studies* 67 (1947): 31–33.

40. *PatriaCP,* 234 and 233.

41. Zonaras, *Epitomae historiarum,* XIII.25, Bonn ed. III, 123–26; Cedrinus, *Historiarum compendium,* Bonn ed. I, 565.

42. Cedrinus, *Historiarum compendium,* Bonn ed. I, 565. Cedrinus does not speak of a Nymphaeum in this passage that I can see, but he does mention the Nymphaeum, see Cedrinus, *Historiarum compendium,* Bonn ed. I, 543.

43. Cedrinus, *Historiarum compendium,* Bonn ed. I, 565; Choniates, *Nicetae Choniatae historia,* CSHB (Bonn), 559. See also Jenkins, "Bronze Athena," 31–33.

44. *PatriaCP,* II, 204–5.

45. Sozomen, *Eccl. Hist.,* I.4; For Eusebius on the Labarum, see *Ecclesiastical History,* 10.4.16 and 9.9.10f., ed. Schwartz (1903–9) and the *Vita Constantini,* 2.8, ed. Winkelmann (1975). For the ornamenting of Constantinople by Constantine, see above. On cross of precious stones in the Imperial Palace, see *Vita Constantini,* 3.49, ed. Winkelmann (1975).

46. This is a direct quote from Prudentius' *Reply to Address of Symmachus* in Prudentius, trans. H.J. Thomson, 2 vols., LCL (1949–53), 386f., ll. 486–88: Christus purpureum gemmanti textus in auro / signabat labarum, clipeorum insignia Christus / scripserat, ardebat summis crux addita cristis. I have used my translation.

47. For Eusebius on the Labarum, see *Ecclesiastical History,* 10.4.16 and 9.9.10f, ed Schwartz (1903–9) and the *Vita Constantini,* 2.8, ed. Winkelmann (1975). The secondary literature on Constantine's vision and his alteration of the Roman standard, or Labarum, is extensive. I consulted, for example: H.A. Drake, *In Praise of Constantine: A Historical Study and New Translation* (Berkeley: University of California Press, 1975), 72f. and notes; Jones, *Constantine and the Conversion of Europe* (New York: Macmillan, 1949), 94f.; Barnes, *Constantine and Eusebius* (Cambridge, MA: Harvard University Press, 1981), 42–43, 306–7; A. Alföldi, *Conversion of Constantine and Pagan Rome* (Oxford: Clarendon Press, 1948), 16f., 72, 75.

48. Gilles' paraphrasing of Tertullian is very strange and difficult to understand; Tertullian, *Apology,* xvi in *The Ante-Nicene Fathers: Translations of the Writings of the Fathers,* ed. Alexander Roberts and James Donaldson, rev. ed. A. Cleveland Coxe (Peabody, MA: Hendrickson Publishers, 1994), vol. 3. I have used the translation in Coxe's edition.

49. More correctly: Minucius Felix; he was a contemporary of Tertullian (whom Gilles also quotes here). His *Octavius* appears as Book VIII in manuscripts of Arnobius, hence Gilles assumption that the two are one and the same; it was not

until 1560 that Franciscus Balduinus discovered the error and corrected it. See *The Ante-Nicene Fathers*, ed. Coxe, vol. 4, Introduction to Minucius Felix, *Octavius*.

50. Translation in part from *The Ante-Nicene Fathers*, ed. Coxe, vol 4, Minucius Felix, *Octavius*, xxix.

51. Or rather *siparum*; Seneca, *Epistulae morales ad Lucilium*, trans. Richard Gummere, LCL, 3 vols. (1967), IX.lxxvii.1.

52. Lucan, M. *Annaei Lucani Pharsalia*, ed. C.E. Haskins (London: George Bell & Sons, 1887), V.429; I have been unable to identify this reference in Affranius.

53. Sextus Pomponius Festus, *De verborum significatu quae supersunt cum Pauli epitome*, ed. Wallace M. Lindsay (Leipzig: Teubner, 1913), xvii.

54. By the "Satiric Poet," Gilles means Horace, from whose *Sermones* or *Satires* he is quoting here; see Q. *Horati Flacci Carmina*, ed. Fr. Vollmer (Leipzig: Teubner, 1907), *Sermones* II.iii.15–22.

55. Apuleius, *Metamorphoses* 10.29, translation in *The Context of Ancient Drama*, trans. William J. Slater and Eric Csapo. (Ann Arbor: University of Michigan Press 1995), 384–85.

56. I have been unable to find this precise reference in Seneca using Gilles' wording.

57. The Arch of Constantine in Rome.

58. Eusebius, *Ecclesiastical History*, 9.9.1ff., ed. Schwartz (1903–9); *Vita Constantini*, 1.27ff., ed. Winkelmann (1975).

59. Nazarius Rhetor, *XII panegyrici Latini* (Leipzig: B.G. Teubner, 1874), Pan. Lat. 4(10).17.2, 37,1ff. See also Alföldi, *Conversion of Constantine*, 72, 75; Barnes, *Constantine and Eusebius*, 73, 323; Samuel N.C. Lieu and Dominic Montserrat, *From Consatantine to Julian: Pagan and Byzantine Views. A Source History* (London & New York: Routledge, 1996), 66.

60. *Anthol. Graeca.* IX.799 and 800.

61. *PatriaCP*, II, 177–78.

62. *Anthol. Graec.*, XVI.39.

63. Socrates, *Hist. Eccles.*, I.38, 169–72.

64. For the preceding paragraph see Dionysius Byzantius, *Anaplus Bospori*, ed. Güngerich, 6 ll. 6–11; 7 ll. 1–3.

65. Gilles, *Bosporo Thracio*, II.ii.

66. *PatriaCP*, 235.

67. Ibid.

68. The Latin here is confused and the reference to Livy is not entirely clear.

69. Cedrinus, *Historiarum compendium*, Bonn ed. I, 647–48; Janin, *CPByz2*, 99.

70. Marcus Terentius Varro, *Varro on the Latin Language*, trans. Roland G. Kent, 2 vols., LCL, 7.2.

71. Gilles' 1561 first edition reads "Naustathmos," a misprint or misspelling.

72. Livy, *Histories*, 37.31.8–14, LCL, 10:382f.

73. Pliny, *Natural History*, III.iv.31 mentions this body of water but does not use the term *"Lamptera"* or *"Lampterum."*

74. Cedrinus, *Historiarum compendium*, Bonn ed. I, 567. See D. Stiernon, "Le Quartier du Xerolophos à Constantinople et les réliques venitiennes du Saint Athanase," *REB* 19 (1961): 165–88; Alice-Mary Talbot, ed., *The Correspondence of Athanasius* (Washington DC: Dumbarton Oaks, 1975), xxvii.

75. Zonaras, *Epitomae historiarum*, XIV.4, Bonn ed., III, 144–45.

76. Evagrius, *Ecclesiastical History*, II.13.

77. Zonaras actually reads Ἀρτοπρατίων, not Artopoleion. See Zonaras, *Epitomae historiarum*, XVI.26, 511.

78. Artopoleion/Bread Market. See Magdalino, *Constantinople Médiévale*, 21f.; Janin, *CPByz2*, 94, 95, 315.

79. Cedrinus, *Historiarum compendium*, Bonn ed. I, 658 in this passage on the the fire relative to the bronze Tetrapylon mentions Julian, not Leo; Janin, *CPByz2*, 329; Mango, "Development of Constantinople," *Studies*, I:129f. and "Columns of Justinian," *Studies*, X:15.

80. *PatriaCP*, III, 243.

81. Evagrius, *Ecclesiastical History*, III.24–28, ed. Allen, 139–40. Evagrius mentions the Sentator Mamianus and the Tetrapylon as being in Antioch — apparently from the Greek Malalas.

82. *PatriaCP*, II, 181.

83. Cedrinus, *Historiarum compendium*, Bonn ed. I, 565–66; Janin, *CPByz2*, 100. (But Janin gives the wrong citation in Cedrinus; it is I, 565–66 not I, 555.) Gilles is speaking here of the monumental weathervane in the shape of a pyramid called the Anemodoulion. See Mango, "Columns of Justinian," *Studies*, X:5; A. Berger, *Untersuchungen zu den Patria Konstantinupoleos* (Bonn: Habelt, 1988), 313–14. As Mango was quick to point out, Berger has mistakenly equated the bronze Tetrapylon with the Anemodoulion for some reason.

84. See the *Parastaseis Syntomoi Chronikon*, I. 65, which Mango calls an unreliable source, but it does mention this similar arrangement of statues, although that of Theodosius was silver, with the images of Arcadius and Honorius lower, closer to the ground. See also Mango, "Columns of Justinian," *Studies*, X:8.

85. Socrates, *Hist. Eccles.*, IV.8, 483–86.

86. Zonaras, *Epitomae historiarum*, XIII.16, Bonn ed. III, 80–82; Cedrinus, *Historiarum compendium*, Bonn ed. I, 543.

87. Socrates, *Hist. Eccles.*, IV.8, 483–86; Cedrinus, *Historiarum compendium*, Bonn ed. I, 566.

88. *PatriaCP*, 235.

89. Ibid.

90. Choniates, *Nicetae Choniatae historiae*, 554–55; Janin, *Églises*, 107f.

91. There were a number of churches to Hagia Irene in Constantinople since the Byzantines venerated several saints with this name. It is difficult to tell, as Gilles shows, which Irene is meant. For instance, relics of St. Irene are recorded by Russian travelers in Kyra Martha as well as Lips monastery, and St. Irene, wife of John II Comnenus, was buried in the Pantocrator monastery, of which she was the foundress. See Majeska, *Russian Travelers*, 311; Janin, *Églises*, 107f.

92. Socrates, *Hist. Eccles.*, II.6, 187 and I.16,103.

93. *PatriaCP*, 235; Procopius, *Buildings*, I.7, Bonn ed. III, 195

94. Sozomen, *Eccl. Hist.*, VII.5.

95. Ibid.

96. *PatriaCP*, 235; Cedrinus, *Historiarum compendium*, Bonn ed. I, 658; Majeska, *Russian Travelers*, 336–37; Van Millingen, *Walls*, 174–77 and 195–96; Janin, *Églises*, 388. Majeska notes that the church of St. Anastasia, which Van Millingen and Janin place in the Blachernae region, is actually the church of the Holy Resurrection, further east than the Blachernae.

97. Gilles, *Bosporo Thracio*, II.ii.

98. Procopius, *Buildings*, I.5, Bonn ed. III, 190. Procopius reads: Ῥησίῳ.

99. *PatriaCP*, 235–36.

100. This main artery was the Mese.

101. Cedrinus, *Historiarum compendium*, Bonn ed. I, 610; Janin, *CPByz2*, 154f.

102. The Ottoman building Gilles refers to in passing here must be the Şehzade Camii complex on the third hill that was built by the great Sinan. Completed in 1548, the mosque was erected in honor of Suleyman's eldest son Prince Mehmet, who perished from smallpox in his early twenties.

103. *PatriaCP*, 236–37.

104. *PatriaCP*, 237.

105. Evagrius, *Ecclesiastical History*, III.13, ed. Allen, 111.

106. The Myrelion, which means The Place of Myrrh, or Bodrum Cami as it is called today, is the Byzantine church erected by Emperor Romanos Lacapenos in the 920s and is one of the earliest known quincunx-plan churches in the city. See Thomas Mathews, *The Byzantine Churches of Istanbul: A Photographic Survey* (University Park-London: The Pennsylvania State University Press, 1976), 209f.; and especially, Cecil L. Striker, *The Myrelaion (Bodrum Camii)* (Princeton: Princeton University Press, 1981).

107. Suda, *Lexikon*, III.616; Janin, *CPByz2*, 394–95; Janin, *Églises*, 364–66.

108. *PatriaCP*, II, 179 and II, 202; Janin, *CPByz2*, 66.

109. Cedrinus, *Historiarum compendium*, Bonn ed. I, 566–67.

110. Ammianus Marcellinus, *Rerum gestarum libri*, XXVI.6.14, ed. John C. Rolfe, LCL, 606–7.

111. Sozomen, *Eccl. Hist.*, VI.9.

112. *PatriaCP*, 237–38.

113. *PatriaCP*, 236–38.

114. Sozomen, *Eccl. Hist.*, VIII.21.

115. Suda, *Lexikon*, II.238; Janin, *CPByz2*, 220.

116. Socrates, *Hist. Eccles.*, IV.8, 483–86; Socrates, *Hist. Eccles.*, PG, 219, 476–77. The translation is by Hussey.

117. Cedrinus, *Historiarum compendium*, Bonn ed. I, 543; Socrates, *Hist. Eccles.*, IV.8, 483–86.

118. Socrates, *Hist. Eccles.*, IV.8, 483–86; Cedrinus, *Historiarum compendium*, Bonn ed. I, 543–44.

119. Zonaras, *Epitomae historiarum*, XIII.16, Bonn ed. III, 80–82; The Nymphaeum Baths were erected under Valens c.372–73. See Müller-Wiener, *Bildlexikon*, 258.

120. Cedrinus, *Historiarum compendium*, Bonn ed. I, 543–44.

121. *PatriaCP*, 237–38.

122. Theophanes, *The Chronicle of Theophanes*, 608; Müller-Wiener, *Bildlexikon*, 273–74.

123. Niketas Choniates, Bonn ed., 428; Janin, *CPByz2*, 140–41.

124. Procopius, *Buildings*, I.4.25–26, Bonn ed. III, 190–91. Gilles appears to have had access to various manuscripts of Procopius, but unfortunately, he does not tell us where he obtained these works — in Rome or Constantinople or elsewhere.

125. Cedrinus, *Historiarum compendium*, Bonn ed. II, 240 and also I, 679. Yet he refers to Heptascalion here by the name of the adjacent district and palace of Kaisarius. Van Millingen, *Walls*, 302f.; Janin, *CPByz2*, 229f.; Janin, *Églises*, 17–18 on the two St. Acacius churches' possible locations; *Theophanes Continuatus*, Bonn ed., 324; Ioannes Cantacuzenus, *Historia-Historiarium*, ed. L. Schopen, 3 vols. (Bonn: Weber, 1828–32), III, 72, 165, 212.

126. Janin, *Églises*, 17–18; idem, *CPByz2*, 396–97.

127. In other words a fame-seeker, from δοξομαν ἧς; Suda, *Lexikon*, I, 74; Janin, *Églises*, 17ff.

128. Agathias Scholasticus, *Anthol. Planud.*, XVI.41, Bonn ed., 388.

129. Dionysius Byzantius, *Anaplus Bospori*, ed. Güngerich, 7 ll. 7–12; 8 ll. 1–5.

130. Strabo, *Geography*, VII.6.2.

131. Zosimus, *New History*, II.35 (pp. 39–40).

132. Dionysius Byzantius, *Anaplus Bospori*, ed. Güngerich, 8 ll. 6–11.

133. Ibid., 8 ll. 10 and 11.

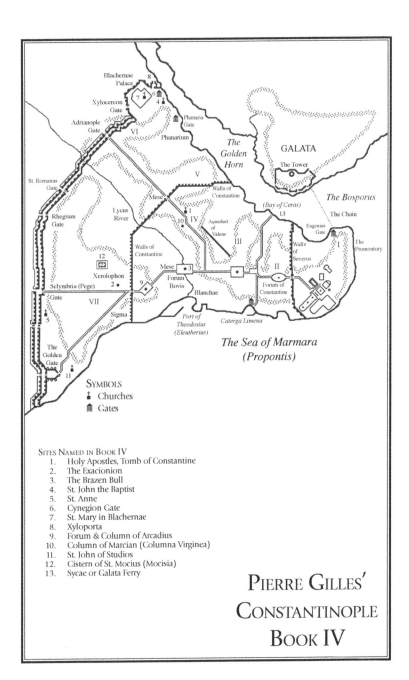

SYMBOLS

🜊 Churches

🏛 Gates

PIERRE GILLES'
CONSTANTINOPLE
BOOK IV

BOOK IV

I would have barely recognized the Eleventh Ward from the *Description of the Wards of the City*, which says that its area was spread out rather freely; in no part was it joined to the sea.[1] In fact, its extent is just as flat as it is uneven with hills, except the *Description* adds that the Eleventh Ward contained the church of the Martyred Apostles. Although nothing remains today, nevertheless I learned from the recollections of older Constantinopolitans that it was on the ridge of the fourth hill that declined onto the ridge of the third valley near the workshops of the saddle-makers and the tomb of Sultan Mehmet. I took note of this and concluded that the Eleventh Ward was on the back of the fourth hill and on the side of it that inclines to the north just as much as it is situated on the back side of it. I will show below that this ward reached the Land Walls of the city, which divided the Eleventh Ward from the Fourteenth Ward, which was also separated from the city by an intervening space and fortified with its own wall, which was on the sixth hill outside the Constantinian city walls and later enclosed by Theodosius II.

The Constantinian walls are reported to have extended from the tower of Eugenius to the church of St. Anthony and the church of St Mary, who was called Rabdos, and from here to have risen up to the land wall, the Exacionion, which had been named because of the fact that outside the land walls there was a column supporting a statue of Constantine the Great. Recent writers say Constantine erected a church to the Holy Trinity in the place called the Exacionion, now called the church of the Holy Apostles. These writers, if I correctly understood them, say that the Constantinian walls were constructed on the border of the fourth and fifth hills near the Exacionion.[2] George Cedrinus says that the walls of the city, the decorated churches and splendid palaces were in parts of the city in the Exacionion that were demolished in a horrible earthquake.

These same authors are not consistent among themselves in another place where they say porticos extended from the Miliarium to the Taurus and to the Bronze Bull and the gates of the church of St. John of the Hippodrome, which are more than 1000 Roman paces away from the church of the Holy Apostles, and almost equally far from the walls set up by Constantine.[3] This can be deduced from Sozomen. He says that Theodosius, leading his army against Eugenius, marched out one mile outside Constantinople to the church of St. John the Baptist, which he had constructed in the Hebdomon suburb, and there prayed that the outcome of the war was fortunate for himself and the army. For in fact a Greek codex of Sozomen has the following:

Θεωδόσιος λέγεται δὲ τοτε τῆς Κωνσταντινουπόλεως ἐκδημῶν, πρὸς τῷ Ἑβδόμῳ μιλίῳ γενόμενος, προσεύξασθαι τῷ θεῷ ἐν τῇ ἐνθάδε ἐκκλησία, ἥν ἐπὶ τιμῇ Ἰωάννου τοῦ Βαπτιστοῦ ἐδείματο, αἰτῆσαί τε αἰσίαν αὐτῷ τῆκαί στρατι ᾶ καὶ Ῥωμαίοις ἅπασι γενέσθαι τὴν ἔκβασιν τοῦ τολέμου....[4]

Leaving Constantinople and coming to the Hebdomon milestone, Theodosius prayed in that church built in honor of John the Baptist to ask that the outcome of the war be good for himself, the army and the Romans....

Those who do not know that the Hebdomon was a suburb of Constantinople think this meant that Theodosius went seven miles outside of the city. But it is not clear from the same Sozomen that the Hebdomon was a suburb since he says elsewhere that Theodosius transferred the head of John the Baptist from the village called Coslaus, which bordered the neighborhood of Chalcedon, and put it before Constantinople in the place called the Hebdomon, which we said was once a suburb.[5] But in fact, now I will say that it was inside the city walls on the sixth hill.[6]

If the column after which they call the place the Exacionion was the one discussed earlier that towered far higher on the ridge of the fifth hill above all the houses, then we might easily understand that the walls that Constantine set up did not proceed beyond this column, which was located approximately four stadia distant from the church of the Apostles. I saw this column transferred for use in the construction of a religious building that Sultan Suleyman ordered built. Its shaft was of fiery, intricate marble, about 60 feet high, its perimeter 13¾ feet, with a Corinthian capital of white marble. Its pedestal, stylobate and base were even of white marble. The stylobate was so tall I would have needed a ladder to climb it. The stylobate was 4 feet 9 digits tall, and the plinth one foot 6 digits high. The Greeks and Turks, in both languages, call this the Column of the Virgin, which I assume is the same celebrated by recent writers who say that it was set up on a hill and supported a stone statue of Venus. They also say it distinguished virgins suspected of lust from those who were untouched by it. For if virginal and pure women approached it, they departed unharmed, but if corrupted women approached, they stripped themselves and exposed their private parts.[7]

Since the *Ancient Description of the Wards of the City* says that the Eleventh Ward does not touch the sea at all, one ought to suppose that the plain situated between the Golden Horn and the base of the fourth hill was outside the city. And although this *Description of the Wards* says the width of the city extended 6,150 feet, that is, one mile and 230 paces, in fact the width of the isthmus, running across the fourth and seventh hills (through which the ancient wall ran), exceeds the width described.[8] But the ancient historian Zosimus has it that Constantine the Great encircled the city with walls that cut off the whole isthmus from sea to sea.[9] And so it is fitting to place in the Tenth Ward the plain situated between the bay and the foot of the fourth hill.

II. The Church of the Holy Apostles, the Tomb of Constantine the Great, the Cisterns of Arcadius and Modestus, the Palace of Placilla, and the Bronze Bull

Eusebius writes that Constantine the Great raised the church of the Apostles to an immense height and covered it with all kinds of marbles, various and glittering, from the bottom to the top. He decorated it with a delicate, gilded coffering and covered it with bronze roof-tiles, heavily gilt, emitting splendor even to those who looked at it from far away. The upper portion of the church, distinguished by elaborately worked bronze and gold, had lattices and windows all around the church. Surrounding the church there was a beautiful courtyard standing open and uncovered to the pure air. Its porticos, arranged in a square, bordered an open area. Next to the portico were spread royal palaces, baths, ἀναλαμπτηρία,[10] and many other residential buildings constructed to facilitate the caretakers and ministers of the church. The pious emperor handed down all these to posterity in memory of the Apostles of Our Savior. Here he consecrated twelve small coffins, like holy stars, to the memory of the Apostles, and he put the coffin in which he was enclosed after death in the center of the Apostles so that he would be accompanied by six Apostles on each side.[11] Socrates adds that the body of Constantine was placed in a gold coffin and his friends bore it into the city of Constantinople, and they interred it in the church of the Apostles.[12] Zonaras, it appears, did not read Eusebius, for he says that this tomb was in the portico of the church of the Apostles, which Constantius claims had been built for the burial of his father.[13]

Following the wide street that travels across the back of the promontory from the church of Hagia Sophia to the Adrianople Gate, near the spot where I said the Apostoleon used to stand, one sees a sarcophagus made of porphyry marble but empty and without a lid, ten feet long and five and a half feet wide, which the Greeks and the Turks say is that of Constantine the Great. They will have to decide whether they speak truly. It seems doubtful to me because Eusebius and Socrates say that he was placed in a golden coffin, unless perhaps the golden coffin was placed inside this porphyry sarcophagus.[14]

Zonaras says Justinian's wife Theodora built the church of the Apostles. He adds that there had once been a church built by Constantine before the church of the Apostles, not such as is there now but less beautiful and inferior by far.[15] Procopius says that there was still a church from ancient times in Constantinople dedicated to all of the Apostles, already decayed from age and in danger of falling down. Justinian completely demolished it and was eager to rebuild it, enlarged and beautified, and in the shape of a cross. Part rose straight east and west. The other transverse section ran north and south, enclosed from the outside with walls on either side decorated on the interior all the way around with upper and lower columns.[16] Evagrius, it seems, was ignorant of the fact that Constantine the Great built it since he says that it was built by Justinian, who, as with many of the buildings, did not build it first.[17] Likewise, Procopius declares in the fashion of the rhetoricians. But he [Justinian] only renovated old buildings, or restored those that had collapsed, or restored those that were burnt.[18] There are no remaining traces of this building, not even of its foundations, except some foundations of a cistern, which supplied the church of the Holy Apostles with water. On the side of the cistern there are about 200 workshops and stalls of saddle-makers, where they manufacture and sell not only saddles and Turkish equestrian ornaments, but also leather bags for drawing water, skillfully made, and also quivers and chests covered with leather.

Above this cistern an Islamic temple with a building for travelers, the poor or ill stands on a plain. Mehmet, who captured the city, built this nearby with the same design as Hagia Sophia using the ruins of other sacred Christian churches including the church of the Apostles. It is built with finished stone and covered with a semicircular roof, made of brick and roofed with lead, as all Turkish public buildings are. He decorated it with an extremely ornate vestibule as wide as the building itself, with pavement shining with marble, and with a portico laid out in a square. The portico's arches, supporting the roof, are themselves supported by huge columns of the most exquisite marble. In the center of the entrance courtyard or atrium is a fountain cascading down into a large marble basin. Around the mosque is a huge area, enclosed partly by walls and partly by long buildings, some of which are inhabited by religious men and scholars of literature. A garden closes off the eastern part with walls, in the center of which is the tomb of Sultan Mehmet I. This is built in the shape of a cylinder, like a domed shrine, covered with shining marble, roofed with lead, illuminated with grated windows and provided with a door with a porch. In the center of this mausoleum is the sarcophagus of Mehmet, entirely covered with silk. The floor is covered with Attalic carpets upon which religious officials continuously sit, comrades attending the tomb night and day. Outside the courtyard are medresses built in the same way with squared stone, with courts at their centers and porticos encircled with marble columns. Large gardens are attached to these buildings, enclosed with walls. In short, this mosque with all its surrounding structures, including the atrium and the medresses, encloses an area of about six stadia in circumference.

Below the enclosure of these buildings the same Mehmet constructed the largest baths in the entire city on the site of an ancient cistern, which I think is either the cistern of Arcadius or of Modestus, which the *Description of the Wards of the City* places in the Eleventh Ward.[19] These baths are double and are twins, with one side for men and the other for women, of course. They are joined but have separate doors on opposite sides of the building that do not give access from one bath to the other bath. I will therefore describe the men's baths, since the women's are similar. First they have the entrance, the Apodyterium, which leads into the Tepidarium, and from the Tepidarium to the Caldarium, with which three sections the baths are connected by an entrance, but are separated by ceilings and walls arranged in proper order. The Apodyterium is a square room built with squared stone up to the circular ceiling, which is made of brick. Its interior circumference measures 240 feet 8 digits. It is encircled with a raised stone platform more than six feet wide and three feet high.

The walls of the Apodyterium, from the pavement to the springing of the ceiling arches, are 37 feet high. In the center of the Apodyterium on the marble-covered floor is a vast marble basin measuring 37 feet in circumference, three feet deep and full of springing water. With two doors a passage opens from the Apodyterium to the Tepidarium room, the interior of which measures 100 feet in circumference. It is arranged with four arches supporting the domed ceiling and making eight small rooms, one of which is made half a size smaller, with latrines in back, into which all the water from the baths flows for flushing them clean. There is a pipe in the wall of this room by which the Turks, as is their custom, wash away their excrement. Of these eight chambers there are six, each with a basin but so arranged that they each have two arches in the middle, from which one can pass into the next cell to the right and left. The other two arches of these cells are made so that what faces the doors (from which I said there was access from the Apodyterium into the Tepidarium) has a chamber as large as itself, in which there are basins where the Turks wash their clothes on the marble pavement. The fourth arch supporting the wall divides the Tepidarium from the Caldarium. In the center of the Tepidarium is a basin with gushing pipes of water. From the Tepidarium one door leads into the third part, the Caldarium, which has eight arches supporting its dome, making eight chambers going around the outside of the dome and receding into and encircling the Caldarium. It is about 90 feet in circumference and has a floor paved in marble, which in the middle is built up in an octagon, like a platform. It is 57 feet nine digits in circumference, two feet four digits tall. A trough runs around between the octagon and the pavement the same height as the octagon, by which access is had to the chambers.

The four innermost chambers are arranged in four corners, and each are 11 feet 3 digits on each side, performing the function of Laconica, in which sweat is drawn out by the dry heat. The size of the two chambers that extend beyond the two arches is the same. The other six chambers are semicircular, constructed with six arches, situated around the circumference of the dome of the Tepidarium, and between the lowest pillars of the arches they are 11 feet long, and 5 feet 9 digits wide. Each cell has a marble tub. Moreover, in one of these rooms is a great marble tub. In the walls of the Caldaria, Tepidaria and chambers there are no windows, but there are in the domed ceilings, which are full of holes. These are covered with glass projecting over the roof and bearing a similarity to inverted lamps.

Outside of the baths is the opening to the furnace, two and a half feet long and the same in width. A perpetual fire constantly heats a bronze heating element ejecting the vapor of flames into straight conduits that crisscross underground, heating the floor of the baths above.[20] A stream drawn from a field in the suburbs not far from the furnace opening forms a channel six paces wide. Channels or tubes lead away from this stream and run through the walls around the baths. One of these, passing over a shallow heating pan, sends in hot water to the fountain in the basin of an enclosure with openings. It goes across the arched ceiling of the first canal providing cold water to the same basin with the higher pipes, whose faucet they open whenever the bathers wish to cool the hot water. However, the Turks' use of bathing and their reason for building baths will be dealt with in a separate place.

I return now to establishing the Eleventh Ward, which contained the Palace of Placillana. Procopius mentions this when he says that Empress Theodora consoled Emperor Justinian with these words: "We have other royal palaces." These are called Hellenae and Placillianae after Placilla, wife of Theodosius the Great, whom, just as Justin made his wife Sophia famous with royal palaces called Sophiana, so it seems likely that Theodosius honored Placilla by the Placillan Palace.[21] How passionately Theodosius loved Placilla he showed the entire world with his anger against the Antiochenes, whom he handed over to the Laodenses to rule because the Antiochenes had overturned the statues of Placilla that he had erected in his forum, because a new tax had been imposed.[22] I will not add here at this time what Chrysostomus Andriantes has written. However, it can be read that there was a Flacillan Palace built by Flacilla, about which Claudian has written:

SOLA NONUM LATIIS VECTIGAL HIBERIA REBUS
CONTULIT AUGUSTOS, FRUGES AERARIA MILES
UNDIQUE CONUENIUNT, TOTOQUE EX ORBE LEGUNTUR
HAEC GENERA, QUI CUNCTA REGANT, NEC LAUDE VIRORUM
CENSERI CONTENTA FUIT, NISI MATRIBUS AEQUE
VINCERET, ET GEMINO CERTATIM SPLENDIDA SEXU
FLACCILLAM MARIAMQUE DARET, PULCHRAMQUE
SERENAM.[23]

But Spain alone pays that rarest tribute: the gift of emperors. Corn, money, soldiers come from all the world over and are gathered together from every quarter of the globe; Spain gives us men to govern and direct over all this. Nor was she content to be esteemed only for her famous horses. Did she not also excel in heroines, and emulous to win glory from either sex, bestow upon us Flacilla, Maria and the fair Serena?[24]

The Bronze Bull was in the Eleventh Ward. We could deduce what part of the ward it was in from the great cistern that recent historians say was built by Nicetas the Eunuch near the Bronze Bull in the time of Emperor Theophilus if it were still extant, or if it retained its name, or if the forum were extant, which some recent writers call the Forum of the Bull.[25] John Tzetzes writes in his history that the Forum of the Bull was the same place called "the Bull," named such after the Bronze Bull.[26] What it was like can be learned from Zonaras. He says that the body of the unfortunate tyrant Phocas was burnt in the place called the Bull, where there was a furnace made bearing the figure of a large bull, brought from Pergamum.[27] Cedrinus writes that in this bull the martyr Antypas was burned.[28] How great was the cruelty with which some tyrants of Constantinople sometimes operated, who tortured offenders by this torment, is shown from the Bull of the Agrigentines. The Athenian bronze sculptor Perillus, as he is called by Pliny, or Perilaus as others more correctly call him, made this for the tyrant Phalaris. Promising that it would make a lowing sound from men when fire was put under it, he was the first to endure this torture, which was just for the cruelty of its maker. Pliny says that no one praised his work, and for a long time afterwards it was preserved so that whoever saw this might curse the hand that made it.[29] As to what inspired the artist to fashion the furnace in the shape of a bull, I find nothing else more telling than the Greek language, which is accustomed to call bulls with good flanks and excelling in strength "furnaces." In fact, just as furnaces have access on the side like a door, so too Perilaus fashioned a door on the side of that bull.[30]

I conclude that this Bronze Bull was taken to Constantinople from Sicily or Italy rather than from Pergamum, on the basis of the pillaging of the emperors of Constantinople, who plundered the entire world in order to decorate their New Rome. In fact, I asked many citizens where this Bronze Bull used to be, but I was unable to find out from anyone.

However, they are not completely unaware that there was a certain Bronze Bull in Constantinople; a great many of the oldest of these are accustomed to recount the oracle of this Bronze Bull just as if it were handed down to them directly. They attribute the interpretation of it more correctly to their times than John Tzetzes. Indeed an educated man who, in his *Historiarum variarum*, written 370 years earlier, interprets it as follows. He says the oracle was discussed in these words: Βοῦς βοήσει τε καὶ Ταῦρος δὲ θρηνήσει — the bull lows and the ox will wail. Because of this the Constantinopolitans believed disasters would happen, and they feared that a huge army of Germans and other nations would move against Constantinople. They were all stunned, expecting an overthrow and pillaging of the city, and they were uneasy and sleepless. The wife of the Megaletaerarch [the great heteriarch] was thoroughly terrified by false verses predicting this enormous army. Her mind fashioned what she dreaded, and in her dream she thought she saw what the words of men feared. First she saw that Constantinople had walls of brick. Indeed, near the Forum of the Bull, or the "Bull Place," she seemed to see the army and armed soldiers, and near the Taurus a sad man declaring his grief with beating hands and mourning voice. Dreaming this and thinking that it foretold a great impending disaster for the city, she told it to Tzetzes, who interpreted her dream to mean that the brick walls foretold an abundance of produce and copious provisions for Constantinople. He said,

> You who are present know the abundance of our crops that existed then. Certainly you know that this army and numerous armed forces are around the Bull, and that a sad man sits by the Bull. He said that it was the end of the oracle's being spread publicly. I speak of the prophecy that announces that the Bull is about to clamor and to lament, but not as they who dwell on fear imagine, but it is the end of its usefulness for all of us citizens. And so listen, Augusta, and make others aware too, and say Tzetzes instructed me in this way: We Greeks call a female cow a "bos," but sometimes we call a bull *taurus* or a cow *vitulius*. But we speak more correctly calling a male cow a bull. But the Latins call this a bull in Italian. Therefore, let our cow [*bos*] — that is, our city Constantinople, constructed by the Roman bulls of Italy and filled with all kinds of arms, provisions and armies — sound the battle call against our enemies. Indeed the Italian bull, the army of the Latins, will grow pale with great fear, and will mourn, as long as the emperor is not seduced by powerful words.[31]

Certainly this interpretation of Tzetzes' was witty, since the man was a flatterer of the empress, easily persuading her as she desired. Such is the ingenious weakness of men in ensnaring themselves.

But far stronger was that interpretation of the prophecy going about, which Tzetzes tried to refute and which pervaded the minds of the Constantinopolitans: that the army of the Latins would conquer Constantinople, as it actually did a little later. It plundered and burnt the city and threw some of the other tyrants of the city off of the top of the Column of Theodosius in the Forum Taurus, and burnt others in the Bronze Bull. Likewise the same subtle Tzetzes wanted to seem to be the interpreter of another prophecy, which he told and interpreted himself, but feebly and ridiculously. He gave his conclusion as follows:

οὐ αἰ σοὶ ὦ ἑπτάλοφε ὅτι οὐ χιλιάσεις, that is, "Woe to you, Constantinople, dwelling on seven hills, you won't last a thousand years!" This other prophecy made to the Constantinopolitans, as I mentioned before, said that the bull will cry out and the ox will lament. Then he said, "I would have refuted that itself in my interpretation beautifully and advantageously," and another was offered: "O Constantinople, which resides on seven hills, you will not last a thousand years." I interpret this not to be understood as the common people understand οὐ αἰ, as a mournful adverb, for it is not a single word, but rather there are two parts of the phrase. Everyone knows οὐ is a negative, but αἰ stands for "or if…" And therefore it can be rendered, "If, O Constantinople, you don't last a thousand years." Yet even if you are destroyed within a thousand years, nevertheless there will be no woe and grief for you, but there will be joy, since you will grow larger and become more splendid. For you will have been destroyed for the good of those who destroyed you. [32]

Tzetzes secretly supported principle citizens of the factions struggling for power, for if he had discerned the city's destruction by external enemies, this interpretation would be foolish. But whatever way he understood it, he was foolish. For whether the city was overtaken by its citizens or by outside forces, there was no joy for Constantinople, nor was it only predicted by the divine pronouncement of the oracle that Constantinople would not endure for a thousand years, but even by the presentiments of the astronomers. Some historians of note, so says Suidas, report that after he had completed the city Constantine the Great summoned the astronomer called Valens, at that time the most excellent of men who devoted themselves to astronomy, and he ordered him to identify the birth star and observe the horoscope of the city in order to find out how many years the city would last. Valens predicted it would endure 690 years, but these passed by long ago.[33] Therefore, Zonaras says he believes Valens' prediction ought to have been wrong and the art of astronomy ought to have differed from the horoscope, or else it is appropriate to suppose that Valens meant these 690 years to be those in which the rules of politics were observed, there was peace and the Senate was honored, the citizens of Constantinople flourished, and the imperial administration was legitimate and did not belong to domineering tyrants or to those considering their own good to be the common good, or to those abusing the common good to satisfy their own desires.[34]

Now, in order to finish the prophecy that great men have handed down concerning this city, I come to Zosimus an ancient author if you compare him with John Tzetzes and Zonaras. For this man says that Constantinople grew so huge that no other city could be compared to it, neither in size nor in prosperity. Nevertheless, he says that

after considering seriously for a long time that there were no divine predictions from our elders that predicted for Constantinople an increase of good fortune, I read many historians and when I had spent a long time on these questions, I stumbled upon the oracle of a Sibyl called Heritrea, or Phaellis, or Phaennus of Epirus. So it is said that this woman, being divinely inspired, was moved to utter oracles that Nicomedes, son of Prussias, obeyed, and being favorable to those things that appeared useful to himself, he started a war against his father Prussias, who was serving Attalus. Thus runs the oracle of the sibyl[35]:

Ὦ βασιλεῦ Θρῃκῶν, λείψεις πόλιν ἐν προβάτοισιν,
αὐξήσεις δὲ λέοντα μέγαν, γαμψώνυχα, δεῖνον,
ὅς ποτε κινήσει πατριάς κειμήλια χώρας,
γαῖαν δ αἱρήσει μόχθων ἄτερ. Οὐδέ σέ φημι
σκηπτούχοις τιμαῖσιν ἀγάλλεσθαι μάλα δήρον,
ἐκ δὲ θρόνων πεσεείν, οἷοι κύνες ἀμφίς ἔχουσι.
Κινήσεις δ εὕδοντα λύκον γαμψώνυχα, δεινόν.
οὐδ ἐθέλοντι γὰρ εἴσω ὑπὸ ζυγὸν αὐχένα θήσει.
Δὴ τοτε Βιθυνῶν γαῖαν λύκοι οἰκήσουσι,
Ζηνὸς ἐπιφροσύναισι. Ταχὺ δ ἐπιβήσεται ἀρχὴ
ἀνδράσιν οἵ Βύζαντος ἕδος καταναιετάουσι.
Τρισμάκαρ Ἑλλήσποντε, θεόκτιτα τείχεά τἀνδρῶν,
...θείαισιν ἐφετμαις
ἢν λύκας αἰνόλυκος πτήξει κρατερῆς ὑπ ἀνάγκης.

ὤμε γὰρ εἴσασίν τε ἐμὸν ναίοντες ἔδεθλον.
Οὐκέτι σιγήσω πατρὸς νοον, ἀλλ ἀναδείξω
ἀθανάτων λογίων θνητοῖς εὔσημον ἀοιδήν.
Θρῆσσα κύει μέγα πῆμα, τόκος δέ οἱ οὐκέτι τηλοῦ,
πείρα παῖδα κακὸν … καὶ τῇδε φέρουσα.
Τρηχὺ παρ ἠπείρου πλευρὰς ἐπινείσεται ἕλκος,
καὶ μέγ ἀνοιδήσει, ταχὺ δὲ ῥαγὲν αἱμοροήσει. ³⁶

O King of Thrace, you will leave your city. Among the sheep
You will rear a great lion, crooked-clawed and terrible,
Who will plunder the treasures of your country
And take the land without toil. I say to you, not long
Will you enjoy your royal honors
But will fall from your throne which is surrounded by columns.
You will disturb a sleeping wolf, crooked-clawed and terrible,
Who will put the yoke on your unwilling neck.
Wolves will the make their lair in the land of Bithynia
By Zeus' decree. But power will soon pass to
The men who dwell in Byzas' seat.
Thrice-blessed Hellespont, walls built for men by the gods
At the gods' behest,
Before whom the terrible wolf must submit, compelled by necessity.
O inhabitants of Megara's city, my holy place,
I will no longer keep silent about my father's intentions but reveal
The divine oracles' message clearly to mortals.
Thrace will bring forth a great woe, and the birth is imminent,
A serpent child bringing evil to the land sometime.
A savage ulcer will grow on the side of the land
Which will swell and swell until, suddenly bursting,
It will pour blood.³⁷

Zosimus says that this prediction — and I agree — actually manifests and enigmatically offers information and mentions all the future troubles of the Bithynians because of the most burdensome tribute later exacted from them, and foretells that their empire will quickly fall to men who reside in Byzantium. But even though these predictions did not come to pass for a long time later, let no one suppose them invalid. All time, indeed, is brief to God who exists forever and in the future. Zosimus also says, "I have conjectured these things from the words of the oracle and from the outcome of events, but if other things seem to have been meant by the oracle to anyone, he may pursue it."³⁸ Then, in order to confirm his own opinion concerning this prophecy, he writes that

Constantine the Great and his sons oppressed Bithynia and the entire world with severe tributes, so that cities have remained deserted.[39] John Tzetzes, the famous grammarian and historian many generations after Zosimus, interpreted the oracle another way, having been informed by time, the revealer of things. "In fact," he says, "some say that this oracle is from the Sibyl. However, others say that it was from Phanno the Epirote." He says that

the Epirotes predicted to Phanno so many ages ago events that took place shortly before our own age: how the Persians would defeat the Roman emperor, and they would trample on his neck just like a man bound for slavery, and how this [emperor] would be driven out from his empire by his people and nobles, and how the Persians would capture all of Bithynia, and how the Scythians would start a war and fight against the Roman people: ... κατὰ ἔπος λέγουσα ταύτη στοματὶ διειρμένω.[40]

The oracle speaks above about the conquest by the Turks. I will pass over other verses and select a few:

Δὴ τότε Βιθυνῶν γαῖαν οἰκήσουσι Ζηνὸς ἐπιφρουναίσι
Κακὸν δ ἐπιβήσεται ἄνδρας οἳ Βύζαντος ἔδος κατανοιετάουσι.[41]

They make their lair in the land of Bithynia by Zeus' decree
But evil will come upon men dwelling in Byzas' seat.

Although this oracle is very ancient, nevertheless it never seemed more apparent than now in the ruins of the city under Turkish rule.

On the brow of the fourth hill inclining towards the east can be seen the church of the Pantocrator, made famous in the memoirs of recent historians, the interior walls of which are variously covered with sheets of marble, and which has double doors and many domes covered in lead, of which the largest is supported by four porphyry columns that each measure seven feet in circumference. Another dome is supported by four arches that are held up by four columns of Theban marble.

Also on the fourth hill, on the south side, is a column equal and similar to the one I said stood in the Exacionion until recently, but it was transported to Sultan Suleyman's merchants' hall. Circling its base it has laurel wreathing and spokes, bearing a similarity to the labarium cross, just as is seen on the spiral column of Arcadius in the Xerolophon.

42. Zeyrek Camii/Church of the Pantokrator. Eastern side, apses.

At the base of the fifth hill is a double wall enclosing a neighborhood of homes that is now commonly called Phanarium because it was constructed in one night by candlelight during a siege. I learned from Dionysius where the place was, which is called Mellacopias. Why it was called this I explained in my book *On the Thracian Bosporus*.[42] On the back of the fifth hill is the palace of Sultan Selim with a building for travelers, the poor or ill and his tomb. And nearby is a huge cistern being converted into a meadow, looted of columns and roofing.

III. The Seventh Hill and Fourteenth Ward [43]

The *Description of the Wards of the City* claims that the Fourteenth Ward was counted as part of the city. Nevertheless, because it has been separated by the intervening space, it is protected with its own fortifications, appearing to look like another city. For those going from its gate it is on a modest plain, but on the right side it rises up a slope, up to the wall nearly as wide as a street and steep. It contains its own church, palace, nymphaeum, baths, theater and a wooden bridge resting on piles.[44] Probably anyone who had not seen Constantinople would think it easy to know from this description in which part the Fourteenth Region was located, especially since now the Eleventh is identified, and the Thirteenth and Twelfth are very soon to be identified. But the dispute remains over determining where it was since nothing is left of what was said to be here, not even the wooden bridge. Nor can the water that the bridge spanned easily be determined. I do not know where that gate was, from which the *Description* said there were hillocks projecting out on to a modest plain, and that it said rises up a slope on the right side. It might easily be determined if I knew what the author meant by the right side. But in fact this Fourteenth Ward does not appear to be on the fifth hill. The *Description* says it is separated by an interjecting space; by what space it does not advise us. But at least it was distinguished by its own wall from the neighboring wall of the city.[45] It comes down to the fact that it was not possible to build a bridge on the fifth hill nor on the sixth or seventh hills, nor does any bridge exist outside the city, nor does the valley lying between the fifth and third hills have any bridge or water, unless we assume there was some other stream that was spanned by a bridge and that is now filled in. However, if we suppose that it was past the sixth hill where today there is a village called Aibasarium [Eyüp Ensari], it will easily be confirmed, in fact, that there had been a bridge at that place that spanned the Golden Horn. Near here the foundation piles of a bridge can be seen. But on the other hand it seems likely that the sixth hill had been an inhabited neighborhood because of the convenience of the roads from Thrace. And besides, before being a village it was considered to be within the wards of the city, particularly since most writers say the sixth hill was inhabited by a suburb called the Hebdomon because there were other suburban buildings that were considered as being included in the city; and the nearness of the place caused Theodosius II to extend the city walls.

IV. The Hebdomon Suburb of Constantinople and the Magnara Triclinium; the Cyclobion; Statue of Mauritius and His Armory; the Place Called Cynegion

That the suburb called the Hebdomon was on the sixth hill, which is now inside the city, is clear from the church of St. John the Baptist, whom the Greeks commonly call Prodromos. This is on the side extending to the east, demolished for the most part by the Turks, where a few marble columns remain, awaiting their final plunder. But these are few of the many that have been taken away. While other remains indicate how sumptuous this church was, so does the cistern called Bonus (which was so called because a patrician named Bonus constructed it), situated a little above it. This cistern is 300 paces in length. Its columns and roof have been despoiled, and a garden now grows there.

Sozomen claims that Emperor Theodosius I translated the head of John the Baptist from the village called Coslaus, which was near Panteichion, an area in Chalcedon, and placed it in front of the city of Constantine in the place called the Hebdomon, and erected there a large and beautiful church to God. Sozomen also reports that when Theodosius led his army out against Eugenius, he set out from the city of Constantinople, and, so that the war might come out well and favorably for himself and his army, he prayed to God in the church that he had built in honor of John the Baptist in the Hebdomon.[46] Procopius is overly rhetorical praising Justinian, whom he says was the founder of this church in the suburb called the Hebdomon.[47] Zonaras says that in the reign of Constantine Pogonatos the Agarenes [Rhodians] besieged the city with a strong fleet that held an attack position by the promontory of the Hebdomon to the west as far as the Cyclobion.[48] Other historians speak similarly of the promontory called the Hebdomon extending to the west, that is, they say that the Agarene fleet — looking to the east from the Magnara Palace — extended all the way to the Cyclobion Palace. From this account, incidentally, I noticed that the Magnara was in the Hebdomon.[49]

Cedrinus writes that King Philip built the round Solarium of the Magnara, placed his own statue there in the atrium, and constructed an armory.[50] Other authors write that the Emperor Maurice erected the Triclinium of the Magnara, and in its atrium placed his statue and constructed an armory there. On the Triclinium of the Magnara there are these verses by an unknown poet:

'Οτραλέως τολύπευσαν τονεδ δόμον Βασιλῆες,
αἰχμὴν ὀλβοδότειραν ἀπὸ σταυροῖο λαχόντες,
αὐτὸς ἄναξ Ἡρακλῆς σὺν Κωνσταντίνῳ υἷ.[51]

This house was rapidly constructed
By the emperors Heraclius and his son Constantine,
Power given them under the auspices of the Cross.

Heraclius destroyed the Cistern of Magnara, which was in the palace, and which, according to Cedrinus, the Macedonian emperor [Basil] cleaned and restored it to its original state.[52] Some, lacking in truth, nevertheless say that the Magnara Triclinium was named because, when Emperor Anastasius might have died there in a horrible storm with winds, thunder and lightening, he said in a clear voice: "We die by a mighty blast." Pulcheria, sister of Theodosius II, had been removed from the administration of the realm and lived in the Hebdomon by herself.[53] Zonaras says that when Nicephorus Phocas approached the city he was met with great applause by the popular faction called the Greens, and he was crowned in the Hebdomon by the patriarch of Constantinople.[54]

Why, indeed, this suburb was called the Hebdomon I judge because there were seven suburbs, which retained their names even after being included in the city. Procopius claims that Justinian built a church to St. Anna in the ward of the city that should be called the Deuteron [the Second].[55] The anonymous author of the Patria of Constantinople gives the reason as to why it is called the Deuteron. He says that in the place called the Deuteron stood a statue of Justinian Rhinotometos. This was shattered and destroyed by Bardas Caesar Michael, grandfather of Theophilus.[56] The place is called the Second because Justinian II was sent into exile in the Chersonese and Leo the Patrician became in charge. After living in exile for ten years, he set out to Terbelus the king of the Bulgarians, whose daughter, named Theodora, he took in marriage. An army was given to him, which he led against Constantinople in order to resume his rule. When the citizens did not want to receive him, he entered the city through an aqueduct channel to a place where the foundations of his own column remained, which had been toppled by his adversaries, and he seized the kingdom a second time. Here he set up a second column and built a church to St. Anna, for which reason the place is called the Second.[57] Yet, as I already said, Procopius claims that Justinian the Great built this church in the Deuteron, which Theodosius II had extended the city walls around earlier.

I surmise that the suburb was on the seventh hill, in other words, in the Twelfth Ward, as Cedrinus and others maintain.[58] They say that horrendous earthquakes, which destroyed the city walls at the Exacionion, threw down magnificent churches and splendid palaces near the city's Golden Gate, the symbol of victory, and in the Second Ward the places shook to the church of St. Anna.[59] I told this to many, lest anyone believe the δεύτερον χώριον be counted as one of the wards of which the Ancient Description says there were fourteen in the city. I am surprised that Procopius, in describing so many of the city's buildings, mentions none of them, although they are mentioned in the Constitutions of Justinian.

Between the Palace of Constantine[60] and the Adrianopolitan Gate of the city, on the seventh hill, there remains a building that, though it has stood now for many ages inside the city, nevertheless was called Χριστὸς Χώρας. This is because it was once outside the city on three of its sides, as was customary for Greek church buildings.[61] It is enclosed by a portico, and its interior walls are encrusted over with squared sheets of various marble, so joined that they are distinct from the bottom to the top, with small beaded moldings, in some places with moldings of pearls, and in others smooth, without beadings. Above the squared sheets of stone run three fascia bands and three rows of beads, with dentils above the fasciae, and finally Corinthian foliage above the dentils. The marble is designed so that it shows off Corinthian work at the joints — but this appears better in Hagia Sophia.

Now, from what I will discuss below, it will be seen that the Hebdomon suburb was in the Fourteenth Ward of the city, containing its own palace. Not even the names remain of so many ancient palaces today, except for the palace sitting on the seventh hill, which is still called the Palace of Constantine, from whose buildings there remains one with some columns and a cistern, in which elephants are stabled.

On the shore plain at the base of the sixth hill, stretching northeast, is the Palatine Gate, also called the Cynegion. Outside the gate are plane trees. Near the gate, within the wall, there are three great arches, now blocked up, but once open, through which triremes entered to a man-made port built inside the enclosure of the walls for the convenience of the nearby palace. Now it is filled in and used as a garden. The Cynegion is celebrated by recent writers so that even Suidas did not think it unsuitable to put this story in his Lexicon. He says that those condemned to death were thrown into the place called Cynegion, and there were some statues in that place. Theodorus Anagnostes, going there with Imerius the Chartophylax, saw a statue, small in height but huge in bulk.

> "As I see it," said Imerius, "you are thinking, who built the Cynegion?" At which I [Theodorus] responded, "Maximinus built it, Aristides planned it." Suddenly a column fell and crushed Imerius so that he was found dead. Struck with fear, I fled to the church and reported what had happened. I affirmed it on oath because men hardly believed me. Servants done with their duties and some ministers of the emperor went to the place with me. When they marveled at the fallen man and column, John, a certain philosopher, told them that he had discovered from a small animal that a famous man was about to buried. King Philip

believed this and ordered this small animal be buried in the ground in this place.[62]

Justinian III ordered that Tiberius and Leontius, who had ruled three years, be taken from their imprisonment and bound together, and that they be dragged by horses through the forum and theater, and that they be killed at his feet, pulled apart when he tread on their necks, with the people watching this in the Cynegion.[63] This theater, through which I said they were dragged bound together, I think is the Theater of the Hunts, for there was at Rome a θέατρον κυνήγιον. And so there was one in Byzantium, according to Procopius, who claims that by the avarice of Justinian the theaters, hippodromes and cynegia were in great part neglected.[64]

V. The Blachernae, the Triclinium of the Blachernae, The Palace, Aqueduct and Many Other Ancient Places

The *Ancient Description of the Wards* says that the Fourteenth Ward contained a certain sacred building but does not name nor even

43. *Palace of Constantine Porphyrogenitus at the Blachernae (Tekfur Sarayı).* DAI R 2590.

mention the Blachernae, even though it was named before Severus sacked Byzantium, as I will clarify below.[65] The Blachernae was outside the city not only at the time that he who wrote this description of the wards lived, but even in the lifetime of Justinian, who, writes Procopius, built a church to the Virgin Mary in front of the city walls in a place called Blachernae. He says that upon entering, one marvels at this church, at its huge mass built this side of any danger, and perceives its very magnificence to be free of arrogance.[66] I think Justinian restored this church, for Zonaras claims that Pulcheria, wife of Marcian, erected a church in the Blachernae and dedicated it to the Virgin Mary.[67] Pomponius Laetus says that this was built by Theodosius.[68] Cedrinus testifies that Justinian's nephew Justin added two arches to the Blachernae church.[69] It is clear that Blachernae was outside the city, from what Procopius said before and also from Agathias.[70] He says that when the barbarians besieged the city, by order of Justinian all of the churches sitting outside the city, which started with the Blachernae and spread all the way to the Black Sea, were stripped of their ornaments, which were carried into the city to be kept safe.[71] Today near the Xylo Gate and the western corner of the city, between the base of the sixth hill and the bay, there is a holy building inside the city, which they say was the church consecrated to the Virgin. The Greeks show a flowing fountain still sacred to her and they call the place Blachernae. Its ruins were still there when I came to Byzantium. They are now almost entirely ransacked and obliterated.

From the bottom slope of the sixth hill, rising above the Blachernae church, an aqueduct projects with two pipes. Its water still flows. One of the two is stopped by a faucet, the other flows continually. I stated earlier that Emperor Andronicus brought this aqueduct from the Hydrales River into the Blachernae region where no river water flowed before. Emperor Anastasius built the great Triclinium in the Blachernae, which even in the age of Suidas was called Anastasiacum.[72] Zonaras and others have recorded that Emperor Tiberius constructed a public bath in the Blachernae.[73] In the Blachernae region there was an imperial palace even from the time of Zonaras and later, up to Emperor Manuel, as appears from recent histories.[74]

Why is the place called Blachernae? In his *Anaplus Bospori* Dionysius of Byzantium tells us that he describes places from the base of the fifth hill to the furthest angle of the city and the sixth hill. I cite a few of his descriptions. He says that

> past the spot called Mellacopsas (this I said earlier was below the foot of the fifth hill) there are two places for year-round fishing near the furthest depressions that the tongues of land extending from the hill make, and near the deep bays, generously offering rest from winds. One of them is called Indigena, the other Piraeics, from Piraeus of Athens, or as others say, from some ancient inhabitant. In the middle of these is a place called Cittos because of the copious ivy that grows easily here. Next to the Piraeics is the place called Camara. It has hills and a shore exposed to winds and is therefore pounded a great deal by the sea. Above that place is the sea. At this furthest edge of the entire Ceretine Bay, the rivers start to flow into the bay. It is named either because of those rivers mixing with the water of the sea, or because it is still and little affected by wind, or rather from the continual flowing of rivers bringing a constant mass of material that makes the sea muddy. Nonetheless there are many fish there. The first place on this languid sea is called Polyrrhetius, from the man Polyrrhetus. Past this is Vateiascopia, named for the deep sea. The third is Blachernae, a barbarian name, taken from someone ruling there. The last is Paludes [marshes].[75]

VI. THE BRIDGE WHICH IS NEAR THE CHURCH OF ST. MAMAS AND ITS HIPPODROME; THE BRONZE LION; THE TOMB OF EMPEROR MAURICE

Not only the historians but even Suidas the Grammarian claim that near the church of St. Mamas there was a bridge supported by twelve arches, for a lot of water flowed there. There also was a Bronze Serpent set up there because it was believed that a serpent lived in that place before, where many virgins were made pregnant. Indeed, a certain man Basiliscus, who was fond of this place and who was a member of the bodyguard of Caesar Numerianus, lived in that place and erected a church, which Zeno later demolished.[76] Constantine Iconomachus had Andreas Calybites, a man famous in Blachernae, whipped to death in the Hippodrome of St. Mamas.[77] Zonaras reports that Emperor Maurice was interred in the church of St. Mamas near the wall that was built by the eunuch Pharasmenes, cubicularios to Justinian.[78] Cedrinus says the church of St. Mamas was near the gate called the Xylokerko.[79] Others claim that Crunna [Krum], the Bulgarian king, surrounded Constantinople from the Blachernae to the Golden Gate. When he despaired of being able to capture the city, he fled to the church of St. Mamas, burnt a palace in that place, and carried off a Bronze Lion set up in the Hippodrome [of St. Mamas] together with a Bronze Bear, a Serpent, and choice marbles as he retreated.[80]

Sozomen, in mentioning those who were expelled on account of Chrysostom, writes that when they left the city they met in a place situated in front of the city, which Emperor Constantine had cleaned and encircled with wooden walls to make a Hippodrome for public spectacles.[81] I believe this was later called the Hippodrome of St. Mamas. Zonaras adds that Emperor Leo, in fear of the fire that was burning the city, left the city and stayed a long time in the church of St. Mamas.[82] Cedrinus says that the Emperor Theophilus was entertained by horse races near the church of St. Mamas the Martyr, situated in the Stenon.[83]

Its seems obvious from the summary collected above that St. Mamas was near the Blachernae, and that there was a bridge in this place, which is confirmed by John Tzetzes in his *Historiarum variarum* when he says that the Straights of Abydus all the way to the Blachernae bridge were called the Hellespont. From this it is clear that this bridge was where the stone pilings of an ancient bridge can be made out, though they do not rise above the water except at some times in the summer.[84] They are located between the Blachernae corner of the city and the suburbs that the Turks call Aibasarium.[85] We can conclude that this is that bridge that the *Ancient Description of the Wards of the City* called a wooden bridge and placed in the Fourteenth Ward, in which we said the Hebdomon suburb was. Note this one thing from Suidas: that the bridge at St. Mamas had twelve arches, and so these were of stone, or Suidas is speaking of some other church of St. Mamas located elsewhere.[86]

VII. The Seventh Hill and the Twelfth Ward; the Column of Arcadius

The Column of Arcadius still exists on the seventh hill called Xerolophon, which is divided from the other six hills by a wide valley. On the basis of this column I reckon where the Twelfth Ward had been, which includes the Golden Gate for those seeking the city.[87] It is all on a long plain, but the left side is drawn out by gentle slopes, and it is bordered by the sea. It contains the Golden Gate, the Trojan Portico, the Forum of Theodosius, Port of Theodosius and a column with an interior staircase, which Emperor Arcadius erected in the Xerolophon. Even now in our time the name is retained, and on top of this he set up his own statue, which in the reign of Leo Conon fell down during an earthquake that strongly shook Byzantium and toppled many churches and houses and crushed many people. Cedrinus declares that the Column of Arcadius was in every way similar to the Column of Theodosius situated in the Taurus.[88]

It has a stylobate, base and capital, its shaft with its coil, and capital made up of twenty-one stones. Moreover, two stones remain on top of the capital; the stylobate contains five stones all connected together by joints done in such a way that if neither earthquakes nor times had damaged it, the entire column would appear to consist of one and the same stone. These stones are set one on top of the other and are connected like vertebrae carved out inside, while the whole outside of the column is uniform, and they supply constant light through windows, and they make steps. Each single stone makes part of the stairs, and the outside of the shaft is like a wall. I began to measure from the highest stone at the top of the column all the way to the bottom step. The uppermost stone contains a passage, by which one ascends to the abacus of the capital, about thirteen paces and nine digits high. Roofed and vaulted it covers the entire column. The door is six feet and two digits tall and three feet and nine digits across. The second stone is six feet high; it has the top step set up above the abacus of the capital. The third is five feet four digits tall and contains the abacus and all of the capital. The fourth is two digits under five feet in height. The fifth has a height of five feet minus two digits. The sixth is four feet nine digits; the seventh five feet two digits; the eighth four feet four digits; the ninth six feet; the tenth is five feet. The eleventh is four feet fourteen digits; the twelfth is four feet nine digits; the thirteenth is five feet; the fourteenth is five feet two digits; the fifteenth is five and a half feet; the sixteenth is five and a half feet; the seventeenth is five feet ten digits; the eighteenth is six and one half feet; the nineteenth five feet four digits; the twentieth six and one half feet. The twenty-first, which forms the beginning of the shaft, is six feet four digits. Below the shaft there are six stones containing the coil and stylobate, of which the uppermost is four feet nine digits high; the

44. *Drawing of Column of Arcadius. J. Kollwitz.*

second-most is the same. The third is four feet high; the fourth four and a half feet; the fifth is the same; the sixth and last is four feet. The individual stones make steps, and the outside is like a wall, decorated with fifty-six windows. However there are 233 steps of two types circling around. For some just bend, and some spiral in the manner of a shell.

The stylobate is ascended by five spiral steps rising up regularly, and each spiral step has a single open space by which one ascends from one spiral step to the next. The first turn has six steps, the second the same, the third has eight steps, the fourth nine, and the fifth also nine. The lowest of all, near the bottom threshold of the door, is ten digits tall, one foot wide, and two feet nine digits long. The five windings are all similar, with a square area two feet nine digits long on each side. Past the fifth winding is the beginning of the shaft, of which the first steps are ten digits tall, a foot wide near the wall of the shaft, in the middle one foot nine digits wide, in length two feet nine digits. The highest steps are nine digits high. The interior of the column shaft has a circumference of 28 feet. The thickness of the wall, by which the stairway is enclosed as if by a breastplate, is two feet eight digits; at the base of the column it is a foot and nine digits thick.

If someone were to say that I am strange for measuring each stone, he would also say that that man is stranger, whom Thucydides praises, who had counted the bricks of the enemy's walls so that he could calculate their heights.[89] I did not dare to measure its exterior circumference lest the barbarians catch the lowered plum-line determining its height. It was necessary to take measurements from the inside of individual interior stones, from which I added up their number and determined the height of the spiral column. What at first appeared to rise above the earth is really two steps composed of many stones. Next came the third step; it is a stone three feet four digits high and 33½ feet on each side. On top of this stone, which forms the third step, is the stylobate, the beginning of which, from the threshold of the door, is five and one-half feet high. On this stone is a flat plinth three feet five digits tall, a small *torus* five digits tall, an *apophyge* with *regula* nine digits tall, another *regula* above two digits, and a sculpted wreath nine digits high. The splendid *sophorus* [frieze] is wonderfully

45. Drawing of the base of the Column of Arcadius. Archaeologia *72 (1921/22).*

sculpted with memorials on three of the sides, yet the side facing north containing the door is not decorated with sculpture. The *coronis* of the stylobate inclines like a roof in which there is first a *regula*, a vined *astragal* above, an *echinus* in the third position, and fourth, an astragal wound like a rope.

The remaining part all the way to the curved top is foliage, formed in a regimented way, that is, straight and curved and twisted on itself. The stylobate sticks out like an abacus, on which crown-like work is a pair of wreathed bands on one side, of which the largest is curved all the way to the lowest part of the abacus. On the sides of this same abacus, crowning the summit, there are seven nude youths holding laurel wreaths. An eagle extends out

46. Column of Arcadius. Remains of base.

from each and every corner of the abacus. Above the crowning of the garlanded abacus of the stylobate is the plinth of the column that projects less with outlined foliage. Above the plinth is a *torus* wreathed in laurel and bound with a twisted band. On top of the *torus* is the *apophyge*. From there the shaft starts to be carved with various battles. The sculpture proceeds in the same way as the column in Rome that was dedicated to Trajan, spiraling up the column between twin grooves. The top of the shaft, or the *trachelium*, is distinguished by vertical fluting; the bottom part of the capital is distinguished by an *apophyge*, then an *echinus*. In the third position an abacus projects beyond the shaft two feet and 14 digits. The abacus is 17 feet nine inches on each side. Above the abacus is the door, and then the cone of the column contains another door, ten paces higher. I can identify this as a Tuscan column since the base and capital are decorated with Tuscan work.

VIII. The Statues and Ancient Tripod of Apollo Set up in the Xerolophon

Suidas writes that the Xerolophon was initially called "Thema" by some on account of its having fifteen *cochlea*, a statue of Diana, a statue of Severus, its builder, and a Themation, that is, a tripod where Severus offered his sacrificial victims, and where once many oracles were announced, and a virgin girl was sacrificed.[90]

Priscian, of whom Benedictus Aegius, an acute investigator of antiquity, reminds me, relates that the Oeles had the custom of inserting the digamma, "ϝ," which appears in epigrams that I myself read on the most ancient tripod of Apollo, which is in the Xerolophon of Byzantium, thus inscribed: δημοφάϝων, λαϝοκάϝων. The same author says in another place that with the Aeolians it is common to put the digamma between two vowels of the same word, which we find in many places: ὄϝις, ovis; δάϝος, davos; ὠϝόν, ovum.[91] Ancient inscriptions show that this is true, and I have read it written in antique letters on many tripods, above all the tripod of Apollo that is in Constantinople in a place they call Ξηρόλοφον [Xerolophon], for they are written as follows: δημόϝων for δημοφόων, and λαϝοκόϝων for λαοκόων. Others add that on the Xerolophon near the base of the Column of Arcadius there had been a column of Theodosius II, a column of Valentinian and a column of Marcian, which fell in an earthquake.[92]

Zonaras says that the Bulgarian Prince Symeon, a cruel man never at rest, led his army against the nation of the Chrobatians, by whom he was vanquished, and he lost his army because of the difficulties of the terrain. In the meantime someone pointed out to the emperor in Constantinople that the statue set up above the arch in the Xerolophon, facing west, represented Symeon of Bulgaria, and if anyone were to cut off the head from the column, the death of Symeon would follow. So by order of the emperor the head of the column was cut off, and Symeon died of a violent stomach ailment. This was made known to the emperor in Constantinople as he diligently awaited the time of this death.[93]

Now, in fact, the Port of Theodosius was in the gardens that are today called Blancha, enclosed by walls and situated on the coastal plain of the Propontis. This plain is situated below the base of the seventh hill, the entrance of which stretched northeast, from which a pier extended northwest.[94] Walls that were added now stand on this pier. The city's pier still existed, twelve feet wide and 600 of my paces long, that is, paces I usually make while walking. The port is filled in, having very extensive gardens planted with herbs but few trees, for which reason, Fabius would say, "the veils do not hang down, but the fruits."[95] The gardens are irrigated by pools, which they have all year, doubtless the remnants of the ancient port. From the pier the circumference of this place is over one mile, and I understand this from the situation of the place. In the port's entrance, which is even now spacious enough for ships, outside the city walls even now a tower surrounded by the sea is seen as well as the remaining stones of its ruins. The unknown author of the *Patria of Constantinople* claims that it was first known as the Thema, where I said there were fifteen *cochlea*, then it was called the Forum of Theodosius.[96] It seems to me rather to be the Forum of Arcadius, on account of the nearby Column of Arcadius, for it seems more likely that the Forum of Theodosius was near the Port of Theodosius, because of the rules of architecture, which prescribe that a forum be built next to a port, and also from the name of the founder Theodosius, who could not have built his forum in a more suitable place than adjacent to a port with his name. I believe this port was once called the Port of Eleutherius, if they speak the truth who hold that Constantine the Great erected a stone wall against the waves from the point of the first hill up to the Port of Sophia and the Port of Eleutherius, built in the time of Constantine the Great. Eleutherius the Patrician presided over the work. A marble statue of Eleutherius had been set up in this port, bearing a load of marble on his shoulder and also holding a marble spade in his hand.[97]

They also say that Irene and her son Constantine built the Palace of
Eleutherius. From this palace all the way to the Amastrianum Theodosius
the Great built a Hippodrome, which was destroyed by Irene.[98] Zonaras
writes that Irene, when she was removed from the imperial throne by her
son Constantine, lived in her own house, which she built on part of the
Eleutherius.[99] The porticos that the *Description of the Wards of the City* calls
the Troadeae, others call the Toadesiae, saying that Constantine the Great
extended the walls as far as the Troadesias.[100] I believe that the Golden Gate,

*Golden Gate. Clockwise from upper
left: 47. General view from southwest
corner. 48. Detail: portal in exterior
wall. 49. Detail of pilasters to left of
portal in exterior wall. 50. Detail of
pilasters and frames to right of portal
in exterior wall.*

which was contained in the Twelfth Ward, was called the Troadeae because
they contained something of the same type as Plutarch claims the Porticus
Varia contained. He says, "they say that in the Portico formerly called
Plesiactia, now in fact called the Poecila Portico, Polygnotus the Painter,
painting the Troadeae, made Laodice in the image of Elpinicia."[101] I would

not have identified it by this name, which has been changed, except that I deduced that the Trojan Porticos were in this location from a spring near the gate that is now called the gold πηγή, retaining its name from the Golden Gate.[102] It still flows here continually and is religiously imbibed by the Greeks, who believe and call sacred all the springs situated near churches. The church that Procopius describes no longer exists. He says that Justinian constructed two churches to the Theotokos in front of the city walls, one in the region called Blachernae, the other in a place called Πηγή, where there is a great grove of cypress trees, a meadow of flowers, a garden producing seasonable and beautiful fruits, and a noiseless spring emitting calm and drinkable water. In fact, he built these two churches in front of the city walls so that one[103] was on the sea shore and the other[104] was near the Golden Gate. Concerning these churches, Procopius adds that they were near the end of the walls, so that both would be impregnable defenses for the city.[105]

From this I gather that in the time of Justinian the corner of the city that they call the Seven Towers was not inside the city. But the Land Walls from the Golden Gate had made a corner further inside the city, as is possible to assume from the formerly suburban Studios Monastery, which now is further inside the city than the corner of the Seven Towers.[106] The same Procopius says that Justinian restored at great cost the church of Hagia Ia, which had collapsed from age, at the entrance to the Golden Gate on the right.[107]

Now I understand that the Golden Gate was in the area of the seventh hill called the Xerolophon, not only from what was discussed above, but also from Zonaras, who claims that during the reign of Leo many churches and many houses were destroyed by an earthquake, including the statue of Arcadius set up on a column in the Xerolophon, the statue of Theodosius the Great on the Golden Gate, and the walls of the city that ran out into the continental plain.[108] Cedrinus says that the statue of Victory near the Golden Gate was toppled by the same earthquake.[109] Others add that this same earthquake, occurring on the fifth of the calends of November, destroyed many holy and public buildings and killed many people, and the statue of Constantine the Great that stood on top of the Attalus Gate fell along with the Gate of Attalus itself.[110]

Therefore, they err greatly who maintain that the Golden Gate is the same one they now call the Porta Oria, located in the northern part of the city, which I said before was the Neorium Gate, since it is clear from what I have written earlier that the Golden Gate was in the northwest part of the city. This is also in the Ancient Description of the Wards of the City, which holds that the length of the city, in a direct line from the Golden Gate to the shore of the sea, was 14,075 feet.[111] Cedrinus says that stabled in the Porta Aurea were elephants that were similar to those on which Theodosius sat in while entering the city.[112] To these they ascribe the statues of those elephants set up on the Golden Gate, taken from the Temple of Mars in Athens by Theodosius II, who built the walls of the city up to the Blachernae. Cedrinus says that the Macedonian emperor [Basil] built the great church of St. Mocius the Martyr and a church to St. Anne in a place called the Second.[113] Procopius writes that Justinian built both of these churches.[114] I saw the remains of the church of St. Mocius near a cistern situated on the back of the seventh hill. It is vast, not smaller than the one of which I wrote earlier that Justinian constructed, and supported by fewer columns, of which now it is seen despoiled, retaining only its name. For there is a place called Mocia that not only the historians, but also Suidas the Grammarian says, was built by Anastasius Dicorus.[115]

Judge whether the Moneta [Mint], which the *Ancient Description of the Wards of the City* places in this ward, was the Temple of Juno Moneta or the Treasury.[116] For even today the sultans use the castle on the seventh hill called the Seven Towers as a Treasury. Suidas adds that a bronze arch held up a statue of Juno, posed in a position as if cutting her hair, but in which place he does not explain.[117] I just mention in passing what I have added about the Moneta.

51. *Plan of Yedikule and the Golden Gate.* A. Gabriel.

IX. REGARDING THE COLUMNS NOW EXTANT ON THE SEVENTH HILL

The Studios Church is named after Studios, a leading citizen of Constantinople. Suidas says that he built this with its famous monastery.[118] Justinian mentions Studios in his *New Constitutions* when he says that there were two litters with which they bore the dead out for burial. They were litters located in the sacred treasury to the brilliant memory of Studios and to the magnificent memory of Stephanus. One understands the monastery is called the Studion, which now no longer exists. The church survives and has been converted for the Islamic faith. In its vestibule are four columns with splendidly worked beams. In the interior part of the building on each side there are seven green columns, distinct with black spots as if made with inlay from fragments of other kinds of stone. Each is six feet six digits in circumference. Moreover, the style of their capitals and epistyles, worked out with Corinthian details, is the same as that of the columns in the vestibule. Above these there are the same number of columns in

52. 17th-century drawing of Yedikule. Cod. Cicogna 1971. Photo Museo Correr, Venice.

the upper part of the church. In an open space of the Studion Church is a cistern, the brick roof of which is supported by 23 lofty Corinthian columns.[119] The Studion Monastery once stood outside the city but now is inside the city next to the road that goes from the Column of Arcadius to the Gate of the Seven Towers, which the walls of the city enclose. There is a gate now obstructed but once passable. Its jambs are two Corinthian columns of spotted marble, decorated with green veins, supporting eight smaller columns making three arches.

On the left side of the Golden Gate six marble panels remain. Each one has its sides bordered by small columns, some that are rounded and others squared. They contain excellently and cunningly carved sculptures, naked, fighting with clubs, of which the highest have above them cupids as if poised for flying. On the right side are six more panels similarly bordered with pilasters. On the first of the lowest panels a youth holding a musical instrument with pan pipes is in a reclining position, above him hangs a little figure like a cupid, and above the cupid a woman. On the uppermost panel is a nude statue holding an uplifted club with a lion skin flung over his arm and leading dogs with his left hand. Above him a lioness with swollen teats is prominent. Another panel contains two farmers bearing baskets filled with grapes. On another panel is a flying horse

Church of Constantine Lips (Fenari Isa Camii).
53. View of south side.
54. Detail of apse (east end) of main church.

Church of St. Savior in Chora (Kariye Camii).
55. Western side.
56. East side, detail of apse with flying buttress.

with a woman holding the horse's bridle. Behind her are two women; at the top part of the panel another female reclines, and a youth lies near her. I have included these on account of the antiquity of these images and the superior quality of their workmanship.[120]

Next, I saw on the seventh hill, with other Islamic buildings, four extraordinary buildings having marble vestibules decorated with marble columns. Two of these buildings were on the eastern side. Two of these buildings had six wonderfully tall and solid columns in their vestibules, of which two were of Theban marble and the remaining four of assorted types of marble covered with green. The other building is near the Column of Arcadius and was just recently built by the wife of Emperor Suleyman, with a splendid building for travelers, the poor or ill and a school teaching Turkish and Arabic literature in which I counted more than sixty different columns. On the back of the hill two other buildings can be seen, one of which has baths and schools of literature next to it. In the vestibule of this mosque are six columns of Theban marble, each of which is seven feet in circumference, of which the bases and capitals are worked in the Turkish manner, as if shod in bronze, but the shafts are most ancient, especially the two flanking the entrance to the mosque. They have delicate *hypotrachelions* that are more refined than the rest of the shaft. The lower parts of the *hypotrachelions*, even with the shaft, have a rounded ring, and above the ring is another broad band sunken into the column, and then the uppermost *hypotrachelion* is left more slender than the rest of the shaft, just like the neck of a man, more narrow between the head and shoulder. I never saw another *hypotrachelion* extant in Byzantium that came so close to the model of Vitruvius, who maintains that the *hypotrachelion* of a Doric column should narrow, as is recorded in the third book of *De Ionicis*.[121]

Another Islamic temple is on this same hill, in whose vestibule there are six wonderfully tall columns; in the atrium of the college there are fourteen, and as many in a nearby portico.

X. The Thirteenth Ward of the City, which Is Called Sycae, and the Town of Galata, Also Known as Pera

The town of Galata was part of Constantinople, as appears from the *Ancient Description of the Wards*. It says that the Thirteenth Ward of New Rome is Sycae. Separated by a narrow inlet from the sea from the society of the city it would be made part of the city because of the frequency of shipping. All of it clings to the side of a mountain except for one tract of land. Stephanus says that the city of Sycae was situated across from New Rome and was called Justinianae in his day, but he does not explain why it was so called.[122] But it may be because Justinian embellished it with buildings or restored collapsed buildings. For this reason cities tend to change names.

I am surprised that Procopius does not mention these buildings when he precisely describes all of the buildings erected or restored by Justinian along the bay called the Horn, unless there is an error in Procopius' writings: *Jucundianae* instead of *Justinianae*. For he records that Justinian restored the suburban palaces in the Bronze Quarter and in the place that they call Jucundianae.[123] Or if there is no error in Procopius, the error can be seen in the codex of Stephanus, which has *Justinianae* for *Jucundianae*; but Stephanus wrote long before the time of Justinian.[124] Therefore, if there is a mistake, it is not from Stephanus, but from Hermolaus the Grammarian of Constantinople, who collected a selection of the *Commentaries* of Stephanus, which he dedicated to Justinian. But in fact it seems likely that Sycae was named *Justinianae* rather than *Jucundianae* as appears from the collation of many codices, not only of Procopius but even of editions and manuscripts of Justinian.[125] Justinian says this in his *New Constitutions*: "It is obvious that if there would be a greater pause, there should be more attendants accompanying the bier and more ease as just a small amount of weight ought to be given to them." And a little later it appears he adds that: "If there should be a funeral inside the new walls of the city and a crossing τῶν Ἰουστινιανῶν ἤτοι Συκῶν, that is to Sycae, or Justinianae, since they are not distant, there is no need for much time or labor to proceed over there. But if a funeral be led outside the walls of this fortunate city, or a crossing carried out to another place than a funeral crossing to Sycae...." I omit what follows.[126] Notice that where it reads περάσμα the Latin equivalent should be *traiectum* and not *terminum* as the Latin has been given.[127]

From what was said above it is clear that the town named Sycae is across the bay from Constantinople, but across from which part of Constantinople, Stephanus does not indicate. However, I understand its position from the *Ancient Description of the Wards of the City*, which says that the Sixth Ward extended from the Forum of Constantine to the Sycae crossing, that is, to Pera, or Galata as it is now called.[128] And lest I seem to discount them, I apply to recent authors. There are several of these who claim that Absimarus, commander of the enemies besieging Constantinople, retreated to the Port of Sycae, outside a region of Constantinople.[129] Evagrius writes that the heads of Longinus and Theodore were placed upon poles and dispatched to Constantinople by John the Scythian, and were set up on the shore of Sycae opposite Constantinople, erected by the Scythian emperor's command, to be an entertaining spectacle for the Byzantines.[130] The same adds that Vitalianus advanced as far as the place called Sycae, against whom the Syrian navy, stationed in Sycae, was sent to fight by Emperor Anastasius. It seems that both fleets prepared themselves, one with Sycae to the stern, and the other Constantinople.

Initially they held back their oars, then after some excursions and light skirmishes were conducted by both sides, the naval battle commenced near the place called Vitharia. Vitalianus fled and lost a greater part of his men, so that none of the enemy remained in the Bosporus.[131] I am not convinced by Strabo, who appears to locate Sycae far from the bay. He says that, "from the Promontory confining the channel of the Bosporus for five stadia as far as the port below Sycae is 30 stadia, and from Sycae to the Horn of the Byzantines it is five stadia,..." which does not differ from what I said earlier, if one understands the "Horn of the Byzantines" as Pliny understood the Promontory to be the Bosporus Promontory itself, on which Byzantium was located.[132] But Strabo goes on straightaway, asserting that the Horn was a bay 60 stadia long.[133]

I think that either there is an error in the codex of Strabo or Strabo himself was mistaken, because of what was written earlier, especially by the very ancient author Dionysius Byzantius, a native writer of the city. Dionysius maintains that Sycae is the place near the bay called the Horn, in which place Galata exists today, as I have clearly illustrated in my *Circumnavigation of the Bosporus*.[134] For the people of Pera, who are wont to claim that the Genoese first established the town of Pera, are greatly mistaken because it was founded many ages before the Genoese set out for Pera, or rather they accepted the reward of this place from an emperor of Constantinople for the use of their navy in war. Justinian places Sycae inside the city walls, and Agathias claims it was enclosed inside walls when he says that, with the approach of the enemy, the citizens of Constantinople were so very afraid that Emperor Justinian's armed soldiers stood upon the walls of Sycae, so they were readily able to resist the enemy.[135] What Stephanus calls the city of Sycae is what recent writers, but authors more ancient than when the Genoese took

Galata, call the Castle of Galata, stating that the Saracen navy had anchorage from the Magnara to the Cyclobion. But two days later, when the wind blew violently at the Castle of Galata as far as the Clydion, part of the fleet was torched by fire that the emperor hurled down from the Acropolis.[136]

Zonaras reports that when Emperor Michael was besieged by land and sea, he came to such a point of desperation that he stretched a chain from the Acropolis to the small town on the opposite shore.[137] Still there is a gate of Galata called "the chain" after the chain that used to be extended from the Acropolis to the port. Indeed, that Galata was enlarged by the Genoese not once, but repeatedly, can be seen by the walls that they have often moved forward, still extant, doubled on the east and tripled on the west, illustrating the various increments of the city. Ancient Sycae can still be seen in the center of Galata, enclosed by walls, located across from the Sixth Ward and the ferry of Sycae, built entirely on the side of the hill, as described in the books surveying the wards of the city, except for one tract that the flatness of the surrounding shore at the base of the same hill exceeds. This plateau was purported to be at least a hundred Roman feet wide.[138] And today a plain of probably larger size remains between the hill and the bay. After so many years it has become wider, as we can see daily from the discarding of waste used as landfill held in by piles stabilizing wooden arches. The residents diligently drive these piles in by force with a ram to increase the shore plain and to produce maritime landings that are more appropriately deep. In order to more clearly explain where the ward of Sycae formerly was, I will describe the location of Galata as it now is.

XI. Description of Galata; the Temples of Amphiarius, Diana and Venus; the Theater of Sycae; the Forum of Honorius

The ward of Sycae, which is usually called Galata, or more correctly Pera, ought to be called Peraea, just as Josephus calls the Judean Trans-Jordan Peraea, and Strabo calls the Trans-Euphrates region Peraea.[139] All the Constantinopolitans (they are influenced by the allusion of the name) explain that it is called Galata because milk used to be sold and produced there. I have no doubt that if they knew that Galata used to be called Syca they would dare to say its name came from the milk of the fig. And then they would be able to cover their mistake with the authority of Dionysius Byzantius, who states that it was originally called Syca, "fig" in Greek, on account of the abundance and quality of the fig trees that grew there.[140] But they would have conjectured better if they had judged that the name of Galata comes from the Galatae people, based on the authority of John Tzetzes (a resident of Constantinople and very prolific grammarian) in his *Historiarum variarum*, which was composed more than 400 years ago and says that Brenus the Gaul, general of the Gauls, whom the Greeks call *Galatas*, set out for Byzantium and crossed the sea at this place. From this the place on the Byzantine side had been called Pera, after the crossing of the Gauls, by whom I suppose it was also named Galata.[141] This place is located partly on a hill and partly on a plain at the base of it.

The hill is defined on the east and the west by two valleys, each approximately a mile long. The ridge of the hill extends from north to south and is nowhere less than two hundred paces across and equal in length with the valleys that border it; then it connects with the remaining plain on the continent. The south side of the hill as well as the plain beneath is bordered by the bay of Ceras, which makes it almost an isthmus and semicircular peninsula. So if you drew a line from the mouth and jaws of the bay to the middle inlet of the valley into which winds the bay that the hill of Galata closes off on the west, you would see a semi-circle enclosed inside. Thus Galata takes a shape of a drawn bow, except that the western tip is half as large and not so long as the eastern end. The curve of Galata enclosed inside the wall stretches four miles and 400 paces. Its width varies; in the center of the city it is 600 paces across. The bay and the walls stand 20 paces apart. The plain that separates the bay and the hill is 180 paces wide and the hill is itself 400 paces wide.

The eastern side of Galata, at its entrance, is 400 paces wide, after which it narrows to a width of only 260 paces. The western side, which stands outside of old Galata, inclines upon a gentle rise, which bends almost entirely to the south except for a brief decline sinking to the west near the walls of old Galata. The slopes of the Galatine hill decline with a double fall, one into the valley, the other toward the bay. And so the city of Galata stands tipped on a triple decline, of which one bends from north to south, the other to the east, and another to the west. The decline that stretches across the middle width of Galata runs north to south and is so steep that in many places the slope is eased by stairs. Just so houses are mounted from the lower parts, and from above one proceeds on a flat foot to the first floor. The side facing both the east

and west has a double descent, one north to south and the other to the
east or west, so that both the road sloping straight up the ridge line and
those parts that go across the sides have a slope. But the eastern side of
the town is more steep than either other side. The west slope has a gentle
incline both up and across it.

In brief, Galata is so steep that if all the houses were of equal height
the upper stories would all have a complete view of the sea and of the
ships sailing up and down. And not merely Galata, but nearly all of
Constantinople would enjoy the same benefit if the law, first promulgated
by Zeno and later supported by Justinian, were fully enforced. This law
expressly forbade anyone within 100 paces to interrupt or obstruct an
open and complete sea view or even a partial sea view.[142] The flat part
of the town, which extends from the base of the hill and the bay, is
nowhere less that 200 paces wide, and in some places opens out to 400
paces wide. The town is three times as long as it is wide. It stretches in
width from north to south and in length from east to west. The western
end is wider than the eastern and almost as wide as the middle of the
city, for in a length of 500 paces it is never under 500 paces wide. The
eastern side of Galata is narrower as its end is brought down in the shape
of a wedge — not over 260 paces across.

The shoreline around the town is full of ports. Between the walls and
the bay is a plot of land where there are numerous stalls, shops, eating
places and also a number of open places where ships are unloaded. It has
six gates, three of which have frequent ferries to Constantinople. Galata
lies so much to the north of Constantinople that it faces the first, second
and third hills and the first and second valleys of Constantinople, with
the Golden Horn and Constantinople in front and some buildings of
the suburbs behind it. Above Galata there are many suburban buildings,
some on the top of the hill, some on three sides of the hill. For the town
of Galata itself does not extend up to the summit of the hill. At the
highest point in Galata, where there is a very tall tower, there still stands
to this day a stairway about 300 steps high, crowded with structures, and
beyond that is the flat ridge stretching south to north, approximately
200 paces wide and 2000 paces long. Through the center runs a broad
street bound on both sides by houses, gardens and vineyards. Here is
the nicest part of Galata; from here and from the sides of the hill one
has an unobstructed view of the Golden Horn, the Bosporus and the
Propontis, the seven hills of Constantinople, the land of Bithynia and
the mountain of Olympus, always snow-covered. In addition, there are

buildings both on the Galatine hill and in the area set on the shore across from Constantinople. It has the same number of hills and valleys as does Constantinople, so that they could make the city half again as large as it is. And if the good fortune of the Turkish Empire continues another 100 years, Galata it is going to be another Constantinople.[143]

Those who record that Byzas, founder of Byzantium, built the Temple of Amphiaraus in Sycae, are mistaken, but not utterly so. For Dionysius Byzantius relates that behind Sycae stood the Temple of Amphiaraus, which was erected by those who established the leaders of a colony at Constantinople, the leader of whom was Byzas. Both the Greeks and the Megarians revered Amphiaraus as a god.[144] Yet even though the Temple of Amphiaraus was not located in the place Dionysius calls Sycenum, the word had been extended after Sycena became a city, so that the Temples of Amphiaraus, and of Diana Lucifera and Venus Placida, all stood within Sycae, as I have sufficiently explained in my book *On the Thracian Bosporus*.[145] But there is nothing left of these buildings today nor of those buildings that the *Ancient Description of the Wards of the City* says were in the region of Sycae. Nor does the memory of any living man record traces of where they had been. Indeed, not only is there no memory of these things, but there is no one who has even heard or read the name of the Sycena region. Yet we can extrapolate from the *Rules of Architecture* where the theater and the Forum of Honorius stood.[146] The former was at the foot of the hill, where every theater is usually built, as I have seen from the ruins in Greece.

The forum was on flat ground near the harbor, where there is now a building for travelers, the poor or ill built on the foundations of a church dedicated to St. Michael, which was still extant when I arrived. This forum was amply supplied with water by an ancient underground aqueduct. But basically there is nothing visible today of old Sycae. The columns that used to be visible in some Galatine temples are said to have been exported by the Genoese, not a few of which were worked with ancient craftsmanship. The cistern of St. Benedict, now missing its roof, and the three hundred columns that supported it, had been converted into a garden feeding the priests of the church, which proves that it had been a very ancient and costly work.

From what has been written you can see what monuments Constantinople formerly had. It would require another book to describe the public buildings owned by the Turks and to explain for what reason some of them were built. I shall just mention a few. The city, as it exists today, has more than 300 mosques, the most magnificent of which were constructed by the sultans and their pashas. All of them are roofed with lead tiles and are decorated with marble and marble columns plundered from Christian churches, just as these had been decorated with the spolia of the old gods. It has more than 100 public baths, of which fifty are very spacious, and twinned, very like the ones I described constructed by the Sultan Mehmet. Their buildings for travelers, the poor or ill and their public houses number more than 100; the most famous being those that have fountains in the middle of a courtyard, supplied from suburban fields. The sultans of the Turks have excelled in bringing water into the city. Likewise Eusebius particularly praises Constantine. In the middle of the forums, he states, one may see their fountains adorned with the symbols of the good shepherd, well understood by those who know the sacred scriptures, such as the story of Daniel and the Lions depicted in bronze and glistening with gold plates.[147] Valens and Andronicus built rivers at great expense and at a great distance from the city, in part on arches standing above ground, and in part in underground channels. With just as great expense a number of other emperors, fearing siege by hostile neighbors, constructed fishponds and underground reservoirs, called cisterns in later times, in every region of the city.

But the enemies of Constantinople are now so far away that the Turks have either left the cisterns entirely to ruin or converted them to other uses. The city enjoys an abundance of water running from conduits leading from every suburban field, even remote ones. There is not a single famous mosque, public building, public hospital or decent bath that does not have a fountain in a central area. I will not discuss the grand houses of the Turkish nobles and pashas nor the sultan's palace, whose property, occupying old Byzantium, is always supplied with rivers that flow into it from outside the city. I will pass over their lakes and fountain houses everywhere in forums and streets, which are not only famously generous with water for them to drink but also drain away the city's sewage to the sea, and they carry away unhealthy air and the things that thicken the air, for which great cities are usually considered infamous. At this point I will not elaborate upon the fact that almost all the buildings in Constantinople are low in height, constructed out of the remains left over from fires and earthquakes. Not many are even two stories in height. They are rebuilt with unfinished stones or with baked, sometimes unbaked, bricks. I also leave out the Genoese houses of Galata and some of those of the court attendants. The Christian Greeks have lost 600 churches and have not a single one left of any importance, except the church of the monastery where their patriarch resides. The remainder are either utterly ruined or converted for Islamic worship. The churches that they still hold sacred are an obscure lot of some 70 buildings. The French have about ten churches, the Armenians seven. The Jews have almost thirty synagogues, which are hardly enough to hold the numerous assemblies of that populous race. For what anyone will find who tries to investigate after me — seeing as anyone could be more enterprising — I would direct him right away to the work on the regions of New Rome, Constantinople, a little book written before the time of Justinian.[148]

First Ward

The First Ward contains the Palace of Placidia Augustus, the Palace of the most noble Marina, the Baths of Arcadius, twenty-nine neighborhoods, 118 large houses, two porticos of great length, fifteen private baths, four public and fifteen private mills, and four stairways. It was governed by one curator who had the entire ward under his control. There was also one vernaculus [policeman], who was like a servant to all and a mediator of the ward. It likewise had 25 colleagiati [firemen] chosen out of several organizations of tradesmen, whose job it was to help in case of fires. There were also five vicomagistri whose job was to watch the city at night. P. Victor and Sextus Ruffus say that they had been slaves in ancient Rome, here in New Rome they call them "informers." Neither Ruffus nor Victor mentions the collegiati, but both mention the guards, whom it seems the *Description of Constantinople* separates into collegiati and vicomagistri.[149] In Latin some of the street-monitors are named on an inscription still extant on the capitol at Rome:

IMP. CAESARI DIVI.
TRAIANI PARTHICI FIL.
DIVI NERVAE NEPOTI.
TRAIANO ADRIANO.
AUG. PONTIF. MAXIMO.
TRIBUNIC. POTESTAT. XX.
IMP. II. CON. III. P.
MAGISTRI VICORUM XIIII.

To the Emperor Caesar, Trajan Hadrian,
Son of Trajan Parthiens,

Grandson of Divine Nerva,
August Pontifex Maximus
With tribunician power 20 times,
Emperor two times, consul three times,
The fourteen night-guards of the streets have set [this] up.

SECOND WARD

The Second Ward, starting from the Smaller Theater, rising imperceptibly with a gentle slope beyond its plain, soon falls sharply down to the sea. This ward contains the great church of Hagia Sophia, the Old Church, the Senate House, a tribunal with steps of porphyry, the Baths of Zeuxippus, a theater, an amphitheater, 34 neighborhoods, 98 large residences, four large porticos, thirteen private baths, four private mills and four stairways. It also has one curator, one vernaculus, 35 collegiati and five vicomagistri.

THIRD WARD

The Third Ward is flat in its upper part, in as far as the area of the circus is spread out for some distance in it, but descends at the end with great steepness down to the sea. It contains the same Circus Maximus, the house of Pulcheria Augusta, the new port, a portico of semi-circular shape, which, because of the similarity of its shape, is called the Sigma in the Greek language, the Tribunal of the Forum of Constantine, seven neighborhoods, 94 great houses, five large porticos, eleven private baths and nine private mills. It had one curator, one vernaculus, 21 collegiati and five vicomagistri.

FOURTH WARD

The Fourth Ward stretches from the golden milestone over hills on the right and on the left over hills rising through a valley to a plain. It contains the Miliarium Aureum, the Augusteon, a basilica, a nymphaeum, the Portico of Phanio, the Marble Ship — a monument of a naval victory — the church of the martyr St. Mena, a stadium, the dock of Timasius, 35 neighborhoods, four large porticos, seven private baths, five private mills and seven stairways. It is overseen by one curator, assisted by one vernaculus, 40 collegiati and five vicomagistri.

FIFTH WARD

A large part of the Fifth Ward is stretched out on slopes, with a plain following along. There are many structures useful to the city in this ward. It contains the Baths of Honorius, the cistern of Theodosius, the Prytaneum, the Baths of Eudoxia, the Strategium (in which the Forum of Theodosius and the squared Theban Obelisk stand), oil-storage depots, a nymphaeum, the Troadentian Granaries, the Granaries of Valens and Constantius. It also contains the Probosphorian Port, the docks of Chalcedon, 23 neighborhoods, 184 great houses, four large porticos, 11 private baths, seven public and two private mills, nine stairways and two meat markets. It had one curator, one vernaculus, 40 collegiati and five vicomagistri.

SIXTH WARD

The Sixth Ward proceeds briefly on level ground. The remainder is on an incline, for it runs from the Forum of Constantine to the stairs or ferry station to Sycena. It contains the Porphyry Pillar of Constantine, the Senate House in the same place, the Neorion Port, the wharf of Sycaena, 22 neighborhoods, 484 houses, one large portico, nine private baths, 17 private and one public mill. It also has one curator, one vernaculus, 49 collegiati and five vicomagistri.

SEVENTH WARD

Compared to the Sixth Ward, the Seventh Ward is flatter, although on the edge of one side it drops off steeply into the sea. It runs along with continuous porticos from the right-hand side of the Column of Constantine to the Forum of Theodosius, just as it does on the other side as far as the sea, by porticos running in the same fashion. The Seventh Ward contains three churches: St. Irene, St. Anastasia and St. Paul. It also contains the Column of Theodosius, which one can climb up in the interior by spiral stairs; two large equestrian statues; part of the Forum of Theodosius; the Baths of Corosia; 85 neighborhoods; 711 houses; six large porticos; 11 private baths; 12 private mills; and 16 stairways. It is governed by one curator, one vernaculus, 80 collegiati and five vicomagistri.

EIGHTH WARD

The Eighth Ward is not bordered by the sea on the side of the Taurus. It is narrow rather than wide. Yet this is made up for by its great length. It contains part of the Forum of Constantine, a portico on its left side that runs as far as the Taurus, the Basilica of Theodosius, the Capitol, 22 neighborhoods, 108 houses, five large porticos, ten private baths, five private mills, five stairways and two meat markets. It has one curator, one vernaculus, 17 collegiati and five vicomagistri.

NINTH WARD

The Ninth Ward is entirely sloped and faces south. It terminates at the shores of the expansive sea. It contains the two churches of Cenopolis and Omonoea, the Granaries of Alexandria, the house of the most illustrious Arcadia, the Baths of Anastasia, the granaries of Theodosius, 16 neighborhoods, 116 houses, two large porticos, 15 private baths, 15 private mills, four public mills and four stairways. It is governed by one curator, one vernaculus, 38 collegiati and five vicomagistri.

TENTH WARD

The Tenth Ward, on the other side of the city, is separated from the Ninth Ward by a broad street intervening like a river, yet is much flatter, and not in any part uneven except near the shore of the sea. Its length and width are in proportion, and it contains the Martyrium of St. Achatius, the Baths of Constantine, the Palace of Augusta Placidia, the Palace of Augusta Eudoxia, the mansion of the most illustrious Arcadia, a greater nymphaeum, 20 neighborhoods, 636 houses, six large porticos, 22 private baths, two public and 16 private mills and 12 stairways. It has one curator, one vernaculus, 90 collegiati and five vicomagistri.

ELEVENTH WARD

The Eleventh Ward is much broader in size than the Tenth, but is not bordered by the sea at all. The whole ward is just as flat as well as it is uneven with hills. It contains the Martyrium of the Apostles, the Palace of Flacilla, the House of Augusta Pulcheria, the Bronze Bull, the Cistern of Arcadius, the Cistern of Modestus, 503 houses, four large porticos, 14 private baths, one public and three private mills and seven stairways. It has one curator, one vernaculus, 37 collegiati and five vicomagistri.

TWELFTH WARD

The Twelfth Ward has, on a long plain, the gate for those leaving the city. On its left side it is led down by a gentle descent, and it is bordered by the sea. This ward contains the part of the walls that a more sublime ornamentation decorates, that is, the Golden Gate. It also has the Trojan Porticos, the Forum of Theodosius, a column of the same man with an interior spiral staircase, the Mint, the Port of Theodosius, 11 neighborhoods, 363 large houses, three large porticos, five private baths, five private mills and nine stairways. It has one curator, 17 collegiati and five vicomagistri.

THIRTEENTH WARD

The Thirteenth Ward is called the Sycaene Ward, which is separated from the city by a narrow bay of the sea, and maintains connection with the city with frequent boat traffic. It stands completely on the side of a mountain, except for a piece of land that the flatness of the shore surrounding the mountains barely surpasses. It contains one church, the baths and forum of Honorius, a theater, a dockyard for shipbuilding, 431 large houses, one large portico, five private baths, one public and four private mills and eight stairways. It has one curator, one vernaculus, 34 collegiati and five vicomagistri.

FOURTEENTH WARD

Even though the Fourteenth Ward is considered to be the fourteenth part of the city, it is separated from the other wards by an intervening space of land and is enclosed by its own walls, appearing to be a small city by itself. For those going outside its gate it is somewhat flat. But with the right side of the ward ascending nearly to the middle of its broad thoroughfare, it is very steep. Then it descends sharply and ends finally in a plain near the sea. This flatness, which contains part of the city, contains a church, a palace, a nymphaeum, baths, a theater, a mime theater, a wooden bridge, 11 neighborhoods, 167 houses, two large porticos, five private baths, one public and one private mill and five stairways.

GENERAL SUMMARY OF THE CITY

Now that the city is understood in terms of wards, it is proper to reveal the layout of its entire area so that its unique beauty and grandeur can be seen not only as made by skill and workmanship, but also as fortified by the elements of nature conspiring with good fortune. Divine providence looks after it, taking care of future homes with a big area situated on a promontory. There the land is more spacious, set opposite openings to the Pontic Sea and full of harbors along its curvy shores. Narrow in width, it is greatly protected by the sea that flows around it. And this part, which alone the sea leaves unprotected, a line of towers guards, stretched out with a double wall. Among the things the citizenry possesses we will mention in turn, but they are summarized here to aid unsound memory.

The ancient city of Constantinople had five palaces, 14 churches, six divine residences of the Augustae, three most noble houses, eight baths, two basilicas, four forums, two senates, five granaries, two theaters, two mime theaters, four harbors, one circus, four cisterns, four nymphea, 322 neighborhoods, 4,388 large houses, 52 porticos, 153 private baths, 20 public mills, 120 private mills, 117 stairways, five meat markets, 14 curatores, 13 vernaculi, 560 collegiati, 65 vicomagistri, one porphyry column, two columns with interior stairs, one colossus, one gold tetrapylon, the Forum of Augustus [Augusteon], the Capitol, the Mint and three ports. The city is 14,075 feet long from the Golden Gate in a direct line to the sea shore, and is 6,150 feet wide.

However, it is important to know that the 14 wards did not contain only 4,388 houses. This figure should be understood with respect to the larger houses of the principal citizens. As Sextus Ruffus and P. Victor say, the 14 wards of Rome contained about 1,755 houses. It must be that only fine and spacious homes are meant since both Old Rome and New were very large and extremely crowded.[150] And so, while I pass over Old Rome, indeed Constantinople, New Rome, was so populous at the time when the *Ancient Description of the Wards of the City* was written that even those who inhabited the forums and the broad streets were crowded. Buildings were so closely built together that the sky above their roofs was barely visible. And regarding the buildings in the suburbs, they were stretched out widely all the way to Selymbria and the Black Sea. A considerable part of the nearby sea was even covered over with houses supported underneath by piers.

Constantinople was long famous for these and for many other monuments. None of these remain today, except the Porphyry Column of Constantine, the Column of Arcadius, the church of Hagia Sophia, the Hippodrome (now in ruins) and a few cisterns. No one, historian or otherwise, had recorded the antiquities of old Byzantium before it was destroyed by Severus. It is reasonable to assume that there were very many, especially if one considers how it flourished in those heroic times when the talent of every craft was held in high regard and when Rhodes, in no way superior to Byzantium, was adorned with no fewer than 3,000 statues. Based on the walls, built with such skill, we can judge how much the inside would have gleamed.

It is certain, however, that Darius, Philip of Macedon and Severus destroyed many of these antiquities, and the Byzantines themselves, when they had used up everything else, resisted the soldiers of Severus with wood that they pulled from buildings and with statues that they threw on the enemy. But the Byzantines, who were built back up by Constantine, lost so many monuments, which I list partly in summary, partly [Attici?]. The primary of these causes was the emperors quarreling, then the frequency of fires, not only accidental, but also set just as much by enemies from abroad, as by their own factions, as by internal civil conflicts. Some of these raged constantly for three or four days in a row. Not only did they burn what was genuinely combustible but also the marble statues and likenesses and all buildings constructed of any materials whatsoever. It was like a heaping into a pile of junk whatever was good for burning, like a mountain built up out of every sort of material, so confusing its prior appearance that even the one who built it could not recognize what or where it was before the fire.

Nor were old Byzantium's ancient monuments destroyed only by their enemies, but even by those emperors who had the greatest love for the city. The worst of these was Constantine the Great, who, as Eusebius relates, demolished the temples of the pagan gods and destroyed their beautiful porches and completely removed their roofs and their statues of bronze, for which they were famous for so many ages. In all the forums of Constantinople he set them up, not as an honor but for cheap pleasure. He filled the entire city bearing his name with bronze works executed with the highest and most ancient skill, so that spectators could be amused by them. He took from the public gold statues of gods, and silver ones, and plundered other things made of precious material — indeed, statues made of bronze were considered vulgar. Eusebius adds that Constantine was so hostile to pagan monuments that he took care that they be destroyed throughout the empire and decreed by law that pagan temples should be torn down.[151] To what extent Eusebius himself as well as other Christian writers were hostile to them is quite clear in their works. They preached with the same rigor against images of the gods as Muslims do now against our statues. The leaders Basilius and Gregorius were bitterly hateful not only toward the stone images of the gods but also against the books of those who wrote lasciviously about them.

Why should I recall other imperial successors of Constantine, who were so disgusted even with Christian images that they not only destroyed them but even attacked those who created, painted or engraved them? From this attack on them they were called the Iconomachi [iconoclasts], just like the Parthici from conquered Parthia. I will not mention the earthquakes recorded by history that occurred in the reigns of Zeno, Justinian, Leo Conon and Alexius Comnenus, and in which not only the most important buildings of Constantinople but almost the entire city and its walls were destroyed. They were barely able to find its ancient foundations had it not been for the Bosporus and Marmara, the permanent boundaries enclosing Constantinople, circumscribing the place they were before. I pass over the large regions of Constantinople that lay deserted with a paucity of residents, after frequent conflagrations and the ravages of war until finally they were reconstructed. But they were built indiscriminately, without care for straightening out the streets, on the ruins of the fires and earthquakes. Just as Livy says concerning Rome's burning, this was the reason the old sewers and even the aqueducts and cisterns were set through the public areas the way they were. Now everywhere private things are under roofs, and it is like a city occupied rather than divided.[152]

I will pass over the immense grounds of the Turkish sultans, occupying the center of the city, the enclosing of the courtiers' palaces, the closing of separate city blocks and taking over public roads, or the things toppled long ago, and foundations extant above ground, and even those below ground, extremely well hidden, carefully sought out and destroyed. And in the time I spent in Byzantium, unless I had seen palaces utterly destroyed to their lowest foundations I would not have recognized their original position. I would not so easily understand what they had been able to destroy in a captive city. Although they are eager to decorate it with public buildings, nevertheless it is more awful and dark than night was formerly when, as Marcellinus says, the brightness of the night lights, accustomed to imitate the brilliance of day, lit up the splendor of the buildings.[153] Now the brightness of the day reveals the darkness of ruins and reflects darkness. So even if Constantine had restored and decorated it, or others had increased it, and brought it back to life, they would still not know the location of the ancient buildings.

How had I, a foreigner, been informed? Not by the traces of ancient buildings, nor statues, nor inscriptions, nor coins, nor by inhabitants curious about antiquity. Indeed, these last were so unfamiliar with antiquity that they rather impeded my inquiry. How did I dare to measure anything or ask anything freely, not only of the barbarians, but even of the Greeks? For them nothing is more hateful than the Latin name; and they bite like a dog, they hate and curse with a dog's tooth. Nor would you be able to mollify them with any bone. But you could assuage them with a lot of juice from the grape. But unless, as you pour, you make numerous invitations or unless you yell in the Greek way like a drunk, you will have wasted your effort and your wine. Nor will you get back anything from them, except trivial things or the habit of drinking, which alone they retain from the ancient Byzantines.

Add to these inconveniences that ancient Greek authors cannot help you. Not even Dionysius Halicarnassus, not Livy, Strabo, Vitruvius, Varro or countless others. For understanding New Rome like Old Rome, Blondus was no help, nor Fulgosius, nor did many others put their fingers in the fountains for me. The anonymous author of the *Patria of Constantinople* was not able to teach me. He spouts pure drivel, and while he teaches who built sacred structures, he does not say where they were located. If he came back to life, he would not know the parts of the city. Everything is so changed that not only are we unable to say what ancient things remained above ground in the memory of the living, but also we cannot say what ancient things can be said to be above ground in the course of a single summer. Indeed, every day the ancient things are so laid to waste that an old man does not know what a boy sees.

Not only are ancient buildings destroyed, but even their place names have been lost. Barbarian ones take their place, and even unheard-of Scythian ones. This Turkish race so loves its own tongue that it immediately changes the names of every place it invades, imposing a new, unrecognizable one without bearing on the original name, and signifying something else. They do not think they rule a place unless they control the names. Hence they suspect Greek and Latin, as they are afraid of the names themselves. So what's the point of investigating?

Indeed, traces are scant from both human memory and the writings of recent authors who follow ancient practice. Whatever is beyond our memory we can say derives from the recognition of ancient places.

From these few sources, as from the claws of a lion, I learned there were fourteen regions instead of from descriptions of them, which were not specific but general and ambiguous, or I learned from the traces of the buildings that they contain. And their memory will be blotted out soon if the Turks succeed. So it happens that not even those far more diligent than I will find any more traces of the regions of the city and of its monuments. If indeed I have erred here, I should be excused, since I have tried to assist future scholars and to preserve things about to disappear.

And my delay at Byzantium was longer than I wanted. The fate into which the death of the French king threw me should not be blamed but cursed. It was by his permission that I went to Greece, not for so long a time at Byzantium as I desired but so that I could consult ancient Greek texts, so that I could describe the layout of many different places, not just Byzantium, and so that I could benefit the literary world if I were able. Once I was urged on by this project, I feared to return before I accomplished something related to the reason I came. Therefore, on my meager budget I tried to travel around Asia and Greece, to describe illustrious cities. But I wanted to add certain comments and to address those who prefer to slander my fortunes rather than approve my eagerness, in case anyone thinks my return was delayed by Byzantine myrrh or Asiatic delicacies. For there was no utility, no reputation to be gained. I would have been able to offer better, more famous things at home, with peace of mind and a healthy body.

It was not the pleasantries of Leo the Byzantine or of Pasias that held me, or Python the Byzantine's vehemence for proclaiming, which even Demosthenes is said to have shuddered at among the dead. It was not the harsh, violent voices of the barbarians, which are able to arouse not only slow-paced monsters but even the Byzantine Python himself[154] who were able to drive me into leaving my country. I do not know if my speedy return was on account of fate, which realized I was in these dangers, seized me, and provided providence and wisdom in almost every danger. Or perhaps constancy, or the worthiness of the affair drove me on, confirmed by the judgment of the Platonists that there is no way of tracking down the truth unless you come to it, and that tiring of searching is shameful when what is sought is the most beautiful thing there is.

*Church of the Theotokos
Pammakaristos (Fethiye
Camii).
57. View of Parekklesion,
south side.
58. East end (apse) of
Parekklesion with figures for
scale.*

NOTES TO BOOK IV

1. *Notitia urbis CP*, ed. Seeck, 238–39.

2. *PatriaCP*, III, 281.

3. Cedrinus, *Historiarum compendium*, Bonn ed. II, 173; Van Millingen, *Walls*, 18–19; Janin, *CPByz2*, 351–52. As usual, Gilles does not name specifically all of the "other writers" from whom he has drawn his information.

4. Sozomen, *Eccl. Hist.*, VI.21.22; Van Millingen, *Walls*, 318–19. Sozomenos, *Kirchengeschichte*, ed. Bidez, 337. Van Millingen says that Gilles is in error here and misidentified the location of the Hebdomon (which is located at the modern village of Bakırköy three miles outside the Golden Gate). Van Millingen says that since Gilles thought Sozomen's account that the Hebdomon was seven Byzantine miles outside the walls was too far outside the city for a suburb Gilles opted to read the distance as one mile. See also Robert Demangel, *Contribution à la topographie de l'Hebdomon* (Paris: de Boccard, 1945).

5. Sozomen, *Eccl. Hist.*, VII.21; Panteichion is modern Pendik. See Janin, *CPByz2*, 500.

6. On this famous relic see Van Millingen, *Walls*, 338f.

7. *PatriaCP*, II, 185–87; Janin, *CPByz2*, 84–85; see also: Albrecht Berger, "Imperial and Ecclesiastical Processions," *Byzantine Constantinople: Monuments, Topography and Everyday Life* (Leiden: E.J. Brill, 2001), 82.

8. *Notitia urbis CP*, 238–39; 243.

9. Zosimus, *New History*, II.30, (p. 37).

10. Both Gilles and, later, Ball leave this word untranslated, as do present scholars. The meaning of *analampteria* is uncertain. See Mango, "Constantine's Mausoleum," *Studies*, V:55.

11. This famous passage from Eusebius' *Vita Constantini*, 4.58–60 (Winkelmann, 144–45) is originally in Greek and Gilles has rendered it much changed and abbreviated in Latin. Gilles or his editor obviously made substantial alterations. Gilles' own grasp of Greek must have been formidable so the reason and source of his changes needs further investigation. For an alternative translation and discussion of the Apostoleon under Constantine see Mango's article, "Constantine's Mausoleum," *Studies* V.

12. Socrates, *Hist. Eccles.*, I. 40.1–2, ed. Hussey, 174–75.

13. Zonaras, *Epitomae historiarum*, XIII.23, 58, which actually reads that Constantius placed the body of his father in the naos of the Holy Apostles. As Mango has noted, it is entirely possible that Constantius II built the Apostoleon — or finished it, as Zonaras, but especially Philostorgius (5c), Procopius, and others claim. See Mango, "Constantine's Mausoleum," *Studies*, V:58, and G. Downey, "The Builder of the Original Church of the Apostles at Constantinople," *DOP* 6 (1951): 51–80.

14. Eusebius, *Vita Constantini* 4.56ff., ed. Winkelmann (1975); Socrates, *Hist. Eccles.*, I.40.1–2., ed. Hussey, 174–75. And see article by Mango, "Three Byzantine Sarcophagi," *Studies*, VI:397–402.

15. Zonaras, *Epitomae historiarum*, XIV.6, Bonn ed. III, 159–60.

16. Procopius, *Buildings*, I.4.9–12, Bonn ed. III, 187–88; LCL, 49f.

17. Evagrius, *Ecclesiastical History*, IV.31 (181, 10–13) per Allen, 198.

18. Procopius on Apostoleon: *Buildings*, I.4.9–12, Bonn ed. III, 187f.; LCL, 49f.

19. *Notitia urbis CP*, ed. Seeck, 238.

20. It seems clear Gilles is describing a hypocaust.

21. Procopius, *Persian Wars*, I.24, Bonn ed., 125.

22. Gilles seems to be quoting still from some source regarding these palaces, but it does not appear to be from Procopius any longer. One gets the sense of a lacuna of some kind in Gilles text here.

23. Claudian, *Claudii Claudiani Carmina*, ed. J.B. Hall (Leipzig: B.G. Teubner, 1985), C.M. 30 (29), 63–69.

24. It is unclear to me what this quotation has to do with the Palace of Flacilla. There was a Palace of Flacilla in Constantinople, however, but not in Gilles' day. See: Janin, *CPByz2*, 135; Procopius, *Persian Wars*, I.24. I have used the translation of M. Platnauer, *Claudian*, LCL, C.M. 30.163–69, pp. 242–43.

25. Janin, *CPByz2*,.218. This information on a bath, which Gilles calls a cistern, constructed by Nicetas the Trapezas of the Palace of Theodophilus comes from Pseudo-Codinus (Th. Preger, III, 269).

26. Tzetzes, *Historiae*, IX.608–78, ed. Leone (Naples: Libreria scientifica editrice, 1968), 369–71; Janin, *CPByz2*, 69–71.

27. Zonaras, *Epitomae historiarum*, XIV.14, Bonn ed. III, 203.

28. Cedrinus, *Historiarum compendium*, Bonn ed. I, 566; PG, CXXI, 616C; Janin, *CPByz2*, 69–71.

29. I believe the correct reference here should be to Diodorus Siculus, who mentions the bronze, bull-shaped furnace and gives the lines: "by his groanings the bull will be thought to bellow and / his cry of pain will give you pleasure / as they come through the pipes in the nostrils," Diodorus Siculus, *Bibliotheca historica*, 9.19.1 (LCL). See also Pliny, *Natural History*, VI.61.200.

30. Janin, *CPByz2*, 69–71.

31. Tzetzes, *Historiae*, IX.608–78, ed. Leone, 369–71.

32. Tzetzes, *Historiae*, IX.649, ed. Leone, 370.

33. The original sources is *PatriaCP*, I, 142–43, n. 55; See also Janin, *CPByz2*, 23.

34. Zonaras, *Epitomae historiarum*, XIII.3, Bonn ed. III, 15–16.

35. Zosimus, *New History*, II.35, (pp. 39–40). Ridley's translation runs:

I have often wondered why, since the city of Byzantium has grown so great that no other surpasses it in prosperity or in size, no divine prophecy was given to our predecessors concerning its progress and destiny. After thinking about this for a long time and reading through many historical works and collections of oracles and spending time puzzling over them, I finally came across an oracle said to be of the Sibyl of Erythrae or Phaennis in Epirus.

36. Zosimus, *Historia Nova*, ed. L. Mendelssohn (Hildesheim: Olms, 1963), 93f.

37. Zosimus, *New History*, trans. and ed. Ridley, II.35–37 (pp. 39–40). I used Ridley's translation of the oracle here.

38. Zosimus, *New History*, II.37 (p. 40).

39. Zosimus, *New History*, II.35–40 (pp. 39–41). Ridley's translation, end of II. 37, p. 41: "By such exactions the cities were exhausted; for as these demands persisted long after Constantine, they were soon drained of wealth and most became deserted."

40. This line in Tzetzes actually reads: κατ᾽ ἔπος λέγουσα ταυτὶ στόματι διηρμένω; Tzetzes, *Historiae*, VII.549, ed. Leone, 277.

41. In fact these lines seem to come from Zosimus II, 37 (above) as much as from Tzetzes. I believe Gilles has slightly confused the two authors, or he may have been using a poor copy of the latter. The lines in a modern edition of Tzetzes are: Δὴ τότε Βιθυνῶν γαῖαν λύκοι οἰκήσουσι Ζηνὸς ἐπιφροσύνῃσι κακὸν δ ἐπιβήσεται ἄνδρας οἳ Βύζαντος ἕδος καταναιετάουσιν (note that Tzetzes does include λύκοι so the translation is virtually the same, except in Tzetzes κακὸν or evil will come upon the men dwelling in Byzas' seat. Tzetzes, *Historiae*, IX.817–19, ed. Leone, 378.

42. Dionysius Byzantius, *Anaplus Bospori*, ed. Güngerich, 8, ll. 11–16 through 9, ll. 1–2; Gilles, *Bosporo Thracio*, II.ii.

43. Gilles makes a valiant attempt to identify the exact the location of the Fourteenth Ward and suggests that it was at Eyüp because piers of a bridge were still extant in the area when he visited it. But he seems to prefer the sixth hill as its more likely location given that it was closer to the walls of Constantinople and since he also deduced (mistakenly, as it turns out, see above) that the Hebdomon was on this hill, i.e. the hill of the Blachernae. As Mango has pointed out in his "The Fourteenth Region of Constantinople," Gilles was mistaken in settling on the sixth hill as its most likely location, and was closer probably to the truth in mentioning Eyüp. Mango himself feels that either Eyüp or Silâhtarağa, further up the Golden Horn, are more probable locations, and favors the latter. See: Mango, "The Fourteenth Region of Constantinople," *Studies*, VIII.

44. *Notitia urbis CP*, ed. Seeck, 240–41.

45. *PatriaCP*, 240–41.

46. Sozomen, *Eccl. Hist.*, VII.21–22.

47. Procopius, *Buildings*, I.8.15–16, Bonn ed. III, 198.

48. Zonaras, *Epitomae historiarum*, XIV.20, Bonn ed. III, 223–24.

49. This Magnara is not the one in the Great Palace near the Hippodrome, but another. Theophanes, *Chronicle*, 494–95; Janin, *CPByz2*, 139.

50. Cedrinus, *Historiarum compendium*, Bonn ed. I, 709 mentions Phocas, not Philip in this regard: "idem Phocas armamentarium extruxit Magnaurae propinquum, statua supra id collocata." Gilles may also be confusing the Magnara and the Mangana (Arsenal) here and Philip's role in that. See also Van Millingen, *Walls*, 250.

51. *Anthol. Graec.* IX, no. 655. Anonymous.

52. Cedrinus, *Historiarum compendium*, II.237–41.

53. Zonaras, *Epitomae historiarum*, XIII.23, Bonn ed. III, 109; Janin, *CPByz2*, 139f.

54. Zonaras, *Epitomae historiarum*, XIV.13, Bonn ed. III, 196.

55. Procopius, *Buildings*, I.3, Bonn ed. III, 185.

56. *Patria CP*, II.61, ed. Preger, 184 on Bardas.

57. *Patria CP*, III.79, ed. Preger, 244 on the Deuteron.

58. Procopius, *Buildings*, Bonn ed. III, 185; Cedrinus, *Historiarum compendium*, Bonn ed. II, 240.

59. Cedrinus, *Historiarum compendium*, Bonn ed. II, 240; Janin, *Églises*, 40.

60. By the "Palace of Constantine" Gilles probably means the Palace of Constantine Porphyrogenitus (Tekfur Sarayı in Turkish), which is in the Blachernae area.

61. Gilles is speaking here of the Kariye Camii, the church of Christ in the Chora. See Commentary.

62. Suda, *Lexikon*, III:213.

63. This information does not come from the Suda entry on the Cynegion as does the passage above. Gilles clearly read of this grisly episode in Theophanes, *The Chronicle of Theophanes*, 523, but note that Theophanes claims event occurred in the Hippodrome, not in the Cynegion.

64. Procopius, *Secret History*, 26, Bonn ed. III, 143–44; *The Secret History* of Procopius was unknown in the West until the seventeenth century yet Gilles is certainly quoting from it here; even though he doesn't name the book itself. This can only mean that he found a manuscript of this work (or excerpts at the very least) while in Constantinople. See Cameron, *Procopius and the Sixth Century*, 4. The story of Theodore and Himerius comes from the *Parastaseis Synt. Chron*. See: Preger, ed., *Script. Orig CP*, I, page 35f. = II p. 163, par. 24; and Mango, "Antique Statuary," 60ff. The Kynegion was a theater from ancient times located on today's Sarayburnu, per Mango.

65. *Patria CP*, 240–41.

66. Procopius on the Blachernae Church, see: *Buildings*, I.3, Bonn ed. III, 183–85. Janin, *Églises* (1969), 161ff. Cameron, *Procopius and the Sixth Century*, 100 and footnote 116 same page.

67. Zonaras, *Epitomae historiarum*, XIII.24, Bonn ed. III, 115.

68. Müller-Wiener, *Bildlexikon*, 223–24; *OBD*, 293. Pomponius is mistaken. Pulcheria, wife of Emperor Marcian and sister of Theodosius II, founded the church of the Virgin at Blachernae between 450 and 453.

69. Cedrinus, *Historiarum compendium*, Bonn ed. I, 684.

70. Procopius, *Buildings*, I.3.1–5. Gilles is correct in assigning this church not to Justinian but to Justin I.

71. Agathias, *Histories*, V.14.8–9; Cameron, *Agathias*, 85.

72. Suda, *Lexikon*, I:188.1.

73. Zonaras, *Epitomae historiarum*, XIV.11, Bonn ed. III, 180–81.

74. Zonaras mentions the Blachernae for the last time during the reign of Alexius I Comnenos. See *Epitomae historiarum*, XVIII.18, Bonn ed. III, 719.

75. Dionysius Byzantius, *Anaplus Bospori*, ed. Güngerich, 9, l. 3–11, l. 1.

76. Suda, *Lexikon*, III:315.

77. Theophanes, *Chronicle*, 598; Janin, *CPByz2*, 140, 189.

78. Zonaras, *Epitomae historiarum*, XIV.13, Bonn ed. III, 197–98.

79. Cedrinus, *Historiarum compendium*, Bonn ed. I, 707; II, 25; Janin, *CPByz2*, 474.

80. Theophanes, *Chronicle*, 686. See also, Janin, *CPByz2*, 140; and Janin, *Églises* (1953), 325–31.

81. Sozomen, *Eccl. Hist.*, VIII.21.

82. Zonaras, *Epitomae historiarum*, XIV.1, Bonn ed. III, 125.

83. Cedrinus seems to have gotten this line from Zonaras, *Epitomae historiarum*, XVI. 4, Bonn ed. III, 404 and XVI.7, Bonn ed. III, 415; Cedrinus, *Historiarum compendium*, Bonn ed. I, 707 and II, 25; Janin, *CPByz2*, 474 and 479–80, where he indicates that "Stenon" was a term the Byzantines commonly used to refer to the Bosporus. On the hippodrome, the Xylokerkos, near St. Mamas, see Janin, *CPByz2*, 195–96 and 440–41 and Van Millingen, *Walls*, 88–94, esp. 89 n. 4.

84. Tzetzes, *Historiae*, I.840–43, ed. Leone, 37.

85. Aibasarium is modern Eyüp.

86. Suda, *Lexikon*, Vol. III:315.

87. The Latin here is not entirely clear.

88. Cedrinus, *Historiarum compendium*, Bonn ed. I, 566 and 567; on destruction of Arcadius' statue, see Cedrinus, *Historiarum compendium*, Bonn ed. I, 801.

89. Thucydides, *Peloponnesian War*, trans. Rex Warner (New York: Penguin, 1954, Revised 1985), III.9.20.

90. Suda, *Lexikon*, III:496–97.

91. Priscian, *Institutiones grammaticae*, ed. Martin Hertz, in *Grammatici latini*, ed. Heinrich Keil, Vols. I–VII (Leipzig: B.G. Teubner, 1855–1923), II:11, 15. Priscian was an important Latin grammarian who lived in the sixth century CE and worked

as a teacher and prolific author in Constantinople. His *Institutio de nomine et pronomine et verbo* was known in western Europe in the early Middle Ages, and his longer *Institutiones grammaticae* circulated throughout Europe in the Carolingian period and after. Thus, Gilles need not have consulted these works in Constantinople; he was probably already familiar with them; *OCD*, 1247–48. For further information on the consonantal digamma, see *OCD*, "Greek language," 655.

92. *Patria CP*, II.19, ed. Preger, 160–61.

93. Zonaras, *Epitomae historiarum*, XVI.18, Bonn ed. III, 473.

94. On the Vlanga and the Jewish Quarter, see Majeska, *Russian Travelers*, 268f.

95. I remain uncertain as to where Gilles read this line. Could he be referring to Quintus Fabius Pictor (3C BCE), whose history of Rome survives only in fragments, or the Spaniard, Fabius Rusticus? It could be the latter as it was his *History* that earned the praise of Tacitus, but I have not been able to pinpoint the reference; *OCD*, 583.

96. *Patria CP*, ed. Preger, II.105 and 207.

97. *PatriaCP*, II.63, 184; III.91, 248; and III.215, on Port of Eleutherius. On the Eleutherius Port near the Vlanga see also Majeska, *Russian Travelers*, 268f.

98. *Patria CP*, III.173, ed. Preger, 269.

99. Zonaras, *Epitomae historiarum*, XV.11, Bonn ed. III, 292 and XV.13, p. 301.

100. *Patria CP*, ed. Preger, 239.

101. Plutarch, *Lives*, Cimon, 4.1.5; Livy mentions that Polygnotus (before 420 BCE) was also a gifted painter as well as a sculptor; *OCD*, 1212–13.

102. The spring of the church of the Virgin Pege.

103. The Blachernae.

104. Zoodochos Pege.

105. On Zoodochos Pege see Procopius, *Buildings* I.3, Bonn ed. III, 184 and on the Blachernae 184–85 of same.

106. Having walked this area extensively myself, I can state that Gilles is quite accurate about all of this. -K.B.

107. Procopius, *Buildings*, I.9.16, Bonn ed. III, 201.

108. Zonaras, *Epitomae historiarum*, XV.4, Bonn ed. III, 263–64.

109. Cedrinus, *Historiarum compendium*, Bonn ed. I, 675 on the Victory statue that fell during an earthquake under Michael III; Van Millingen, *Walls*, 64.

110. See sources in Van Millingen, *Walls*, 29–30, 33.

111. *PatriaCP*, 243.

112. Cedrinus, *Historiarum compendium*, Bonn ed. I, 567; Janin, *CPByz2*, 270.

113. The Deuteron. See Cedrinus, *Historiarum compendium*, Bonn ed. II, 239.

114. Procopius, *Buildings*, I.3, Bonn ed. III, 185 on St. Anna; and *Buildings*, I.4, Bonn ed. III, 190 on St. Mocius.

115. Suda, *Lexikon*, I:187–88.1.

116. *PatriaCP,* 239.

117. Suda, *Lexikon*, III:408.

118. Suda, *Lexikon*, IV:438.

119. Today there are remains of a cistern, not in the atrium or forecourt of Imrahor Camii, but along the southwest (i.e. Marmara) side.

120. None of these reliefs survive on the Golden Gate, although some of the cornices and pilasters that once framed them are still in situ. Notice that Gilles only describes the right, or south side sculptures in any detail. See Cyril Mango, "The Triumphal Way of Constantinople and the Golden Gate," *DOP* 54 (2000), 183f.; and Van Millingen, *Walls*, 65–66 and especially, 66 n.1.

121. Vitruvius, III.3, 12, translation in *Vitruvius: The Ten Books on Architecture*, trans. M. Morgan (Cambridge, MA: Harvard University Press, 1914), 84–86.

122. Stephanos Byzantinii, *A Geographical Lexicon*, 590–91.

123. Procopius, *Buildings*, I.11, Bonn ed. III, 207; Procopius wrote his *Buildings* before all of Justinian's projects were complete. For an example of such a structure (albeit not in Constantinople itself) and concerning the date of Procopius' *Buildings*, see Michael Whitby, "Justinian's Bridge over the Sangarius and the Date of Procopius' *De aedificiis*," *Journal of Hellenic Studies*, 105 (1985): 129–48.

124. See n. 122 above.

125. Procopius, *Buildings*, I.11, Bonn ed. III, 207.

126. Justinian, *Corpus iuris civilis,* ed. Kruger, I (1902), 11.7, 155–58 and II (1889), 47.6, 789; also, the *Codex Justinianus* I.2.4 mentions the "Parabalanoi" or "Paraboloi" responsible for burial of the dead.

127. More correctly, *perama*, "the crossing." See Majeska, *Russian Travelers,* 353 and n. 114 on that page.

128. *PatriaCP,* 234.

129. Gilles is referring to Emperor Tiberius III Apsimar (698–705), Theophanes, *Chronicle,* 517.

130. Evagrius, *Ecclesiastical History,* III.35 ed. Allen, 154–55, who points out that Evagrius is confused here on which heads were sent back.

131. Evagrius, *Ecclesiastical History,* III.43 and IV.3 ed. Allen, 163–64, who points out that Evagrius again following Malalas here; Allen, 175–76.

132. Pliny, *Natural History,* IX.51; Strabo, *Geography*, VII.6.2.

133. Strabo, *Geography*, VII.6.2.

134. Dionysius Byzantius, *Anaplus Bospori*, ed. Güngerich, 15, ll. 5–13 and notes below; Gilles, *Bosporo Thracio*, II.v.

135. Agathias, *Histories*, V.15.

PIERRE GILLES' CONSTANTINOPLE ᏋᏮ

136. *PatriaCP,* II,265; Theophanes, *Chronicle,* 545–47, 547n.

137. Zonaras, *Epitomae historiarum,* XV.22, Bonn ed. III, 342–43.

138. *Notitia,* ed. Seeck, 239.

139. Josephus, *Jewish Wars,* III.3.3, IV.7.3, 6; Strabo, *Geography,* XIV.2.29, XVI.1.1; and Pliny, *Natural History,* V.83.

140. Dionysius Byzantius, *Anaplus Bospori,* ed. Güngerich, 15, ll. 9–10.

141. Tzetzes, *Historiae,* VI.661–69 and XI.380–407, ed. Leone, 236; 443–44; Gilles is getting his information from different parts of Tzetzes for this sentence, but nowhere that I can see does Tzetzes use the word Pera for Galata.

142. *Corpus iuris civilis, Codex Iustinianus,* 8.10.12–2–4; *Corpus iuris civilis, Nov.* 63.

143. Gilles' use of the future conditional here is difficult to render into English.

144. Gilles also includes here the words "sed Amphiarai templum," which I am unable to fit into the translation of this sentence and make it meaningful.

145. Gilles, *Bosporo Thracio,* II.v and II.vi. Dionysius Byzantius, *Anaplus Bospori,* ed. Güngerich, 15, ll. 5–13 and notes below on that page. There is no uniformity in Gilles' spelling of Sycae; for some reason he keeps switching the gender and number. For the most part I have consistently used "Sycae," but this single sentence contains several variants so I decided to put in a comment here.

146. Vitruvius, V.4.3, Morgan, 138.

147. Eusebius, *Vita Constantini,* 3.49, Winkelmann (1975).

148. Gilles refers to the *Notitia urbis Constantinopolitanae* (his *Ancient Description of the Wards of the City*). What follows is Gilles' transcription of that document. The modern critical edition of this fifth-century text remains *Notitia urbis Constantinopolitanae,* ed. O. Seeck, *Notitia Dignitatum* (Berlin: Weidmann, 1876).

149. In fact, the *vernaculi* were slave-policemen. The *vicomagistri* were night-guardsmen. See *ODB,* 1496–97; *Notitia urbis CP,* 229–43.

150. Ibid.

151. For Eusebius on Constantine's treatment of pagan worshippers and their temples, see *Vita Constantini,* 3.54.4, 3.55, and 3.57.4, ed. Winkelmann (1975).

152. Livy, *Histories,* XXVI.27.1.

153. It is possible that this a reference to the feast of the Epiphany from Ammianus Marcellinus, *Rerum gestarum libri,* XXI.2, ed. Rolfe, also mentioned by Zonaras, *Epitomae historiarum,* XII.11, but the precise reference is unclear to me.

154. Python of Byzantium was a rhetor sent to Greece in 343 BCE by Philip of Macedon to persuade the Athenians to accept Philip's proposals. See Plutarch, *Lives,* Demosthemes, IX.1.

ᏋᏮ ᏋᏮ

BIBLIOGRAPHY

ABBREVIATIONS

AB = *Art Bulletin*. New York: College Art Association, 1919–.

Agathias, *Histories*. = *Agathias Myrinaei Historiarum libri quinque*. Ed. Rudolf Keydell. *Corpus Fontium Historiae Byzantinae*. Vol. 2. Berlin: W. de Gruyter, 1967.

AJA = *American Journal of Archaeology*. New York: Macmillan Co., 1897–.

Anthol. Graec. = *Greek Anthology*. Trans. W.P. Paton. 5 vols. LCL, 1925–27.

Anthol. Palat. = *Epigrammatum Anthologia Palatina cum Planudeis et appendice nova epigrammatum veterum ex libris et marmoribus doctorum; annotatione inedita Boissonadii, Chardonis de la Rochette, Bothii, partim inedita Jacobsii, metrica versione, Hugonis Grotti et apparatus critico instruxit Fred. Dübner.* 3 vols. Paris: Didot, 1864–80.

BMGS = *Byzantine and Modern Greek Studies*. Oxford: Blackwell, 1975–.

Bonn ed. = *Corpus Scriptorum Historiae Byzantinae*. Ed. B.G. Niebuhr et al. Bonn: Impensis Ed. Weberi, 1828–.

Byz. Forsch. = *Byzantinische Forschungen*. Amsterdam: A.M. Hakkert, 1966–.

BZ = *Byzantinische Zeitschrift*. Munich: C.H. Beck, 1892–.

CA = *Cahiers Archéologiques*. Paris: A. & J. Picard, 1945–.

CFHB = *Corpus Fontium Historiae Byzantinae*. 1967–; in progress. Series Berolinensis: Berlin: Novi Eboraci: W. de Gruyter; Series Washingtonensis: Washington, DC: Dumbarton Oaks; Series Vindobonensis: Vienna, Verlag der Österreichischen Akademie der Wissenschaften; Series Bruxellensis: Brussels; Byzantion Series Italica: Rome, Accademia nationale dei Lincei; Series Atheniensis: Athens, Apud Institutum Graecoromanae antiquitatus auctoribus edendis destinam, Academiae Atheniensis.

CSCO = *Corpus Scriptorum Christianorum Orientalium*. Louvain: Peters, L. Durbecq, Secretariat du Corpus SCO, E. Typographeo Linguarum Orientalium; Paris: E. Typographeo Reipublicae Poussielque.

PIERRE GILLES' CONSTANTINOPLE ॐ

CSHB = *Corpus Scriptorum Historiae Byzantinae*. Ed. B.G. Niebuhr et al. Bonn: Impensis Ed. Weberi, 1828–.

DOP = *Dumbarton Oaks Papers*. Cambridge, MA: Harvard University Press, 1941–.

EO = *Échos d'Orient*. Paris: Maison de la Bonne Presse, 1897–1940. From 1943, *Études Byzantines*. Paris: Institut français d'études Byzantines, 1943–.

IstMitt = *Istanbuler Mitteilungen*. Tübingen: E. Wasmuth.

Janin, *CPByz2* = Raymond Janin. *Constantinople byzantine: Développement urbain et répertoire topographique*. 2nd ed. Archives de l'Orient Chrétien, 4A. Paris: Institut français d'études byzantines, 1964.

Janin, *Églises* = Raymond Janin. *La géographie ecclésiastique de l'Empire byzantin 3: Les églises et les monastères*. Paris: Institut français d'études byzantines, 1953; 2nd ed., 1969.

JÖB [G] = *Jahrbuch der Österreichischen Byzantinischen Gesellschaft*. Graz (etc.): H. Bölhaus. From 1969, *Jahrbuch der Österreichischen Byzantinistik*. Vienna: Verlag der Österreichischen Akademie der Wissenschaften.

JRA = *Journal of Roman Archaeology*. Ann Arbor, MI: Editorial Committee of the Journal of Roman Archaeology, c. 1988–.

JRIBA = *Journal of the Royal Institute of British Architects*. London: The Institute.

JRS = *Journal of Roman Studies*. London: Society for the Promotion of Roman Studies, 1941–.

Kleiss, *Plan* = W. Kleiss, *Topographisch-archäologischer Plan von Istanbul. Verseichnis der Denkmaler und Fundort*. Tübingen: E. Wasmuth, 1965.

Krautheimer, *Early Christian and Byzantine Architecture* = Richard Krautheimer and Slobodon Curcic. *Early Christian and Byzantine Architecture*. New Haven: Yale University Press, 1986.

LCL = Loeb Classical Library. Cambridge, MA: Harvard University Press; London: W. Heinemann; New York: G.P. Putnam's Sons; et al.

Mainstone, *Hagia Sophia* = Roland J. Mainstone. *Hagia Sophia: Architecture, Structure and Liturgy of Justinian's Great Church*. New York: Thames and Hudson, 1988.

Majeska, *Russian Travelers* = George Majeska. *Russian Travelers to Constantinople in the Fourteenth and Fifteenth Centuries*. Dumbarton Oaks Studies 19. Washington DC: Dumbarton Oaks, 1984.

Mango, *Brazen House* = Cyril Mango. *The Brazen House: A Study of the Vestibule of the Imperial Palace of Constantinople*. Copenhagen: I. Kommission hos Munksgaard, 1959.

Mango, *Le développement*: = Cyril Mango. *Le développement urbain de Constantinople, IVe–VIIe siècles*. Paris: Diffusion de Boccard, 1985; 2nd ed., Paris, 1990.

Mango, *Studies* = Cyril Mango. *Studies on Constantinople*. Aldershot: Variorum, 1993.

Mathews, *Early Churches of CP* = Thomas Mathews. *The Early Churches of Constantinople: Architecture and Liturgy*. University Park: The Pennsylvania State University Press, 1971.

MGH = Monumenta Germaniae Historica.

Müller-Wiener, *Bildlexikon* = Wolfgang Müller-Wiener. *Bildlexikon zur Topographie Istanbuls*. Tübingen: E. Wasmuth, 1977.

NachGött = *Nachrichten von der Akademie [Gesellschaft] der Wissenschaften zu Göttingen. Philologisch-historische Klasse*. Göttingen: Vandenhoeck & Ruprecht, 1941–.

Necipoğlu *BC* = *Byzantine Constantinople: Monuments, Topography and Everyday Life*. Ed. Nevra Necipoğlu. Leiden: J. Brill, 2001.

Notitia urbis CP = *Notitia dignitatum, accedunt notitia urbis Constantinopolitanae et Laterculi provinciarum*. Ed. O. Seeck. Berlin: Weidmann, 1876.

OCD = *Oxford Classical Dictionary*. Ed. Simon Hornblower and Antony Spawforth. 3rd ed. Oxford: Oxford University Press, 1996.

ODB = *Oxford Dictionary of Byzantium*, Ed. Alexander Kazhdan et al. 3 vols. Oxford: Oxford University Press, 1991.

PatriaCP = *Patria Constantinopoleos*. Ed. T. Preger. *Scriptores Originum Constantinopolitanarum*. Vol. 2. Leipzig: B.G. Teubner, 1907.

PG = *Patrologia cursus completus, Series graeca*. Ed. J.-P. Migne. 161 vols. in 166 Parts. Paris: Petit-Mountrouge, 1857–66.

PL = *Patrologia cursus completus, Series latina*. Ed. J.-P. Migne. 221 vols. in 222 Parts. Paris: Petit-Mountrouge, 1844–80.

Pliny, *Natural History* = Pliny. *Natural History*. Trans. H. Rackham. 10 vols. LCL, 1938–63.

Preger, *Scriptores* = *Scriptores originum constantinopolitarum*. Ed. T. Preger. Leipzig: B.G. Teubner, 1901–7.

REB = *Revue des Études Byzantines*. Paris: Institut français d'études byzantines, 1943–.

Schneider, *Byzanz* = A.M. Schneider. *Byzanz. Vorarbeiten zur Topographie und Archäologie der Stadt*, Istanbuler Forschungen 8. Berlin, 1936.

SLNPNF = *Select Library of the Nicene and Post-Nicene Fathers*. New York: The Christian Literature Co., 1887–1900.

Socrates, *Hist. Eccles.* = *Ecclesiastica Historia.* 3 Vols. Ed. Robert Hussey. Hildesheim–New York: George Olms Verlag, 1992.

Sozomen, *Eccl. Hist.* = *Kirchengeschichte.* Ed. J. Bidez and J.C. Hansen. Berlin: Akademie-Verlag, 1960.

Strabo, *Geography* = *Geography of Strabo.* Trans. H.L. Jones. 8 vols. LCL, 1917–33.

Suda, *Lexikon* = *Suidae Lexikon.* Ed. A. Adler. 5 vols. Leipzig: I. Bekker, 1928–38.

Van Millingen, *Walls* = Alexander van Millingen. *Byzantine Constantinople: The Walls of the City and Adjoining Historical Sites.* London: J. Murray, 1899.

Zosimus, *New History* = *New History.* Trans. with commentary by Ronald T. Ridley. Australian Association for Byzantine Studies, *Byzantina Australiensia* 2. Sydney: Australian Association for Byzantine Studies, 1982.

☙

WORKS BY PIERRE GILLES

Gilles, Pierre (Petrus Gyllius). *De Bosporo Thracio libri tres.* Lyon Guillaume Rovillium, 1561; Leiden: Elsevier, 1632, 1635.

—. *De Bosporo Thracio libri tres.* Lyon: Guillaume Rovillium, 1561. Facsimile ed. Athens: Vivliopōleion N. Karavia, 1967.

—. *De topographia Constantinopoleos et de illius antiquitatibus libri quatuor.* Lyon: Guillaume Rovillium, 1561; Leiden: Elsevier, 1661.

—. *De topographia Constantinopoleos et de illius antiquitatibus libri quatuor.* Lyon: Guillaume Rovillium, 1561. Facsimile ed. Athens: Vivliopōleion N. Karavia, 1967.

—. *The Antiquities of Constantinople.* Trans. John Ball. London: Private printing, 1729. Rev. ed., New York: Italica Press, 1988.

—. "Elephanti nova descriptio missa ad reverendissimum cardinalem Armaignacum ex urbe Berhoea Syriaca." In *Ex Aeliani de Historia animalium libri xvii,* p. 499.

—. *Ex Aeliani de Historia animalium libri xvii de vi et natura animalium.* Lyon: Sebastien Gryphius, 1533.

—. *Lexicon graecolatinum.* Basil: V. Curio, 1532.

—. *Liber unus de Galicis et Latinis nominibus piscium.* Lyon: Sebastien Gryphius, 1533.

PRIMARY SOURCES

Agathias Scholasticus. *Agathias Myrinaei historiarum libri quinque.* Ed. Rudolf Keydell. *Corpus Fontium Historiae Byzantinae.* Vol. 2. Berlin: W. de Gruyter, 1967.

—. *Historiae.* Ed. L. Dindorf. *Historici Graeci minores 2.* Leipzig: B.G. Teubner, 1871.

Agnellus. *Liber pontificalis.* PL 106:459–750.

Ammianus Marcellinus. *Ammianus Marcellinus. Rerum gestarum libri.* Ed. John C. Rolfe. 3 vols. LCL, 1935–39.

—. *Inscriptionis latinae selectae.* Ed. Hermann Dessau. 3 vols. Berlin: Weidmann, 1892–1916.

—. *Rerum gestarum libri qui supersunt.* Ed. W. Seyfarth. 2 vols. Leipzig: B.G. Teubner, 1978.

Ante-Nicene Fathers: Translations of the Writings of the Fathers. Ed. Alexander Roberts and James Donaldson. Rev. ed. A. Cleveland Coxe. 10 vols. Peabody, MA: Hendrickson Publishers, 1994.

Anthologia graeca. Ed. H. Stadtmüller. Leipzig: G.T. Teubner, 1894–1906.

Anthologia graeca: The Greek Anthology. Trans. W.P. Paton. LCL, 1916.

Anthologia graeca. With German translation. Ed. Hermann Beckby. 4 vols. Munich: E. Heimeran, 1958.

Apollonius Rhodius. *Argonautica*. Ed. Herman Frankel. Scriptorum Classicorum Bibliotheca Oxoniensis. Oxford: Oxford University Press, 1961.

___. *Argonautika: The Story of Jason and the Quest for the Golden Fleece.* Trans. Peter Green. Berkeley: University of California Press, 1997.

Apuleius. *Metamorphoses*. Ed. and trans. Arthur Hanson. 2 vols. LCL, 1989.

___. *Metamorphoses*. Translation in *The Context of Ancient Drama*. Trans. Slater and Csapo. Ann Arbor: University of Michigan Press, 1995.

Athenaeus. *Deipnosophistae*. Trans. Charles Burton Gulick. 7 vols. LCL, 1927–67.

Bibliotheca Hagiographica Graeca. Ed. François Halkin. 3rd ed. Brussels: Société des Bollandistes, 1957.

Buondelmontius, Cristophorus. *Description des iles de l'archipel: Version grecque par un anonyme*. Ed. and trans. E. Legrand. Paris: Ernest Leroux, 1897.

—. *Librum insularum archipelagi*. Ed. G. de Sinner. Leipzig: G. Reimer, 1824.

—. "Le vedute di Constantinopoli di Cristoforo Buondelmonti." Ed. G. Gerola. *Studi Bizantini e Neoellenici* 3 (1931): 247–79.

Callimachus. *Callimachus II: Hymni et epigrammata*. Ed. R. Pfeiffer. Oxford: Clarendon Press, 1953.

—. *Opera Omnia*. Ed. R. Pfeiffer. 2 vols. Oxford: Clarendon Press, 1949–53.

Cantacuzenus, Ioannes. *Historia–Historiarum*. Ed. L. Schopen. 3 vols. Bonn: Impensis Ed. Weberi, 1828–32.

—. *The History of John Cantacuzenus (Book IV): Text, Translation and Commentary*. Ed. T.S. Miller. Washington, DC: Dumbarton Oaks, 1975.

Cassiodorus (Senator). *Chronica ad a. DXIX*. Ed. T. Mommsen. MGH, Auctores antiquissimi 11. *Chronica minora*, 2:109–61. Berlin: Weidmann, 1894.

—. *Variae*. Ed. Theodore Mommsen. 3 vols. MGH. Berlin: Weidmann, 1894.

Cedrinus, Georgius. *Historiarum compendium*. Ed. Immanuel Bekker. 2 vols. Bonn: Impensis Ed. Weberi, 1838–39.

Chalkokondyles, Laonikos. *Atheniensis, Historiarum libri decem*. Ed. Immanuel Bekker. Bonn: Weber, 1843.

——. *Historiarum Demonstrationes*. Ed. E. Darko. Budapest: Sumptibus Academiae Litterarum Hungaricae, 1922.

——. *Laonikos Chalkokondyles: A Translation and Commentary of the "Demonstrations of Histories," Books I–III*. Ed. Nicolaos Nicoloudis. London: Kings College, 1992.

Choniates, Niketas. *Nicetae Choniatae historia* 1. Ed. J.L. Van Dieten. Berlin-New York: De Gruyter, 1975.

——. *O City of Byzantium: Annals of Niketas Choniates*. Trans. Harry J. Magoulias. Detroit: Wayne State University Press, 1984.

Chronicon paschale. Ed. L. Dindorf. CSHB. 2 vols. Bonn: Weber, 1832.

——. *Chronicon Paschale 284–628 A.D.* Trans. Michael and Mary Whitby. Liverpool: University Press, 1989.

Claudian. *Claudian*. Trans. M. Platnauer. 2 vols. LCL, 1922.

——. *Claudii Claudiani Carmina*. Ed. J.B. Hall. Leipzig: B.G. Teubner, 1985.

Clavijo, Ruy Gonzalez de. *Embassy to Tamerlane, 1403–1406*. Trans. G. LeStrange. London: The Broadway Travellers, 1928. Repr. in *The Islamic World in Foreign Travel Accounts* 1. Ed. F. Sezgin. Frankfurt and Mainz: Publications of the Institute for the History of Arabo-Islamic Science, 1994.

Codinus, Georgius. *Excerpta de antiquitatibus Constantinopolitanis*. Ed. Immanuel Bekker. Bonn: Impensis Ed. Weberi, 1834.

Comnena, Anna. *Alexiad*. Trans. Elizabeth Dawes. London: Kegan Paul, 1928.

——. *Alexiad*. Ed. and trans. B. Leib. 3 vols. Paris: Société d'édition Les Belles Lettres. 1937–67.

Constantine IV, Patriarch. *Ancient and Modern Constantinople*. Trans. J.P. Brown. London: Steven Bros., 1868.

Constantine Porphyrogenitus. *De cerimoniis aulae byzantinae*. Ed. J. Reiske. Bonn: Impensis Ed. Weberi, 1829–40.

——. *De cerimoniis: Le Livre des ceremonies*. Ed. Albert Vogt. 2 vols. Paris: Les Belles Lettres, 1935–40.

Constantinople, Ecumenical Patriarchate of. Τὸ ἁγίασμα τῆς Πατριαρχικῆς. Istanbul: Ecumenical Patriarchate, 1952.

Corpus inscriptionum latinarum. 18 vols. Berlin: G. Reimer, 1862–1989.

Cosmas Indicopleustes. *The Christian Topography of Cosmas, an Egyptian Monk*. Trans. J.W. McCrindle. London: The Hakluyt Society, 1897.

——. C. Stornajolo, ed. *Le Miniature della topografia cristiana di Cosma Indicopleuste: Codice Vaticano Greco 699*. Milan: U. Hoepli, 1908.

—. *Topographie Chrétienne.* Trans. Wanda Wolska-Conus. 3 vols. Paris: Éditions du Cerf, 1973.

Dio Cassius. *Historia Romana.* Trans. Earnest Cary. 9 vols. LCL, 1914–27.

Diodorus Siculus. *Bibliotheca historica.* Trans. C.H. Oldfather. 10 vols. LCL, 1933–.

Dionysius Areopagita. *Ecclesiastica hierarchia.* PG 3:369–584.

Dionysius Byzantius. *Anaplus Bospori. De Bospori Navigatione. Quae supersunt una cum supplementis in geographos minores aliisque eiusdem argumenti fragmentis.* Ed. Charles Wescher. Paris: E. Typographeo Publico, 1874.

—. *Epistulae imperatorum pontificum aliorum. Corpus scriptorum ecclesiasticorum latinorum* 35.2. Vienna: F. Tempsky, 1898.

—. *Anaplus Bospori.* Ed. R. Güngerich. Berlin: Weidmann, 1958.

Du Cange, Charles. *Constantinopolis christiana, seu descriptio urbis Constantinopolitanae.* Paris: L. Billaine, 1680.

—. *Glossarium ad scriptores mediae et infimae graecitatis.* Lyons: Anissonios, J. Posuel & C. Rigaud, 1688.

Emperors, Patriarchs and Sultans of Constantinople, 1373–1513: An Anonymous Greek Chronicle of the Sixteenth Century. Ed. Marios Philippides. Brookline, MA: Hellenic College Press, 1990.

Epigrammatum Anthologia Palatina cum planudeis et appendice nova epigrammatum veterum ex libris et marmoribus doctorum; annotatione inedita Boissonadii, Chardonis de la Rochette, Bothii, partim inedita Jacobsii, metrica versione, Hugonis Grotti et apparatus critico instruxit Fred. Dübner. 3 vols. Paris: Didot, 1864–80.

Eunapius Sardianus. *Historia: Fragmenta historicorum graecorum.* Ed. K. Müller. 5 vols. Paris: A. Firmin Didot, 1841–85. Repr. Frankfurt-am-Main: Minerva, 1975.

—. *Lives of the Philosophers.* Trans. W.C. Wright. LCL, 1952.

—. *Vitae Sophistarum.* Ed. G. Giangrande. Rome: Typis Publicae Officinae Polygraphicae, 1956.

Eusebius of Caesarea. *Historia ecclesiastica.* In *Eusebius Werke* 2.1–3. *Die Kirchengeschichte.* Ed. E. Schwartz. 3 vols. Leipzig: J.C. Hinrichs, 1903–9.

—. *Ecclesiastical History.* Trans. Kirsopp Lake. 2 vols. LCL, 1926–32.

—. *Vita Constantini.* In *Eusebius Werke* 1.1. *Über das leben des Kaisers Konstantin.* Ed. F. Winkelmann. Berlin: Akademie-Verlag, 1973.

—. *In Praise of Constantine: A Historical Study and New Translation of Eusebius' Tricennial Orations.* Trans. and commentary by H.A.

Drake. University of California Publications: Classical Studies 15. Berkeley: University of California Press, 1975.

——. *Eusebius Werke*. Ed. F. Winkelmann. Berlin: Akademie-Verlag, 1975.

Eustathius of Thessalonika. *De emendanda vita monachia*. PG 136.

——. *Eustathii metropolitae Thessalonicensis opuscula*. Ed. T.F.L. Tafel. Frankfurt: Sumptibus Sigismundi Schmerber, 1832.

——. *Commenatrii ad Homeri Iliadem pertinentes*. Ed. M. Van der Valk. 4 vols. Leiden: J. Brill, 1979.

Eustratius. *Vita Eutychii Patriarchae*. PG 86.2:2273–2390.

Eutychius Patriarcha. *Sermo de paschate et eucharista*. PG 86.2:2391–2402.

Evagrius Scholasticus. *Historia ecclesiastica*. PG 86.2:2415–2886.

——. *Ecclesiastical History*. Ed. J. Bidez and L. Parmentier. London: Methuen & Co., 1898.

——. *Evagrius Scholasticus the Church Historian*. Ed. Pauline Allen. Spicilegium Sacrum Lovaniense, Études et Documents 41. Louvain: Spicilegium Sacrum Lovaniense, 1981.

Festus, Sextus Pomponius. *Sexti Pompei Festi De verborum significatu quae supersunt cum Pauli epitome*. Ed. Wallace M. Lindsay. Leipzig: B.G. Teubner, 1913.

Germanus Constantinopolitanus. *Historia ecclesiastica*. Ed. A. Galland. Paris, 1779. Also in PG 98:384–453.

——. *Il commentario liturgico di s. Germano patriarca constantinopolitano e a versione latina di Anastasio bibliotecario*. Ed. Nilo Borgia. Grottaferrata, 1912.

Glycas, Michael. *Annales*. Ed. Immanuel Bekker. CSHB. Bonn: Impensis Ed. Weberi, 1836.

Greek Anthology. Trans. W.P. Paton. 5 vols. LCL, 1916–.

Gregorius Nazianzenus. *Oratio 43 in laudem Basilii Magni*. PG 36:493–606.

Gregorius Thaumaturgus. *Epistola canonica*. PG 10:1019–48.

Gregorius Turonensis. *Libri miraculorum*. PL 71:705–828.

Gyraldus, Lilius Gregorius (Giraldi, Giglio Gregorio). *Historiae deorum gentilium*. Basel: Oporinus, 1548.

Herodian. *Histories*. Trans. C.R. Whittaker. 2 vols. LCL, 1969–70.

Herodotus. *History*. Trans. A.D. Godley. 4 vols. LCL, 1926–38.

—— *Histories*. Trans. A. De Selincourt. New York: Penguin, 1963.

Ho megas synaxaristēs. Ed. K. Dukake. Athens: Ek tou Typographeiou M. Papagēorgia, 1889–97.

Horace. *Q. Horati Flacci carmina.* Ed. Fr. Vollmer. Leipzig: B.G. Teubner,
1907.

Ibn Batuta, *Voyages.* Trans. B.R. Sanguinetti and C. Defremery. 4 vols.
Paris: Imprimerie Imperiale, 1858.

——. with introduction and notes by S. Yerasimos. Paris: F. Maspero,
1982.

Ignatius Deaconus. *Vita s. Nicephori.* PG 100:41–168.

Ioannes Chrysostomus. *Opera.* PG 47–64.

Iustinianus I (Justinian I). *Corpus iuris civilis.* Ed. T. Mommsen, P.
Kruger et al. 3 vols. Berlin: Weidmann, 1899–1902; 2nd ed.
Berlin: Weidmann, 1928–29.

Jerome. *Contra vigilantium.* PL 23:353–67.

——. *Dedicatur Constantinopolis omnium paene urbium nuditate in
Chronicon.* Ed. J.K. Fotheringham. London: H. Milford, 1923.

——. *Opera.* Ed. G. Morin and P. Antin. CCSL 22–30. Turnhout: Brepols,
1958–59.

Jordanes. *The Gothic History of Jordanes.* Introduction and commentary
by Charles C. Mierow. New York: Barnes & Noble, 1960.

Josephus. *The Works of Flavius Josephus.* Trans. William Whiston. 4 vols.
Grand Rapids, MI: Kregel Publications, 1995.

Justin, Marcus Junian. *Epitome of the Philippic History of Pompeius
Trogus.* Trans. J.C. Yardley with commentary by Waldemar Heckel.
Oxford: Clarendon Press, 1997.

Lactantius. *De mortibus persecutorum.* In *The Works of Lactantius.* Trans.
W. Fletcher. Edinburgh: T. & T. Clark, 1871.

Leo VI. *Les nouvelles de Leon VI le Sage.* Ed. P. Noailles and A. Dain.
Paris: Les Belles Lettres, 1944.

Leo Grammaticus. *Chronologia.* Ed. Immanuel Bekker. Bonn: Impensis
Ed. Weberi, 1842.

Leontius Byzantius, *Opera.* PG 86:1185–2016.

——. *Leontius of Byzantium.* Ed. D. Evans. Dumbarton Oaks Studies 13.
Washington, DC: Dumbarton Oaks, 1970.

Liber pontificalis. Ed. L. Duchesne. 3 vols. Paris: E. Thorin, 1886.

Liutprand of Cremona. *The Works of Liudprand of Cremona: Antapodosis,
Liber de Rebis Gestis Ottonis, Relatio de legatione Constantinopolitana.*
Trans. F.A. Wright. London: Routledge & Sons, 1930.

Livy. *Histories.* Trans. Frank G. Moore. 14 vols. LCL, 1958.

Lucan. *M. Annaei Lucani Pharsalia.* Ed. C.E. Haskins. London: George
Bell & Sons, 1887.

Lydus, Ioannis (John the Lydian). *Ioannis Laurentii Lydi liber de mensibus*. Ed. Richard Wünsch. Leipzig: Teubner, 1898.

Malalas, John. *The Chronicle of John Malalas: A Translation*. Trans. Elizabeth Jeffreys, Michael Jeffreys, and Roger Scott, with Brian Coke et al. Melbourne: Australian Association for Byzantine Studies, 1986.

Malchus. See P.A. Brunt. "On Historical Fragments and Epitomes." *Classical Quarterly* 30.2 (1980): 477–94.

Marcellinus Comes. *Chronicon*. PL 51:917–48.

Maximus Confessor. *Mystagogia*. PG 91:657–717.

—. *S. Massimo Confessore, a Mistagogia ed altri scritti*. Ed. Raffaele Cantarella. Testi cristiani 4. Florence: Testi Cristiani, 1931.

Menander Protector. *Historia*. CSHB 9. Bonn: Weber, 1829.

Menavino, Giovantonio. *I costumi et la vita de Turchi*. Florence: Apprezzo Lorenzo Torrentino, 1561.

Narratio de structura templi s. Sophiae. Script. Orig. Const. Ed. T. Preger. 1:74–108. Leipzig: B.G. Teubner, 1901.

Nazarius Rhetor. *Opera quae existant universa Constantini Magni*. PL 8.

—. *XII panegyrici Latini*. Ed. A. Baehrens. Leipzig: B.G. Teubner, 1874.

—. *Poetae latini minores*. Ed. Emil Baehrens. 5 vols. Leipzig: B.G. Teubner, 1879–83.

Nestor-Iskander. *The Tale of Constantinople: Of Its Origin and Capture in the Year 1453*. Trans. Walter Hanak and Marios Philippides. Late Byzantine and Ottoman Studies 5. New Rochelle: A.D. Caratzas, 2000.

Nicephorus Callistus. *Ecclesiastica historia libri xviii*. PG 145–47.

Nicephorus Gregoras. *Byzantina historia*. 3 vols. Ed. L. Schopen and Immanuel Bekker. Bonn: Weber, 1828–55.

Nicephorus Patriarcha. *Breviarum historicum*. PG 100:875–994.

Nicolaus Andidorum. *Protheoria* = Theodorus Andidorum, *Brevis commentatio de divinae liturgiae symbolis*. PG 140:417–68.

Nicolaus Mesarites. "Description of the Church of Holy Apostles at Constantinople." Trans. Glanville Downey. *Transactions of the American Philosophical Society* 47 (1957): 857–924.

Notitia dignitatum, accedunt notitia urbis Constantinopolitanae et Laterculi provinciarum. Ed. O. Speeck. Berlin: Weidmann, 1876.

Ordines romani du haut moyen-âge. 2, Les textes. Ed. Michael Andrieu. Louvain: Spicilegium sacrum lovaniense, 1948.

Pachymeres, Georgius. *De Michaele et Andronico Palaeologis*. 2 vols. Ed. Immanuel Bekker. Bonn: Weber, 1835.

—. *Georges Pachymeres Relations Historiques*. Ed. Albert Failler. Trans. Vitalien Laurent. Paris: Belles Lettres, 1984.

Palladius. *Dialogus de vita sancti Ioannis*. PG 47:5–82.

—. *Palladii dialogus de vita s. Ioannis Chrysostomi*. Ed. P.R. Coleman-Norton. Cambridge: Cambridge University Press, 1928.

Panegyrici Latini. Trans. Mark Vermes. In *From Constantine to Julian: Pagan and Byzantine Views*. Ed. Samuel N.C. Lieu and Dominic Montserrat. London: Routledge, 1996.

Papinius, Statius P. (Publius Papinius). *Silvae*. Trans. J.H. Mozley. 2 vols. LCL, 1928.

Parastaseis Syntomoi Chronikae. Παραστάσεις σύντομοι χρονικαί. Ed. Theodor Preger. *Scriptores Originum Constantinopolitanarum*. Leipzig: B.G. Teubner, 1901.

—. *Constantinople in the Early Eighth Century: The Parastaseis Syntomoi Chronikai*. Ed. Averil Cameron and Judith Herrin. Leiden: E.J. Brill, 1984.

Patria Constantinopoleos. Ed. Theodor Preger. *Scriptores Originum Constantinopolitanarum*. Leipzig: B.G. Teubner, 1901–7.

Paulus Silentiarius. *Descriptio ecclesiae Sanctae Sophiae et ambonis*. Ed. Immanuel Bekker. Bonn: Imprensis Ed. Weberi, 1837.

—. *Descriptio s. Sophiae et ambonis*. In Paul Friedlander, *Johannes von Gaza und Paulus Silentiarius, Kunstbeschreibungen justinianischer Zeit*. Leipzig: B.G. Teubner, 1912.

Pausanias. *Description of Greece*. Trans. W.H.S. Jones. Volumes 1-4. LCL, 1918–35.

Philostratus. *Lives of the Sophists*. Trans. W.C. Wright. LCL, 1952.

Photius, Patriarch. *The Homilies of Photius*. Trans. Cyril Mango. Cambridge MA: Harvard University Press, 1958.

—. *Logoi kai homiliae*. Ed. S. Aristarches. Constantinople: Typos Tēe Annuaire Oriental, 1900.

Pindar. *Odes*. Trans. J. Sandys. LCL, 1937.

—. *Scholia vetera in Pindari carmina. III*. Ed. A.B. Drachmann. Leipzig: Teubner, 1927.

Pliny. *Natural History*. Trans. H. Rackham. 10 vols. LCL, 1938–63.

Plutarch. *Lives*. Trans. Bernadette Perin. 11 vols. LCL, 1914–26.

—. *Plutarchii libellus de fluviis*. Ed. Rudolf Hercher. Leipzig: Weidmann, 1851.

Pollux, Iulius. *Pollucis Onomasticon*. Ed. Eric Bethe. 3 vols. Leipzig: B.G. Teubner, 1900–1937.

Polybius. *Historiae*. Ed. L. Dindorf and T. Buettner-Wobst. 5 vols. Rev. ed. Stuttgart: Teubner, 1962-63.

—. *The Histories*. Trans. W.R. Paton. 6 vols. LCL, 1960-64.

Pomponius Laetus, Julius. *Compendium historiae Romanae*. Venice: Bernardinus Venetus de Vitalibus, 1499.

Priscian. *Institutiones Grammaticae*. Ed. Martin Hertz. *Grammatici latini* 2. Ed. Heinrich Keil. Vols. 1-7. Leipzig: B.G. Teubner, 1855-1923.

—. *De laude Anastasii imperatoris*. Ed. Emil Baehrens. *Poetae Latini minores*. Leipzig: B.G. Teubner, 1883.

Procopius. *Anecdota*. Trans. H.B. Dewing. LCL, 1935.

—. *Buildings*. Trans. H.B. Dewing and Glanville Downey. LCL, 1959.

—. *Opera omnia*. Ed. J. Haury and G. Wirth. 4 vols. 2nd ed. Leipzig: B.G. Teubner, 1962-64.

Prudentius. *Prudentius*. Trans. H.J. Thomson. 2 vols. LCL, 1949-53.

Psellos, Michael. *Fourteen Byzantine Rulers: The Chronographia of Michael Psellus*. Trans. F.K.A. Senker. Baltimore: Penguin Books, 1966.

Pseudo-Codinus. *Patria Konstantinoupoleos. Script. Orig. Const.* Ed. T. Preger. 2. Leipzig: B.G. Teubner, 1906, 135-289.

Regesten der Kaiserurkunden des oströmischen Reichs. Ed. Franz Dolger. Hildesheim: H.A. Gerstenberg, 1924-.

Robert of Clari. *La Conquête de Constantinople*, Ed. Philippe Lauer. Paris: E. Champion, 1924. Trans. E. McNeal. New York: Columbia University Press, 1936.

Les saints stylites. Ed. H. Delehaye. Brussels: Société des Bollandistes, 1923.

Schedel, Hartmann. *Liber chronicarum cum figuris et imaginibus ab initio mundi*. Nuremberg: Anton Koberger, 1493.

Scholarius, Georges. *Oeuvres completes de Georges Scholarios*. Ed. L. Petit, et al. Paris: Maison de la Bonne Presse, 1928-36, 428.

Select Library of the Nicene & Post-Nicene Fathers of the Church. Ed. H.P. Wace and P. Schaff. Oxford-New York: The Christian Literature Co., 1887-.

Seneca. *Epistulae morales ad Lucilium*. Trans. Richard Gummere. 3 vols. LCL, 1967.

Socrates Scholasticus. *Ecclesiastica Historia*. 3 vols. Ed. Robert Hussey. Hildesheim-New York: George Olms Verlag, 1992.

—. *Historia ecclesiastica*. PG 67:30-843.

—. *Socrates of Constantinople: Historian of Church and State*. Ed. Theresa Urbainczyk. Ann Arbor: University of Michigan Press, 1997.

Sophronius Hierosolymitani. *Commentaria liturgicus*. PG 87.3:3981-4002.

Souda–Suidas. *Souda.* Ed. A. Adler. 5 vols. Leipzig: I. Bekker, 1928–38.

Sozomen. *Kirchengeschichte.* Ed. J. Bidez and J.C. Hansen. Berlin: Akademie- Verlag, 1960.

—. *Historia ecclesiastica.* PG 67:844–1630.

Stephanos Byzantinii. *A Geographical Lexicon on Ancient Cities, Peoples, Tribes and Toponyms.* Chicago: Ares, 1992.

Strabo. *Geography of Strabo.* Trans. H.L. Jones. 8 vols. LCL, 1917–33.

Sybilline Oracles. *Oracula Sibyllina.* Ed. A. Rzach. Vienna: F. Tempsky, 1891.

Symeon Magister. *Annales.* In *Theophanees Continuatus.* Ed. Immanuel Bekker. Bonn: Weber, 1838.

Symeon Metaphrastes. *Vita et conversios. Ioannis Chrysostomi.* PG 114:1046–1210.

Symeon Thessalonicensis. *De sacra liturgia.* PG 155:253–304.

—. *De sacro templo.* PG 155:305–62.

—. *Expositio de divino templo.* PG 155:697–750.

Synaxarium Ecclesiae Constantinopolitane, Propylaeum ad Acta Sanctorum, Novembris. Ed. Hippolyte Delehaye. Brussels: Société des Bollandistes, 1902.

Synesius Cyrensis. *Epistola 67.* PG 66:1411–32.

Testamentum domini. Ed. I. Rahmani. Mainz: Kirchheim, 1899.

Theodoretus Cyrensis. *Ecclesiasticae historiae.* PG 82:879–1278.

Theodorus Lector. *Excerpta ex ecclesiastica historia.* PG 86.1:165–216.

Theodorus Mopsuestiae. *Les Hoelies catechetiques.* Ed. R. Tonneau and R. Devreesse. Studi e testi 145. Vatican City: Biblioteca apostolica vaticana, 1949.

Theodorus Studita. *Descriptio constitutionis monasterii Studii.* PG 99:1703–20.

Theodosius I. *Theodosiani libri xvi.* Ed. T. Mommsen. Berlin: Weidmann, 1905.

Theophanes. *The Chronicle of Theophanes the Confessor, Byzantine and Near Eastern History AD 284–813.* Trans. and ed. Cyril Mango and Roger Scott. Oxford: Clarendon Press, 1997.

—. *Chronographia.* Ed. John Classen. 2 vols. Bonn: Weber, 1839–41.

Theophanes Continuatus. Ed. Immanuel Bekker. Bonn: Weber, 1838.

Theophrastus. *Theophrastus De Causis Plantarum I.* Ed. B. Einarson and G.K.K. Link. LCL, 1976–90.

Thucydides. *The Peloponnesian War.* Trans. Rex Warner. New York: Penguin Books, 1954.

Tzetzes, Ioannes. *Epistulae*. Ed. P.A.M. Leone. Leipzig: B.G. Teubner, 1972.

—. *Historiae*. Ed. P.A.M. Leone. Naples: Liberia scientifica editrice, 1968.

—. *Historiarum variarum chiliades*. Ed. T. Kiessling. Leipzig: F.C.G. Vogel, 1826.

Varro, Marcus Terentius. *Varro on the Latin Language*. Trans. Roland G. Kent. 2 vols. LCL, 1938.

Vita et acta S. Maximi confessoris. PG 90:67–222.

Vita Nicolai Studitae. PG 105:864–925.

Vitruvius. *The Ten Books on Architecture*. Trans. M. Morgan. Cambridge: Harvard University Press, 1914.

Xenophon. *Anabasis*. Trans. C.L. Brownson. 4 vols. LCL, 1930–38.

—. *Expeditio Cyri (Cyropaedia)*. Trans. Walter Miller. 2 vols. LCL, 1914.

—. *Hellenika. Historica Graeca*. Ed. Charles Hude. Stuttgart: Teubner, 1969.

Zonaras, Ioannes. *Annalium*. Ed. Moritz Pinder. CSHB. Bonn: Weber, 1894.

—. *Epitomae historiarum*. Ed. L. Dindorf. 6 vols. Leipzig: B.G. Teubner, 1868–75.

—. *Epitomae historiarum*. Ed. T. Buttner-Wobst. CSHB. Bonn: Weber, 1897.

Zosimus. *Historia nova*. Ed. L. Mendelssohn. Leipzig: B.G. Teubner, 1887. Repr. Hildesheim: Olms, 1963.

—. *New History*. Trans. with commentary by Ronald T. Ridley. Australian Association for Byzantine Studies, Byzantina Australiensia 2. Sydney: Australian Association for Byzantine Studies, 1982.

—. *Zosimus: Historia Nova. The Decline of Rome*. Trans. James J. Buchanan and Harold T. Davis. San Antonio: Trinity University Press, 1967.

SECONDARY WORKS

Aetos: Studies in Honor of Cyril Mango. Stuttgart, Leipzig: B.G. Teubner, 1998.

Ahunbay, Metin and Zeynep. "Restoration Work at the Zeyrek Camii, 1997–98." In Necipoğlu BC, 117–32.

Alexander, Paul J. *The Byzantine Apocalyptic Tradition.* Berkeley: University of California Press, 1985.

—. *The Oracle of Baalbek: The Tiburtine Sibyl in Greek Dress.* Dumbarton Oaks Studies 10. Washington, DC: Dumbarton Oaks, 1967.

Alföldi, Andrew. *Conversion of Constantine and Pagan Rome.* Trans. Harold Mattingly. Oxford: Clarendon Press, 1948; repr. 1969.

Allen, Pauline. *Evagrius Scholasticus the Church Historian.* Spicilegium Sacrum Lovaniense 1. Louvain: Spicilegium Sacrum Lovaniense, 1981.

Alpatov, Mikhail. "Die Fresken der Odalar-Djami in Konstantinopel." *BZ* 26 (1926): 373–79.

—, and Brunov, Nikolai. "Une nouvelle église de l'époque des Paleologues à Constantinople." *EO* 24 (1925): 14–25.

Ambraseys, Nicholas N. and Caroline F. Finkel. *The Seismicity of Turkey and Adjacent Areas: A Historical Review, 1500–1800.* Istanbul: M.S. Eren, 1995.

And, Metin. *Istanbul in the 16th Century: The City, The Palace, Daily Life.* Akbank Culture and Art Publication 59. Istanbul: Akbank, 1994.

Andreas, G.A. "Die Sophienkathedrale von Konstantinopel." *Kunstwissenschaftliche Forschungen* 1. Berlin: Frankfurter Verlag-Anstalt, 1931, 33–94.

Antoniades, E. *Ekphrasis tes Hagias Sophias.* 3 vols. Athens: Typois P.D. Sakellariou, 1907–83.

Asgari, N. "Roman and Early Byzantine Marble Quarries of Proconessus." In *Proceedings of the Tenth International Congress of Classical Archaeology, 1973.* Ankara: Türk Tarih Kurumu, 1978.

Aspropoulos, Stavros. "Aegyptiaca in Istanbul." *Minerva* 2 (1991).

Babinger, Franz. *Die Geschichteschreiben der Osmanen und ihre Werke.* Leipzig: O. Harrasowitz, 1927.

—. *Mehmed the Conqueror and His Time.* Ed. W.C. Hickman. Trans. R. Manheim. Bollingen Series 96. Princeton: Princeton University Press, 1978.

Bakır, Mevlüde. "Impact and Consequences of Earthquakes in Byzantine Constantinople and Its Vicinity, AD 342–1454." Master of Arts Thesis. Istanbul: Bosporus University, 2002.

Bals, G. "Contribution à la question des églises superposées dans le domaine byzantin." *Actes du IVe Congrès international des études byzantines (Bulletin de l'institut archaeologique bulgare 10)* 2. Sofia: Imprimerie de la cour, 1936, 156–67.

Banduri, Anselmo Maria. *Imperium orientale; sive, Antiquitates Constantinopolae in quator partes distributae quae ex variis scriptorum graecorum operibus et praesertim ineditis adornatae, commentariis, et geographicis, topographicis.* Paris: J.B. Coignard, 1711.

Bardill, Jonathan. "A Catalogue of Stamped Bricks in the Ayasofya Collection." *Anatolian Archaeology* 1 (1995): 28–29.

—. "The Palace of Lausus and Nearby Monuments in Constantinople: A Topographical Study." *AJA* 101 (1997): 67–95.

Barisic, F. "Le siège de Constantinople par les Avares et les Slaves en 626." *Byzantion* 24 (1954): 371–95.

Barkan, O.M., and E.H. Ayverdi. *İstanbul Vakıfları Tahrir Defteri 953* (1546). Tarih İstanbul Fetih Cemiyeti İstanbul Enstitiüsü 61. Istanbul: Sayi, 1970.

Barnes, Timothy D. *Constantine and Eusebius.* Cambridge: Harvard University Press, 1981.

Basgelen, Nezih. "The Ancient Land Walls of Istanbul." *Sanat* 3 (1993): 16–31.

—. *The Wall in Anatolia through the Ages.* Trans. Bahar Atlamaz. Istanbul: N. Basgelen, 1993.

Bassett, Sarah Guberti. "The Antiquities in the Hippodrome of Constantinople." *DOP* 45 (1991): 87–96.

—. "*Historiae custos:* Sculpture and Tradition in the Baths of Zeuxippos (Constantinople: Iconography for the New Capital of the Roman Empire)." *American Journal of Archaeology* 100 (July 1996): 491–506.

—. "*Paene Omnium Urbium Nuditate:* The Reuse of Antiquities in Constantinople, Fourth through Sixth Centuries." PhD diss., Bryn Mawr College, 1985.

Becatti, Giovanni. *La colonna coclide istoriana: Problemi storici icono-graphici stilistici.* Studi e material del Museo dell'Impero romano 6. Rome: L'Erma di Bretschneider, 1960.

Beck, Hans-Georg. *Das byzantinische Jahrtausend.* Munich: Beck, 1978.

—. *Geschichte der byzantinischen Volksliteratur.* Munich: Beck, 1971.

—. *Kirche und theologische Literatur im byzantinischen Reich.* Munich: Beck, 1959.

—. "Konstantinopel: Zur Sozialgeschichte einer frühmittelalterlichen Haupstadt." *BZ* 58 (1965): 11–45.

—, ed. *Studien zur Frühgeschichte Konstantinopels.* Munich: Institut für Byzantinistik und Neugriechische Philologie der Universität, 1973.

Belting, Hans. "Ein Gruppe Konstantinopler Reliefs aus dem 11. Jahrhundert." *Pantheon*, 30.4 (1972): 263–71.

—. "Zur Skulptur aus der zeit um 1300 in Konstantinopel." *Münchener Jahrbuch der Bildenden Kunst* 23 (1972): 3, 63–100.

Berger, Albrecht. *Das bad in der Byzantinischen Zeit.* Munich: Insitut für Byzantinistik und neugriechlische Philologie der Universität, 1982.

—. "Die Altstadt von Byzanz in der vorjustinianischen Zeit." *Poikila Byzantina* 8. Varia 2. Bonn: Habelt, 1987: 8–30.

—. "Imperial and Ecclesiastical Processions." In Necipoğlu BC, 73–87.

—. *Untersuchungen zu den Patria Konstantinupoleos.* Bonn: Habelt, 1988.

Berzobohaty, Peter and Werner Jobst. "Mosaikenforschung, 1988. Bericht über die Arbeiten am Palastmosaik von Konstantinopel." *Anzeiger der phil-hist. Klasse der Österreichischen Akademie der Wissenschaften* 126. Vienna: Verlag der Österreichischen Akademie der Wissenschaften, 1989–1990, 225–37.

Bierman, Irene, Donald Preziosi, and Rifaat Abou al-Haj. *The Ottoman City and Its Parts: Urban Structure and Social Order.* Subsidia Balcanica, Islamica et Turcica 3. New Rochelle: A.D. Caratzas, 1991.

Birge, John K. *A Guide to Turkish Area Study.* Washington, DC: Committee on Near East Studies. American Council of Learned Societies, 1949.

Bittel, Kurt, and Alfons Maria Schneider. "Das Martyrion des hl. Euphemia beim Hippodrom." *Archäologischer Anzeiger* 56 (1941): 296–315.

Blair, Sheila and Jonathan Bloom. *The Art and Architecture of Islam 1250–1800.* New Haven: Yale University Press, 1994.

Blockley, R.C. *Ammianus Marcellinus: A Study of His Historiography and Political Thought.* Brussels: Latomus, 1975.

—. *The Fragmentary Classicising of Historians of the Later Roman Empire: Eunapius, Olympiodorus, Priscus and Malchus.* ARCA Classical and Medieval Texts, Papers and Monographs 6. Liverpool: F. Cairns, 1981.

Borrelli, Licia Vlad. "La porta dell'orologio di s. Sofia a Istanbul: Reismane dopo un restauro." *Annuario della Scuola Archeologica di Atene e delle missioni Italiane in Oriente* 57–58. Rome: Istituto Poligrafico dello Stato, 1979–80, 375–419.

—, and A. Guidi Toniato. "The Origins and Documentary Sources of the Horses of San Marco." In *The Horses of San Marco, Venice.* Exhibition Catalogue. London: Royal Academy, 1979, pp. 87–96.

Bouras, Charalambos. "Houses and Settlements in Byzantine Greece." In *Settlers in Greece.* Ed. O.B. Doumanis and P. Oliver. Athens, Ekdose "Architektōn Thematōn," 1974, 30–50.

Bradley, D.R. "The Composition of the *Getica.*" *Eranos* 64 (1966): 57–79.

Braudel, Fernand. *The Mediterranean and the Mediterranean World in the Age of Philip II.* 2 vols. New York: Harper and Row, 1972–73.

Brett, Gerard, Gunter Martiny, and R.B.K. Stevenson. *The Great Palace of the Byzantine Emperors: Being a First Report on the Excavations Carried out in Istanbul on behalf of the Walker Trust (University of St. Andrews) 1935–1938.* London: Oxford University Press, 1947.

Brown, T.S., Anthony Bryer, and David Winfield. "Cities of Heraclius." *BMGS* 4 (1978): 39–53.

Browning, Robert. *Medieval and Modern Greek.* London–New York: Cambridge University Press, 1969.

Brubaker, Leslie. "The Chalke Gate, the Construction of the Past, and the Trier Ivory." *BMGS* 23 (1999): 258–85.

Brun, Richard. "An Urban Design Imported from Rome to Constantinople." *Byzans och Norden: Akta for norkiska forskarkursen; byzantinsk konsuetenskap.* Uppsala: Almqvist, 1986.

Brunov, Nikolai. "Die Gul-Djami von Konstantinopel." *BZ* 30 (1929–30): 554–60.

—. "Die Odalar-Djami von Konstantinopel." *BZ* 26 (1926): 352–72.

—. "Ein Denkmal der Hofbaukunst von Konstantinopel." *Belvedere* 51–52 (1926): 217–36.

—. "L'église a croix inscrite a cinq nefs dans l'architecture Byzantine." *EO* 26 (1927): 257–86.

—. "Über zwei byzantinische Baudenkmaler von Konstantinopel aus dem XI Jahrhundert." *Byzantinisch-Neugriechische Jahrbucher* 9 (1931–32): 129–44.

—. "Zur Erforschung der Byzantinischen Baudenkmaler von Konstantinopel." *BZ* 32 (1932): 49–62.

Bruns, Gerda. *Der Obelisk und seine Basis auf dem Hippodrom zu Konstantinopel.* Istanbuler Forschungen 7. Istanbul: Universum-Druckerei, 1935.

Brunt, P.A. "On Historical Fragments and Epitomes." *Classical Quarterly* 30.2 (1980): 477–94.

Bryer, Anthony, and Heath Lowry, eds. *Continuity and Change in Late Byzantine and Early Ottoman Society*. Washington, DC: Dumbarton Oaks, 1986.

Buckton, David, ed. *The Treasury of San Marco Venice*. Milan: Olivetti, 1984.

Byzance retrouvée: Érudits et voyageurs français XVI–XVIII siècles. Paris: Sorbonne, 2001.

Byzantine Constantinople: Monuments, Topography and Everyday Life. Ed. Nevra Necipoğlu. Leiden: J. Brill, 2001.

Byzantios, Scarlatos. Ἡ Κωνσταντινούπολις I. Athens, 1851.

Byzantium and the Classical Tradition. Ed. M. Mullett and R. Scott. Spring Symposium of Byzantine Studies 13. Birmingham: University of Birmingham Centre for Byzantine Studies, 1981.

Çakmak, Ahmet, and Robert Mark, eds. *Hagia Sophia from Justinian to the Present*. Cambridge–New York: Cambridge University Press, 1992.

Cameron, Alan. *Circus Factions: Blues and Greens at Rome and Byzantium*. Oxford: Clarendon Press, 1976.

—. "Sir Thomas More and the Greek Anthology." In *Florilegium Columbianum: Essays in Honor of Paul Oskar Kristeller*. Ed. Karl-Ludwig Selig and Robert Somerville. New York: Italica Press, 1987, pp. 187–98.

—. *The Greek Anthology: From Meleager to Planudes*. Oxford: Clarendon Press, 1993.

—. *Porphyrius the Charioteer*. Oxford: Clarendon Press, 1973.

Cameron, Averil. *Agathias*. Oxford: Clarendon Press, 1970.

—. "The Artistic Patronage of Justin II." *Byzantion* 50 (1980): 62–84.

—. "Notes on the Sophiae, the Sophianae and the Harbor of Sophia." *Byzantion* 37 (1967): 11–20.

—. "Procopius and the Church of St. Sophia." *Harvard Theological Review* 58 (1965): 161–63.

—. *Procopius and the Sixth Century*. Berkeley: University of California Press, 1985.

—, and Judith Herrin. *Constantinople in the Early Eighth Century: The Parastaseis Syntomoi Chronikaiu*. Leiden: E.J. Brill, 1984.

Capizzi, Carmelo. "Anicia Giuliana (462ca–530ca): Ricerche sulla sua famiglia e la sua vita." *Rivista di studi bizantini e neoellenici* 5 (1968): 191–226.

Carnoy, H., and J. Nicolaïdès. *Folklore de Constantinople*. Paris: Bureaux de la Tradition E. Lechevalier, 1894.

Casson, Stanley, David Talbot Rice, and Arnold H.M. Jones. *Preliminary Report upon the Excavations Carried out in the Hippodrome of Constantinople in 1927 on Behalf of the British Academy*. London: Published for the British Academy by H. Milford, Oxford University Press, 1928.

—. *Preliminary Second Report upon the Excavations Carried out in and near the Hippodrome of Constantinople in 1927–1928 on Behalf of the British Academy*. London: Published for the British Academy by H. Milford, Oxford University Press, 1929.

Cecen, Kazim. *The World's Longest Water Supply*. İstanbul: Türkiye Sinai Kalkinma Bankası, 1996.

Celik, Zeynep. *The Remaking of Istanbul: Portrait of an Ottoman City in the Nineteenth Century*. Seattle: University of Washington Press, 1986.

Cezar, M. *Osmanli Devrinde Istanbul Yapilarinda Tahribat yapan Yanginlar ve Tabii Afetlerk, Turk Sanati Tarihi Arastirma ve Incelemeleri I*. İstanbul: Berksoy Matbaası, 1963.

Charanis, Peter. "The Significance of Coins as Evidence for the History of Athens and Corinth in the Seventh and Eighth Centuries." *Historia* 4 (1955): 163–72.

Chesnau, Jean. *Le Voyage de Monsieur d'Aramon*. Paris: Ernest Leroux, 1887.

Ciggaar, Krijnie. "Une description de Constantinople dans le Tarragonensis 55." *REB* 53 (1995): 117–40.

—. "Une description de Constantinople traduite par un pelèrin anglais." *REB* 34 (1976): 211–67.

Cirac, Sebastián. "Tres monasterios de Constantinopla visitados por Espanoles en el ano 1403." *REB* 19 (1961): 374–77.

Claude, D. *Die byzantinische Stadt im 6. Jahrhundert*. Munich: Beck, 1969.

Conant, Kenneth J. "The First Dome of St. Sophia and Its Rebuilding." *AJA* 43 (1939): 589–92.

Constantelos, Demetrios. *Byzantine Philanthropy and Social Welfare*. New Brunswick, NJ: Rutgers University Press, 1968.

Crow, James, and Alessandra Ricci. "Investigating the Hinterland of Constantinople: Interim Report on the Anastasian Long Wall (Thrace, Turkey)." *JRA* 10 (1997): 235–62.

Dagron, Gilbert. *Constantinople imaginaire*. Paris Universitaires de France, 1984.

—. *Naissance d'une capitale*. Paris: Presses Universitaires de France, 1974.

Dalman, Knut Olof. *Der Valens-Aquadukt in Konstantinopel*. With an Appendix by Paul Witteck. Istanbuler Forschungen 3. Bamberg: J.M. Reindl, 1933.

De Beylie, Léon Marie Eugène. *L'habitation byzantine*. Grenoble: Falque & F. Perrini; Paris: E. Leroux, 1902–3.

Deichmann, Friedrich W. *Studien zur Architektur Konstantinopels*. Deutsches Beitrage zur Altertumswissenschaft. Baden-Baden: B. Grimm, 1956.

Delehaye, Hippolyte. *Deux typica byzantines de l'époque des Paleologues*. Brussels: M. Lamertin, 1921.

—. "L'Invention des réliques de S. Menas à Constantinople." *AB* 29 (1910): 1–34.

Demangel, Robert. *Contribution à la topographie de l'Hebdomon*. Paris: E. de Boccard, 1945.

—, and Ernest Mamboury. *Le quartier des Manganes et la première Région de Constantinople*. Paris: E. de Boccard, 1939.

Denny, Walter. "A Sixteenth-Century Architectural Plan of Istanbul." *Ars Orientalis* 8 (1970): 49–63.

Dernschwam, Hans. *Istanbul ve Anadolu'ya Seyahat Günlüğü*. Trans. Y. Önen. Ankara: Kültür Bakanlığı Yayınları, 1992.

Dethier, Philipp A., and Andrea D. Mordtmann. *Epigraphik von Byzantion und Constantinopolis von den ältesten Zeiten bis zum Jahre Christi 1453*. Denkmalschriften 13. Vienna: A. Hölder, 1864.

Diehl, Charles. "Les fouilles du corps d'occupation français à Constantinople." *Académie des inscriptions et belles-lettres, Comptes rendues*. Paris: Académie des inscriptions et belles-lettres, (1922): 198–207; (1923): 241–48.

Diller, A. *The Textual Tradition of Stabo's Geography*. Amsterdam: A.M. Hakkert, 1975.

Dirimtekin, Feridun. "Adduction de l'eau à Byzance." *CA* 10 (1959): 217–43.

—. "Les fouilles dans la région des Blachernes pour retrouver les substructions des palais des Comnènes." *Turk Arkeoloji Dergisi* 9.2 (1960): 24–31.

—. "Les fouilles faites en 1946–47 et en 1958–60 entre Sainte-Sophie et Sainte-Irene à Istanbul." *CA* 13 (1962): 161–85.

—. "14. Minitika (Blachernae) Surlar, Saraylar ve Kiliseler." In *Fatih ve İstanbul* I. İstanbul: İstanbul Fethi Derneği, 1953, pp. 192–222.

—. "Le local du patriarchat à sainte Sophie." *IstMitt* 13–14 (1963–64): 113–27.

—. "Leylekkale, un aquéduc byzantin à 60 km au Nord-Ouest d'Istanbul." *ByzForsch* 3 (1968): 117–19.

—. *Saint Sophia Museum.* Istanbul: Türkiye Turing ve Otomobil Kurumu, 1971.

—. "Le skeuphylakion de Sainte-Sophie." *REB* 19 (1961): 390–400.

Djuric, Ivan. "La Fortune de Theodore Metochite (Family Clans and Political Administration in Constantinople under Andronicus II)." *CA* 14 (1996): 149–68.

Dmitrievskij, Aleksei. *Opisanie Liturgiceskike Rukopisei* 1. *Typica.* Kiev: Tip. Universiteta sv. Vladimira, 1895; repr. Hildesheim: G. Olms, 1965.

Downey, Glanville. "The Builder of the Original Church of the Holy Apostles at Constantinople." *DOP* 6 (1951): 51–80.

—, ed. and trans. "Description of the Church of the Holy Apostles at Constantinople by Nicholas Mesarites." *Transactions of the American Philosophical Society* 47 (1957): 855–924.

—. "Imperial Building Records in Malalas." *BZ* 38 (1938): 1–15, 299–311.

—. "Justinian as Builder." *AB* 32 (1950): 262–66.

—. "Notes on the Topography of Constantinople." *AB* 34 (1952): 235–36.

—. "The Tombs of the Byzantine Emperors at the Church of the Holy Apostles in Constantinople." *Journal of Hellenic Studies* 79 (1959): 27–51.

Drake, H.A. *In Praise of Constantine: A Historical Study and New Translation.* Berkeley: University of California Press, 1975.

Durliat, Jean. *De la ville antique à la ville Byzantine: Le problème des subsistances.* Rome: École française de Rome, 1990.

Duyuran, Rüstem. "First Report on Excavations on the Site of the New Palace of Justice at Istanbul." *İstanbul Arkeoloji Müzeleri Yıllığı* 5. Istanbul: Pulhan Matbaası, 1952: 33–38.

—. "Second Report on Excavations on the Site of the New Palace of Justice at Istanbul." *İstanbul Arkeoloji Müzeleri Yıllığı* 6. Istanbul: Pulhan Matbaası, (1953): 47–80.

Ebersolt, Jean. *Les anciens sanctuaires de Constantinople.* Paris: E. Leroux, 1951.

—. *Constantinople Byzantine et les Voyageurs du Levant.* Paris: E. Leroux, 1918.

—. *Le Grand Palais de Constantinople et le Livre des cérémonies.* Paris: E. Leroux, 1910.

—. *Sanctuaires de Byzance.* Paris: E. Leroux, 1921.

—. *Sainte-Sophie de Constantinople: Étude de topographie d'après les cérémonies.* Paris: E. Leroux, 1910.

—, and Adolpe Thiers. *Les Églises de Constantinople.* Paris: E. Leroux, 1913.

Emerson, W., and Robert L. Van Nice. "Hagia Sophia: The Collapse of
the First Dome." *Archaeology* 4 (1951): 94–103.

—. "Hagia Sophia: The Construction of the Second Dome and Its
Later Repairs." *Archaeology* 4 (1951), 162–71.

Engemann, Josef. "Melchior Lorichs Zeichnung eines Saulensockels in
Konstantinopel." In *Quaeritur, inventus colitur: Miscellanea in onore
di U.M. Fasola* 1. Vatican City: Pontificio Instituto di Archeologia
Cristiana, 1989.

Erzen, Jale. "Imperializing a City: Istanbul of the Sixteenth Century."
Environmental Design 1–2 (1987): 88–97.

Ettinghausen, Elizabeth. "Byzantine Tiles from the Basilica in the
Topkapı Sarayi and St. John of Studios." *CA* 7 (1954): 79–88.

Eyice, Semavi. "Aslanhane ve Cevresinin Arkeolojisi." (With French
translation). *İstanbul Arkeoloji Müzeleri Yıllığı* 11–12 (1954): 23–
33, 141–46.

—. *Bizans devrinde Bogazici.* Istanbul: Edebiyat Fakultesi Basımeyi,
1976.

—. "Les Fragments de la decoration plastique de l'église des Saints-
Apôtres" *CA* 8 (1956): 63–74.

—. "Istanbul'da Bias Imparatorlarinin Sarayi: Buyuk Saray." *Sanat
Tarihi Arastirmalari Dergisi* 1–3 (1988): 3–35.

—. *Istanbul: Petit guide à travers les monuments byzantins et turcs.*
Istanbul: Istanbul Matbaasi, 1955.

—. *Son Devir Bizans Mimarisi: İstanbul'da Palaiologoslar Devri Anıtları.*
Istanbul: Edebiyat Fakultesi Basımeyi, 1969.

Feld, Otto. "Beobachtungen in der Küçük Ayasofya zu Istanbul."
Istanbuler Mitteilungen 18 (1968): 264–69.

—. "Zu den Kapitellen des Tekfur Saray in Istanbul." *IstMitt* 19–20
(1969–70): 359–67.

Firatli, Nezih. "Decouverte de trois églises byzantines a Istanbul." *CA* 5
(1951): 163–78.

—. "Notes sur quelques hypogées paleo-chrétiens de Constantinople."
*Tortulae: Studien zu altchristlichen und byzantinishen Monumenten.
Römische quartalschrift für Altertumskunde und Kirchengeschichte* 30.
Supplementheft 20. Rome: Herder, 1936, 31–39.

—. *La Sculpture byzantine figurée au Musée Archéologique d'Istanbul.* Paris: Librarie d'Amerique et d'Orient Adrien Maisonneuve, Jean Maisonneuve Successeur, 1990.

Fischer, Erik. *Melchior Lorck: Drawings from the Evelyn Collection at Stoner Park, England and from the Department of Prints and Drawings, The Royal Museum of Fine Arts, Copenhagen.* No. 13. Copenhagen: Statens Museum für Kunst Kobberstiksamlingen, 1962.

Forcheimer, Philipp. *Die byzantinischen Wasserbehaelter von Konstantinopel: Beitraege zur Baukunst und zur Topographie von Konstantinopel. Byzantinische Baudenkmaeler 2.* Vienna: Verlag der Mechitharisten Congregation, 1891.

Foss, Clive. "Archaeology and the 'Twenty Cities' of Byzantine Asia." *AJA* 81 (1977): 469–86.

—. "Late Antique and Byzantine Ankara." *DOP* 31 (1977): 29–87.

—, and David Winfield. *Byzantine Fortifications.* Pretoria: University of South Africa, 1986.

Fossati, Gaspard. *Aya Sofia, Constantinople, As Recently Restored by Order of H.M. the Sultan Abdul Medjid.* London: Colnaghi & Co., 1852.

Fossati, Giuseppe. *Rilievi storico-artistici sulla architettura bizantina dal IV al XV secolo, notizie intorno alle scoperte fatte in Santa Sofia a Constantinopli, Maggio 1847–Luglio 1849.* Milan: Tipografia Bernardoni di C. Rebeschini e C., 1890.

Fowden, Garth. "Constantine, Silvester and the Church of S. Polyeuctus in Constantinople." *JRA* 7 (1994): 274–84.

—. "Nicagoras of Athens and the Lateran Obelisk." *Journal of Hellenic Studies* 107 (1987): 51–57.

Freely, John. *Istanbul.* Blue Guide. 4th ed. London: A.C. Black, 1997.

Frend, William C.H. *The Archaeology of Early Christianity: A History.* Minneapolis: Fortress Press, 1998.

Freshfield, Edwin. "Notes on the Church now Called the Mosque of the Kalenders at Constantinople." *Archaeologia* 55 (1897): 431–38.

Frolow, Anatole. "La Dédicace de Constantinople dans la tradition Byzantine." *Revue de l'Histoire des Religions* 127 (1941): 61–127.

From Constantine to Julian: Pagan and Byzantine Views. Ed. Samuel N.C. Lieu and Dominic Montserrat. London: Routledge, 1996.

Gates, M-H. "Archaeology in Turkey." *AJA* 99 (1995): 207–55; 100 (1996): 277–335.

Gautier, Paul. "Le typikon du Christ Sauveur Pantocrator." *REB* 32 (1974): 82–113.

Georg, J. "Darstellung Mariä als Zoodochos Pigi." *BZ* 18 (1909): 183–85.

George, W.S. *The Church of Saint Eirene at Constantinople*. London: Oxford University Press, 1912.

Gerlach, Stephan. *Tage-buch der von zween gorwurdigsten römischen Kaysern Maximiliano und Rudolpho…an die ottomanische Pforte zu Constantinopel abgefertigten…Gesandschaft*. Frankfurt: Verlegang Johann-David Zunners. Getruct bey Heinrich Friesen, 1674.

Giglioli, Giulio. *La Colonna di Arcadio a Constantinopoli*. Naples: G. Macchiaroli, 1952.

Glück, Heinrich. *Das Hebdomon und seine Reste in Makriköi*. Beiträge zur vergleichenden Kunstforshung 1. Vienna: Österr. Staatsdrukerei, 1920.

Göllner, Carl. *Turcica: Die europäischen Turkendrucke des XVI. Jahrhunderts*, Band 1: 1501–1550. Band 2: 1551–1600. Bucharest-Baden: Edituro Academiei R.P.R., 1961–68.

Gourlay, C. "Minor Churches of Constantinople." *JRIBA* 14.18 (1907): 637–49.

Grabar, André. "Études critiques: R. Naumann, Die Euphemiakirche." *CA* 17 (1967): 251–54.

—. *Martyrium: Recherches sur le culte des reliques et l'art chrétiene antique*. 2 vols. Paris: College de France, 1943–46.

—. *Sculptures byzantines de Constantinople IVe–Xe siècle*. Paris: Dépositaire A. Maisonneuve, 1963.

—. *Sculptures byzantines de Moyen Âge XIe–XIVe siècle*. Paris: Dépositaire A. Maisonneuve, 1976.

Grape, Wolfgang. "Zum Stil der Mosaiken in der Kilise Camii in Istanbuls." *Pantheon* 32 (1974): 3–13.

Greatrex, Geoffrey. "The Nika Riot: A Reappraisal." *Journal of Hellenic Studies* 117 (1997): 60–87.

Grélois, Jean-Pierre. "Pierre Gilles." In *Byzance Retrouvée: Érudits et voyageurs français XVI-XVIII siècles*. Paris: Sorbonne, 2001, pp. 30–31.

Grelot, Guillaume J. *Relation nouvelle d'un voyage à Constantinople*. Paris: D. Foucault, 1680.

Grierson, Philip. "The Tombs and Obits of the Byzantine Emperors (337–1042)." With an additional note by Cyril Mango and Ihor Sevcenko. *DOP* 16 (1962): 1–63.

Grossman, Peter. "Beobachtungen an der Kefeli-Mescid in Istanbul." *IstMitt.* 16 (1966): 241–49.

—. "Zum Atrium der Irenenkirche in Istanbul." *IstMitt.* 15 (1965): 186–207.

Grosvenor, E.A. *Constantinople*. Boston: Roberts Brothers, 1895.

Grumel, Venance. "Le 'Miracle habituel' de Notre-Dame des Blachernes." *EO* 30 (1931): 129–46.

—. *Les regestres des Actes du patriarcat de Constantinople*. Paris–Istanbul: Socii Assumptionistae Chalcedonesis, 1932.

Guidoni, E. "Sinan's Construction of the Urban Panorama." *Envrionmental Design* 1–2 (1987): 20–32.

Guilland, Rodolphe. "La chaine de la Corne d'Or." *Epetēris Hetaireias Byzantiōn Spoudōn* 15 (1955): 88–120.

—. "Constantinople Byzantine: Le port palatin du Boukoleon." *Byzantinoslavika* 11 (1950): 187–206.

—. *Études byzantines*. Paris: Presses Universitarires de France, 1959.

—. *Études de topographie de Constantinople Byzantine*. Berlin: Akademie-Verlag; Amsterdam: Hakkert, 1969.

—. "Études sur la topographie de Constantinople byzantine." *Hellenika* 17 (1962): 95–104.

—. "Études sur la topographie de Byzance: Les Thermes de Zeuxippe." *JÖBG* 15 (1966): 261–71.

—. "Études sur le Grand Palais de Constantinople: La Terrasse du Phare." *JÖBG* 13 (1964): 87–101.

—. "Études sur le palais d'Hormisdas." *Byzantinoslavica* 12 (1951): 210–37.

—. "Études sur l'Hippodrome de Byzance: Les Courses de l'Hippodrome." *Byzantinoslavica* 27 (1966): 6–8, 26–40.

—. "Études sur l'Hippodrome de Byzance 6. Les Spectacles de l'Hippodrome." *Byzantinoslavica* 27 (1966): 289–307.

—. "Études sur l'Hippodrome de Constantinople 10. La Déchéance et la ruine de L'Hippodrome." *Byzantinoslavica* 30 (1969): 209–19.

—. "Études sur l'Hippodrome de Byzance 11. Les Dimensions de l'Hippodrome." *Byzantinoslavica* 31 (1970): 1–11.

—. "The Hippodrome at Byzantium." *Speculum* 23 (1948): 679–82.

—. Περι τὴν Βασίλειον τάξιν Κωνσταντίνου Ζ τοῦ Πορφυρογεννήτου. 'Η Χαλχῆ καὶ τὰ πέριξ αὐτῆς.'Ο Αυγυστεων." In 'Επετηρὶς 'Εταρείας Βυζαντινῶν Σπουδῶν 18 (1948): 153–72.

—. "Les portes de Byzance sur le Propontide." *Byzantion* 23 (1953): 181–204.

Gülekli, Nurettin.C. *Hagia Sophia*. Ankara: Turkish Press, Broadcasting & Tourist Dept., 1947.

Gurlitt, Cornelius. *Die Baukunst Konstantinopels*. 2 vols. Berlin: E. Wagmuth, 1912.

—. "Zur Topographie Konstantinopels im 16. Jahrhunderts." *Oriental Archiv* 2 (1911–12): 1–9, 51–65.

Haldon, John, and Bryan Ward-Perkins. "Evidence from Rome for the Image of Christ on the Chalke Gate in Constantinople." *BMGS* 23 (1999): 286–96.

Hallensleben, Horst. "Zu Annexbauten der Kilise Camii in Istanbul." *IstMitt* 15 (1965): 208–17.

Hamy, E.T. "Le père de la zoologie française: Pierre Gilles d'Albi." *Revue des Pyrénées* 12 (1990): 561–88.

Harrison, R. Martin. "The Church of St. Polyeuctos in Istanbul and the Temple of Solomon." In *Okeanos: Essays Presented to Ihor Sevcenko.* Harvard Ukrainian Studies 7. Cambridge, MA: Ukrainian Research Institute, Harvard University, 1983: 276–79.

—. *Excavations at Sarachane in Istanbul.* 2 vols. Princeton: Princeton University Press; Washington DC: Dumbaron Oaks, 1986.

—. *A Temple for Byzantium: The Discovery and Excavation of Anicia Juliana's Palace-Church in Istanbul.* Austin: University of Texas Press, 1989.

—, and Nezih Firatli. "Discoveries at Sarachane, 1964." *İstanbul Arkeoloji Müzerleri Yıllığı* 13–14 (1966): 128–34.

—, and Nezih Firatli. "Excavations at the Sarachane in Istanbul." *DOP* 19 (1965): 230–36.

Heisenberg, August. *Grabeskirche und Apostelkirche* 2. Leipzig: J.C. Hinrichs, 1908.

Hellenkemper, G. "Salies, die Datierung der Mosaiken im Grossen Palast zu Konstantinopel." *Bonner Jahrbucher* 187 (1987): 273–86.

Hemmerdinger, B. *Essai sur l'histoire du texte de Thucydide.* Paris: Les Belles Lettres, 1955.

Herges, A. "Le monastère du Pantocrator à Constantinople." *EO* 2 (1898–99): 70–88.

Hillenbrand, Robert. *Islamic Architecture: Form, Function and Meaning.* Edinburgh: Edinburgh University Press, 1994.

Humphrey, John H. *Roman Circuses.* London–Berkely: University of California Press, 1986.

Hunger, Herbert. *Die hochsprachliche profane Literatur der Byzantiner.* 2 vols. Munich: Beck, 1978.

—. "Der Kaiserpalast zu Konstantinopel: Seine Funktionen in der byzantinischen Aussen- und Innenpolitik." *JÖB* 36 (1986): 1–11.

İnalcık, Halil. "The Hub of the City: The Bedestan of Istanbul."
    International Journal of Turkish Studies 1 (1980): 1–17.
—. "Istanbul: An Islamic City." *Journal of Islamic Studies* 1 (1990): 1–23.
—. *The Ottoman Empire: The Classical Age 1300–1600.* London:
    Weidenfeld & Nicolson, 1973.
—. "The Policy of Mehmed II toward the Greek Population of Istanbul
    and the Byzantine Buildings of the City." *DOP* 23 (1970): 213–49.
Irigoine, J. *Histoire du texte du Pindar.* Paris: C. Klincksieck, 1952.
Istanbul: City of Seven Hills. Istanbul: Ertug & Kocabiyik, c.1994.
Istanbul, World City, Habitat II. Istanbul: Türkiye Ekonomik ve
    Toplumsal Tarih Vakfı, 1996.
Iversen, Erik. *Obelisks in Exile 2: The Obelisks of Istanbul and England.*
    Copenhagen: Gad, 1972.

Jacoby, David. "La population de Constantinople à l'époque
    Byzantine." *Byzantion* 31 (1961): 81–110.
—. "Les Juifs Venetiens de Constantinople et leur communauté de
    XIIIe au milieu du XVe siècle." *Revue des Études Juives* 131 (1972):
    397–400.
—. "Les quartiers juifs de Constantinople à l'époque Byzantine."
    Byzantion 37 (1967): 189–205.
—. "The Urban Revolution of Latin Constantinople (1204–1261)." In
    Necipoğlu BC, pp. 277–97.
James, Liz. "'Pray Not to Fall into Temptation and Be on Your Guard':
    Pagan Statues in Christian Constantinople (Ninth-Century
    Texts)." *Gesta* 35 (1996): 12–20.
Janin, Raymond. *Constantinople Byzantine: Développement urbain et
    répertoire topographique.* 2nd ed. Archives de l'Orient Chrétien, 4A.
    Paris: Institut français d'études byzantines, 1964.
—. "Les couvents secondaires de Psamathia." *EO* 33 (1933): 326–31.
—. *Les Églises et les monastères des grandes centres byzantines.* Paris:
    Institut français d'études byzantines, 1975.
—. *La Géographie ecclésiastique de l'Empire byzantin 1: Le siège de
    Constantinople et le patriarcat oecumenique. 3: Les églises et les
    monastères.* Paris, 1953; 2nd ed. Paris: Institut français d'études
    byzantines, 1969.
—. "Le palais patriarchal de Constantinople byzantine." *REB* 20
    (1962): 131–55.
—. "Les monastères du Christ Philanthrope à Constantinople." *REB* 4
    (1946): 135–62.

——. "Les sanctuaires de Byzance sous la domination latine." *Études Byzantines* 1 (1944): 134–84.

——. "La topographie de Constantinople byzantine: Études et décou-vertes, 1918–38." *EO* 38 (1939): 136–45.

Jantzen, H. *Die Hagia Sophia des Kaisers Justinian in Konstantinopel.* Cologne: Dumont Schauberg, 1967.

Jenkins, Romily J.H. "The Bronze Athena at Byzantium." *Journal of Hellenic Studies* 67 (1947): 31–33.

Jerphanion, Guillaume. *La voix des monuments: Notes et études d'archéologie chrétienne.* Paris–Brussels: Van Oest, 1930.

Jobst, Werner, Behcet Erdal, and Christian Gurtner. *Istanbul: The Great Palace Mosaic.* Istanbul: Arkeoloji Ve Sanat Yayınları, 1997.

Jones, Arnold H.M. *Cities of the Eastern Roman Provinces.* 2nd ed. Oxford: Clarendon Press, 1971.

——. *Constantine and the Conversion of Europe.* New York: Macmillan, 1949.

——. *The Greek City from Alexander to Justinian.* Oxford: Clarendon Press, 1940.

Kafescioğlu, Çigdem. "The Ottoman Capital in the Making: The Reconstruction of Constantinople in the Fifteenth Century." PhD. Diss., Harvard University, 1996.

——. "Vizerial Undertakings in the Making of Ottoman Istanbul." In *Art Turc–Turkish Art. 10e Congrès International d'art turc.* Geneva: Fondation Max Van Berchem, 1998.

Kalavrezou, Ioli. "Irregular Marriages in the Eleventh Century and the Zoe and Constantine Mosaic in Hagia Sophia." In *Law and Society in Byzantium.* Ed. Angeliki E. Laiou and Dieter Simon. Washington, DC: Dumbarton Oaks, 1991, pp. 241–59.

Karahan, Anne. "The Palaeologan Iconography of the Chora Church and Its Relation to Greek Antiquity (Kariye Camiii, Istanbul)." *Konsthistorik Tidskrift* 66.2–3 (1997): 89–95.

Karatay, Fehmi E. *Topkapı Sarayı Müzesi Kütüphanesi, Türkçe Yazmalar Katalogu.* 2 vols. Istanbul: Topkapı Museum Publications, 1961.

Karayannopulos, J. and G. Weiss. *Quellenkunde zur Geschichte von Byzanz (324–1453).* Wiesbaden: O. Harrassowitz, 1982.

Kautzsch, Rudolf. *Kapitellstudien.* Studien zur spätantiken Kunstgeschichte 9. Berlin-Leipzig: W. de Gruyter, 1936.

Kidonopoulos, Vassilios. *Bauten in Konstantinopel, 1204–1328: Verfall und Zerstorung, Restaurierung, Umbau und Neubau von Profan- und Sakralbauten.* Wiesbaden: Harrassowitz Verlag, 1994.

Kitzinger, Ernst. "The Cult of Images in the Age before Iconoclasm." *DOP* 8 (1954): 83–150.

Kleinbauer, Eugene W. *Saint Sophia at Constantinople: Singulariter in mundo.* Dublin, NH: Wilham L. Bauhan Publishers, 1999.

Kleiss, Wolfram. "Grabungen in Bereich der Chalkopratenkirche in Istanbul, 1965." *IstMitt.* 16 (1966): 217–40.

——. "Neue Befunde zur Chalkopratenkirche in Istanbul." *IstMitt.* 15 (1965): 149–67.

——. *Topographisch-archäologischer Plan von Istanbul: Verzeichnis der Denkmaler und Fundorte.* Tübingen: E. Wasmuth, 1965.

Kollwitz, Johannes. "Zur frühmittelalterlichen Baukunst Konstantinopels." *Römische Quartalschrift* 42 (1934): 233–50.

Kostof, Spiro. "The Primacy of Constantinople." In *A History of Architecture: Settings and Rituals.* New York: Oxford University Press, 1985, pp. 260–69.

Kowalski, Jacek. "L'architecture de Jerusalem et de Constantinople dans le Pélerinage de Charlemagne." *Revue d'Auvergne* 109 (1995): 93–104.

Krautheimer, Richard. "Again Saints Sergius and Bacchus at Constantinople." *JÖBG* 23 (1974): 251–53.

——. *Rome: Profile of a City, 312–1303.* Princeton: Princeton University Press, 1980.

——. *Studies in Early Christian, Medieval and Renaissance Art.* London-New York: New York University Press, 1971.

——. *Three Christian Capitals.* Berkeley: University of California Press, 1982.

——."Zur Kontantins Apostelkirche in Konstantinopel." In *Mullus: Festschrift Theodor Klauser.* Münster: Aschendorffsche Verlagsbuchhandlung, 1964, pp. 224–29.

——, and Slobodan Curčić. *Early Christian and Byzantine Architecture.* New Haven: Yale University Press, 1986.

Kritovoulos. *History of Mehmed the Conqueror.* Trans. C.T. Riggs. Princeton: Princeton University Press, 1954.

Krumbacher, Karl. *Geschichte der byzantinischen Litteratur.* 2nd ed. Munich: C.H. Beck, 1897.

Kuban, Doğan. *Istanbul: An Urban History.* Istanbul: History Foundation, 1996.

Kumbaracilar, Izzet, and Cahide Tamer. *Istanbul Surlari ve Yedikule and Yedikule-Altinkapi,* 1958. Repr. Levent: Turkish Touring and Automobile Assn., 1995.

Kuran, Aptullah. *Sinan: The Grand Old Master of Ottoman Architecture.* Istanbul: Hürriyet Vakfı Yayınları, 1986.

Lackner, Wolfgang. "Ein byzantinisches Marienmirakel." *Vyzantina* 13.2 (1985): 835–60.

Lafond, Jean. "Les vitraux histories du moyen âge découverts recemment à Constantinople." In *Bull. Soc. Nat. Antiquaires de France* (1964): 164–66.

Lampe, Geoffrey W.H. *Patristic Greek Lexicon.* Oxford: Clarendon Press, 1961–68.

Lasareff, Viktor. "Studies in the Iconography of the Virgin." *AB* 20 (1938): 26–65.

Lathoud, D., and P. Pezaud. "Le sanctuaire de la Vierge au Chalcoprateia." *EO* 23 (1924): 36–61.

Laurent, Vitalien. "Une Princesse byzantine au cloître." *EO* 29 (1930): 29–60.

Lavin, Irving. "The House of the Lord." *AB* 44 (1962): 1–27.

Lethaby, William R., and Harold Swainson. *The Church of Sancta Sophia, Constantinople.* New York: Macmillan & Co., 1894.

Lewis, Bernard. "The Ottoman Archives: A Source for European History." In *Report on Current Research.* Washington, DC: Middle East Institute, 1956.

Lewis, Charlton T. *An Elementary Latin Dictionary.* Oxford: Oxford University Press, 1992.

—, and Charles Short. *Latin Dictionary.* Oxford: Oxford University Press, 1879.

Liddell H.C., and R. Scott. *Greek-English Lexicon.* Oxford: Clarendon Press, 1991.

Lieu, Samuel N.C., and Dominic Montserrat. *From Constantine to Julian: Pagan and Byzantine Views. A Source History.* London & New York: Routledge, 1996.

Lifchez, Raymond. "Constantinople – Istanbul: The Making of a Muslim City." *Landscape Architecture* 21 (Winter 1977): 2–14.

Lotz, Corinna. "Hagia Sophia Tottering." *Architectural Review* 190 (March, 1992): 4.

Lowry, Heath. "From Lesser Wars to the Mightiest War: The Ottoman Conquest and the Transformation of Byzantine Urban Centers in the Fifteenth Century." In *Continuity and Change in Late Byzantine and Early Ottoman Period.* Ed. Anthony Bryer and Heath Lowry. Birmingham: University of Birmingham Centre for Byzantine Studies, 1986, pp. 323–38.

Maas, Michael. "Innovation and Restoration in Justinianic Constantinople." Ph.D. Diss. University of California, Berkeley, 1982.

Macridy, Theodore. "The Monastery of Lips and the Burials of the Palaeologi." *DOP* 18 (1964): 253–78.

Madden, Thomas F. "The Fires of the Fourth Crusade: A Damage Assessment." *BZ* 84–85 (1991–92): 72–93.

Magdalino, Paul. "Aristocratic *Oikoi* in the Tenth and Eleventh Regions of Constantinople." In Necipoğlu BC, pp. 53–69.

—. "The Byzantine Aristocratic Oikos." In *The Byzantine Aristocracy, IX–XIII Centuries.* Ed. Michael Angold. British Archaeological Reports. International Series 221. Oxford: B.A.R., 1984, pp. 92–111.

—. *Constantinople médiévale.* Paris: de Boccard, 1996.

—. "Manuel Komnenos and the Great Palace." *BMGS* 4 (1978): 101–14.

—. "Observations on the Nea Ekklesia of Basil I." *JÖB* 37 (1987): 51–64.

Maguire, Henry. "The Beauty of Castles: A Tenth-Century Description of a Tower at Constantinople." *Deltion tēs Christianikēs Archaiologikēs Hetaireias* 17 (1993–94): 21–24.

Mainstone, Rowland J. *Hagia Sophia: Architecture, Structure and Liturgy of Justinian's Great Church.* London: Thames & Hudson, 1988.

—. "Justinian's Church of St. Sophia, Istanbul: Recent Studies of Its Construction and First Partial Reconstruction." *Architectural History* 12 (1969): 39–49.

—. "The Reconstruction of the Tympana of St. Sophia at Istanbul." *DOP* 23–24 (1969–70): 355–68.

Majeska, George. "The Sanctification of the First Region: Urban Reorientation in Palaeologan Constantinople." In *Actes du XVe Congrès international d'études byzantines, Athènes, 1976,* 2. Athens: Association internationale des études byzantines, 1981, pp. 359–63.

—. *Russian Travelers to Constantinople in the Fourteenth and Fifteenth Centuries.* Dumbarton Oaks Studies 19. Washington, DC: Dumbarton Oaks, 1984.

Mamboury, C.E., and Th. Wiegand. *Die Kaiserpalaeste von Konstantinople zwischen dem Hippodrom und dem Marmara-Mer.* Leipzig & Berlin: W. de Gruyter, 1934.

Mamboury, Ernest. "Autour d'Odalar-Djamisi, à Stamboul." *EO* 19 (1920): 69–73.

—. "Les fouilles byzantines à Istanbul et ses environs" *Byzantion* 21 (1951): 433–37.

—. "1945: Les sondages à l'interieur de Ste. Sophie." *Byzantion* 21 (1951): 37–38.

—. "Topographie de sainte-Sophie: Le sanctuaire et la solea, le mitato-rion, etc." In *Atti del V Congresso di studi bizantini* 2. *Studi bizantini e neoellenici*, 6. Rome: Istituto per l'Europa Orientale, 1940.

—, and R. Demangel. *Le Quartier des Manganes et la première région de Constantinople*. Paris: E. Boccard, 1939.

Mango, Cyril. "Ancient *Spolia* in the Great Palace of Constantinople." In *Byzantine East and Latin West: Art Historical Studies in Honor of Kurt Weitzmann*. Princeton: Princeton University Department of Art and Archaeology, 1995, pp. 645–49.

—. "Antique Statuary and the Byzantine Beholder." *DOP* 17 (1963): 53–75.

—. *The Art of the Byzantine Empire, 312–1543: Sources and Documents*. Toronto: University of Toronto Press, 1986.

—. *The Brazen House: A Study of the Vestibule of the Imperial Palace of Constantinople*. Archaeologisk-kunsthustorike Meddeleser, Danske Videnskabernes Selskab IV.4. Copenhagen: I. Kommission hos Munksgaard, 1959.

—. *Byzantine Literature as a Distorting Mirror*. (Inaugural Lecture, Oxford, 21 May 1974). Oxford: Clarendon Press, 1975.

—. *Byzantium: The Empire of the New Rome*. London: Weidenfeld & Nicolson; New York: Scribner's, 1980.

—. "The Church of Sts. Sergius and Bacchus at Constantinople and the Alleged Tradition of Octagonal Palatine Churches." *JÖB* 21 (1972): 189–93.

—. "The Church of Sts. Sergius and Bacchus Once Again." *BZ* 68 (1975): 385–92.

—. "The Columns of Justinian and His Successors." In *Studies on Constantinople*. Aldershot: Variorum, 1993, X:1–20.

—. "Constantine's Column." In *Studies on Constantinople*. Aldershot: Variorum, 1993, III:1–6.

—. "Constantine's Mausoleum and the Translation of Relics." *BZ* 83 (1990): 51–62. Repr. with Addendum in *Studies on Constantinople*. Aldershot: Variorum, 1993, V:51–62; 434.

—. "Constantine's Porphyry Column and the Chapel of St. Constantine." *Deltion tēs Christianikēs Archaiologikēs Hetaireias*, Ser.

4.10 (Athens, 1981): 103–10. Repr. in *Studies on Constantinople*. Aldershot: Variorum, 1993, IV:103–10.

—. "Constantinopolitana." In *Jahrbuch des Deutschen Archäologischen Instituts* 80. Berlin, 1965, pp. 305–36. Repr. in *Studies on Constantinople*. Aldershot: Variorum, 1993, II:305–36.

—. "Daily Life in Byzantium." *JÖB* 31 (1981): 338–41.

—. "The Date of the Studius Basilica at Istanbul." In *BMGS Studies IV: Essays Presented to Sir Steven Runciman*. Oxford: B. Blackwell, 1978, pp. 115–22.

—. "The Development of Constantinople as an Urban Center." In *The 17th International Byzantine Congress: Main Papers*. New Rochelle, NY: A.D. Caratzas, 1986, pp. 117–36. Repr. in *Studies on Constantinople*. Aldershot: Variorum, 1993, pp. 117–36.

—. *Le développement urbain de Constantinople, IVe–VIIe siècles*. Paris: Diffusion de Boccard, 1985; 2nd ed., Paris: de Boccard, 1990.

—. "Le Diippion." *REB* 8 (1951): 159–61.

—. "L'Euripe de l'Hippodrome de Constantinople: Essai d'identification." *REB* 7 (1949–50): 180–93.

—. *Hagia Sophia: A Vision for Empires*. Istanbul: Ertug & Kocabiyik, 1997.

—. "Isaurian Builders." In *Polychronion: Festschrift Franz Dolger*. Heidelberg: C. Winter, 1966, pp. 358–65.

—. "Justinian's Equestrian Statue." Published as Letter to the Editor, *AB* 61 (1959): 1–16. Repr. in *Studies on Constantinople*. Aldershot: Variorum, 1993, XI:1–16.

—. "The Legend of Leo the Wise." *Zbornik radova Vizantoloskog instituta* 6 (1960): 59–93. Repr. in *Byzantium and Its Image*. Aldershot: Variorum, 1984, pt. 16, with Addenda 3–4.

—. *Materials for the Study of the Mosaics of St. Sophia at Istanbul*. Dumbarton Oaks Studies 8. Washington, DC: Dumbarton Oaks, 1962.

—. "A Note on Panagia Kamariotissa and Some Imperial Foundations of the Tenth and Eleventh Centuries at Constantinople." *DOP* 27 (1973): 130–32.

—. "Notes on Byzantine Monuments: Tomb of Manuel I Comnenus." *DOP* 23–24 (1969–70): 327–75.

—. "On the Cult of Saints Cosmas and Damian at Constantinople." In Θυμιαμα στη μνήμη της Λασκαρίνας Μπούρα. Athens: Benaki Museum, 1994, pp. 189–92.

—. "The Palace of Marina, the Poet Palladas, and the Bath of Leo VI." In *Mélanges M. Chatzidakis*. Athens, 1991, pp. 321–30.

—. "The Shoreline of Constantinople in the Fourth Century." In Necipoğlu BC, pp. 17–28.

—. *Studies on Constantinople*. Aldershot: Variorum, 1993.

—. "The Triumphal Way of Constantinople and the Golden Gate." *DOP* 54 (2000): 173–94.

—. "The Work of M.I. Nomidis in the Vefa Kilise Camii, Istanbul (1937–38)." In Μεσαιωνικὰ καὶ νέα ἑλληνικά 3. Athens: Academy of Athens, 1990, pp. 421–29. Repr. in *Studies on Constantinople*. Aldershot: Variorum, 1993, XXII:421–29.

—, and Gilbert Dagron, eds. *Constantinople and Its Hinterland*. Aldershot: Variorum, 1995.

—, and Ernest J.W. Hawkins. "Additional Finds at Fenari Isa Camii, Istanbul." *DOP* 22 (1968): 177–84.

—, and Ernest J.W. Hawkins. "Additional Notes on the Monastery of Lips." *DOP* 18 (1964): 299–315.

—, and Ernest J.W. Hawkins. "The Apse Mosaics of St. Sophia at Istanbul." *DOP* 19 (1965): 3–51.

—, and Ernest J.W. Hawkins. "The Mosaics of St. Sophia at Istanbul: The Fathers in the North Tympanum." *DOP* 26 (1972): 1–41.

—, and Romily J.H. Jenkins. "The Date and Significance of the Tenth Homily of Photios." *DOP* 9–10 (1955–56): 125–40.

—, and Ihor Sevcenko. "Remains of the Church of St. Polyeuktos at Constantinople." *DOP* 15 (1961): 243–47.

—, and Ihor Sevcenko. "Some Churches and Monasteries on the South Shore of the Sea of Marmara." *DOP* 27 (1973): 235–77.

—, M. Vikers, and E.D. Francis. "The Palace of Lausus at Constantinople and Its Collection of Ancient Statues." *Journal of the History of Collections* 4 (1992): 89–98.

Mango, Marlia Mundell. "The Porticoed Street at Constantinople." In Necipoğlu BC, pp. 29–51.

Manners, Ian. "Constructing the Image of a City: The Representation of Constantinople in Christopher Buondelmonti's *Liber Insulum Archipelagi*." In *Annals of the Association of American Geographers* 87.1 (March 1, 1997): 72–102.

Mansel, Arif Mufid. "The Excavations of the Balaban Aga Mesdjidi in Istanbul." *AB* 15 (1933): 210–29.

—. "İstanbul'daki 'Burmali Sutun.'" *Türk Tarih Kurumu Belleten* 34 (1970): 189–209.

Mark, Robert. *Light, Wind, and Structure: The Mystery of the Master Builders*. Cambridge, MA and London: MIT Press, 1990.

—, with A. Westgard. "The First Dome of the Hagia Sophia: Myth vs Technology." In *Domes from Antiquity to the Present: Proceedings of the IASS–MSU International Symposium. Istanbul, Turkey, May 30–June 3, 1988*. Ed. I. Muygan. Istanbul: Mimar Sinan University, 1988, pp. 163–72.

Marlier, Georges. *La Renaissance flamande: Pierre Coeck d'Alost*. Bruxelles: R. Finck, 1966.

Mathews, Thomas. *The Art of Byzantium*. London: Calmann and King, 1998.

—. *The Byzantine Churches of Istanbul: A Photographic Survey*. University Park–London: The Pennsylvania State University Press, 1976.

—. *The Early Churches of Constantinople: Architecture and Liturgy*. University Park: The Pennsylvania State University Press, 1971.

—, and Ernst. J.W. Hawkins. "Notes on the Atik Mustafa Pasa Camii in Istanbul and Its Frescoes." *DOP* 39 (1985): 125–34.

Mayer, Robert. *Byzantion, Konstantinupolis, Istanbul: Ein genetische Stadtgeographie*. Vienna: Holder-Pichler-Tempsky, 1943.

Megaw, Arthur H.S. "Notes on Recent Work of the Byzantine Institute in Istanbul." *DOP* 17 (1963): 335–64.

Mellink, Machteld J. "Archaeology in Asia Minor: Istanbul-Sarachane." *AJA* 69 (1965): 133–49; 70 (1966): 139–59; 71 (1967): 155–74.

Ménage, V.L. "The Serpent Column in Ottoman Sources." *Anatolian Studies* 14 (1964): 169–78.

Mendel, G. *Catalogue des sculptures grecques, romaines, et byzantines*. 3 vols. Constantinople: En Vente au, 1912–14.

Micklewright, Nancy. "Looking at the Past: Nineteenth-Century Images of Constantinople as Historic Documents." *Expedition* 32 (1990): 24–32.

Miller, Timothy S. *The Birth of the Hospital in the Byzantine Empire*. Baltimore: The Johns Hopkins University Press, 1985.

—. "Byzantine Hospitals." *DOP* 38 (1984): 53–63.

—. "The Sampson Hospital of Constantinople." *Byz. Forsch.* 15 (1990): 101–35.

Millet, G. *L'École grecque dans l'architecture byzantine*. Paris: Leroux, 1916.

—. "Sainte-Sophie avant Justinien." *Orientalia christiana periodica* 13 (1947): 587–612.

Miranda, Salvador. *Étude de topographie du palais sacre de Byzance*. Paris: [s.n.], 1976.

—. *Les palais des empereurs byzantins.* Mexico City, 1964.
Modern Greek Culture: A Selected Bibliography in English-French-German-Italian. 4th rev. ed. Athens: National Hellenic Committee, 1974.

Moffatt, Ann. "A Record of Public Buildings and Monuments." In *Studies in Honor of John Malalas.* Sydney: Australian Association for Byzantine Studies, 1990, pp. 87–109.

Moran, Berna. *A Bibliography of the Publications in English Concerning the Turks, XV–XVIIIth Centuries.* Istanbul: İstanbul Matbaası, 1964.

Moran, Neil K. "The Skeuphylakion of the Hagia Sophia." *CA* 34 (1986): 29–32.

Moravcik, Gyula. *Byzantinoturcica.*1-2. Berlin: Akademie-Verlag, 1958.

Mordtmann, Andreas D. *Esquisse topographie de Constantinople.* Lille: Desclée, De Brouwer et Cie., 1892.

Müller-Wiener, Wolfgang. *Bildlexikon zur Topographie Istanbuls.* Tübingen: Wasmuth, 1977.

—. *Die Hafen von Byzantion, Konstantinopolis, Istanbul.* Tübingen: E Wasmuth, 1994.

Musto, Ronald G. "Just Wars and Evil Empires: Erasmus and the Turks." In *Renaissance Society and Culture: Essays in Honor of Eugene F. Rice Jr.* Ed. John Monfasani and Ronald G. Musto. New York: Italica Press, 1991, pp. 197–216.

Naumann, Rudolf. "Ausgrabungen bei der Bodrum Camii (Myrelaion)." *İstanbul Arkeoloji Müzeleri Yıllığı* 13–14 (1966): 135–39.

—. "Der antike Rundbau beim Myrelaion und der Palast Romanos I Lakapenos." *IstMitt* 16 (1966): 199–216.

—. "Vorbericht über die Ausgrabungen zwischen Mese und Antiochus-Palast 1964 in Istanbul." *IstMitt* 15 (1965): 135–46.

—, and Hans Belting. *Die Euphemia-Kirche am Hippodrom zu Istanbul und ihre Fresken.* Istanbuler Forschungen 25. Berlin: Mann, 1966.

Necipoğlu, Gulru. *Architecture, Ceremonial and Power: The Topkapi Palace in the Fifteenth and Sixteenth Centuries.* Cambridge, MA: MIT Press, 1991.

—. "The Life of an Imperial Monument: Hagia Sophia after Byzantium." In *Hagia Sophia from Justinian to the Present.* Ed. Ahmet Çakmak and Robert Mark. Cambridge and New York: Cambridge University Press, 1992, pp. 195–225.

Nesbitt, John, and J. Wiita. "A Confraternity of the Comnenian Era." *BZ* 68 (1975): 360–84.

Nicol, Donald M. *The Byzantine Lady.* New York: Cambridge University Press, 1994.

—. *The End of the Byzantine Empire*. London: E. Arnold, 1979.

Nicolaus Mesarites. "Description of the Church of the Holy Apostles at Constantinople." Trans. Glanville Downey. *Transactions of the American Philosophical Society* 47 (1957): 857–924.

Nicolay, Nicolas de. *Dans l'empire de Soliman le magnifique*. Ed. Marie-Christine Gomez-Geraud and Stephane Yerasimos. Paris: Presses du CNRS, 1989.

Nomidis, Miltiades I. *Notre-Dame d'Ephese* 2.8 (1958): 14–19; 2.11–12 (1959): 36–40.

—.' Η Ζωοδόχος Πηγή. Istanbul: Typois Kephalidou, 1937.

Nordhagen, Per Jones. "Mosaic of the Great Palace." *BZ* 16 (1963): 53–68.

Norwich, John Julius. "The Threat of Tourism to Sublime Byzantine Frescoes (in the Church of Kariye Camii, Istanbul)." *Art News* 5 (Oct. 1994): 21.

—, with Lars Karlsson, Andrew Finkel, and Andrew Byfield. "Istanbul in Peril: The Great Walls." *Cornucopia* 7.2 (1994–95): 28.

Oates, David. "A Summary Report on the Excavations of the Byzantine Institute in the Kariye Camii, 1957–58." *DOP* 14 (1960): 223–31.

Oberhummer, E. *Konstantinopel unter Suleiman dem Grossen*. Munich: R. Oldenbourg, 1902.

Ogan, Aziz. "Les fouilles de Topkapı Saray entreprises en 1937 par la Société d'histoire Turque." *Türk Tarih Kurumu Belleten* 4 (1940): 317–35.

Oikonomides, Nicolas. "Leo VI and the Narthex Mosaic of Saint Sophia." *DOP* 30 (1976): 151–72.

Ostrogorsky, George. "Byzantine Cities in the Early Middle Ages." *DOP* 13 (1959): 45–66.

—. *History of the Byzantine State*. New Brunswick: Rutgers University Press, 1969.

Ousterhout, Robert. *The Architecture of the Kariye Camii*. Washington, DC: Dumbarton Oaks–Harvard University Press, 1988.

—. "Architecture, Art and Komnenian Ideology at the Pantokrator Monastery." In Necipoğlu BC, 133–52.

—. *Master Builders of Byzantium*. Princeton: Princeton University Press, 2000.

—. "A Sixteenth-Century Visitor to the Chora." *DOP* 39 (1985): 117–24.

—, and Nezih Basgelen. *Monuments of Unaging Intellect: Historic Postcards of Byzantine Istanbul*. İstanbul: Arkeoloji ve Sanat Yayınları, 1996.

Oxford Classical Dictionary. Ed. Simon Hornblower and Antony Spawforth. 3rd ed. Oxford: Oxford University Press, 1996.

Oxford Dictionary of Byzantium. Ed. Alexander Kazhdan et al. 3 vols. Oxford: Oxford University Press, 1991.

Özdoğan, M. "Istanbul in Prehistory." In *Istanbul, World City. Habitat 2.* Istanbul: Türkiye Ekonomik ve Toplumsal Tarih Vakfı, 1996.

Palazzo, B. *Deux anciennes églises dominicaines à Stamboul, Odalar Djami et Kefeli Mescidi.* Istanbul: Imprimerie Güler, 1951.

Papadaki-Oekland, Stella. "The Representation of Justinian's Column in a Byzantine Miniature of the Twelfth Century." *BZ* 83 (1990): 63–71.

Papadopoulos, Ioannes V. *Les palais et les églises des Blachernes.* Thessalonika: Imprimerie de la Société commerciale et industrielle de Macédoine, 1928.

Pargoire, Jules. "Constantinople: L'église Sainte-Theodosie." *EO* 9 (1906): 161–65.

—. "Constantinople: La porte basilike." *EO* 9 (1906): 30–32.

Paris, Louis. *Essai historique sur la Bibliothèque du Roi.* Paris: Au Bureau du Cabinet Historique, 1856.

Pasadaios, Aristides. *Epi dyo byzantinon mnemeion tes Konstantinopoleos agnostou Onomasias.* Athens: Athenais Archaiologike Etaireia, 1965.

Pascal, Louis. "Pierre Gilles." In *Nouvelle Biographie Générale* 20. Paris: Didot Frères, 1857.

Paspates, A.G. *Byzantinai meletai topographikai kai historikai.* Constantinople: A. Koroméla, 1877.

Perrin-Henry, M. "La place des listes toponymiques dans l'organisation du livre IV des *Edifices* de Procope." *Geographica Byzantina.* Byzantina Sorboniensia 3. Paris: Publications de la Sorbonne, 1980, 93–106.

Peschlow, Urs. *Die Irenenkirche in Istanbul: Untersuchungen zur Architektur.* With a contribution by P.I. Kuniholm and C.L. Striker. In *IstMitt,* Suppl. 18. Tübingen: E. Wasmuth, 1977.

—. "Die Johanneskirche des Studios in Istanbul." *JÖB* 32.4 (1982): 429–33.

—. "Eine wiedergewonnene byzantinische. Ehrensaule in Istanbul." In *Studien zur spätantiken und byzantinischen Kunst F.W. Deichmann gewidmet* 1. Ed. Otto Feld and Urs Peschlow. Bonn: R. Habelt, 1986, pp. 21–33.

—. *Studien zur byzantinischen Kunstgeschichte: Festschrift für Horst Hallensleben zum 65. Geburtstag.* Amsterdam: Hakkert, 1995.

Piganiol, Andre. "La Loge impériale de l'hippodrome de Byzance et le problème de l'hippodrome couvert." *Byzantion* 11 (1936): 383–90.

Raby, Julian. "Mehmed the Conqueror and the Byzantine Rider of the Augusteon." *Topkapı Sarayı Müzesi Yıllık* 2 (1987): 145.

Ramazanoglu, Muzaffer. "Neue Forschungen zur Architektur-geschichte der Irenenkirche und des Complexes der Sophienkirche." *Atti del VIII congresso di studi bizantini* 2. *Studi bizantini e neoellenci* 8 (Palermo, 1951): 232–35.

Refik, Ahmet. *Istanbul Hayatı: Documents on the Economic and Social History of Istanbul in the Sixteenth and Seventeenth Centuries*. 2 vols. Istanbul: Devlet Matbaası, 1930–31.

Ricci, Alessandra. "I recenti restauri alla Belgrat Kapi nelle mura terrestri di Costantinopoli." *Milion* 2 (1990): 465–68.

Rice, David Talbot. "Excavations at Bodrum Camii, 1930." *Byzantion* 8 (1933): 151–76.

—, ed. *The Great Palace of the Byzantine Emperors. Second Report.* Edinburgh: Edinburgh University Press, 1958.

Rivoira, Giovanni T. *L'architettura romana*. Milan: U. Hoepli, 1921.

Rouillard, C.D. *The Turk in French History: Thought and Literature (1520–1660)*. Paris: Boivin, 1941.

Rudell, Alexander. *Die Kahrie-Dschamisi in Constantinopel: Ein Kleinod byzantinischer Kunst*. Berlin: E. Wasmuth, 1908.

Runciman, Steven. *The Fall of Constantinople*. Cambridge: Cambridge University Press, 1965.

Ryden, Lennart. "The Andreas Salos Apocalypse." *DOP* 28 (1974): 201–14.

Sackur, Ernst. *Sibyllinische Texte und Forschungen*. Halle: M. Niemeyer, 1898.

Safran, Linda. "Points of View: The Theodosian Obelisk Base in Context." *Greek, Roman and Byzantine Studies* 34 (1993): 409–35.

Salaville, Sévérin. "Note de topographie constantinopolitaine: La Porte Basilike." *EO* 12 (1909): 262–64.

Salzenburg, W. *Altchristliche Baudenkmale von Constantinople von V bis XII Jahrhundert*. Berlin: Ernst & Korn, 1854.

Sanderson, John. *The Travels of John Sanderson in the Levant 1584–1562*. Ed. William Foster. London: The Hakluyt Society, 1931.

Sanpaolesi, Piero. "La chiesa dei SS. Sergio e Bacco a Constantinopoli." *Rivista dell'Istituto Nazionale di Archeologia e Storia dell'Arte* [s.n.] 10 (1961): 116–80.

—. *La Chiesa di Santa Sofia a Constantinopoli*. Florence: Sadea-Sansoni, 1965; Rome: Officina, 1978.

Schafer, Hartmut. *Die Gul Camii in Istanbul: Ein Beitrag zur mittelbyzantinischen Kirchenarchitektur Konstantinopels*. *IstMitt* 7. Tübingen: E. Wasmuth, 1973.

Schazmann, Paul. "Des fresques byzantines récemment découvertes par l'auteur dans les fouilles a Odalar Camii, Istanbul." In *Atti del V congresso internazionale di studi byzantini 2*. Rome: Istituto per l'Europa Orientale, 1936.

—. "Die Grabung an der Odalar Camii in Konstantinopel." *AA* 50 (1935): 511–19.

Schneider, Alfons Maria. "Bibliographical Note." *BZ* 45 (1952): 222–23.

—. "Brände in Konstantinopel." *BZ* 41 (1941): 382–403.

—. *Byzanz: Vorarbeiten zur Topographie und Archäologie der Stadt*. Istanbuler Forschungen 8. Berlin: [s.n.], 1936.

—. "Funde in der Buyuk Resit Pasa Caddesi. *Archäologischer Anzeiger* 59–60 (1944–45): 75.

—. "Die Blachernen." *Oriens* 4 (1951): 82–120.

—. *Die Grabung im Westhof der Sophienkirche zu Istanbul*. Istanbuler Forschungen 12. Berlin, 1941.

—. *Die Hagia Sophia zu Konstantinople*. Berlin: Mann, 1939.

—. "Die vorjustinianische Sophienkirche." *BZ* 36 (1936): 77–85.

—. "Grabung im Bereich des Euphemiamartyrions zu Konstantinopel." *Archäologischer Anzeiger* 58 (1943): 255–89.

—. "Mauern und Tore am Goldenen Horn zu Konstantinopel." *NachGött* 5.5 (1950): 65–107.

—. *Strassen un Auartiere Konstantinopels*. Mitteilungen des Deutschen Archäologischen Institut, 1950.

—, and M.I. Nomidis. *Galata: Topographische-archäologischer Plan*. Istanbul, 1944.

Schreiner, Peter. "John Malaxos (16th Century) and His Collection of *Antiquitates Constantinopolitanae*." In Necipoğlu BC, pp. 203–14.

Schweinfurth, Peter. "Der Mosaikfussboden der komnenischen Pantokratoriche in Istanbul." *Jahrbuch des Deutschen Archäologischen Instituts* 69. Berlin: W. de Gruyter, 1954, pp. 253–60.

Schwoebel, Robert S. *The Shadow of the Crescent: The Renaissance Image of the Turk (1453–1517)*. New York: B. de Graaf, 1967.

Sedlmayr, Hans. "Zur Geschichte des justinianischen Architektursystems." *BZ* 35 (1935): 38–69.

Sevcenko, Ihor. "Inscription in Honor of Empress Eudoxia." *Annals of the Ukrainian Academy* 12. New York: Ukranian Academy, 1969–72, 207–8.

———. "Society and Intellectual Life in the Fourteenth Century." In *Actes du XIVe Congrès International des Études Byzantines.* Bucharest: Editura Academiei Republicii Socialiste Romania, 1974, 1:7–30.

———. *Three Byzantine Literatures: A Layman's Guide.* Brookline, MA: Hellenic College Press, 1985.

Sharf, Andrew. *Byzantine Jewry from Justinian to the Fourth Crusade.* London: Routledge & Kegan Paul, 1971.

Shepherd, M.H., Jr. "Liturgical Expressions of the Constantinian Triumph." *DOP* 21 (1967): 57–78.

Sheppard, Carl D. "A Radiocarbon Date for the Wooden Beams in the West Gallery of St. Sophia, Istanbul." *DOP* 19 (1965): 237–40.

Smith, Christine. "Cyriac of Ancona's Seven Drawings of Hagia Sophia." *AB* 69 (1987): 16–32.

Sophocles, E.A. *Greek Lexicon of the Roman and Byzantine Periods.* Boston: Little, Brown & Co., 1870.

Speck, Paul. "Eudoxia-Säule und Pittakia." *Hellenika* 22 (1969): 430–35.

———. *Kaiser Konstantin VI: Die Legitimation einer Fremden und der Versuch einer eigenen Herrschaft.* Munich: Fink, 1978.

Starr, J. *The Jews in the Byzantine Empire 641–1204.* Athens: Verlag der Byzantinisch Neugriechischen Jahrbücher, 1939.

Stephanus Byzantius. *A Geographical Lexikon on Ancient Cities, Peoples, Tribes and Toponyms.* Chicago: Ares, 1992.

Stiernon, D. "Le Quartier du Xérolophos à Constantinople et les réliques venitiennes du Saint Athanase." *REB* 19 (1961): 161–88.

Striker, Cecil L. "The Findings at Kalenderhane and Problems of Method in the History of Byzantine Architecture." In Necipoğlu BC, pp. 107–16.

———. *The Myrelaion (Bodrum Camii) in Istanbul.* Princeton: Princeton University Press, 1981.

———. "Work at Kalenderhane Camii in Istanbul: Second Preliminary Report." *DOP* 22 (1968): 185–93.

———, ed. *Architectural Studies in Memory of Richard Krautheimer.* Mainz: P. von Zabern, c.1996.

———, and Dogan Kuban. *Kalenderhane in Istanbul: The Buildings, Their History, Architecture & Decoration. Final Reports on the Archaeological Exploration and Restoration at Kalenderhane Camii 1966–1978.* Mainz: Verlag Philipp von Zabern, 1997.

Strube, Christine. *Die westliche Eingangseite der Kirchen von Konstantinopel in justinianischer Zeit.* Wiesbaden: O. Harrassowitz, 1973.

Strzygowski, Josef. *Origin of Christian Art.* Trans. O.M. Dalton. Oxford: Clarendon Press, 1923.

Studien zur spätaniken und byzantinischen Kunst. Ed. F.W. Deichmann with Otto Feld and Urs Peschlow. 3 vols. Bonn: R. Habelt, 1986.

Swainson, Harold. "Monograms of the Capitals of S. Sergius at Constantinople." *BZ* 4 (1895): 106–8.

Swift, Emerson H. *Hagia Sophia.* New York: Columbia University Press, 1940.

—. "The Latins at Hagia Sophia." *AJA* 39 (1935): 458–74.

Tafrali, Oreste. *Thessalonique au quatorzième siècle.* Paris: P. Geuthner, 1913.

—. *Thessalonique des origines au XIVe siècle.* Paris: P. Geuthner, 1919.

—. *Topographie de Thessalonique.* Paris: P. Geuthner, 1913.

Talbot, Alice–Mary. "The Restoration of Constantinople under Michael VIII." *DOP* 47 (1993): 243–61.

—. "Saints et leur sanctuaires à Byzance." *Speculum* 70 (1995): 920–22.

—, ed. *The Correspondence of Athanasius I.* Washington, DC: Dumbarton Oaks, 1975.

Taylor, Rabun. "A Literary and Structural Analysis of the First Dome on Justinian's Hagia Sophia, Constantinople." *Journal of the Society of Architectural Historians* 55 (March, 1996): 66–78.

Teall, John L. "Age of Constantine: Change and Continuity." *DOP* 21 (1967): 11–36.

Teteriatnikov, Natalia. *Mosaics of Hagia Sophia, Istanbul: The Fossati Restoration and the Work of the Byzantine Institute.* Washington, DC: Dumbarton Oaks, 1998.

—. "The Place of the Nun Melania (the Lady of the Mongols) in the Deesis Program of the Inner Narthex of the Chora, Constantinople (13th-Century Byzantine Mosaic; with Appendices of Poem and Commentary)." *CA* 43 (1995): 163–84.

Tezcan, Hülya. *Topkapi Sarayi ve Cevresinin Bizans Devri Arkeolojisi.* Istanbul: Türkiye Turing ve Otomobil Kurumu, 1988.

Thibaut, Jean-Baptiste. "L'Hebdomon de Constantinople." *EO* 21 (1922): 31–44.

Thiers, Adolphe, with Jean Ebersolt. *Les Églises de Constantinople.* Paris: E. Leroux, 1913.

Thompson, H.A. "Athenian Twilight, AD 267–600." *JRS* 49 (1959): 61–72.

Tiftixoğlu, V. "Die Helenianai nebst einigen anderen Besitzungen im Vorfeld des frühen Konstantinopel." In *Studien zur Frühgeschichte Konstantinopels.* Ed. H.-G. Beck. Miscellanea Byzantina Monacensia 14. Munich: Institut für Byzantinistik und Neugriechische Philologie der Universität, 1973, pp. 49–83.

Trilling, James. "The Soul of the Empire: Style and Meaning in the Mosaic Pavement of the Byzantine Imperial Palace at Constantinople." *DOP* 43 (1989): 27–72.

Trone, R. "A Constantinopolitan Double Monastery of the Fourteenth Century: The Philanthropic Saviour." *Byzantine Studies–Études Byzantines* 10 (1983): 81–87.

Tunay, Mehmet.I. "Byzantine Archaeological Findings in Istanbul during the Last Decade." In Necipoğlu BC, pp. 217–31.

——. "İstanbul'dan arkeolojik harberler." *Rehber dünyasi* (November 1996): 14–18.

Ülgen, A.S. *Fatih Devrinde İstanbul, 1453–1481.* Ankara: Vakıflar Umum Müdürlüğü, 1939.

Underwood, Paul. *The Kariye Djami.* 4 vols. New York: Pantheon Books; Princeton: Bollingen Foundation, 1966–75.

——. "Notes on the Work of the Byzantine Institute in Istanbul, 1954." *DOP* 9–10 (1956): 299–300.

——. "Some Principles of Measure in the Architecture of the Period of Justinian." *CA* 3 (1948): 64–74.

——, and E.J.W. Hawkins, "The Portrait of the Emperor Alexander." *DOP* 15 (1961): 187–217.

Ursinus, Michael. "Byzantine History in Late Ottoman Turkish Historiography." *BMGS* 10 (1986): 237–43.

Ursu, Ioan. *La politique orientale de François Ier.* Paris: Honoré Champion, 1908.

Van Millingen, Alexander. *Byzantine Churches in Constantinople.* London: Macmillan & Co., 1912.

——. *Byzantine Constantinople: The Walls of the City and Adjoining Historical Sites.* London: J. Murray, 1899.

Van Nice, Robert L. *Saint Sophia in Istanbul: An Architectural Survey.* Washington, DC: Dumbarton Oaks, 1966–86.

Vasiliev, Alexander. "Harun-ibn-Yahya and His Description of Constantinople." *Seminarium Kondakovianum* 5 (1932): 149–63.

——. "The Monument of Porphyrius in the Hippodrome at Constantinople." *DOP* 4 (1948): 29–49.

—. "Pero Tafur: A Spanish Traveler of the Fifteenth Century and His Visit to Constantinople, Trebizond and Italy." *Byzantion* 7 (1932): 75–122.

—. *The Russian Attack on Constantinople in 860.* Cambridge, MA: The Medieval Academy of America, 1946.

Vickers, Michael. "Wandering Stones: Venice, Constantinople and Athens." In *The Verbal and the Visual: Essays in Honor of William Sebastian Heckscher.* Ed. Karl-Ludwig Selig and Elizabeth Sears. New York: Italica Press, 1990, 225–47.

Vryonis, Speros. *The Decline of Medieval Hellenism in Asia Minor and the Process of Islamization from the Eleventh through the Fifteenth Century.* Berkeley: University of California Press, 1971.

Ward Perkins, J.B. "The Building Methods of Early Byzantine Architecture." In *The Great Palace of the Byzantine Emperors, Second Report.* Ed. David Talbot Rice. Edinburgh: Edinburgh University Press, 1958, pp. 52–104.

—. *The Great Palace of the Byzantine Emperors: Being the First Report on the Excavations Carried out on Behalf of the Walker Trust (the University of St. Andrews), 1935–38.* London: Oxford University Press, 1947.

Weiss, Roberto. *Medieval and Humanist Greek.* Padua: Antenore, 1979.

Weitzmann, Kurt. *Die byzantinische Buchmalerei des IX. und X. Jahrhunderts.* Berlin: Mann, 1935.

Wellesz, Egon. "The 'Akathistos.' A Study in Byzantine Hymnography." *DOP* 9–10 (1955–56): 141–58.

Wessel, Klaus. "Byzantinische Plastik der palaiologischen Periode." *Byzantion* 36 (1966): 217–59.

Whitby, Michael. "Justinian's Bridge over the Sangarius and the Date of Procopius 'De aedificiis.'" *Journal of Hellenic Studies* 105 (1985): 129–48.

—. "The Long Walls." *Byzantion* 55.2 (1985): 560–83.

Whittemore, Thomas. *The Mosaics of St. Sophia at Istanbul: Preliminary Reports.* Paris, Oxford: Oxford University Press for the Byzantine Institute, 1933–52.

Wilson, Nigel G. *Scholars of Byzantium.* Baltimore: The Johns Hopkins University Press, 1983.

Wolff, Robert L. "Footnote to an Incident of the Latin Occupation of Constantinople: The Church and the Icon of the Hodegetria." *Traditio* 6 (1948): 319–27.

Wrede, Henning. "Zur Errichtung des Theodosius-Obelisken in Istanbul." *IstMitt* 16 (1966): 178–98.

Wulff, O. *Altchristliche und byzantinische Kunst.* Berlin: Akademisch Verlagsgesellschaft Athenaion, 1913–14.

Wulzinger, Karl. *Byzantinische Baudenkmaler zu Konstantinopel.* Hannover: H. Lafaire, 1925.

—. "Die Apostelkirche und die Mehmedije zu Konstantinopel." *Byzantion* 7 (1932): 7–39.

Xydis, Stephen. "The Chancel Barrier, Solea, and Ambo of Hagia Sophia." *AB* 29 (1947): 1–24.

Yenal, Engin. *The Ottoman City in Comparative Perspective. Istanbul 1453–1923: A Selected Bibliography of the Urban History Compiled from Western Sources.* Monticello, IL: Vance Bibliographies, 1978.

Yerasimos, Stephanos. *La fondation de Constantinople et de Sainte-Sophie dans les traditions turques.* Paris: J. Maisonneuve, 1990.

—. *Les Voyageurs dans l'empire Ottoman. XIVe–XVIe siècles.* Ankara: Société turque d'histoire, 1991.

Yücel, E. *Der Grosse Palast.* Istanbul: Mosaikmuseum, 1988.

Zachariadou, Elizabeth. Δέκα Τουρκικά Έγγραφα για την Μεγάλη Ἐκκλησία (1483–1567). Athens: Byzantine Institute, 1996.

Zaloziecky, W.R. *Die Sophienkirche in Konstantinopel und ihre Stellung in der Geschichte der abendlandischen Architektur.* Studi di antichità christiana 12. Vatican City: Pontificio istituto di archeologia cristiana, 1936.

INDEX

A

forum (of): Arcadius 201; Artopoleion 151; Augustus (Augusteon)
86, 87, 94, 96, 98, 99, 105, 106,
107, 221; Constantine 66, 91,
103–5, 110, 130, 133, 134, 137,
138, 140, 142, 146, 147, 149, 151,
154, 157, 159, 168, 169, 210, 217,
218, 219; Great Forum 107, 164;
Honorius 211, 214, 220; Lacoton
138; Pistorium 151, 152; Placoton 134, 137, 138; Praetorium
132, 133; Taurus (the Bull, Tauri)
104, 151, 152, 153, 154, 155,
156, 159, 182–84; Theodosius
(Theodosiacum) 105, 128, 129,
132, 133, 138, 148, 149, 150, 151,
153, 154, 157, 163, 197, 201, 218,
219, 220; Trajan 80, 137; Trajan
Hispanus 151
Fourth Crusade XVI
François I, king XIII, XVII, XVIII,
XIX, XX, XXIV, 47, 225
Franks 154
French XIII, XVIII, XIX, XX
Fulgosius 224
Fulvius, Ursinius, antiquarian 135

G

Galata XXI, 1, 11, 16, 24, 49, 83, 131,
134, 174, 209–16; castle of 49
Gallo-Grecians 2
gardens (of): Apsasius 166; Blancha
158, 201; Blanchae 159, 160;
(grove of) Rufinus 94; Sultan 17
gates (of): Adrianople 36, 178,
192; Agia 37; Attalus 203 ; Bab-ı
Hümayün 43; Bab-üs Saadet 43;
Bab-üs Selam 43; Blachernae
37; Carsiana 37; Condescala
37; Cynigos 37; Demetrius 37;
Farinaria 37; Golden 36, 38,
151, 191, 196, 197, 202, 203, 204,
205, 220, 221, 227, 233; Jubalica

37; Leonina 37; Leo 21, 66, 83;
Lignaria 37; Myriandros 37;
Neorium 5, 37, 204; Oria 131,
204; Palatine (Palatina) 37, 192;
Phanaria 37; Piscaria 37; Prasina
79; Rhegium 8, 36, 37; Romanus
XVII; Selymbria 36; Seminaria
37; Seven Towers, the 36, 205;
Stercoraria 37; Thracian 37, 49;
Venetia 79; Xylocerum (Xy-
lokerko) 8, 37, 194, 196, 231
Gauls 2, 77, 84, 103
Genoese 1, 210, 211, 214, 216
Genseric, Vandal king 94
Germans 183
Gilles, Antoine XXI, XXV
Gilles, Pierre XIII, XIV, XVIII, XIX–
XXII, XXIV, XXV, XXVI, XXVIII;
Circumnavigation of the Bosporus
210; *Greek-Latin Lexicon* XIX; *On
the Life and Nature of Animals* XIX;
On the Thracian Bosporus XXI, 48,
97, 155, 188, 214; *The Topography
of Constantinople and Its Antiquities*
XX, XXI, XXIII; travels 225
Golden Fountain 151
Golden Horn XIII, XXI, 5, 10, 11,
12, 14, 15, 17, 20, 24, 28, 29, 30,
32, 33, 35, 37, 48, 49, 129, 154,
177, 189, 213, 214, 229
Gorgon 139
Goths 92
granaries (of): Alexandria 158, 219;
Constantius 132, 218; Theodo-
sius 160, 219; Troadentian 218;
Valens 218; Valentinian 132, 164
Grand Bazaar XX, XXIII, XXVII, XXVIII
Greece XX
Greek Anthology XXVI
Greek Patriarchal library XXIII
Gregorius 223
Gregory Nazianzus 155
Gyges 20

Paludes 195
Panteichion 190, 227
Paphlagonians 160
Papinius, Statius Publius, *Sylvae* 92
Parilia 107
Paris, Bibliotheque Nationale XX,
XXIV
Parthia 223
Parthici 216, 223
Pasias 225
Patria of Constantinople XXII, 62, 85,
111, 191, 201, 224
Paul Silentiarius 65, 133
Paulus Florus 56
Pausanias 36, 76, 139
Pausanius the Spartan 1, 2, 39, 75
Peloponnesian War XIV, 39
Pera 210–11. *See also* Galata
Pergamum 182
Pergamus 94
Pericles 111
Perillus (Perilaus), sculptor 182
Perinthians 2, 4
Perseus 2
Persia XV, XX, 110, 146; Persians 6, 76,
88, 136, 148; Persian War 75, 92
Pescennius Niger 39
Pessinus 139, 169
Petrus Gyllius. *See* Gilles, Pierre
Phalaris 182
Phanarium 188
Phanno the Epirote 187
Pharasmenes, eunuch 196
Pharos 62–63, 94–96
Phidalia 97, 160
Phidias 50, 96, 111, 160
Philadelphion 140, 145
Philadelphus 2
Philarkos 2
Philip II of Spain XVII
Philip of Macedon 129, 131, 148,
222, 234
Philostratus, *Life of Marcus* 1

Philoxenos (Philoxenon) 109, 111,
127
Phocaea 150; Phoceans 76, 150
Phocas 230
Phocas the Tyrant 182
Phoenicia 7; Phoenicians 1
Phosphorio 129
Phosphorium. *See* Bosporium
Phrygia 139
Pindar 131
Piraeus of Athens 195
Placidia, empress 50
Placilla, empress 177, 181
Plataea, battle of 76
Plato 77; Platonists 226
Pliny the Elder 105, 110; Bosporus
Promontory 210; Chrysoceras
(Golden Horn) 12, 48; Cyzicus
37; Lampterum 150; *Life of Lucul-
lus* 37; *Natural History* 41, 43,
45, 113, 124, 127, 171, 228, 234;
sculptors 97, 111, 182; Sigeum
Promontory 6
Plutarch 37, 49, 203, 234; *De flumi-
nibus* 49
Politianos 3
Polybius, *Histories* 43
Polydius 50
Polygnotus the Painter 203
Polyrrhetius 195
Pompey 2
Pomponius Laetus 194
Pontic Sea 221
Pontus 164
Porphyry XIX, XXVII, XXVIII
Porta Aurea. *See* gates (of): Golden
Porta Leonis. *See* gates (of): Leo
Porta Palatina. *See* gates. *See
also* Cynigos
portico (of): 103–4; Constantine 89;
Domninus 104; Phanio (Fanio)
105, 218; (Porticus) Varia 203;
Severus 89; Trojan 197, 203, 220

This Book Was Completed on November 1, 2007
at Italica Press, New York, New York
and Was Set in Adobe Giovanna.
It Was Printed on 60-lb
Natural Paper by
BookSurge
U. S. A./
E. U.
₰ ₰
₰

Made in the USA
Coppell, TX
18 December 2020